A HISTORY OF SOUTHLAND COLLEGE

A HISTORY OF SOUTHLAND COLLEGE

The Society of Friends and Black Education in Arkansas

THOMAS C. KENNEDY

The University of Arkansas Press
Fayetteville
2009

Manufactured in the United States of America

ISBN-10: 1-55728-916-6
ISBN-13: 978-1-55728-916-2

13 12 11 10 09 5 4 3 2 1

Designed by Liz Lester

♾ The paper used in this publication meets the minimum requirements of the American National Standard for Permanence of Paper for Printed Library Materials Z39.48-1984.

LIBRARY OF CONGRESS CATALOGING-IN-PUBLICATION DATA

Kennedy, Thomas C. (Thomas Cummins), 1937–
A history of Southland College : the Society of Friends and black education in Arkansas / Thomas C. Kennedy.
p. cm.
Includes bibliographical references and index.
ISBN 978-1-55728-916-2 (cloth : alk. paper)
1. Southland College (Helena, Ark.)—History. 2. Society of Friends—United States—History. I. Title.
LC2851.S662K46 2009
378.767'88—dc22

2009032239

Contents

Preface and Acknowledgments

About the time that Ronald Reagan was first elected president of the United States, I sat in the library at Haverford College, a neophyte Quaker scholar, perusing British Friends' journals. At one point while I scanned the pages looking for any nuggets of information that might help to boost the launching of my new research project on late-nineteenth and early-twentieth-century British Friends, my eyes fixed upon a solitary reference to "Arkansas." Having by that time lived in my adopted state for over a decade without being aware of its having any Quaker connections, I was intrigued and read through a small piece on "Southland College of Arkansas," an educational institution for Negroes near Helena. I suppose that should have been it. After all, I had come to Haverford to discover all I could about English Friends, and I claimed to be an historian of modern Britain. What did I know about Quakers in Arkansas, or black education in the South, or, for that matter, about Arkansas history? Still, I somehow could not let go the beguiling vision of a Quaker school for freedmen near Helena. So, I jotted a few notes, and, searching about, found a few more references to the band of Indiana Friends who had come south to help black people in the Arkansas Delta recover from slavery. So began the process that, over the course of nearly thirty years, has brought me, at long last, to the point of setting out these prefatory remarks to my own chronicle of an amazing, inspiring, though ultimately ill-starred episode linking northern Quakers and southern blacks in a bond of faith, struggle, and sacrifice that, long forgotten, needs to be remembered.

So, having determined to pursue this story, when I returned to Fayetteville, I consulted with Bobby Roberts, a graduate student in the history department I knew to be a Helena native. Bobby, now distinguished director of the Arkansas Central Library, knew enough about Southland to sustain my interest, and furthermore he led me to exactly the right people who could tell me a good deal more. The first of these was Dale Kirkman, a local historian whose brief but informative little article on Southland in *Phillips County Historical Quarterly*[1] caused me to make the fateful leap into an entwining net of personal recollections and documentary evidence gathered slowly but obsessively from many people in many places over many years. Much as I attempted to maintain my concentration on British Quakers, Southland continued to haunt me, and somehow—in pale imitation of a great literary hero, Robert Frost—I kept turning back onto the road less traveled by. I hope that, in the end, this will make at least some difference.

The first journey on this long and twisting path was a trip to the Earlham College Library in Richmond, Indiana, conveniently on the route of our family's semiannual journey to nearby Dayton to visit with parents and relatives. At Earlham gentle Friends, whose names I have forgotten or never knew, directed me first to whatever Southland materials they could find and then to a pair of surviving Southland teachers as well as the school's last principal, living sources who were wonderfully generous with their time and information.[2] The vivid recollections of these good people and the names of surviving teachers and students they provided led me, with my long-suffering wife in tow, on a journey into the Arkansas Delta that might have been quixotic but for guidance of another local historian, Carolyn Cunningham, who led us to the site of the long-defunct school and, more significantly, to a small group of surviving former Southland students who were ready to tell their story. The revelations these proud and honest folk offered provided inspiration for the first bit of Southland's story I was able to get into print.[3]

Having, as I thought, safely disposed of the diverting influence of American Quakers and black Arkansans, I was resolved to redouble my concentration on the Quaker Renaissance in Britain. Still, in the course of another trip to Ohio, I thought I would briefly stop by Richmond to satisfy my curiosity concerning a document mentioned in Quaker sources that might provide the clarifying details of an unpleasant incident at Southland during its final, occasionally turbulent years. This elusive piece of evidence proved not to be where it ought to have been and, indeed, not anywhere that I and a helpful but clueless summer vacation archivist could find. Frustrated, she finally said that someone had told her that there were some materials in the attic at the headquarters of Friends Central Meeting in Richmond. Why didn't I go over there and take a look? Suspecting that this harassed young woman's chief motive was to be rid of me, I decided I would try since I was in town and had nothing to lose. Little did I imagine what was about to be gained.

So, on that sweltering mid-August day I was led up the stairs into an unairconditioned attic where the temperature surely hovered near a hundred degrees. At one end of the dimly lit room was a long table with cardboard boxes piled under and on top of it. Blowing and brushing away an unpleasantly thick layer of dust, I pulled a folder out of one of the middle containers and began to read its contents. Eureka! It was not the particular document for which I had been searching; it was the harbinger of much, much more. What I had been guilelessly led to discover were over a half-century's worth of Minute Books, correspondence, records, and photographs, all pertaining to the life and times of Southland College. I felt like an archeologist who had by the merest accident stumbled upon the lost tomb of an Old Kingdom pharaoh.

What to do? What to do? Rendered half-sensible by the magnitude of my discovery and the intensity of the heat, my first reaction was to begin copying page after page on the Xerox machine I had been told I could use. But in a fleeting moment of clarity, induced perhaps by the clicking and whirling of the machine, I finally deduced that I should talk to somebody about this. What then began was a series of remarkably amiable negotiations with officials at Friends Central and Earlham's Lily Library, ending with their agreement that the Southland papers, neglected by Friends for lo these many years, should be returned to Arkansas where they might be put to some good use. All these generous Friends asked in return was a microfilmed copy of the collection once it was organized. My much-needed and deeply appreciated partner in these delicate talks was the then director of Special Collections, Michael Dabrishus, who, throughout the entire process, could not have been more personally helpful or professionally able.

On a subsequent trip to Richmond, I loaded manifold boxes holding the precious papers into the family van and delivered them to Special Collections Department at Mullins Library. Michael Dabrishus was able to obtain a grant from the Arkansas Endowment for the Humanities that allowed him to hire Fon Gordon, a graduate student with extensive knowledge of African American and Arkansas history as well as special ability as an archivist, to spend a summer superbly organizing and cataloguing the papers into the twenty-eight manuscript boxes they now occupy in the Special Collections Department.

With the Southland Papers safely ensconced in Mullins Library, I returned with renewed determination to my research on British Quakers, but, alas, I could not for long ignore the siren song emanating out from the records of the Indiana Friends' missionary station in Arkansas. Irresistibly called back, I wrote, at intervals, various essays dealing with aspects of Southland's history.[4] Throughout these years, I consoled myself with the thought that I was somehow not allowing Southland to be entirely forgotten. Yet, all the while, there remained a lingering sense of insufficiency, a perception that knowledge of parts of the story did not necessarily lead to an understanding or appreciation of the whole. Gordon Morgan, a colleague in Fulbright College, knew about Southland and periodically asked me when I was going to finish the whole story. So, at long last nearing the completion of my study of British Quakerism[5], I approached Lawrence Malley, director of the University of Arkansas Press, to ascertain his interest in a complete history of the sixty-year struggle of faith, hardship, sacrifice, determination, and disappointment comprised by the Southland story. Possessing in large measure the virtues—imagination, hope, and, above all, patience—of every good and true editor and director, Larry, blessings be upon him, supported the project. And thus he has waited, without complaint, while I missed self-imposed deadlines until, retiring from teaching and shelving still another British history project, I devoted my time and thought almost exclusively to Southland. I hope that the final result of my efforts proves to be as useful and informative as he thought, or hoped, it might be. In any case, having put his patience and good humor to the test, I owe him my sincerest thanks for believing that my sometimes stumbling and sputtering endeavor would finally reach fruition.

In addition to each of the individuals and organizations mentioned above, many others have made invaluable contributions to the study of Southland. The Arkansas Endowment for the Humanities aided in the early days of this project by providing two research and travel grants. Since then my colleagues in the Department of History and successive deans of the Fulbright College of Arts and Sciences, including John Giles, Bernard Madison, Randall Woods, and Don Bobbitt, have aided my efforts with both research funds and off-campus duty assignments. I am grateful to each of them for their support and encouragement. Tom Dillard, current director of the Special Collections Department, and his staff have offered unfailing assistance, promptly fulfilling my every request and forgiving me for the extra work I have on occasion caused them. Early on, Edwin Bronner, the late curator of the Haverford College Quaker Collection, encouraged me to continue my work on Southland and his wonderful staff, especially Elizabeth Potts Brown and Dianna Franzusoff Peterson, offered their most welcome friendship to me and my family during the memorable year I spent at Haverford as T. Wister Brown Fellow. Thomas D. Hamm, professor of history and curator of the Quaker Collection at Earlham College, has made a more significant contribution to this study than even he realizes. I learned more about Friends from his study of *The Transformation of American Quakerism* than from any other single work. And as author and archivist, he has been my model and my inspiration, guiding me to things I would not otherwise have found and offering the sort of constructive criticism that is both always incisive and deeply appreciated.

Finally, I also must express my deepest gratitude to my esteemed colleagues, the successive editors of the *Arkansas Historical Quarterly,* Walter Brown and his associate Denise Kilgore, Jennie Whayne, and Patrick Williams, who bravely supported, frankly criticized, and finally published the Southland essays I submitted for their consideration. For all the help that so many have freely given for so long, any errors, excesses, or omissions that may occur in the work that follows are entirely of my own making.

Throughout its existence, a consistent characteristic one can associate with Southland is isolation. Physically separated from a smallish river port by nine miles of bad road, socially excluded on account of its race-mixing propensities, religiously set apart by the historical eccentricity and exclusivity of its founding religious body, few places were more removed from the main currents of contemporary life. Still, however insular, Southland could not remain immune from the tides of its time. Accidentally born in the murderous, bewildering chaos of war, Southland school and religious meeting matured during a period of traumatic transition for America, for Arkansas, and for the corporate entity that nurtured it, the Religious Society of Friends. Two paradoxical themes of this study are, therefore, Southland's apparently stultifying isolation and its obvious inability to escape from the effects of the political, economic, social, and religious alterations and altercations of the wider world. With few exceptions, the people who were a part of Southland's story have been long forgotten, either because they were born and died in humble circumstances or because they lived out the meaning of their faith without achieving worldly frame. In general, they came together from two different worlds. Over the space of six decades, through the mutual exercise of kindness, generosity, sacrifice, devotion to duty, abiding faith, and, most importantly, enduring love, they were able, at times, to bridge the gulf between those worlds. They deserve to be remembered, not for their impeccable virtue or ultimate success but for their persistent striving and enduring humanity. An author can only hope that his endeavors are in some way worthy of the heroic efforts that make them more than fit subjects for the study that follows.

A HISTORY OF SOUTHLAND COLLEGE

For Adlynn, Jennie, Thomas, Jared, Mateo, Anna, Harry, and Iain, in the hope they will display the same spirit of generosity and goodwill that established and sustained Southland College

Chapter 1

Worlds Apart

Phillips County and Wayne County

I. The Setting

Sometime before sunset on 8 April 1864 the *Argyle,* a side-wheeling steamer of 319 tons,[1] slipped into its mooring at the Mississippi River port of Helena, Arkansas. Among the passengers disembarking at this vital Federal outpost in the midst of the hostile Arkansas Delta were four somberly dressed civilians, a forty-ish couple, and two younger women. Residents of Wayne and Henry counties in Indiana, all were members of the Religious Society of Friends who, intent upon a wartime mission of mercy, had endured an arduous two-week passage from Cincinnati:

> Braving the dangers and difficulties of war, sometimes anchoring in the middle of the river, occasionally running the gauntlet between hostile forces on either side, landing on the way at Fort Pillow, only two days before the fearful massacre.[2]

These Quakers—Calvin and Alida Clark, Susan L. Horney, and Martha Ann Macy—would have been made aware of their impending their arrival at Helena by the sight of "contraband" camps full of escaped slaves that stretched along the Arkansas side of the river. Helena's prewar population had been scarcely two thousand, but after it was occupied in July 1862 by a force of thirteen thousand Union troops under Gen. Samuel Curtis, the town became a magnet for fugitive slaves, thousands of whom crowded within Union lines around the town. By all accounts the result was exceedingly unpleasant: "You never saw so wretched a place as Helena" filled with "wretched, uncared for, sad-looking creatures," living in a "dwelling-place of fever and argue."[3]

Although legally freed by Lincoln's Emancipation Proclamation, the former slaves who gathered at Helena and elsewhere were still generally perceived by Union commanders as "contraband of war" for their obvious value to the economy and military forces of the South if permitted to fall back into Confederate hands.[4] By mid-1863 an estimated 3,600 freedmen had converged on Helena and their dismal situation, "eaten up with vermin" and prostrate from diarrhea, was made more miserable by the usually "barbarous" treatment they received from Union soldiers. John Eaton, an army chaplain handed the monumental task of organizing relief for freedmen in the Mississippi Valley, later noted that it was nearly impossible to find a Union soldier who would show compassion for black people, whatever their condition.[5] Maria Breckenridge reckoned that Northern soldiers harbored a "latent notion" that the freedmen were the cause of the war and, thus, the cause of the "monstrous outrage" of their being posted to such a "malaria-stricken, disease-fostering hole" as "Hell-in-Arkansas," the ordinary soldiers' name for the town.[6]

Such was the physical environment into which the four Indiana Friends had placed themselves. If these circumstances were not sufficiently daunting, the threat of bodily harm being inflicted upon civilians working among the freedmen had been dramatically accentuated by the fate of Dr. Fahenstock, a fellow Indianan come South to give medical aid to freedmen who was killed by Confederate raiders near Vicksburg at about the time the Clarks and their young assistants arrived at Helena. As Elkanah Beard, the chief field agent in the Mississippi valley for the Freedmen's Committee of the Indiana Yearly Meeting of Friends,[7] wrote at the time, "Dangers seen and unseen are crowding round us, we shudder at the thought of remaining. All have concluded best to go north except my wife and I. We do not feel it right to abandon the field at present."[8]

This young couple (Elkanah was thirty and his wife, Irena, twenty-eight) stayed to work among freed slaves because they continued to see "suffering here . . . [too] horrible to relate" and because no one else seemed willing or able to give succor to "these poor people." In early March 1864 while the Beards were working among black refugees at Vicksburg, they were summoned to Helena by Maj. Gen. Napoleon Bonaparte Buford, commander of the Union forces in the District of

Arkansas. Buford, who one Quaker worker called "a very kind old man," and his wife were esteemed by relief workers for the humane concern they exhibited on behalf of distressed freedmen.[9] The Bufords were particularly moved by "the sad condition of a large number of colored orphan children . . . suffering greatly from neglect and exposure." When Beard arrived at Helena, he was, according to one Quaker version of events, removed from the steamer by an armed guard and marched to Buford's headquarters where the General forthwith ordered this gentle Friend to take charge of the thousands of destitute freedmen crowded in and around the town. When Beard protested that it was impossible to abandon his work at Vicksburg, Buford ordered him "in the name of the United States Government" to go at once to Richmond and impress upon his superiors the urgent necessity that "an asylum be established immediately [at Helena] under the care of Friends."[10]

Within ten days of this plead for assistance, Beard had traveled north to meet with Indiana Yearly Meeting's executive committee on freedmen. Upon hearing Beard's report, the committee agreed to "establish an Asylum for this helpless class" under the supervision of Calvin and Alida Clark, members of the Whitewater Monthly Meeting near Richmond. General Buford, "delighted with the prospect that Friends will be stationed here," made provisions for a suitable building to house the Quaker staff and their charges.[11]

Such was the genesis of Calvin and Alida Clark's journey to Arkansas, but upon arriving they had little leisure time to take stock of their situation. After a meeting with the Bufords, they returned to the house appropriated for them to await the appearance of their first charges: "sixteen ragged, filthy, vermin-infested Negro children, brought . . . in a government wagon drawn by six mules . . . the advance guard of hundreds more."[12]

Calvin, Alida, and their young assistants had come to Arkansas for a variety of reasons: religious, patriotic, political, and, in the Clarks' case, eventually even economic.[13] But for all the dangers, difficulties, and possible rewards they had anticipated, nothing could have prepared these northern Friends for what they would find in Phillips County, a strange and hostile world separated from stable and sedate Wayne County, Indiana, not just by physical distance or geographic features or the kinds of products wrested from the soil but also by vastly different political, social, and cultural perceptions of what made for decent, Christian civilization, a gulf of heart and mind that, for all the years they spent in Arkansas, these gentle Friends never fully bridged. Of all the differences that marked the evolution of the pioneer communities in Wayne County and Phillips County, none was more stark than the simple matter of black and white.

II. Two Different Worlds

Both Phillips County, Arkansas, and Wayne County, Indiana, were first occupied by venturesome settlers in the early years of the nineteenth century: the former as a part of the territory acquired by the United States through the Louisiana Purchase of 1803 and the latter as a western section of the Northwest Territory as defined by Congress in 1800. The first inhabitants of both these frontier territories faced the backbreaking prospect of clearing away dense forests before they could begin to cultivate the abundance of fertile soil that lay beneath thick canopies of trees, although the canebrakes and cypress-laden swamps of Phillips County's lowlands probably made the task there even more arduous.[14] Beyond such superficial similarities, however, the development of these two agriculturally rich areas could scarcely have been more divergent.

When Arkansas petitioned for territorial status in 1819, an amendment making Arkansas's admission contingent on the prohibition of further importation of slaves into the territory was narrowly defeated in the U.S. Congress.[15] Thus, when Phillips County was formed by the Arkansas territorial legislature in 1820, a portion of its population (145 of 1201) was unfree. Still, a sizeable influx of yeoman farmers and squatters, drawn by cheap, fertile land, retarded the early growth of the peculiar institution. The overwhelming proportion inhabitants in 1820 were white farmers living on small plots, growing a variety of mainly subsistence crops and serviced by merchants and traders concentrated at Helena, the only community with any resemblance to an urban center.[16] Miserable roads hindered access from the interior to Helena, but development was to some degree facilitated by the availability of relatively cheap and generally fertile soil and by the fact that local rivers emptying into the Mississippi were navigable, providing a means of transporting agricultural products to the port town. Arable areas of the county were divided not only by waterways but also by Crowley's Ridge, a wooded outcropping that stretched hundreds of miles from north to south, with its southern terminus at Helena.[17] As late as 1850 unimproved land was still readily obtainable, some for as little as five dollars per acre, and over half the farms in the county were still smaller than fifty improved acres, few of these being worked by slave labor. But, while Phillips County continued for a time to support this considerable body of yeomen farmers, its subsequent development was broadly illustrative of the social and economic history of the pre–Civil War Arkansas Delta.[18]

Eventually, Phillips County's relative isolation and weak financial structure made its economic development heavily dependent on cotton culture and, therefore, on the rapid expansion of slavery. To illustrate, as late as 1860 the total value of manufactured goods in the county was only $50,350, a reflection of the fact that manufacturing interests represented a mere 1.33 percent of Arkansas's total capital investment. By contrast, according to the census of 1860, Phillips County's cotton production reached 26,993 bales, a five-fold increase since 1850, while the slave population upon which cotton production depended had increased by 245 percent from 2,591 (37 percent) to 8,941 (60 percent).[19]

Not surprisingly, nearly half of this burgeoning cotton crop was grown on the county's eighty-eight plantations of over six hundred acres. In 1860 Phillips County farms (including the Gideon J. Pillow plantation of 6,788 acres with 160 slaves) had an assessed value of $11,490,549, making the county the wealthiest in Arkansas.[20] Thus, as Donald McNeilly has noted, during the 1850s Phillips County was transformed from a society with slaves to a slave society increasingly dominated by a "rough and ready" planter class who made up only 11 percent of the landowning population but, controlling the best land and most of the slaves, produced nearly half the county's cotton.[21]

The census of 1860 also indicated that while the absolute number of landowners had scarcely changed in a decade, over one-quarter of the county's farms were operated by renters or tenants and the number of landless white men had doubled to over 1400 among a total white population of under five thousand. Thus, Carl Moneyhon has concluded that while "elements of economic democracy" remained apparent in Phillips County, the growing dominance of the planter class suggested the possibility of future social and economic instability.[22] Doubtless, many of the landless whites lived in Helena and as the Rev. Otis Hackett, the local Presbyterian minister, noted in 1859, there was evidence of disaffection between town and country:

> Helena will need still more nursing. There are difficulties to contend with here that render it anything but an easy field to work. Our numbers are scattered, most of them living in the country, and the planters look askance upon the town, feel no pride in its growth, and take no interest in building it up.[23]

So, at the outbreak of the Civil War, Phillips County was growing in numbers and prosperity, but, at the same time, its economic base was narrowing as concentration on slave-based cotton gradually squeezed a previously diverse agricultural economy. Furthermore, while Helena remained an important market town and river port, nonagricultural enterprises, as noted above, were practically nonexistent. Agriculture dominated, and cotton, which represented nearly half of the state's farm production ($16 of $33 million) in 1860, was its only significant export and the only means of generating new capital. Since cotton production was dependent on slave labor, slavery was the economic lifeblood of lowland, planter-dominated Phillips County.[24]

Helena's status as a port, of course, explains how pious Indiana Quakers would arrive in Arkansas and subsequently play an important role in lives of black residents of Phillips County. Friends who came into this had been inhabitants of an area that from its inception as territory of the United States had been a free domain, untainted by slavery, a fact that created a vast cultural and moral chasm between the inhabitants of Phillips and Wayne counties. Indeed, the spiritual and political development of Wayne County was at least as important as its economic and social circumstances in illustrating the depth and breadth of separation from its Arkansas counterpart.

The presence of scattered but still-formidable American Indian tribes slowed migration into the part of southeastern Indiana that would incorporate Wayne County, but ten years after the Treaty of Greenville (1795), which reduced the threat of hostile natives, a small party of Kentuckians established a settlement along the banks of the Whitewater River, two miles south of the future site of Richmond, Indiana. These pioneers found a gently sloping landscape full of dense forests that grew from rich, loose soil, well watered by the three forks of the Whitewater and covered with natural springs, an invaluable resource in what was an isolated and rugged wilderness.[25] Within five years of this initial settlement, Wayne County was formed by act of the territorial legislature at Vicennces. With the virtual removal of Indian hostility by 1815, Wayne County grew rapidly, aided in no small way by the hundreds of Quakers who migrated into the area from the southern states, especially North Carolina, not only to escape from the shadow of human bondage but also to purchase cheaper, better land in Indiana's more amenable environs. One Quaker historian has asserted that the early nineteenth century movement of southern Friends to Ohio and Indiana represented one of "the great folk movements in American history."[26] It is estimated that some six thousand Friends migrated from slave states to the Old Northwest. In 1850 a third of Indiana's population was composed of first and second generation North Carolinians, and, in Wayne County, the majority of these were Friends.[27]

By 1850 Wayne County's population had risen to over twenty-five thousand, augmented by easy access from eastern states by the passage of the National Road through the county seat at Richmond, leading into the heart of Indiana's richest farm lands. In 1853 a railroad line from Cincinnati was completed, linking Richmond to the largest Ohio River port and opening the way to a more diversified local economy, ranging broadly from its agricultural base. An historical sketch of Richmond published in 1857 proudly noted that among its enterprises the city could boast of twenty-one grinding mills, twenty-four sawmills, two paper mills, an oil mill, six carriage builders, a cutlery factory, a soap and candle factory, and sundry other establishments, producing over $900,000 in manufactured articles a year.[28]

Still, agriculture remained the vital heart of Wayne County's economic life, and as one admiring commentator noted, "Wayne County leads because of the superior intelligence of its farming community."[29] The county's farms contained nearly 100,000 fewer acres than those in Phillips County, but in 1860 census takers assigned them a cash value $3.5 million higher. Indeed, in nearly every category of production, with the obvious exception of cotton, Wayne County outshone its Arkansas counterpart.[30]

Frugal Quaker farmers certainly played a crucial role in Wayne

County's becoming Indiana's most prosperous area and among the leading agricultural counties in the United States. Within a year of the first settlement, Friends began to arrive in considerable numbers, purchasing land, clearing forests, and beginning cultivation. Because most of the new Quaker migrants were "in poor circumstances," they formed a close-knit and, of necessity, largely self-sufficient community.[31] The county's first Friends meeting house was erected in 1808 and during the next year, with over 250 Quakers already residing in the area, Indiana's first monthly meeting,[32] called Whitewater, was established. In 1816 Whitewater Monthly Meeting became part of a quarterly meeting under Ohio Yearly Meeting, and in 1821 Indiana Yearly Meeting was formed out of two quarterly meetings in Indiana and three others in western Ohio. Six years later, the new yearly meeting's membership was reported to be 13,945.[33]

Within a generation, Friends were among the most substantial and respected citizens of Wayne County. Farming remained their major occupation but weighty Quaker banking families, like the Coffins and the Morrisons, were prominent in the wider community as well as within their own religious society. In keeping with the announced tenets of Quakerism, some Friends also passionately embraced controversial social and political issues. In 1817 Charles Osborn, a member of Indiana Yearly Meeting, published America's first abolitionist newspaper at Mt. Pleasant, Ohio; three additional antislavery papers were established at Newport in Wayne County, the hometown of Friend and abolitionist leader Levi Coffin.[34] The question of slavery and the fate of "colored people" became a central issue for Indiana Friends, both as a rallying cry and as the source of a serious falling out. The complexity of the issues involved and their connection to the Quakers' wartime mission in Arkansas deserve careful consideration.

Immediately following its formation in 1821, Indiana Yearly Meeting appointed a committee to look to the needs of those of African descent and "to endeavour to promote their education, and moral and religious improvement . . . with a view to their elevation to the rank and rights of freemen." Each quarterly meeting was also directed to establish an auxiliary committee "to have charge of the people of color within its limits." These actions were in keeping with early-nineteenth-century Quakers' view of themselves as friends, educators, and protectors of the "colored race."[35] But such a view was misleading or, at least, incomplete.

As Rufus Jones pointed out in his account of American Quakerism, it would was "an historical mistake . . . to imply that the Society of Friends was a unit in the championship of the cause of the slave."[36]

Some eighteenth-century Friends had themselves been slaveholders, and a few were even involved in the slave trade. Indeed, prior to 1750, Philadelphia, the foremost American yearly meeting, was dominated by a group of slave-owning Friends who were able to keep antislavery opinions of their coreligionists under wraps. Before 1753, for example, overseers of the Quaker press forbade the publication of antislavery material within the limits of Philadelphia Yearly Meeting.[37] There was strong opposition to this proslavery oligarchy within and outside of Philadelphia, but the official wall of silence on the issue of human bondage was not breached until 1753 when the essay *Some Considerations on Keeping Negroes* by the courageous and saintly emancipationist John Woolman was endorsed by the meeting.[38]

Under the influence of Woolman, Anthony Benezet, and others, Philadelphia Yearly Meeting, almost simultaneously with the signing of the American Declaration of Independence, made the holding of slaves a basis for removal from the society, disownment in Quaker parlance.[39] This prohibition opened a way for individual Friends to join and often take a leading role in various abolitionists organizations. Still, Jean Soderlund is persistent in a asserting that many Quaker abolitionists, while calling for blacks to be freed from bondage, not did wish that freedom to impinge upon their social or religious exclusivity. Thus, Soderlund says, these Friends maintained "gradualist, segregationist and paternalistic policies . . . for almost a century," policies reflected in the fact that blacks were not permitted to join with Philadelphia Friends until the 1790s and then only as "a separate (and unequal) segment of the Quaker community."[40]

When an antislavery society was formed in 1825 by Friends in Jefferson County, Tennessee, five of its charter members would eventually move on to Indiana.[41] This was, perhaps, a portent of what was to come. For at the same time that slavery was tightening its grip on Phillips County, Wayne County was becoming a vital center of the American abolitionist movement. The focal point of antislavery agitation in the county, and the state of Indiana, was the village of Newport, twenty miles north of Richmond. The central figure in Newport's emergence as an abolitionist Mecca was Levi Coffin, whose family had joined the exodus of Friends from North Carolina to Indiana in 1825. By the late 1830s Coffin was operating a linseed oil mill in Newport and building a reputation for antislavery activism that would eventually result in his acquiring the honorific title, President of the Underground Railway. With the assistance of local Friends, including Benjamin Stanton, Daniel Puckett, Charles Osborn, and Rebecca and Walter Edgerton, Coffin succeeded in making his Newport home (now a national monument) the major stop for three converging lines of escape to freedom. Of the more than two thousand fugitive slaves sheltered by Coffin, none were recaptured. Later, Coffin moved to Cincinnati to operate a store dedicated to the free labor movement that attacked the economic viability of slavery by organizing boycotts of all goods produced by unfree labor.[42] The free labor crusade was subsequently embraced by the Indiana Yearly Meeting's Committee on the Concerns of the People of Color (COCPC), which issued a "declaration" exhorting Friends to avoid "the purchase and consumption of articles produced by slaves."[43]

The dedicated activism of Levi Coffin and his associates was most certainly reflected in a stream of pronouncements circulated by the COCPC, as in these minutes of 1837, which expressed

> a concern . . . that Friends may be stirred up to renewed allegiance in faithfully maintaining our testimony against slavery. . . . We would encourage all to a close examination as to what is required at their hand . . . in the advancement of the blessed work of universal emancipation, by meekly, yet boldly, pleading the cause of the oppressed.[44]

While, to all appearances, the antislavery banner seemed to be flying high within the limits of Indiana Yearly Meeting, a growing undercurrent of apprehension emerged from among some of the most prominent or "weighty" of Indiana Friends. For example, a minute of a yearly meeting of 1838 admonished the faithful against joining with those "not of our Society for promoting benevolent objects" lest Friends, by chance, become associated with activities that did not conform to their society's "high and holy" standard of morality. By 1841 yearly meeting had gone so far as to issue a "restraining document" that advised members against associating with any antislavery society or opening their meeting houses to antislavery lectures. The ostensible reason for such cautious exclusivity was the fear that activists who joined with "the world's people" in the struggle against slavery might suddenly find themselves in the company of "men of blood."[45]

Antislavery Friends became increasingly frustrated by such remonstrances. They believed that self-proclaimed Quaker "moderates" were content to say that Friends should by all means place themselves on the side of the angels by denouncing slavery, but in no circumstances should they do anything rash or offensive in attempting to end it. Furthermore, as one radical Quaker abolitionist noted, many of the most cautious Friends were those who were wealthy and well connected with the "world's people": "If one wished to encounter a bitter opponent of the Anti-Slavery movement, he had but to go to a Friend, a proprietor of a large manufacturing establishment . . . to find one." Finally, there was the over arching problem pointed out early on by Indiana Friend Samuel Charles: "the prejudice against a colored population was as great in Indiana as in North Carolina." Many Friends, Charles contended, claimed to want blacks to be free but not free and living near them in Indiana.[46]

To a considerable extent, the widening schism between staunch abolitionists and more prudent Quakers reflected the old division of town and country. City Friends, whose wealth and respectability often projected them into leadership positions in the yearly meeting and its quaintly named executive committee, the Meeting for Sufferings[47], were understandably concerned about extremist actions that might sully the Quaker reputation for peacefulness and plain dealing while damaging their economic interests as well. Country Friends, with a penchant for agrarian democracy as well as antislavery, grew more and more impatient with what they deemed the temporizing, condescending attitudes of many prominent leaders of the yearly meeting. The incident that provoked a decisive split was the visit in October 1842 of Whig congressman Henry Clay to Richmond where antislavery Friends presented the startled Clay with a petition signed by over two thousand individuals requesting that he lead the nation down the path of moral rectitude by freeing his own slaves.[48]

While many Friends were deeply chagrined by this breach of etiquette, abolitionists claimed political as well as spiritual victory. They believed the controversy set off by the incident would help to undermine Clay's presidential aspirations. On the same day of the Clay incident,

Meeting for Sufferings responded swiftly and conclusively. Noting that those behind this outrage "were not activated by a sincere love of the gospel," they removed eight abolitionist members from their own ranks "as disqualified to fill the stations they occupied."[49] After this censure was approved by the yearly meeting, antislavery Friends met at Newport in February 1843 and announced that, having been virtually driven from their own religious society, they would re-form as the Indiana Yearly Meeting of Anti-Slavery Friends "who adhere to the genuine principles of the Society." The corruption of these principles, especially Friends' testimony against slavery was, they asserted, the work of "a number of the most wealthy and influential Friends in the middle and eastern states" who had close, and apparently sinister, ties to southern slave owners.

> There is far more anxiety to concise the good opinion of slaveholders . . . that you may "retain a place of influence with the rulers of the land," than to identify yourselves in feeling and interest with the humble and devoted, yet despised advocates of the claims of down-trodden humanity.

Charles Osborn, the most prominent of the excluded abolitionists, dramatically declared that because Anti-Slavery Friends had pleaded "the cause of the oppressed, we ourselves are put in bonds."[50]

The formation of the Anti-Slavery Yearly Meeting, claiming two thousand members in a dozen monthly meetings, set off a bitter row that continued for nearly fifteen years. The official yearly meeting, retaining the allegiance of over twenty thousand Friends, may have commanded the numbers, but the dissidents more than held their own in the battle of words.[51] Not only did they control *The Free Labor Advocate,* a monthly journal launched at Newport in 1841, but one of their number also became the only contemporary chronicler of the ensuing struggle. Walter Edgerton, deemed a "rank abolitionist" by his detractors, set down an account of this Quakerly contest that, however biased and polemical, remains an invaluable historical source and an exquisite illustration of the intense passions aroused by the slavery issue as well as a fascinating example of the Quaker capacity for fierce invective and rhetorical extremism, qualities not generally associated with gentle, peace-loving Indiana Friends.[52]

Despite an earnest but seriously botched attempt by British Friends to make peace between the two factions, the Indiana Yearly Meeting remained bitterly divided until 1857.[53] Quaker historian Rufus Jones, for one, believed that, ultimately, the effects of the Indiana separation were positive because they "brought the whole question of slavery and the problem of how to combat it with fresh force and vigor to the consciousness of Friends everywhere." Certainly, during the intervening years, Anti-Slavery Friends continued to find much to criticize in the position of the regular yearly meeting. There may have been some validity in the dissenters' view that holding antislavery opinions while not working vigorously to end slavery was "like faith without works." When the Indiana constitution was rewritten in 1850–51 and Hoosier state voters overwhelmingly approved an amendment, Article 13, that actually forbade blacks from entering their state, antislavery Friends issued a blistering public denunciation of this outrage.[54] The larger yearly meeting has been accused of failing to respond to Article 13 or other so-called black laws.[55] Actually, in 1847 the Orthodox Yearly Meeting had issued a general denunciation of black laws as "irreconcilable with the manifested will of our Great Creator" and had sent a memorial to the state constitutional convention condemning Article 13 and arguing for the legal equality of races.[56]

Despite continued hostility between Friends, however, during the late 1840s and 1850s the slavery issue was being dragged into the political mainstream by the emergence of the "free soil" Republican Party. The nearly universal adherence of Indiana Quakers, both regular and antislavery, to this new party (to which they henceforth showed a "fierce devotion") and the efforts at reconciliation by moderates like the Richmond banker Charles Coffin helped to heal the breach. By 1857 a quiet reunion had been accomplished, although a few hard-line abolitionists like Walter Edgerton held out until after the outbreak of the Civil War.[57]

III. War in the Two Worlds

By 1861 both Phillips and Wayne counties had shaken off the worse economic consequences of the financial panic of 1857 and brief depression that followed, although the short term effects on northern locales like Wayne County had been more severe than in cotton-rich Phillips. But while the terrible war between the states that began that year spared few Americans from the consequences of its deathly ferocity, fewer still suffered more cruelly than the people of Phillips County, Arkansas, especially if they were enslaved blacks or poor whites. Parts of southeastern Indiana experienced some taste of the horrors of war as a result of Gen. J. M. Morgan's daring but ill-fated foray into Indiana and Ohio, but Wayne County itself was spared from the sights and sounds of combat. On the other hand, Helena was too significant a port and its environs too rich in cotton, produce, and slaves to escape from the shattering violence and agonizing deprivations brought by invading Union armies.

Federal troops entered Phillips County in July 1862, quickly captured Helena, and remained in effective control of the area until the end of the war. The county's overwhelmingly "secesh" white population experienced monumental losses, especially if they were poor, as a result of the wholesale confiscation and random theft that nearly denuded the county of every sort of livestock while much of its richest farmland lay fallow throughout the conflict. Edward Redington, a Union officer from Wisconsin, described the western part of Phillips County as "desolation itself." "You cannot conceive," he told his wife, "of the desolation . . . through which we passed . . . The road ran through one continued series of plantations of the best land in the world, all deserted, not an acre under cultivation." As for local white folk, Redington characterized them as "poor, lean, hungry-looking creatures," with a "wild, scared, strange look. . . . Poor things, there is an awful future in store for them. . . . God help them for they do not seem disposed to help themselves." Redington believed that the army would have to open up its storehouses to keep "our erring brethren from dying of actual starvation." But even if none actually starved, no doubt lower resistance resulting from poor diet contributed to the high rates of locals, white and black, who succumbed to various diseases. By contrast, it seems that the county's elite classes, whatever temporary deprivations they may have suffered, generally survived the war with their holdings intact, or even expanded.[58]

In an economic sense at least, citizens of Wayne County, Quakers included, did very well out of the war. Between 1860 and 1865 the assessed value of real estate and personal property rose from nearly $14.7 to $18.5 million.[59] Even allowing for wartime inflation, these figures reflected sizable economic development. Of course, there was always a price to be paid. A considerable number of the county's young men did military service, and a good many of these died. Because of Friends' traditional testimony against fighting with carnal weapons, the cost for Quakers of military age might be, until 1863, a monetary payment to escape service in the state militia. The Indiana constitution contained a provision exempting those "conscientiously opposed to bearing arms," for a payment of two hundred dollars, no small sum. A recent careful examination of the monthly meeting records indicates that 2,170 Indiana Friends registered as conscientious objectors. At the same time, 1,212 Quakers served in the state militia or, after the introduction of a federal draft in 1863, in the regular forces. This number amounted to about one-quarter of all Quakers of military age. In eight Indiana counties more Friends served than registered as "conscientiously opposed" to service. The relationship between war service and strong antislavery opinions does not clearly emerge, but it was subsequently reported that, prior to the imposition of the federal draft, Quakers furnished a higher percentage of volunteers than any other denomination. Certainly, the question of Quaker combatant service brought to the fore the dilemma facing those who opposed both the slavery system and the war it helped to bring on. In most cases, monthly meetings "looked the other way" and did not discipline younger Friends who violated the peace testimony; still, 148 men were disowned (excommunicated) for serving in the forces.[60]

After July 1863 when a federal draft law made all males between the ages of twenty and forty-five eligible for national service, a Quaker delegation, including Indiana Friends, went to Washington to plead their case for special exemption. These weighty Friends interviewed government officials, including President Lincoln and Secretary of War Stanton. Indiana Yearly Meeting also issued a "Memorial to both Houses of Congress" that noted that while their peace testimony was a "vital principle . . . we feel ourselves conscientiously bound to support. . . . We believe there are various ways in which we can discharge the duties of good citizens." Congress responded to this plea with a clause permitting religious conscientious objectors to be assigned noncombatant duties "in hospital, or in the care of freedmen, or to pay a sum of three hundred dollars."[61] This provision afforded an opening for patriotic as well as humanitarian and even spiritual service for Quakers who could not in conscience take up arms. Given the increasing pleas for help in relieving the terrible suffering of freed contrabands throughout the Mississippi valley, it also gave Indiana governor Oliver P. Morton an opportunity to take advantage of Indiana Yearly Meeting's efforts to create an expanded role for its Committee on Concerns of Colored People. Before the war, this committee's activities had concentrated on religious and secular education of people of color in Indiana. In 1863 the committee, while reporting that nearly all colored children within the yearly meeting limits were receiving some "literary instruction," noted that circumstances had changed so drastically that some "more effectual and organized labor" was required for the relieve of blacks throughout the Mississippi valley who had been released from bondage only to be delivered into nearly universal squalor and suffering. After consideration the yearly meeting created a new "Committee for Contraband Relief" charged with looking "to the relief of the physical necessities of Freedmen and their advance in knowledge and religion." The appointment of this committee was concurrent with Governor Morton's plea for Friends to assist in caring for displaced freedmen. Quakers had good political and economic reasons to respond positively to Morton's entreaty, as his intervention had resulted in nearly twenty thousand dollars being restored to Indiana Friends who had paid the two-hundred-dollar exemption fee required by the Indiana state government when the War Department judged these fees to have been illegally collected.[62]

The appointment of the "Contraband Committee" was the first major step by Indiana Friends "to provide more systematically for . . . [the freedmen's] temporal wants; and for the promotion of missionary labor among them." It also reflected an attempt, somewhat belated perhaps, to go beyond negative opposition to slavery and to take positive steps to deal in some substantial way with its evil effects. As the poet John Greenleaf Whittier reminded his Quaker brothers and sisters in 1864,

> We have to undo the accumulated wrongs of two centuries, remake the manhood that slavery has well nigh unmade, to see to it that the long oppressed colored man has a fair field for development and improvement, and to tread under our feet the last vestige of that hateful prejudice which has been the strongest external support of Southern slavery.[63]

These were noble aims, and for three generations Quakers from a distant world endeavored to make them a reality in always-alien and sometimes-hostile Phillips County, Arkansas.

CHAPTER 2

Friends and Freedmen

1863–1866

I. A Menace Difficult to Overestimate

Even before the Emancipation Proclamation, tens of thousands of blacks flocked to whatever parts of Confederate slave states were occupied by Federal forces.[1] "There was no plan for this exodus. No Moses to lead it." In the end, the task of providing some semblance of order to this "menace to soldiers . . . difficult to overestimate" was assumed by John Eaton Jr., an Ohio army chaplain who had been superintendent of schools in Toledo. Chosen, seemingly at random, by fellow Ohioan U. S. Grant as superintendent of contrabands for the Mississippi valley, Eaton faced the staggering task of providing for the welfare of an estimated three-quarters of a million freedmen. In attempting to carry out his responsibilities, Eaton generally received more sympathy than material help from Grant's subordinates in the field who, after all, had a war to fight. Thus, in the beginning things went very badly indeed. Samuel Thomas, Eaton's assistant superintendent, recalled: "I hope I may never be called on again to witness the horrible scenes I saw in those first days of the history of the freedmen."[2] In the circumstances, Eaton's job might have been impossible but for the assistance of religious bodies like the American Missionary Association and philanthropic organizations like the Cincinnati Contraband Relief Commission. The latter group, formed in November 1862 by representative of various denominations, included Levi Coffin and other prominent Quakers from Indiana Yearly Meeting.

Early on Superintendent Eaton was put in touch with prominent anti-slavery Friends like Coffin. Two of the first Friends recruited by the famed abolitionist to answer Eaton's call for assistance were Job and Tacy Hadley of Hendricks County, Indiana, acting on behalf of Miami Quarterly Meeting. With two hundred dollars in personal savings and a letter of recommendation from Indiana governor Morton, the Hadleys traveled to the contraband camp at Cairo, Illinois, where they found hundreds of blacks sunk in "destitution and distress . . . under officers that manifested but little interest in their welfare." Interest was, however, being shown by "river men" seeking "nice little girls" from among the former slaves. As much as the Hadleys wished to rescue these helpless creatures from such lurking dangers, Job feared that sending them north, where color "prejudice was about equal . . . as [in the] south," might create new difficulties. The chaplain of the freedman's camp at Memphis apparently had the same impression; he told a meeting of the Cincinnati Contraband Commission that while freedmen in the south obviously needed looking after, "there need be no fear of them coming North."[3]

A number of Quakers were, like the Hadleys, early visitors to various freedmen's encampments along the Mississippi, but the first official representatives of Indiana Yearly Meeting were Elkanah and Irena Johnson Beard, dispatched by the newly-formed Freedmen's Committee in October 1863. In the summer of that same year, Elkanah, twenty-nine years old and a recorded Quaker minister[4], felt constrained "to spend some time as a missionary among colored people" and for about six weeks acted as a spiritual emissary to refugee exslaves, although it appears unlikely that he actually envisioned bringing blacks into the Society of Friends. After his first sermon to freedmen at Holly Grove, Mississippi, he remarked that "some of the more noisy shouted louder than was pleasant to me." During this same trip, Beard stopped at Helena where in addition to preaching he visited a school for freedmen organized by the army. His appearance there was Quakerism's entree into Phillips County, Arkansas.[5]

When Elkanah Beard was appointed in October 1863 as official field agent to coordinate Indiana Friends' support for freedmen, his charge was threefold: to bring physical aid to deprived exslaves, to hold religious meetings for their "moral uplift," and, wherever possible, to establish schools. As the Beards journeyed down the Mississippi toward what was to be their headquarters at Young's Point, just north of Vicksburg, they again stopped at Helena. There they found black refugees "in a very destitute, suffering condition," and local military officials implored Elkanah to return as soon as possible with whatever aid he could muster. Shortly after the Beards' visit, Samuel Shipley, a prominent Philadelphia Quaker, called at Helena and, shocked by what he saw there, sent an emergency plea to the *Friends' Review* for warm clothing and blankets for exslaves facing the onset of winter. The Indiana Freedmen's Committee responded by sending nineteen boxes of clothing, fifty bedsteads, and other items to the Arkansas port. But while such ad hoc assistance was welcomed, it represented the merest trickle of what was needed even at a single location like Helena.[6] As for Beard, he soon realized that, given the enormity of the task at hand, if he could somehow accommodate the military authorities at various points along the river by dealing with specific refugee problems, he might, in turn, be able to draw upon the considerable resources these men commanded to help him begin to come to grips with the disparity between what was needed and what was available to fill the need. Some military leaders, no doubt impressed by the Beards' earnest simplicity, generously provided both rations and money to support their work.[7]

However incongruous an alliance between pacifist Friends and makers of war may seem, something akin to a mutual admiration society developed between Quaker relief workers and their military counterparts. Elkanah Beard's journal was full of praise for Superintendent Eaton, his assistant superintendent, Col. Samuel Thomas and Maj. William Sargeant, who headed the army's freedmen's relieve efforts in the district of Arkansas. Eaton, for example, supplied Beard with an invaluable six-month pass, signed by both President Lincoln and General Grant, for unimpeded transportation on any steamboat or railway in the Ohio-Mississippi valley. Such generous assistance moved Samuel Shipley to call Eaton "one of nature's noble men." By the same token, Eaton had the highest regard for the Beards, praising their dedicated service through even "the darkest hours" and noting that of all those who worked among the freedmen none had "come more fully up to our wishes."[8]

Another military commander singled out for special commendation by both Colonel Eaton and Elkanah Beard was Maj. Gen. Napoleon Bonaparte Buford, the commandant at Helena who had prevailed upon Indiana Yearly Meeting to establish the orphanage that Calvin and Alida Clark took charge of in April 1864. General Buford, a West Point graduate, was already known to Friends, having come to the aid of Job Hadley at Cario by reversing the order of an unfriendly Union general, "a Democrat," to banish Hadley and his black charges to the unsafe Missouri side of the river.[9]

Once the Helena Orphan Asylum was established, Buford and "his noble wife" continued to manifest "the deepest interest" in its development so long as they remained at Helena.[10] But for the next quarter century, the central figures of the unfolding drama of Friends in Phillips County were Calvin and Alida Clark. Available evidence seems to indicate that in the beginning the Clarks did not intend to stay in Arkansas for any extended period, given their of lifelong attachments to Indiana and the substantial holdings they possessed there. Both were natives of Wayne County whose families had come from North Carolina at about the same time; they were indeed cousins, sharing great-grandparents, John and Ann Clark.[11] After their marriage in 1844, when he was twenty-four and she twenty-two, Calvin, who had taught school during the winter to supplement his farming activities, became a full-time and apparently quite successful farmer. Alida, who had "attended the best schools in the state," remained at home to raise three daughters, but she was active in the Whitewater Monthly Meeting, most prominently as a member its education committee. In 1860 the census of 1860 for Wayne County valued the family's real estate at $5,000 and personal property at $1,200, substantial assets for the time. But the family's relative prosperity was dimmed by the loss of their youngest daughter Anne, whose death at age six in 1860 was followed by the wartime demise of their oldest, Semira (Myra), born in 1845, leaving only Elizabeth, who was twelve when the Civil War began, to survive to adulthood. The Clarks' mission to Arkansas was ample testimony of their ardent abolitionist sentiments, but since they had remained members of Whitewater meeting, it would appear that they were never connected with the antislavery separation. They seemed simple, straightforward, traditional Friends, although a family photograph of Alida with five of her nine siblings, probably taken in the 1850s, shows her wearing a gold chain, a deviation from Quaker plain dress unfavorably commented upon at the time by a censorious older brother.[12] Some reasons for the Clarks leaving a relatively comfortable life in Indiana for arduous and possibly dangerous work in Arkansas seem clear enough. They were devout Friends, strong abolitionists, and devoted Republicans. To do the Lord's work in pursuit of a sacred cause supported by the political party that had, in their view, restored morality and Christian values to the national government would not be unnatural behavior for pious and dedicated Quakers recently and deeply moved by the evangelical renewal that swept through midwestern Quakerism in the late 1850s and early1860s. In journeying to Arkansas to aid lost and neglected black children, Calvin and Alida were exemplary practitioners of the sort of Quaker lifestyle that would, in the words of a wartime editorial in the *Friends' Review,* make them "lights in your community" creating "a tone of soundness and uprightness," apart from the world and yet actively involved in the world's affairs.[13]

Might the Clarks have developed motives beyond religious piety, political commitment, and humanitarian concern? Quaker historian Richard Wood has noted that as evangelical (Gurneyite) Friends increasingly removed the protective hedge that had separated them from the world's people, they became more susceptible to the idea of taking full advantage of economic opportunities, without discarding their commitment to personal piety and social improvement. An important effect of the Civil War on midwestern Friends, Wood says, was an increasing tendency "to replace local and sectarian outlooks with more nationalistic and cosmopolitan ones."[14] Such inclinations seem to have influenced the Clarks' eventual decision to remain in Arkansas after the war ended. During more than twenty-five years in Arkansas, they became substantial Phillips County landholders, eventually owning, in partnership with their son-in-law Theodore F. Wright, seventeen hundred acres, a sawmill, and other business ventures. Wright, a native of Granville, Ohio, and Union officer stationed at Helena, apparently courted the Clarks' surviving daughter Elizabeth (Eliza) when she came to Arkansas to teach in the freedmen's school after the death of her elder sister in June 1865. Late in 1865 a visiting Friend praised Eliza Wright, not more than seventeen at the time, as "a no.1 teacher for the colored children; she loves them, and they in turn love her."[15]

Whatever the eventual range of their motivations, the Clarks took charge at Helena with a will. Barely a month after their arrival Calvin wrote to the *Friends' Review* noting, "We are all exerting every nerve to do honor to the Society, the cause and the truth. . . . Our labors have already been blessed; fruits begin to appear; order is springing out of chaos and system from confusion." Throughout that first summer, reports from military authorities as well as fellow Quakers continued to be encouraging. Capt. J. N. Locke reported to Colonel Eaton in July that the asylum at Helena "was neat and somewhat commodious. . . . Excellent discipline is maintained, and children are learning rapidly." Eaton's own report commented that the "neatness and order of everything [was] . . . as surprising as it is beneficent. These little ones owe a debt of gratitude to . . . the self-denying managers." After a visit to Helena Maj. Gen. A. McCook declared that these "good righteous people . . . cannot be dispensed with here." Such glowing evaluations led the *Friends' Review* to gush that "the success which has attended the efforts of our Friends at Helena has far exceeded our expectations."[16]

The Clarks briefly returned to Indiana some time in late 1864, probably to attend yearly meeting and put personal matters in order, and again from June until August 1865 after their daughter Semira died. Various other Friends, moved by the yearly meeting's exhortation "to labor for the salvation of souls and the spread of the Gospel among men" took temporary charge of asylum, but only Calvin and Alida proved to be as committed to work among Arkansas orphans in peace as in war.[17]

II. A Subject of Vast Magnitude[18]

The end of the Civil War did not end the Quaker commitment to aid freedmen. Late in 1865, there were still thirty Indiana Friends in the South, nearly half of whom were in Arkansas. Besides the Clarks and their associates at Helena, ten workers were serving in the Little Rock area. The activities of all these postwar agents was coordinated through a board of control established in September 1864 by representatives from Indiana, Ohio, Western, and Iowa yearly meetings. This body drew contributions from their respective yearly meetings and also had access to thirty-eight thousand dollars in money and material turned over to the Indiana Freedmen's Committee by the Cincinnati Contraband Commission when it dissolved in late 1864. One of the first actions of this new board was to dispatch two of its members to Washington "to call upon the President and Sec. of War . . . to attempt to obtain such help as they feel able to give."[19] Shortly after the board of control appointed emissaries to Washington, it also sent John May and Joseph Dickinson—the latter of whom would play an important role in the unfolding story of Friends in Arkansas—to examine Quaker operations throughout the Mississippi and

Cumberland valleys. In early 1865 these inspectors reported from Helena that sixty children were living in a five-room house, the smaller ones sleeping five to a bed, receiving daily "scriptural instructions" and drawing rations from the government—"Everything about the Asylum appears to be managed in the most judicious and economical manner." The Quaker school associated with the orphanage met in the Methodist church and also appeared to be thriving. Susan Horney, one of the Clarks' original companions, had opened an industrial school "exclusively for colored women" that eventually employed over two hundred and produced more than a thousand useable garments in about six months. Thus, at Helena at least, Friends seemed to be holding their own. But with the end of the war and the change of leadership following the assassination of President Lincoln, serious concerns arose. For while the responsibilities of Quaker relief workers appeared to be growing—by June 1865 there were eighty-five orphans at Helena—the federal government's role in assisting the freedmen seemed to be rapidly constricting. The Executive Committee on Freedmen reported to Indiana Yearly Meeting that "the Government has concluded to issue no more rations to the freed people," a decision they believed would cause immense suffering, especially among the most helpless classes, the very old and very young. In October 1865 Elkanah Beard foresaw a bleak winter for a devastated and impoverished South wherein few if any whites seemed prepared to aid the freedmen. The board of control also sent a "Letter to the Senate and the House of Representatives . . . representing an appeal from Friends throughout the Nation" and noting that in some respects freedmen were worse off than they had been as slaves.

Although, as General Eaton emphasized, few blacks were likely to return voluntarily to their former masters, "many must perish. . . . unless sufficient provision be . . . made for their protection and relief."[20]

Still, the situation was far from hopeless. In light of the promise from the newly established Freedmen's Bureau of inducements for maintaining existing schools and establishing new ones, the board of control urged Friends to "keep up their schools . . . and look to the importance of Orphan Asylums in desirable locations." As Elkanah Beard mused at the end of 1865:

> Just so long as the great body of freedmen remain uneducated they will more and more partake of the baneful influences of the stagnant and polluted fountains which constantly pour forth streams

> of miasma prejudicial to their growth in grace; and their right to life, liberty, and the pursuit of happiness, will be . . . thwarted.

Indiana Yearly Meeting agreed that education was the "most important necessity of the Freedmen at this time" and expressed the hope that Friends could be found to continue "this great work . . . of elevating and Chrisitianizing these people."[21]

At the same time, glowing reports on the work in Helena from visiting agents continued. In May 1866 William Harvey noted fruitful progress and "a general influence for good round about," even if war, emancipation, and good works had not transformed the attitudes of local whites. Elkanah Beard observed that while Friends' work was prospering, there were two persistent problems. First of all, few white Southerners had accepted the idea of blacks actually having rights, being educated, or accorded equality in any sphere. At Helena, for example, Major Sweeney reported that a local woman had become hysterical when she observed black women in the same hospital room with whites, screaming that "she would not stand such degradation to the white race." Secondly, northern missionaries and teachers were almost universally "held in derision, and scowled at or passed by in silent contempt" by local white people. Gen. Oliver O. Howard remarked that opposition to educating blacks was so great that "teachers, though they may be the purest of Christian people, are nevertheless visited . . . with undisguised marks of odium." One teacher remembered being loudly and publicly denounced by local people who would, however, never speak directly to "Yankee nigger teachers." Ruth Emily Edwards, an early Quaker volunteer in Helena, noted in her diary that northern Friends should be wary about coming South unless they had "reasonably good health . . . able hands" plus the capacity to bear up under difficult physical and social isolation.[22]

Conditions and attitudes at Helena may have been more extreme than in many locations. The town, having endured three years of military occupation and the crowding in of thousands of destitute black refugees was, according to most northern observers, still a squalid, unhealthy place, continuously visited by "fever and argue," small pox, syphilis, cholera, and other medical horrors. Early in 1866 the Rev. Otis Hackett remarked that "the city and county are sadly unlike the old Helena. . . . The old buoyancy of spirit is gone and grave forebodings are entertained for the future."

As late as the spring of 1867, Major Sweeney castigated the city's leaders for "doing nothing" to confront the menace of continuing disease and destitution.[23]

All of the above seemed sufficient reason for Alida Clark's desire to remove the orphan asylum to a more promising location, preferably away from the sin and squalor of the wounded town. But where were they to go? Late in 1865 John Henry Douglas had informed the Indiana board of control that while the Clarks' were "liable to have to give up . . . the house they now occupy, . . . officers informed us that there was no other place that they could give them." Final determination to move was made perforce early in 1866 when, in fulfilling the spirit of Pres. Andrew Johnson's blanket pardon to former rebels, buildings in Helena that had been requisitioned by the federal government were ordered returned to their prewar owners. While this development seemed to threaten the continued existence of the Quaker house of refuge, the Clarks were encouraged by the positive attitude of local military officials. Just as the army, in the person of General Buford who had been instrumental in bringing Friends to Helena, another military leader was the catalyst for establishing a permanent rural sanctuary for Friends and their charges.[24] When Buford's successor, Col. Charles Bentzoni, a Prussian emigrant who had come to Helena in 1864 as commander the Fifty-Sixth Colored Regiment, received orders to return the Friends' quarters to their original owners, he proposed that the officers and men of his command donate money to purchase land and labor to construct suitable buildings on whatever property was acquired. As a Quaker source later observed, "Alida Clark recognized him as God's instrument to meet the difficulties confronting them about which she had spent hours on her knees in prayer."[25]

While Colonel Bentzoni set the asylum's move to countryside in motion, the black soldiers of his command provided both the financial means and physical labor to make the new establishment a reality. Historian Heather Williams has recently provided a detailed account of the vital contributions of the men of the Fifty-Sixth Regiment to the Arkansas experiment of Indiana Friends. These black troopers raised over two thousand dollars through voluntary contributions and musical concerts, of which nine hundred was used to purchase thirty acres nine miles northwest of Helena. Following this initial purchase, Calvin Clark bought fifty adjacent acres and resold it to Indiana Yearly Meeting, which also received the deed for the initial plot. After this eighty acres was secured, remaining funds were spent on lumber, cement, lime, and other building materials as well as two cows and a calf. In the weeks that followed alternating details of forty men from the Fifty-Sixth marched out to the site to clear forty acres on which trees had already been deadened, to dig cisterns and to build rough temporary structures, including a schoolhouse partially fashioned out of wood from dismantled army barracks as well as quarters for students and teachers.[26] Colonel Bentzoni's benevolence in proposing and supervising this project was impressive but, no doubt, he had practical motives as well as humanitarian concerns. Commanding troops stationed in a hostile town with little of consequence to do, he faced a potentially explosive situation. Still, as Heather Williams points out, the men of the Fifty-Sixth, some of whose members attended the Quaker school and religious services in Helena, undertook this work as a labor of love, a stirring example of the nearly obsessive preoccupation with literacy and learning among southern freed people. The regiment was mustered out of service in late 1866 without any serious clashes with local people but not before "it was fearfully visited by cholera," resulting in 187 deaths.[27]

The Clarks and their charges occupied the new premises on 22 May 1866, and Bentzoni marched out his entire command to participate in the dedication ceremonies. When the Colonel handed over of the property deed to Mrs. Clark, she promised that the regiment's generous trust would not be betrayed and that the Bible would be "the foundation of all teaching in the asylum, which called forth hearty amens." As Calvin Clark noted in July, "There is no backing out now, Friends."[28]

So, Quakers from an alien world, undertaking work despised by most of their white neighbors, occupied the site[29] where they and their successors would remain for sixty years providing a beacon of hope and a "Light unto the Lord" for exslaves in the Arkansas Delta. It was a start, but much was left to be done, and, given the time and place, events showed that no one was better qualified to do it than Calvin and Alida Clark.

Photographs of the Clarks taken after they retired from Southland, while not flattering, seem apropos: two elderly bespectacled Friends, unsmiling but somehow serene, who lived without luxury or even leisure to speak of for the last third of their lives.[30] Hard lives they must have been, even by the standards of their austere coreligionists in Indiana, though not in comparison to most of the black people they chose to live among. They must also have been lonely. Alida once wrote that after two decades in Arkansas only "three white women in this Southern land have ever given me a friendly shake of the hand, or an invitation to their homes, or noticed me." There was company—teachers at the school, an intermittent flow of Quaker visitors and always the children, but the close connections with family, friends, and meeting that had characterized life in Indiana were impossible. Instead, Southland became the epicenter of the Clarks' existence. As one visiting Friend noted, Alida "took the lead . . . ably and faithfully supported by her husband" who was responsible for "general oversight of the temporal interests of the institution." She was "the moving Spirit of the place," operating the school, organizing religious and temperance activities, and, not least important, soliciting the thousands of dollars of private money necessary to keep the venture afloat. Quaker sources recall her "somewhat stern expression indicative of an iron will and an indomitable purpose." She must, indeed, have been an impressive, and formidable, woman. Certainly, Colonel Bentzoni thought so. In later years he remembered her as "the grandest woman I have ever known. With unusual executive abilities, she combined a tenderness of heart and unbounded desire to help the lowly and needy." An equally admiring southern neighbor added: "She had more moral courage and invincible determination than any individual I ever met." Certainly, Alida needed all the courage and determination she could muster just to ensure Southland's survival. More than a half century later, Lucy Barnett, an elderly black Friend who worked as a cook during Southland's early years, recalled how "Miz' Clark" had to care for "all those little kids some of 'em just babies. . . . Once there were seventy-two here, and they all had the measles at once. She had some time then."[31]

Some of the first difficulties the Clarks faced at Southland were elemental. For while the Freedmen's Bureau was again providing rations for the children, Quaker missionaries needed to acquire living and teaching facilities that afforded some protection from the erratic local climate, which often tended towards extremes. The original barracks-style schoolhouse, like the teachers' and orphans' quarters, was "a rough frame building, 24 × 50 feet" with an open floor and vertical weather boarding that did little to stop the wind, "so that we all shiver in the cold weather." There must have been abundant shivering that first winter. A Quaker teacher at the Freedmen Bureau's school in Helena reported in late November 1867 that classes were dismissed for two days on account of extreme cold that presented "the risk of health . . . to both ourselves and the pupils." Alida recounted to English Friends: "We have decided to beg for Money . . . so that our lives may not be endangered by exposure."[32]

Buildings were not all that was needed if Friends wished "to educate and train in a guarded, religious and literary sense. . . ." Warm clothing, furniture, desks, and Bibles and other books were always in short supply. And while the number of orphans being looked after and educated continued to grow, more and more black children living in the immediate area flocked to Southland for instruction. At the same time, despite the efforts of the combined Friends' Relief Committee, monetary support from that source gradually diminished. On 31 May 1867 the relief committee was dissolved and its remaining assets divided among the four constituent yearly meetings, with Indiana's share amounting to less than seven hundred dollars. Thereafter, as the immediate postwar crisis abated and the lives of Friends and other northerners returned to normal, Quaker contributions for freedmen's relief rapidly declined. The Indiana Freedmen's Committee reported in 1866 that it had been able to collect only seventeen thousand dollars of the thirty thousand that was needed and had only been saved from further embarrassment by large donations from England. In 1870, despite the continued appeals from the Clarks and other Quaker teachers and missionaries, the Indiana committee received only about eleven thousand dollars, one-fourth of its peak collection in 1865. Still, the importance of the work being done by Friends like the Clarks was acknowledged by the establishment in 1869 of a missionary board whose charge was to stimulate spiritual and social activism among Indiana Friends. Daniel Salemson has made the important point that the campaign to bring relief and spread the gospel to freedmen "fundamentally altered orthodox Quakerism." Missionaries like the Beards became leaders of a dynamic revivalist movement among midwestern and western Friends that resulted in a dramatic reversal of the Society of Friends' numerical decline over several decades. Calvin and Alida Clark were also intimately involved with this movement, although, as will be seen, their efforts to gather lost and abandoned black sheep into the Quaker fold would not result in universal approbation among Indiana Friends.[33]

While Southland slowly took shape as a educational and religious institution, Phillips County was experiencing the legacy of despoliation and defeat. Times were hard for whites as well as blacks. In 1867 one Helena planter thought that half the county's population was petitioning for bankruptcy, and it is doubtful he included exslaves in his calculations. As for the county's blacks, some local white people believed that the situation was exacerbated by government policy to treat "the negro as better than a white man & protect him first." Whites of the prewar elite were generally pessimistic with regard to freedmen doing anything useful for themselves or others. Judge Henry Hanks was convinced "that negroes will never learn any thing for their own good," and Rev. Otis Hackett felt that blacks could not "be depended upon. As their own masters they are restless, shiftless and idle."[34]

Certainly, not all freedmen were idle. Indeed, by 1866 over four thousand Phillips County black people were working under 650 sharecropping agreements. Still, in the postwar struggle for getting or keeping land, prewar planters, regardless of their wartime allegiance, were, by and large, able to retain their holdings as President Johnson's pardon to former rebels "drastically reduced the lands available" for redistribution to former slaves and placed the landless black labor force at a considerable disadvantage, as the vast majority of exslaves were forced to seek a livelihood according to whatever terms white landowners dictated. After early experiments with wage or wage-share arrangements, the sharecrop or crop-lien system was widely adopted in Phillips County as it was throughout the South. The overall effect of this system was to lock black sharecroppers into ironclad contracts that required they grow cotton. Their situation was further compromised in 1868 when the Arkansas legislature passed a law establishing the superiority of the landlord's crop lien over claims of his tenants.[35]

In the summer of 1867 Alida Clark noted that "very few of the colored people who worked for the cotton last year have ever received a dime for it." Given the circumstances, she feared most farm laborers and sharecroppers in Phillips County would remain as poor as when they were liberated from slavery, regardless of how hard they worked. The planters, she said, "will not be encumbered with them." When Mrs. Clark attempted to solicit funds "from Northern and Southern citizens" of Helena to provide assistance for sick and indigent blacks, her collection was meager to say the least—five dollars, some yard goods, kitchen utensils, some brown sugar, and a Biblical text.[36]

Even the most dedicated missionary, surrounded by such poverty and indifference, might have been disheartened, but as one visiting Friend noted, the Clarks appeared to be "cheered with the prospect before them." One cause of this cheerfulness may have been the praise Freedmen Bureau officials continued to heap upon them. Major Sweeney, the Bureau's chief agent in Helena, expressed his hope to Indiana Yearly Meeting that Calvin and Alida's "reward be large in the world to come, as their labor is great in the present" and Gen. C. H. Smith, assistant commissioner for Arkansas, expressed "a *decided* wish that Friends should continue in charge of the Asylum." More important for Alida was the fact that they had proven that "the work of educating, elevating and Christianizing these colored people could readily be done and upon this depended the success or failure of emancipation, and the welfare of our Country South." Still, there were times, as noted by Walter Carpenter, treasurer of the Indiana Freedmen's executive committee, when even Calvin and Alida felt that "the work was too great."[37] Certainly, their burden was not lightened by the fact that in August 1866 the postwar Arkansas legislature came under the control of former Confederate leaders who passed laws denying blacks certain fundamental liberties, including the right to vote or to have access to public education. Thus, the only educational opportunities available for these supposedly freed people were a handful of schools maintained by religious and philanthropic associations from the north and operated on a shoestring in an extremely hostile environment. In Arkansas, a year after the fall of the Confederacy and the abolition of slavery, lately oppressed blacks seemed once again at the mercy of their former oppressors who, in the words of one ex-Confederate officer, appeared to have "recovered by the ballot what they had lost by the sword."[38] The gentle Quakers who had come South under the protection of the Union Army to aid in the education and "moral uplift" of freedmen, were, like their charges, thrown back on their own resources.

CHAPTER 3

The Curse of Slavery and War

1866–1870

> *The curse of slavery and war . . . rests upon this country. . . . The fruits grown from such seed, sown by such hideous monsters are ripening. So, why wonder that murders, thefts, robberies, and other rampant wickedness flourish in high places; that some legislative halls become pandemoniums of the covetous, the ignorant, and vicious lovers of self, and the greed for gold, power, and place!*[1]

I. This Land of Distress

Early in 1868, in the midst of her fourth year in Arkansas, Alida Clark vividly expressed her frustrations and concerns to the *Friends' Review*:

> I again address thee from this land of distress, want and suffering . . . all is one continued wail of affliction and destitution. The cry of *unrequited toil* . . . of oppressing the hireling in his wages and taking advantage of that ignorance and stupidity which oppression and servitude have entailed upon millions.[2]

Mrs. Clark spoke not just from the heart but from hard experience. In the spring of 1867 the levee at Helena had broken, and while Crowley's Ridge sheltered Southland from the flood, she witnessed the "indescribable" suffering of the poorest inhabitants, "driven from their wretched hovels into the pitiless storm, without shelter, blanket, or anything to eat." By the summer of that year one result of the flood that had "piled people up into heaps" was the visitation of cholera and other diseases from which Southland apparently was not protected. As Alida reported in July, Calvin, worn down by his "constant superintendence" of the farm, buildings, and financial accounts, had been stricken, "seemingly unto *death*" with symptoms she diagnosed as "strongly *typhoid*, very bilious, a deep cold, and almost predisposed to cholera." Calvin subsequently improved, perhaps, as Alida believed, in response to the "fervent, earnest and agonizing prayer" of Henrietta Kitterall, an orphan rescued by the Clarks who they later called their daughter, but the general situation did not. The rains continued unabated, making it impossible for the black people to put in a crop or for the recovering Calvin even to remove weeds from the fields.[3] Freedmen as a class, Alida lamented, were "flat upon their backs," but still they scrimped and sacrificed to educate their children, even as their debts to unscrupulous planters grew.

> True these poor people are safe from the auction block and bill of sale but they are beholden to their former masters and owners for labor. . . . Am I not a slave if I am dependent upon some one to do my thinking for me? I think so—and therefore I endeavor to work assiduously with my hands, tongue and pen for the true freedom of these people, and their elevation from the slough of hopeless oppression, by the ladder of Education, with its sisters Religion, Morality and Justice.[4]

Alida Clark's ringing attestation of the need for fair play and justice for Arkansas blacks would seem to confirm historian Ronald Butchart's contention that Quakers, unlike most representatives of the various denominations that came south, consistently "taught equality." Butchart holds that most northern Christian missionaries and teachers maintained condescending attitudes towards the blacks among whom they proselytized, whereas Friends looked upon education as "a logical, unquestioned corollary to freedom" and believed that if given "the opportunity to practice the arts of civilization," black people would prove themselves equal to "'their Saxon oppressors.'" Quakers, he contends, responded in this singular way not only because they believed that all white Americans had been "'unwilling participants'" in the sin of slavery and, thus, owed a debt to their black brethren but also because Friends "resisted the tendency to subordinate the freedmen and their schooling to the dictates of denominational imperialism."[5]

Butchart contrasts this enlightened Quaker approach with the "fundamentally flawed" philosophical imperative of the American Missionary Association (AMA), that is, "to plant New England in the South" and to establish schools that would tame black people through sectarian instruction "as a means of using the freedman for white ends." Such an agenda, he asserts, no matter how earnestly pursued, amounted to "cultural imperialism" and "helps us understand the failure of Reconstruction, the betrayal of emancipation, and the subsequent history of American race relations." On the other hand, Friends who came South should be absolved from blame because they never sought "parochial schools and denominational indoctrination." The idea that their efforts "might lead to more black members or black churches," he concludes, "never seems to have occurred to them."[6]

In his definitive study of change among American Quakers in the later nineteenth century, Thomas Hamm seems to support Butchart's impressive arguments about the contrast between Quaker and other post–Civil War missions to redeem southern blacks. Hamm asserts that most Quaker workers in the postwar South "showed little interest in proselytizing among the former slaves" perhaps even because "elements of racism may have been involved." Still, the attitudes and actions of the Friends who stayed at Southland to create Quakerism's first black monthly meeting would seem to indicate that, for apparently contradictory reasons, both Butchart's and Hamm's conclusions about the nature of the Society of Friends' mission to the freedmen are, at best, only half correct.[7]

II. Light in the Lord

There were, in fact, Friends who consistently advocated bringing the Quaker message to any who were ready to hear it, including southern black people. These were, by and large, younger leaders of the evangelical revival which swept through southern and western Quakerism in the decades surrounding the Civil War, climaxing in an extreme revivalist or holiness movement which spawned serious theological disputes among Friends during the 1870s and 1880s. Indeed, Hamm believes that the division between those who wished to recruit blacks members and their more traditional (or more racist) brethren foreshadowed a wider split among Orthodox Friends.[8]

As noted above, when Elkanah Beard first ministered to freedmen in 1863, he was not confident in their ability to adopt Quaker beliefs and methods of worship. Beard's experience was that black worship services often lasted "longer than is profitable" and were louder than was comfortable. Therefore, he advised Friends who ministered to the freedmen to forget about Quaker traditions like silent worship and instead to concentrate on being "always devotional [and] fervent in prayer." Events would show that such a nontraditional approach was the direction in which revivalist Friends wished to take their entire religious society, that is, away from the stylized preaching and often stifling silence of traditional Quaker meetings and toward a more direct and all-embracing form of Bible-based Gospel ministry. Thus, when John Henry Douglas (1832–1919), who would become one of Quakerism's most powerful holiness evangelists, visited Helena in 1865, he rejected the view that "we cannot make Quakers of these people. . . . If we *would* we *can*. . . . If the right kind of ministers would settle in Helena, they could make Quakers of nearly every one of them." For over twenty years, Alida Clark ministered in Arkansas attempting to fulfill John Henry Douglas's vision.[9]

Indeed, the concept of attracting hundreds or thousands of freedmen into the Society of Friends in the chaotic aftermath of the Civil War was perhaps less radical or visionary than it might first seem. For while it is true that Quakers had from the late seventeenth century virtually ceased to proselytize among the world's people, by the mid-nineteenth century American Friends, as they moved west had come to share many attitudes about the nature of Christian life with their Protestant neighbors. As made clear in Thomas Hamm's seminal work on the *Transformation of American Quakerism,* during the 1860s and 1870s midwestern Quakers were caught up in a strongly evangelical revival movement. Thus, the sort of emotional evangelicalism that southern whites had preached to black slaves was an increasing common aspect of Quaker worship in Indiana Yearly Meeting. At the same time, Friends continued to maintain the "watchful care" reflected in their traditional *Discipline,* emphasizing a strong sense of social responsibility and family stability. Such a religious message, delivered with the fire and passion by a powerful and sympathetic personality like Alida Clark, might indeed have a ready audience.[10]

During the two years Susan Horney spent in Helena after arriving there with the Clarks, she came to believe that black people were more inclined to religion than whites because they were "a more praying people." Certainly, most of those who came under Alida Clark's charge fit this description, whatever their previous religious associations. From the beginning orphans at Southland were required "to attend the preaching service, the prayer meeting, the Sunday School, [and] the temperance meeting." This emphasis appeared to have the desired effect. When a representative of the Indiana Freedmen's Committee inspected the orphan asylum in November 1866, he took special note of local people's growing interest in the meeting Mrs. Clark had established and of her decision to "take the names of such as desired to become members of our Society." As Alida recounted to readers of the *Friends' Review,* "We have opened books & received seventy-six names for members in our meeting here, preparatory to being attached to Indiana Yearly Meeting at some future time."[11]

In a religious, as indeed in every other sense, Mrs. Clark was always a woman of action; in this instance, however, her actions may have appeared precipitous if not reckless to some more cautious Friends. Four months after the initial announcement of Alida's intention to establish a regular, recognized Quaker meeting at Southland, the *Friends' Review* gave considerable space to making clear "that there has been no attempt to introduce persons into membership with the Religious Society of Friends in an irregular way." For her part, Mrs. Clark felt the need personally to dispel "a wrong impression in the minds of some" that freemen at Southland had been admitted to the society *en masse,* without first being subjected to rigorous inquiries as to the fitness of each candidate. Obviously, the *Review* believed it was entirely in order to trust the judgment of the Clarks' own Whitewater Monthly Meeting to give direction to the "vital, aggressive, convincing and converting Quakerism" that Calvin and Alida were pursuing in order "to persuade even the dark-browed descendants of Africa to become 'light in the Lord.'" Mrs. Clark was moved to admonishment in tones reminiscent of the evangelistic fervor of seventeenth-century Friends:

> Let me say to the followers of George Fox everywhere, rouse up, and let us shake ourselves from the dust of the earth, from a love of ease and too great pursuit of riches, from luxury and pomp, and endeavor to fill up the programme that Fox . . . marked out for us in all its bearings, especially toward the Negro race. The whole

> *South* is spread open to the Quakers and they are invited to come into it and labor and settle. . . . I want to see a great *Black Yearly Meeting* all over this benighted and truly heathen land. Because I love Friends in all their *faith* and purity of doctrine, I want others to enjoy the fullness of the religion of Jesus . . . regardless of color.[12]

C. S. Hubbard, a representative of Indiana Yearly Meeting who visited the Asylum early in 1867, found many of the children there "earnest and anxious to know about Divine things." Indeed, Hubbard encouraged Indiana Friends to raise "an army" of teachers and preachers to come South to spread the gospel, although he did not go so far as to explicitly welcome dark-skinned, "less favored brethren" into the Society of Friends. The Clarks, however, had no hesitation. Reporting that over seventy freedmen had enrolled in the meeting "to build one another up in the most holy faith . . . and instruct each other in the way of life everlasting," they added the startling request that one of these members, Daniel Drew, a former slave and Union army veteran, should be recorded as a Quaker minister. "We know it will seem to you a formidable and weighty step, but dear friends we are convinced that the cause of Truth will be advanced thereby and his way opened for more effectual service among his poor people." Mrs. Clark had taken Drew, a surviving veteran of the Fifty-Sixth Colored Infantry in his mid-twenties, under her wing early on, recognizing his special abilities as an inspiring preacher. She described him as "a chosen vessel of no ordinary qualifications and talent" with a deep knowledge and understanding of the Bible, a gift of ministry, and a clear grasp of Quaker principles, including the peace testimony. He had, she said, "parted company with all carnal weapons" and become a soldier of the Lord.[13]

When the petition to record Daniel Drew as a minister was presented, neither he nor any other black person attending Southland Meeting had even been accepted as a member of Indiana Yearly Meeting. Taken aback by the novelty, let alone the propriety of such a request, members of the freedmen's committee, which was still supervising yearly meeting's southern field operations, agreed only to take the matter under advisement. In the meantime, in late May 1868, Whitewater Monthly Meeting received seven "colored members," including Daniel Drew and Henrietta Kitterall, into its ranks, the first of several hundred Southland blacks to embrace

Quakerism.[14] For Mrs. Clark the reception of these black Friends was obviously an opening wedge, and thereafter she lost no opportunity to push forward the possibilities for Southland Meeting and the virtues of its members or to single out the work of "our dear Friend Daniel" for praise. Over the next two years nearly every letter she dispatched to the Quaker press or officials in Indiana celebrated Drew's devotion to his calling and his success in following it. Citing his "mission of love" up the White River to save souls in Clarendon, "the *hardest* place anywhere," to his service to prisoners at the Phillips County jail, to his dangerous travels in the ministry among hostile whites, Alida termed him "a Friend indeed." The same, she said, could be said of many other freedmen who, in addition to faithfully attending meeting, "show forth in their daily work . . . and in the ordering of their families the religion of Jesus."[15]

The leadership of Indiana Yearly Meeting eventually found Alida Clark's pleas for a separate and official preparatory meeting at Southland impossible to resist. In 1870 Southland was officially recognized as a particular meeting under the auspices of Whitewater Monthly Meeting. Not only was Southland the first Friends meeting in Arkansas, it was also the first predominately black Quaker meeting established in North America. During that same year, "Daniel Drew, a colored man," was one of thirteen persons recorded in the ministry by Indiana Yearly Meeting, becoming Southland's first recorded minister and almost certainly the first black person to be so recorded since Friends took up the practice in 1722. While no confirming evidence exits, it seems likely that Alida Clark, who was clearly the dominant force at Southland, held off petitioning to be recorded as a minister until her protégé was so recognized.[16]

In any case, Mrs. Clark did not use the occasion of Drew's official endorsement as a Quaker minister to rest from her labors, physical or spiritual. There were, she said, "many counteracting influences" hindering their work, including local black preachers, "especially a bad man from the North. . . . preaching . . . heathenism and barbarism." But although local folk still liked to hear "their own peculiar rambling stormy sermons of two hours length with excitement and noise," she was endeavoring "to teach and preach the plain precepts of the Gospel" and the quiet solemnity of Friends meetings was "telling fast upon them."[17]

Alida's infectious enthusiasm, and the glowing reports of visiting Friends who described religious meetings at Southland as "seasons of

Divine favor," may have diminished lingering doubts among some Friends about the efficacy of the Clarks' missionary enterprise. Subsequently, supervision of Southland Meeting was placed directly under the newly established missionary board rather than Whitewater Monthly Meeting. This board had been established to develop a "definite plan for more direct and extended efforts for the evangelizing of this people."[18] Mrs. Clark, it seemed, had carried the day.

In the interim, however, Alida, having been made aware that certain influential eastern Friends were expressing doubts about the nature and efficacy of the new black meeting, resumed the offensive in a letter to the executive board of Philadelphia Yearly Meeting's Freedmen's Aid Committee. It was, she said, "an unaccountable mystery" that those who shared the faith of John Woolman, Anthony Benezet, and other Quaker prophets of emancipation should be "the very last" to welcome "these sable fellow beings."

> Many *good* people profess to believe that *the colored people* are too emotional and impressible ever to become Friends . . . [but] thorough and deep work of grace is just the same in the heart, no matter the color of the skin. . . . and I would affectionately call the serious attention of Friends everywhere to the consideration of the great subject. . . . Let us examine ourselves and see if there is not a prejudice and jealousy (cruel as the grave) against color that is hindering our ultimate success.

The time was long past, Alida declared, for Quakers "to wake up and rouse themselves . . . to an aggressive movement." In her mind there was "no code more perfectly adapted to the lowly . . . and the poor" than Quakerism. Thus, she audaciously, and perhaps in some minds even heretically, declared, "If our system of worship is unsuited to the lowly, let it be altered." Given the predominant historical, social, and theological status of Philadelphia Yearly Meeting, this was a considerable blast, coming as it did from a western Friend of no particular prominence or weight. Alida's admonition also reflected the growing discrepancy between western evangelical Friends and their more staid eastern brethren.[19]

Obviously then, Mrs. Clark's foremost interest was in advancing "Friends' Free Gospel ministry and church organization . . . to the helpless, ignorant and poor condition of these once enslaved creatures." For an example of the healing power of grace through Quaker faith and practice she offered the words of Henrietta Kitterall, a mulatto girl whom was among the first orphans abandoned to their charge:

> When I first came here I knew nothing of the Bible and its truths. . . . since I have been here I have learned how to read the Bible, and I have learned to love my Saviour. . . . I want to . . . make myself useful in the service of the Lord. . . . and useful to my people, who have been so long under cruel bondage.[20]

Alida also believed that local white people, especially the poor, were yearning to hear the redeeming Word. To this end, she joined with Daniel Drew in carrying Friends' message to the area surrounding Southland, and late in 1870 she was able to report the successful establishment of a "large and remarkable" meeting attended by whites as well as blacks at Hickory Ridge (later renamed Marvel), fifteen miles from the school. In this regard, she surmised that a great multitude of sinners "might be gathered by pastors and ministers and be added as stars in their crowns" if northern Friends would only "come over into Macedonia" (Acts 16:9) to aid in the cause. There were, she noted, "good plantations and woodlands for sale . . . enough to form a Quaker colony." The field was ripe for harvest, if only the laborers would come gather the crop of eager souls.[21]

III. A Good Schoolhouse

For all their religious concerns, the Clarks had more to worry about than Southland's spiritual condition. By the spring of 1867 there were over eighty children at the Southland Asylum to be fed, clothed, and educated. This was proving to be a physically trying experience for Calvin and Alida as well as an expensive proposition for Indiana Yearly Meeting, which was also maintaining freedmen's schools in the town of Helena and in Little Rock. As contributions for the support of freedmen diminished, the leadership of Indiana Friends became increasingly concerned about their ability to sustain commitments in Arkansas. One means of easing this financial burden was the attempt to find homes in the North for some of the orphans, with the government providing for the cost of their transportation. At the time it was felt that placing them in the South might put them in "no better condition than slavery." Some places were found for children in St. Louis, but this apparently did not significantly diminish the scope or expense of the venture. When school began at Southland in fall 1867, Alida, bemoaning the "hot and dry and sickly weather," confessed that while she did not feel her work in Arkansas was finished, the experience was proving "very *wearing* both to body and mind." So much so, she said, that Calvin believed "he must soon be relieved" and, indeed, even heretofore irrepressible Alida, felt that her "energies have been so long *overtaxed* . . . that I cannot hold out much longer. . . . to do justice to ourselves we are really unable for service just now."[22]

Given the apparent paucity of financial resources and the obvious difficulty of finding anyone to replace the Clarks, it seemed as if the future of the entire Southland experiment was imperiled. But, in fact, Alida's lament proved to be more a product of momentary frustration than an actual threat of resignation. Furthermore, at this crucial juncture, the federal government, wielding the power of three Reconstruction Acts passed by a Republican-dominated Congress in the spring and summer of 1867, stepped forward to provide a helping hand. Since the orphans at Southland were effectively wards of the Freedmen's Bureau, the Clarks as teachers and managers of the institution were technically federal employees, and bureau officials did not wish to be deprived of their services. In May 1867 the Rev. Enoch K. Miller, an AMA official who was also inspector of Freedmen's Bureau schools in Arkansas, visited Southland and found the school there to be "a grand affair," heaping praise on Quaker teachers there as well as those in Helena. Indeed, William Colby, director of freedmen's schools in Arkansas, ranked the Clarks and other Friends as the most efficient teachers among the thirty-two employed by bureau-sponsored schools in the state. Furthermore, Calvin was singled out as "the best practical farmer in Arkansas."[23] Thus faced with even the outside possibility of a Quaker withdrawal, officers of the Bureau proposed to reduce Friends' expenditure for food by designating Southland as a hospital, thereby making the institution eligible for "hospital rations" rather than the much less generous "contraband rations" it had been receiving.[24]

Buoyed up by this subsidy, by continued optimistic reports from Southland visitors like Elkanah Beard, and by the apparent determination of radical Republicans to ensure that exrebels would not achieve a political victory that might reverse their military defeat, the executive board of Indiana Yearly Meeting affirmed its commitment to the asylum, noting that, in addition to their compelling spiritual mission, Friends at Southland had an eight-thousand-dollar investment in property that was beginning to become productive.[25] Furthermore, the institution was in the center of an area, mainly populated by exslaves, where no public schools existed.[26]

This appalling situation arose from the fact that Arkansas's conservative or "rebel" legislature elected in 1866 not only had barred exslaves from, among other things, voting, sitting on juries, or serving in the militia but also had failed to establish even a separate school system for blacks. The inadequacy of the scattered schools operated by the Freemen's Bureau to close this educational gap was reflected in the fact that in the first half of 1867, the bureau spent only a little over eight thousand dollars all told on construction and maintenance of schools in Arkansas. Even after a new Republican-dominated state legislature had met the provisions of the Reconstruction Acts and Arkansas was readmitted to the union in June 1868, a survey conducted by the state's commissioner of immigration indicated that only four schools (presumably including Southland) were operating in all of Phillips County.[27]

By way of contrast Mrs. Clark reported early in 1868 that their school was flourishing, with a Quaker staff of three teaching 130 scholars arithmetic, geography, and grammar in addition to Bible reading and right living.

> We hope to see some of these continued in school till qualified for teachers, as we believe there is no other way for the *masses* of four millions ever to be reached except by teachers of their own color *taught and drilled in normal schools South*, so that all their interests, associations and attachments will be there.

Officials in Indiana, their optimism restored, agreed, envisioning a school that could accommodate two hundred or more local students whose parents, understanding the importance of education, might in time be able to contribute at least something for their children's schooling. But before this shining Quaker vision could be realized, Southland had to have a proper physical plant, the first perquisite being a new schoolhouse as the one being used was "open as a northern barn" and unfit for human habitation in cold weather.[28]

Southland's children were still shivering in their woeful schoolhouse, however, when the Quakers were informed of the impending shutdown of the Freedmen's Bureau. Yearly meeting officials responded to this new crisis with a renewed effort to find homes in the immediate vicinity of the school for the ninety orphans still housed there while at same time reiterating its commitment to keep Southland open as both a school and "Missionary station." In the meantime, Alida Clark was dispatched to Little Rock to make a last ditch plea to Freedmen's Bureau officials specifically for funds "towards a good schoolhouse at the Asylum" and generally for the means to build new schools for blacks throughout the state. Before setting out on this vital mission, Alida wrote to E. K. Miller, who represented the AMA as well as the bureau, asking for whatever assistance he might render. It was, she said, "the duty of ambassadors to watch over each other for good." Whether or not from Miller's intercession, Mrs. Clark was received in Little Rock with "the utmost kindness and attention." Shortly thereafter, William Colby, general superintendent for Arkansas schools, recommended to his superior, Gen. C. H. Smith, that "it would be good policy" to aid Friends in replacing the "shabby" schoolhouse at Southland with "a good one."[29]

What emerged was a plan for a building suitable for ninety students to be constructed at a cost of three thousand dollars, half of which would be paid by the Freedmen's Bureau. The orphans who still remained at Southland were to be placed in local homes, except for fifteen to twenty "selected to be trained as teachers," whose upkeep would be maintained by Friends. But before this scheme could be implemented, Calvin Clark informed authorities in Indiana that despite Southland's having been given a "very favorable account" by local officials, the Freedmen's Bureau had subsequently notified him of its inability to appropriate the $1,500 that had been pledged for the school building. Where now could Friends turn?[30]

Fortunately for Indiana Yearly Meeting, and for the future of Southland, they did not, in the end, have to provide an answer to that crucial question. Early in 1869 J. W. Alvold, national director for freedmen's schools, wrote to William Colby, informing him that "nothing hitherto gained should be lost" and that schools that had been successfully conducted by religious bodies would continue to be aided by the bureau "by all means and facilities remaining in its possession." Thus,

Southland got its "good school house," a 70' × 32' structure, with the Freedmen's Bureau footing $2,500 of the $3,500 bill, ensuring the Quaker mission would continue as "a centre of great interest, fully appreciated by Freedmen and other citizens" in the area.[31] But there were also "other citizens" whose expressed desire was the prompt removal of Quakers and all northern agitators of their ilk.

From the beginning of their mission the Clarks and their associates had, as already noted, borne "taunts, ignominy and even ostracism" from many white residents of Phillips County. Moreover, in the immediate postwar period the circumstances facing the freed people Quakers had befriended became extremely precarious. Racist feeling was probably even stronger than before the war, and historian Carl Moneyhon believes that in the Arkansas Delta this tendency was exacerbated by a conscious campaign of planters to maintain control of the black labor force, a task made somewhat more difficult from the fact that Arkansas was one of only two ex-Confederate states without the sort of vagrancy law that gave local authorities power to detain any black person who did not possess a labor contract. The elite elements in Phillips County and elsewhere in the Delta therefore played the race card, stressing white race superiority and enlisting poor whites as racial allies if not social or economic equals. Illegal intimidation and unequal law enforcement were among the tactics used to maintain control over the majority black population of Phillips County. Judge James Hanks of Helena was "mortified to see the frivolous and malicious prosecutions against the negroes. . . . It must be stopped or they will produce an unenviable state of affairs."[32]

Freedmen's Bureau records in 1868 indicated that Phillips County had the third highest rate of violent crimes in Arkansas, mainly whites assaulting blacks. Not surprisingly, ill-feeling and even violence spilled over to "nigger teachers" and their schools.[33] One conspicuous cause for continuing white violence was the perceived threat arising from the complicity of northern whites in the registration of nearly twenty-two thousand black Arkansas voters under provisions of the Reconstruction Acts of 1867. Although male freedmen constituted less than a third of all Arkansas voters, in Phillips County they formed a distinct majority (2681 black to 955 white).[34] In the spring of 1867 the Republican Party, to which the Clarks and Indiana Friends in general were devoted, was established in Arkansas. The Union League, a "carpetbagger" organization that encouraged black political participation, was also active in Phillips County. For example, two thousand blacks attended a Union League meeting in Helena in May 1867. The prospect of being overwhelmed by a wave of black Republicans disturbed even moderate local whites like Judge Hanks who believed that the freedmen "poor, deluded, ignorant, superstitious creatures" were "the dupes and victims of sharpers of all sorts. . . . Poor fellows—how terribly they will be . . . made to suffer by their friends."[35] Late in 1867 these new black voters were a key factor in securing overwhelming statewide approval (27,000 to 13,558) for a Republican-dominated constitutional convention intent on complying with the requirements of the Reconstruction Acts in order to secure Arkansas's readmission to the union. The constitution crafted by this convention, which included eight black delegates, gave exslaves full civil and political rights and established a tax-supported system of free public schools available to all persons between five and twenty-one. The animosity aroused by these actions may be garnered from the pronouncements of a "Conservative" or re-reconstructed Democratic counterconvention that proclaimed its advocacy of a "white man's government in a white man's country" and refused to "recognize that the negro has any political rights whatever."[36]

In the circumstances it is not surprising that Alida Clark reported in April 1868 that impending elections for endorsement of the new state constitution and new state officials were causing "much stir and anxiety." Local blacks came, "some . . . for miles," to seek advice from the Clarks.

> Their troubles and perplexities about voting are perfectly inconceivable to the northern person. The planters know how to scare and deceive them, and . . . use every means in their power, even to hiring them not to vote the Republican ticket. . . . Many will lose their situations and be put to every inconvenience possible . . . for voting . . . Republican.[37]

Besides the resentment she elicited for urging blacks to vote the straight (and victorious) Republican ticket, Alida may have evoked as much or even more animosity from local people for directing those who sought her guidance to vote dry in local referenda on the liquor trade. As the elections of November 1868 neared, she dispatched a dramatic communication to the Quaker press, noting that although she and Calvin had "remained steadily on duty at this frightful post through the long, weary, hot season," their political situation was "but 'a reign of terror.'"

> Our Institution's life and existence are threatened by the "Ku Klux" and only spared . . . by fear and dread of insurrection by the blacks . . . we are surrounded by a class of persons who burn colored orphan asylums . . . and nothing but a measure of the overshadowing presence . . . of the orphan's eternal Father could . . . carry us through such ordeals. . . . We live in earnest hope and eager expectation that the fortnight may sound from Indiana, Ohio and Pennsylvania such an overwhelming voice for Republicans as will strike Rebels and Ku Klux dumb.[38]

The answer to Mrs. Clark's prayer, a Radical Republican victory in national elections as well as in Arkansas and even in Phillips County, did seem to bring about an abrupt change in attitude or approach among at least some of the white population. The Indiana Freedmen's Committee in its final report before being replaced by the missionary board noted that "quiet and harmony very generally prevail" in the vicinity of the school and that previously scorned Quaker teachers were being "welcomed and respected" by local white people. For example, Dr. A. A. Horner, a former slave owner, was providing "gratuitous medical services" at Southland despite having to travel ten miles on bad roads to reach the school. Furthermore, at a time when financial assistance was badly needed, English and Irish Friends had sent contributions of over $3,500 in support of Southland's work.[39] On the other hand, Alida Clark's final report for the 1860s, while emphasizing the positive achievements of their mission and the growing generosity of private donors, contained a grim statistic that underscored the tempestuous and tragic nature of that decade as well as necessity for the good Dr. Horner's services. From the time of its opening in 1864, the asylum had received 360 children into its care, of these 10 percent had died from various causes. The image of one or the other of the Clarks lifting three dozen small, lifeless bodies from their beds to prepare them for burial was perhaps less startling to an age more accustomed to the death of children, but such a vision may serve as a reminder of the fundamental nature of Southland's early role as a refuge for "the most hopeless class" of the lost and abandoned.[40] Still, at the dawning of a new decade, there were signs that the somber past might be giving way to a glowing future.

Certainly, one of the most promising developments was the comprehensive restructuring of Arkansas's educational system during the late 1860s. Before the launching of Radical Reconstruction in 1867, the state's postwar committee on education had drafted a bill establishing a new tax-supported school system, "believing that the people are willing to be taxed to educate their children." But the proposed taxes would be paid only by whites, and only white children would be admitted to the schools. In fact, that system never got off the ground because Gen. E. O. C. Ord, commander of the Fourth Military District established by the Military Reconstruction Act of March 1867, suspended the state superintendent of education, and in 1868 the Republican administration of Powell Clayton, passed a public school act providing for the establishment of a system of free public schools for all from ages five to twenty-one to be financed by a one-dollar poll tax on all adult males, revenues from the sale of public lands, and other state and local taxes. School districts were set up throughout the state, and in December 1868 trustees were elected for each district. Early in 1869 Alida Clark pridefully reported that Calvin had been "unanimously elected as Trustee for white and colored schools in this district" and the whites as well as blacks were

> jubilant over the free school systems. . . . The bitter prejudices are gradually passing away, and those who have shown themselves contemptuous towards *us* and our *work* are becoming familiar, affable, sociable, hospitable and *irksome*. I need grace to endure such forced *kindness*.[41]

For all of Alida's discomfiture, things were most assuredly looking up for Friends' work in Arkansas. Republicans had gained control of the state's government, a new school system had been initiated, local whites were accepting rather than threatening Quaker teachers, and, as a parting gratuity, the Freemen's Bureau promised a special appropriation of five thousand dollars for the building of "ampler school buildings" at Southland. In addition, a new barn had been built from proceeds garnered from the sale of farm produce. As the total value for this expanding campus reached nearly ten thousand, Indiana Yearly Meeting determined to extend and deepen its commitment to the institution. Alida Clark's continued reports of progress in advancing religion as well as learning seemed to justify continued financial and personal sacrifices. As one visiting Indiana Friend reported:

> Socially and intellectually, there is a very marked difference between the orphans who have been for some years under the training and

> instruction of the Superintendent [Calvin] and teachers and those whose surroundings have been less favorable to development. . . . The Orphan Asylum is a center of intelligence and Christian influence in a locality where such influences are very much needed.[42]

Had the curse of slavery and war finally been lifted from the selfless Quakers and their destitute charges? Friends, as always, were inclined to hope. Certainly, their influence for good seemed to have been recognized in Arkansas. Elkanah Beard, while visiting with public officials in Little Rock on behalf of Indiana Yearly Meeting early in 1869, received a special vote of thanks from the Republican-dominated legislature for the role Friends had played in pioneering educational development for the state's freedmen—a signal honor for a northern ambassador. Nevertheless, Beard, for one, remained wary. In his travels through the state, he had discovered that many individuals in "responsible positions" seemed determined to hinder the progress of education for exslaves while other elected officials, including blacks, had proved themselves unfit for public office. Beard's unhappy, and ominous, conclusion was that even "the dreadful scourge of war and bloodshed that has swept our beloved country does not seem to have lessened the prevailing vices of the Southern people."[43]

Chapter 4

The Bible and the Spelling Book

Living and Learning

> *Let His truly baptized and anointed believers pray that a special shaking might quicken up the dark hearts of the benighted inhabitants of this slave-cursed, war-ravaged land. . . . O! send us the means and the money to disseminate a knowledge of the Bible and the spelling book.*[1]

I. Carrying On

Observing the moral and spiritual landscape of the Arkansas Delta from her isolated rural post at the turn of a new decade, Alida Clark believed that only remedies offered by the Society of Friends could elevate the condition of the place and its people. The Bible as the symbol of Southland's Quaker meeting and the spelling book as the foundation of its educational program were, of necessity, fundamental instruments for fulfilling the society's spiritual and temporal mission. Mrs. Clark could feel that a good start had been made. A new schoolhouse was under construction that augured well for the educational effort that had already served nearly two hundred orphans and local students. The establishment of Southland as an officially recognized preparatory meeting for worship was a fulfillment of another of her dreams. Politically, things were less glowing. Although Republican governor Powell Clayton had taken strong measures to put down the Ku Klux Klan and other lawless elements, the nascent Arkansas Republican

Party was already divided over accusations that the Clayton administration was becoming both oppressive and corrupt. The ensuing intraparty struggle, eventually leading to political chaos, internecine violence, and the end of Radical Reconstruction in Arkansas, could only have an ominously negative influence on Southland's mission.[2]

Still, for the time being, there seemed cause for optimism. The schoolhouse was completed in 1870 and the deed handed over to the missionary board as trustees for the asylum. The orphans, in addition to their academic training, were "industrious out of school," working on the farm, "sewing for the Institution and improving" in all branches of housewifery."[3] But there were setbacks as well.

In the summer of 1872 serious illness, no doubt abetted by overwork, nearly killed Calvin Clark for the second time. When Elkanah Beard visited Southland in late August, he reported that Calvin was not expected to live. Indeed, his eventual recovery was looked upon locally as something of a miracle. Nearly as miraculous was the ability of the Clarks somehow to balance their diverse responsibilities and concerns so as to allow Southland school and meeting not only to survive but, eventually, to thrive.[4]

There was more to Calvin and Alida than hard bark and probably less than unalloyed candidacy for sainthood. Close consideration of Southland's early development as a school and a center of spiritual life can, in Quaker parlance, allow "way to open" to an deeper understanding of Southland's founders and of the religious, educational, and social milieu they fashioned at their primitive, arduous, and alien post in Arkansas.

II. Soldiers of the Cross

Northern visitors continued to describe Southland as "a center of intelligence and Christian influence" promoting "much needed" scriptural instruction. In light of such reports the Indiana Missionary Board was "encouraged to proceed with the arduous and responsible labor" that lay before them.[5] In the autumn of 1872 Daniel Drew journeyed with Calvin and Alida Clark to the annual gathering of Indiana Yearly Meeting in Richmond where Drew also attended a meeting of the missionary board. Both these bodies were obviously impressed by their novel, dark-skinned visitor. Reports from yearly meeting commented effusively on the dignity of his bearing and the eloquence of his speech. All agreed that he seemed "a man of good sense and a sound Gospel minister;" the missionary board gave their new black minister carte blanche to "attend to any call of duty."[6] No doubt Daniel Drew's presence at yearly meeting, adding luster to the glowing reports of progress at Southland, led Indiana Friends at last to issue an unambiguous endorsement of efforts to reap a harvest of black members into their religious society:

> Our sympathy has been enlisted for the dear Friends who are . . . laboring in this work, and we desire to encourage them to continue faithfulness. . . . The question as to the practicability of gathering into . . . our religious Society those who have been brought under the influence of their instructions . . . has been forcibly and earnestly brought before us, and the Meeting desires that our dear Friends . . . may be faithful in endeavoring to throw around them the arms of the Church as way may open, bearing in mind "to lay upon them no greater burden" than they are able to bear.[7]

This pronouncement was followed by visits to Southland from several prominent representatives of the yearly meeting, all of whom observed the "favorable condition" of the school and meeting. During that same year (1872) Alida Clark was duly recorded as Southland's second gospel minister, and Calvin was appointed as the meeting's first elder. The next year, after the meeting's membership had risen to sixty-one souls, the missionary board recommended to yearly meeting that Southland be granted status as a full-fledged monthly meeting, able to conduct business, grant membership, and form subordinate meetings for worship. Southland Monthly Meeting was directed to gather for business on the third Wednesday of each month and to report directly to the missionary board, which, having "special and extraordinary authority" to pursue work among the freedmen, obviously wished to ensure close supervision of this unique meeting. Thus, on 17 December 1872 Southland Monthly Meeting, the first Quaker congregation in Arkansas, "proceeded to business under a solemn covering of the overshadowing presence of the great Head of the Church," with Alida and Calvin Clark acting as clerks for the day.[8]

What might an observer have seen and heard on that third Wednesday and during subsequent meetings of Quakerism's first predominately black monthly meeting? To begin, in the early days at least, both the shape of the business conducted at the monthly meeting and the form of the sabbath or "First Day" worship services were molded less by the black majority than by the experienced and strong-willed Clarks, especially Alida. Their deportment, one may safely assume, was influenced by the evangelical renewal movement that had swept through midwestern Quakerism during the 1860s and with which the Clarks had solid connections. Thus, religious services at Southland, unlike those in, say, Philadelphia at about same time, would probably have incorporated such hitherto un-Quakerly rites as evangelically inspired hymn singing and readings from scripture and probably a prepared sermon on some Biblical theme. On the other hand, available evidence indicates that shouting, speaking in tongues, and other manifestations of "extreme emotionalism" were generally avoided at Southland and that traditional silent waiting upon the "Light of Christ Within" to give direction and power to the meeting was to some degree preserved. For example, Alida's description of Southland's first monthly meeting referred to a "most precious covering of Divine silence" that at times prevailed.[9]

Events, however, would reveal that however isolated, Southland Meeting could not entirely escape the major late-nineteenth-century influences on mainstream evangelical Quakerism west of Philadelphia. For example, even before the official recognition of Southland Monthly Meeting, Elkanah Beard, who had become a leader in spreading the renewal among western Friends, announced that a "general meeting" had been arranged to coincide with the anniversary celebration of Southland's founding. General meetings, another recent innovation for American Friends, were gatherings, often lasting several days, during which dynamic preachers used revivalist methods to bring about conversions among participants who declared their acceptance of Jesus as their savior. One of the strongest arguments for this unconventional form of Quaker worship was its power in drawing new souls into the Religious Society of Friends. Indiana Yearly Meeting reported over nine hundred new members in 1873, including the sixty-one at Southland, significantly bolstering what had long been a numerically declining Quaker community.[10] In June 1873 during a general meeting at Southland, the "truly edifying" Gospel ministry of visiting Indiana evangelist Jesse C. Johnson resulted in the "conversion of several persons" who "after a time of solid deliberation & prayer" were "recorded members of the Religious Society of Friends."[11] Still, whatever the attractions of revivalism to the Clarks and their prominent visitors, Alida had other considerations to bear in mind, and the descriptions of Southland meetings for worship she passed on to the Quaker press had an oddly dichotomous quality. Rather than emphasizing the enthusiasm or intensity of even general meetings, Mrs. Clark stressed the "solid, reverential deportment" of black Friends who, in stark contrast to the "semi-savage gesticulations" common at Baptist and other local churches, where "screams might have been heard for a mile," conducted their services without "boisterous shoutings and unsightly gymnastics." Even "the most wonderful revival ever known amongst us," said Mrs. Clark, had been remarkable for the "quiet stillness" that eventually prevailed: "no emotion, no excitement, none at all. . . . I write the more of this because so many good Friends know how noisy and excitable the colored people are as a race. But education and Quaker teaching and training regulate them, as it does our own children."[12]

Alida's emphasis on the historic aspects of Quaker worship at Southland meetings, even when these were conducted by revivalist preachers, no doubt reflected her concern that voluntary support for the entire Southland project might be jeopardized if northern, eastern, and British Quakers got the idea that freedmen could not sufficiently restrain themselves to worship in the traditional manner of Friends. But while Southland meetings were doubtless more tranquil and composed than local Baptist services, there must, at times, have been the sort of unrestrained singing, shouting, and testifying that characterized contemporaneous Quaker revivals among traditionally staid and laconic midwestern and western Friends.

In any case, Southland Meeting continued its impressive growth during the 1870s. The attraction of Quakerism to local blacks, beyond gratitude for the personal sacrifices the Clarks and other Friends were making in their behalf, may have arisen from the exslaves' perception that Quaker ministry and worship services were superior to the more primitive local variety, while at the same time the evangelical accouterments of Southland Meeting prevented it from being too uncomfortable or alien. Beyond such surface attractions, however, the activist, aggressive personality of Alida Clark clearly came into play. The stream of letters, articles, sermons, and exhortations that she poured forth visibly demonstrated that Mrs. Clark's mind, tongue, and pen were seldom at rest. She not only supervised Southland school and ministered to the meeting but also, on occasion, took to the road to solicit money from stay-at-home northern Friends as well as to hot-gospel her way through every black community in Phillips County and beyond. It is hard to imagine how any meeting where she was present could have remained silent for very long.[13]

Alida Clark's spirit is clearly etched into the Southland Monthly Meeting's minute book. The theological tone of the minutes, in so far as it emerges, reflected a orthodox Gurneyite emphasis on the propitiatory doctrine of the atonement and the ultimate and inerrant authority of the Bible.[14] But even more obvious is the practical and energetic nature of Mrs. Clark's gospel ministry. At the initial gathering of the monthly meeting, for example, the first order of business was the formation of a committee for scriptural instruction that was directed

> to Labour to promote Sabbath school work throughout our borders . . . . [so] that while many are necessarily deprived of going to week day school . . . all may lay hold of the instruction freely offered and given in application and regular attendance a useful store of knowledge.[15]

When Southland Monthly Meeting reconvened on the twenty-first day of first month (January) 1874, the minutes noted that because of the isolated condition of some members, a visitors' committee was being formed "to take the subject in all its weighty responsibilities and bearings" to families in remote locations

> for their help and encouragement, strengthening them in a Christian life and if a way open for it in the Truth, hold a series of meetings in all those neighborhoods laboring to build up and strengthen believers in the Lord everywhere. That by the preaching of the Gospel, sinners may be turned from "darkness to light and from the power of Satan to God," a knowledge of the Gospel life and free salvation by faith in the love of Jesus increased amongst those who may still be sitting in darkness and in the shadow of death.[16]

One traditional aspect of Southland Meeting was its adherence to the practice of Friends' "Christian Discipline" through regular responses to the "Queries" sent by Indiana Yearly Meeting to ascertain the state of the subordinate particular meetings. These responses generally followed the formal, ritualistic patterns into which nineteenth-century Quakers had fallen, as, for example, the answers to the yearly meeting's "Annual Queries" read in the second month (February) 1874:

> First Query: Are your Meetings for worship regularly held, and how are they attended? Are they occasions of religious solemnity and edification . . . ?
>
> First Answer: All the meetings for worship and Discipline have been attended and generally by the greater part of our members. . . . Unbecoming behavior in meeting is avoided: and the hour of meeting is pretty well observed.
>
> Second Query: Do Friends walk in love, "as Christ also hath loved us" and do Friends avoid tale-bearing and detraction?
>
> Second Answer: Friends are preserved in Christian love one toward another: Talebearing and detraction discouraged and mostly avoided.[17]

Sometimes, however, Southland's clerk, adhering to the Quaker propensity for scrupulous honesty, had to owe up to certain imperfections:

> Fourth Query: Are Friends clear of indulgence in intoxicating liquors? Are they clear of attending places of diversion?
>
> Fourth Answer: Friends are clear of importing, vending, distilling and the unnecessary use of all intoxicating liquors except two cases of drinking. So far as appears, clear of attending places of diversion, but not quite clear of attending circus shows.[18]

Perhaps it was those "two cases of drinking" that induced the monthly meeting's passionate charge to its temperance committee

> to use every . . . means that can consistently be brought to bear upon the monstrous evil and enormous crimes resulting from the drinking customs of our country with a view to the entire suppression thereof . . . and [to] induce the people to sign the Total Abstinence Pledge, with a view to building up strong public opinion in favor of Temperance in order that not only dram drinking but . . . the traffic may be entirely swept from our land . . . thus liberated from the blighting and demoralizing effects of the greatest sin now existing in our country, we may rejoice in a more perfect freedom than we now do.[19]

From the beginning of Friends work in Arkansas, the temperance cause, strongly supported by the Freedmen's Bureau, had been a feature of their mission. In 1870, two visitors to Southland from Whitewater Quarterly Meeting noted that local Friends had "labored diligently . . . to abolish the use of intoxicating liquors" but that intemperance remained "a besetting sin" throughout the area. Because Alida Clark regarded the total abstinence pledge "as essential to safety in this vicinity," Southland Meeting consistently waged "unabated war against King Alcohol." She could, for instance, cite the case of Morris Brown as an example of the saving and redeeming power of abstinence. From the time this exsoldier joined the meeting and signed the temperance pledge, his life had been transformed. By avoiding the debilitating affects of hard liquor, he had saved enough to purchase thirty acres near the school and to build a "nice frame house" for his family while simultaneously growing in faith as "a sound Christian and a minister," a status eventually accorded him by Indiana Yearly Meeting.[20]

Alida believed that if Southland Meeting was to grow sufficiently to continue serving the needs of the freedmen, Friends needed to mount a full-scale effort: "Missionary work is greatly needed and a wide door is set open before us." In this regard she was encouraged by such "favorable signs and bright spots" as were provided by Daniel Drew and Morris Brown, both veterans of the late war turned soldiers of the cross. Brown's reformation by way of the temperance pledge had created a formidable team of Quaker missionaries. Drew's accomplishments continued to be impressive, and his fame as a preacher spread throughout the area. He had, for example, taken chief responsible for ministering to the "large and remarkable" biracial meeting at Hickory Ridge.[21]

Still, pleased and proud as Mrs. Clark was with the religious and temperance work of black Friends like Drew and Brown, there was more to do than a small band of Southland Quakers could manage. She was convinced that with the assistance of a few experienced northern ministers and workers, thousands of souls could be permanently garnered for Quakerism through the increased establishment of black meetings. Such ministry was essential to draw the freedmen away from local black churches that "reflect a very poor light," with members and ministers alike indulging in "all the vices of which ignorance is the mother." The most grievously injurious of these vices remained "drinking and drunkenness" that prevailed "to a frightful extent . . . exacerbated by the presence of whiskey drinking ministers who . . . strive to obstruct the formation of temperance societies."[22]

Over time a considerable number of weighty Indiana preachers made brief sojourns to Southland, conducting revivals that inevitably brought numerous declarations for Christ, but, just as inevitably, many fervent new converts, unable to maintain a close relation to Friends due to time or distance, joined other churches or drifted back into spiritual indifference.[23] Then, during the summer of 1873, while Calvin was "away recruiting his health" after his second death-threatening illness, Lydia M. Chace (1823–1915) of Shawnee, Kansas, arrived at Southland in the company of another female Friend. This visit not only produced the first notable response to Alida's "Macedonian cry" but also afforded her the sort of close Quaker female companionship of which she had been deprived since coming to Arkansas. A New Englander by birth, Lydia Chace and her equally Yankee husband Amasa (1823–1888) came west before the Civil War seeking religious repose and economic security, but apparently they found neither until Lydia discovered Southland.[24] Sharing both a call to ministry and the energy to answer that call, Alida Clark and Lydia Chace wasted little time in pursuing their mutual vision of "educating, elevating and Christianizing" freed people throughout the Delta. Shortly after Mrs. Chace arrived at Southland, she and Alida traveled together by buggy over two hundred miles through the oppressive heat of an Arkansas Delta summer ("the mercury ranging from 96 to 120"), surrounded by "the marks and brands of bushwhackers," visiting schools and families, holding religious meetings, distributing tracts, and laboring "in every way that opened in the Truth. . . . It was exceedingly satisfactory to me and my dear friend to witness such marked results. . . . The Gospel in all its fullness and convincing baptizing power, has been proclaimed to thousands and acknowledgments made." Such progress was heartening, especially because these unaccompanied women, in addition to enduring physical hardships, had also to overcome serious prejudices against female ministers. As Alida noted, once the local people heard Lydia Chace preach, dissenters and detractors "generally shut their mouths." They were a formidable pair, these Quaker ladies, and their personal and spiritual partnership endured for over a decade.[25]

Having discovered tasks worthy of her faith and her enthusiasm, Lydia Chace returned to Kansas to fetch her husband and make plans for their return to the Arkansas missionary station. In the meantime, describing her recent experiences in the *Friends' Review,* Mrs. Chace warned readers that it was "impossible . . . to comprehend the ignorance and degradation the terrible education of slavery had entailed upon its victims, both white and black." With Alida Clark, she had "witnessed scenes which filled our hearts with sorrow and our eyes with tears . . . a mixture of error, superstition and false doctrine." Still, she felt secure in the knowledge that the "solid, reverential deportment of . . . the little company of Friends" at Southland had clearly illustrated that Quakerism could fulfill the spiritual needs of southern black people. Still, for every soul that had been saved, thousands awaited the redeeming word. If only sufficient Friends would come out to minister among freedmen, their influence could take a substantial hold not just in Arkansas but throughout the South. "The fields are ripe to harvest, and the laborers so few, and we know how soon the grain is wasted if not gathered when ready for the reaper."[26]

In the autumn and winter months of 1873–74 the Chaces, having gathered tools for the harvest—Bibles, tracts, and temperance brochures—spent nearly six months in a buggy traversing southern Kansas and parts of Indian Territory before crossing the Boston Mountains and traveling the length of Arkansas to reach the Delta. On 20 May 1874 they brought "minutes of unity and concurrence" from Shawnee Monthly Meeting to their new meeting at Southland wherein both would eventually be recorded as ministers. Later that year their services in and around Southland were officially endorsed by the Indiana Missionary Board, which further agreed to purchase a wagon for use in their missionary activities. Amasa also took on the very practical job of supervising activities on what Mrs. Chace called the Clark and Wright plantation.[27]

As "members and co-laborers for the Master," the Chaces proved to be "faithful and devoted helpers," taking up the spiritual burden for Alida while she toured eastern states during the summer of 1874 to solicit funds for the continuation and expansion of their work.[28] When reporting to the missionary board on their activities between November 1874 and September 1875, Lydia and Amasa noted that, while they had done "nothing of which to boast," they had managed to travel 2,412 miles, visiting 500 families, distributing 50,000 pages of tracts, and selling or donating 275 Bibles to the spiritually famished freedmen. During the same time they had attended over 250 meetings at Southland and elsewhere, assisted at 80 sabbath schools, and held 65 temperance gatherings. In the midst of these labors Lydia dispatched a letter, reprinted in Quaker and other evangelical journals, admonishing stay-at-home Friends not to ignore "the cry that goes up from these benighted millions for light and truth." Most of those being gathered to the fold were under thirty, many of whom had been "wild reckless characters," but under Quaker influence they were so transformed in deportment and character that even local whites admitted that "the only salvation of the colored people is to become Quakers."[29]

During the same period, Daniel Drew's traveling ministry had taken him twenty miles beyond Hickory Ridge to the town of Holly Grove where he organized still another local meeting for worship whose satisfactory progress was reflected in a temperance society that swiftly enlisted 125 members. Such temperance activity helped to reinforce the prohibitionist victories Alida reported "over the colored Baptist ministers . . . who have opposed us for seven years." Indeed, by Alida's account, Southland was virtually surrounded by "protracted Baptist meetings in which are preached shameful lies and willful perversion of the Gospel by men who are filthy, lying, drinking, adulterers. . . . whose influence threatened to lead their followers 'back to barbarism.'"[30]

Baptists were not the only rivals for the souls of black folk. In the spring of 1875 Lydia Chace wrote to Daniel Hill, editor of the evangelical *Christian Worker*, recounting her "fear [of] the persistent influence of Catholicism on this people." An earlier visitor to Southland, after observing the "human weakness, folly and depravity" of Carnival Day (Shrove Tuesday) in the town of Helena, concluded that this shameful exhibition was "probably a relic of Popery." Mrs. Clark's annual report to the missionary board in 1875 noted that "the Church of Rome is extending her influence and exerting greater energy" in enrolling black children in their schools and convents.[31]

Certainly, in the face of such challenges, Friends' causes did not always prevail, even in the near vicinity of abstentious Quaker strongholds. For every battle won, another might be lost. For example, in March 1874 the Southland Temperance Committee reported an encouraging visit to Hickory Ridge, the railroad settlement where Daniel Drew's ministry had laid the groundwork for the establishment of a preparative meeting under

Southland's auspices. Amidst their exhorting saloon keepers "to forsake their wicked and destructive business," Southland's emissaries had obtained forty-one signatures to the total abstinence pledge. Three years later, however, Alida Clark confessed that at Hickory Ridge Friends were still "waging a steady warfare against six liquor saloons in this village of about seventy inhabitants." Such dens of iniquity were, in the words of the Southland minutes, "sapping the very germ of improvement by taking away the money and means of education and civilization from the youth."[32]

There were other disappointments. Occasionally, Southland Meeting had to face up to the presence of "disorderly walkers." As the minutes for June 1877 admitted, "Several in membership with us have violated their temperance pledge & have walked disorderly in some other particulars when subjected to temptation." In keeping with longstanding Quaker practice, the task of detecting such violations and reporting them was assigned to the meetings' overseers. This watch committee was justified on the grounds that it protected Friends' reputation for upright living and enabled the meeting to bring "the spirit of meekness & love . . . with frequent counsel & Christian forbearance" to those who had strayed, "laboring to reclaim them from the error of their way."[33]

Members accused of serious offenses who, after visitation and counsel by representatives of the meeting, refused to acknowledge their guilt and ask forgiveness were "disowned" or excommunicated. Southland had its share of such disownments, mainly for drinking, fighting, or sexual immorality; most of these occurred during the years while the Clarks dominated the meeting.[34] Such a close moral police reflected Alida and Calvin's determination that Southland Friends should remain a "beacon light" to surrounding communities. Thus, from the perspective of Southland trustees, reports from Arkansas gave the missionary board reason to believe that "our laborers there are . . . winning souls to Christ."[35]

In the final analysis, the impact of Southland's example on surrounding areas is difficult to gage, but the community that grew up in the immediate vicinity of the school was long reputed a peaceful, upright area seldom visited by law enforcement officers. More significantly, Southland's long struggle to block the local drink or "jug" trade and to control alcoholic consumption can only have worked to the moral and economic well-being of the general population. Still, these earnest efforts also created bitter resentment and even violent hostility towards Friends. Again, Mrs. Clark painted a vivid canvas:

> Whiskey dealers and Satan have tried too successfully to run riot with everything good, civil, moral and Christian throughout this land. . . . Purses have been raised and runners sent out after temperance men to induce them to violate their pledges; praised be the Lord, they failed in most cases.[36]

There were limits. Even the redoubtable Alida backed off from attempting to induce local whites to sign the temperance pledge because she and Calvin were "so well known to them . . . as 'Nigger Teachers & nigger spoilers' [that] we did not dare offer the Pledge" to them.[37]

While most local white people remained hostile, a few, for a variety of reasons, offered their assistance to Southland Friends. For example, at Hickory Ridge local whites volunteered to donate land upon which to erect a meeting house because, as Mrs. Clark indelicately put it, "they say *Quaker 'niggers'* are so much more godly, industrious, sober and intelligent that they want us to push forward the work of proselytizing and elevating." For these and all the other reasons she recounted in letters to the Quaker press, Alida pleaded with Friends to join their Arkansas brethren in preaching, teaching, and converting "the colored people of the South" or at least "to contribute money . . . to aid Southland College and Monthly Meeting in spreading the doctrines of the Gospel as . . . professed, preached and lived by Friends."[38]

For a time, the Quaker Gospel seemed to have taken root at Hickory Ridge Meeting. Early in 1876 Mrs. Clark announced that the "first meeting-house in the world [exclusively] for 'Colored Friends'"[39] would be opened on first day (Sunday), 2 April, for Bible school and meeting for worship. "We have reason to believe that many souls will be gathered . . . who are asking for better *food* than they are getting from amongst their own people." The inauguration of the meeting house at Hickory Ridge came in close proximity to the celebration of the twelfth anniversary of Indiana Friend's mission in Arkansas. According to the minutes of Southland Monthly Meeting results from this occasion were "of no ordinary character. . . . upbuilding and sanctification of believers, healing and restoration of backsliders and the awakening and conversion of sinners."

> Many hearts commemorated the goodness and special providence of Almighty God in . . . connection with this Institution and that through the influence thereof they had attained unto a knowledge of the Gospel of Life and Salvation. . . . and acquired a guarded Religious & Literary Education.[40]

In the meantime, Lydia and Amasa Chace continued their efforts to ensure that Southland remained an expanding Quaker missionary station. Their report to the missionary board for 1876 listed an even more prodigious religious service than in the previous year. Laboring under "great privations and much bodily discomfort" they had "travelled 3,387 miles" in a one-horse carriage especially fitted up for distribution of Bibles (247) and tracts (160,000 pages) as well as holding over a hundred meetings for worship and forty-three temperance gatherings. With such a record of spiritual endeavor, they might well claim to speak with "personal knowledge of the . . . experiment . . . of receiving the colored people into society with us." The Chaces were "more and more convinced of the propriety and wisdom of the undertaking." Was it not time, Lydia asked, "to extend the loving (not cold) arms of Church fellowship . . . here where way has been opened?"[41]

After a dozen years Southland Meeting had gathered 142 souls ("all but nine colored") to its bosom and sent dozens of students out into the world, many of whom had chosen as their "life work" the instruction and elevation of "their long oppressed and ignorant people." Friends in Arkansas could be excused for believing that their mission station had indeed become "Light Unto the Lord."[42]

III. Training Mind and Body

> *The aim is not to push rapidly through many studies but thoroughness in training mind and body for future usefulness.*[43]

After Joseph Moore, the president of Earlham College, visited Southland in the spring of 1871, he came away impressed with the progress of the school, "especially the *reading* of some of the more advanced pupils."[44] Encouraged by such reports and by the Freedmen's Bureau's aid in erecting an adequate new schoolhouse, the Indiana Missionary Board enthusiastically pushed ahead. By the summer of 1871, a two-room building costing six thousand dollars had been connected to the structure built three years earlier to form "a very commodious" three-room academy suitable for instructing both "inmates" and local children. But just as students, freed for study by the completion of the cotton harvest, poured in for a short summer term, the board was informed by Freedmen's Bureau director general O. O. Howard that parsimonious congressional appropriations would permit him to contribute only half the promised five-thousand-dollar subvention. Thus placed in "a very embarrassing situation," the missionary board contemplated "making a considerable change in the management of the Institution," whatever that implied. In the end, however, the Clarks' "earnest entreaty not to dismiss any of the students" caused the board to reconsider, despite being "stripped of money" by the bureau's default. In this case the solution was to close the Little Rock school Indiana Yearly Meeting had been supporting and to use the proceeds from the sale of this property to replenish missionary board coffers. At the same time, various other sources of income were forthcoming: a $2,500 allocation from Indiana Yearly Meeting, $800 in contributions from Friends in Ireland, $600 from the Peabody Fund to support teacher training at Southland, and $600 in tuition paid by the minority of local black parents who could contribute something for their children's schooling.[45]

Thus, rescued from financial ruin and heartened by the yearly meeting's message exhorting them to continue their "arduous and responsible labor," the missionary board determined not just to continue but to expand the educational mission at Southland. An Indiana Friend, W. A. Syms, was hired to take charge of the normal class with a mandate to produce "native" teachers who would spread the message of the Bible and spelling book to an ever widening circle of freed people. A few months later Alida Clark reported that forty normal school pupils were making significant progress under Syms's "efficient drill."[46]

In the autumn of 1871 the Quaker press proudly reported that Earlham College, with an enrollment of 138 students, was "in a prosperous condition" and likely to remain so, given a forthcoming endowment of fifty thousand dollars. Perhaps it was this notice, trumpeting the well-being of a Quaker educational institution similar in size to her own, that galvanized Mrs. Clark. In any case, the following spring she embarked upon a campaign, or more aptly a crusade, to raise funds designed specifically to aid students training in Southland's normal department. It was, she informed readers of the *Friends' Review,* virtually "impossible for these people to educate children" without outside support. Most black families in the Delta could scarcely survive without their children's labor, let alone pay for their schooling. Furthermore, after the withdrawal of the Freedmen's Bureau, the state-supported free schools that operated for only three to four months between harvest and planting were "taught by such poor, indifferent and unqualified teachers" as to be nearly worthless. By contrast, Southland, with sufficient support, could "train, drill and qualify" hundreds of "thorough scholars, and apt teachers . . . in all the primary and higher branches" and thereby prevent an entire generation of black children from being dragged

> down in their ignorance and poverty to disgrace and ruin—strong drink, urged upon them by the whites, and extravagance and profligacy in dress, idleness incurred by these habits, leading to theft, robbery and murder.[47]

Furthermore, the Clarks could offer independent evidence to show that their struggle against this frightful prospect was bearing fruit. When Elkanah Beard revisited Southland in September 1872, he declared himself "highly delighted" with the school's "complete success . . . in nearly every particular." One manifestation of this success was that nearly thirty Southland students passed the state teachers' examination and were issued teaching licenses. Although the circuit superintendent of schools balked at recommending many of the newly certified as teachers in local free schools because they were so young and small, through the advocacy and determined efforts of Calvin Clark, twenty-eight Southlanders were eventually placed in schools, drawing salaries of thirty to fifty-five dollars per month while teaching over a thousand students. During the ensuing months Calvin visited each of these aspiring teachers, and though he found many assigned to "very poor" schoolhouses, some even out of doors, all the classes he attended were "in complete order and well classified." Alida was proud to add that both white and colored people complimented them on the "nice set of youngsters" Southland had sent forth, especially because none was seen to "drink a drop of spirits, nor use snuff or tobacco."[48] Still, for all the earnest efforts of the school's directors and their charges, the most notable feature of the situation was the generally miserable condition of Arkansas public schools. Given the circumstances, it is not surprising that the emphasis appeared to be more directed to well-behaved students than experienced and effective teachers for those students.[49]

For all the difficulties facing Friends' Arkansas enterprise, Southland continued to gather momentum. The Indiana Missionary Board began looking into the possibility of enhancing the Southland campus with the addition of a new administrative building and teachers' quarters. They soon discovered, however, that even with the funds ($2,777) garnered from the sale of property in Little Rock, such a project was beyond their means. This apparent barrier to continued development brought forth another of Alida's rhetorical flourishes designed to illustrate the necessity for keeping the Quaker mission alive in a place where

> The earth has opened her mouth and swallowed up innocent blood . . . that is still crying for vengeance. The fruits grown from such seed, sown by such hideous monsters are ripening. So why wonder that murders, thefts, robberies and other rampant wickedness flourish in high places; that some legislative halls become pandemoniums of the covetous, the ignorant and vicious lovers of self, and the greed for gold, power and place! . . . Crops are backward, weather rainy, supplies exhausted. Laborers subsisting on credit—*pernicious system.*[50]

Because of the evolution of a malevolent, cotton-based, crop-lien system and the freedmen's general ignorance of progressive farming methods, any profit that might be forthcoming from one year's crop was often used up while that crop was still in the ground, leaving sharecroppers worse off with each passing year. Alida Clarks believed that one great bulwark against the imposition of this iniquitous scheme on nearly helpless people was "the wonder working power of this Institution" that might be a source of "greatest power and influence over the State" if proper funding was forthcoming.[51]

While no single eleemosynary angel appeared bearing the coveted financial resources, Alida's special pleading did bring some results. In September 1873 the missionary board announced receipt of contributions totaling nearly five thousand dollars, most coming from English and Irish Friends. At about the same time, Calvin Clark, journeying to Indiana to attend yearly meeting and recover his health, convinced the board that a proper house, even half-completed, could better stand the next winter than the tumble-down barracks-like quarters Southland's staff were currently occupying. The board responded with a promise of three thousand dollars "the extent of our ability to furnish means for this purpose." As work on the new quarters progressed, Mrs. Clark announced an enrollment of 186, supplemented by the dozens of students trained and sent out among their people to teach, "tinctured at least with Quakerism as well as qualified to give instruction in all ordinary studies."[52]

But while Alida Clark seemed able to guide Southland toward spiritual and pedagogical success, and even fiscal solvency, against nearly impossible odds, two of the earth's least predictable elements, nature and Arkansas politics, were beyond her capacity to effect. The former seemed yearly to conspire against all Southland's best efforts as in 1874 when "owing to . . . the spring overflow of the rivers, and unusual drought, and the hot winds sweeping over the country about the time the cotton crop was laid by, very few will be able to raise the necessary funds for sending their children here." Temperatures according to Mrs. Clark ranged from 102 to 106 degrees in the shade, leaving "not a drop of water on this yard fit to drink." Crossing Arkansas from west to east that summer on their journey to Southland, Lydia and Amasa Chace "saw much poverty and ignorance . . . the blighting effects of slavery, noticeable even after a lapse of ten years."[53]

Slavery and its aftermath had other blighting effects on Arkansas. Hopes for financial prosperity and civic advancement under a progressive Republican government were dashed in 1872 by a bitter division between regular or "Brindletail" Republicans supporting the freedmen's champion Joseph Brooks and "Liberal" Republican dissidents led by Elisha Baxter. Baxter's narrow victory, with the support of Conservative/Democratic votes, in the hotly contested and highly suspect gubernatorial election of that year set off a violent power struggle reminiscent of the late Roman Republic. Armed clashes between supporters of the two antagonists led not only to virtual anarchy and fiscal disaster for the state but also contributed mightily to the eventual victory of the so-called "Redeemer" Democratic Party, which would hold political power for the next century. After the Democratic victory in the election of 1874, a Democratically-controlled conventional convention laid the groundwork for the effective end of Reconstruction in Arkansas and the beginning of "Redeemer"-era governments that did little on behalf of impoverished rural people, black or white.[54]

Law-abiding Indiana Republicans like the Clarks were, of course, shocked and dismayed by the untoward turn of events that led to "the overthrow of our republican government." No one, said Mrs. Clark, could "travel through this country and mingle with, and behold the depravity, ignorance and wickedness of the people, without being seriously impressed with fearful forebodings."[55] For Phillips County such portents took ominous material form. In a referendum supporting the call for what would be a "Redeemer"-dominated convention, official returns from Phillips County, with a considerable majority of black voters, allegedly endorsed the proposed convention by 3,296 votes to none.[56] Obviously, either die-hard Republicans like the Clarks were scared away from the polls or, more likely, their votes were simply not counted.

Besides the "threatening mob-like spirit that prevails over [the] South," Mrs. Clark was equally distressed over the fact that Arkansas's "*free-school* system . . . if not entirely destroyed" had been "rendered inefficient and unavailing." During the political crisis, most teachers were paid in state scrip whose value rapidly fell to twenty-five or thirty cents on the dollar, school sessions were cut to three months, and many teachers, unable to live on their greatly reduced salaries, simply picked up and left the state. Historian John Graves has noted that in the years that followed both white and black schools were "separately and equally starved for funds." As Alida Clarke pointed out at the time, the disastrous consequences of these developments fell, first and foremost, upon the "poor creatures remaining in ignorance" that Friends were attempting to aid.

> We have never seen more rags and patches, dirt filth, drinking, drunkenness, misery and crime, than are now rife amongst these people as a mass. Poor crops for three successive seasons, a credit system of labor; mortgaging all live stock and growing crops for supplies that are used up before the crops are gathered.[57]

Southland Friends had, of course, long denounced the iniquity of the crop-lien system that dominated the not only the economic but every other relationship between blacks and whites in the rural South. As an article in the *Friends' Review* pointed out:

> If Cotton be King, he is a poor master. . . . [who] omits his subjects in the knowledge of the arts of life. He does not permit them to know the value of rotation of crops; cotton, *all the time, and, everywhere*, is his motto. . . . This arbitrary, circumscribed, ignorant way not only impoverishes the soil, and shortens the crops . . . which a rotation of crops . . . would supply; but it entails a condition of filthiness and semi-starvation, shocking to people of humane feelings.[58]

Another Quaker traveler in Arkansas noted that the country around Helena was ideal for growing wheat but none was harvested on account of the lack of a mill where it could be ground.[59]

The Clarks sought to alleviate this shortcoming by establishing their own grinding mill, one of several local enterprises launched in partnership with their son-in-law, Theodore Wright. More significantly, they introduced an innovation in the area around Southland designed both to increase the self-sufficiency of local black people and to enlarge their school's potential clientele. Calvin and Alida began providing five-year leases to selected individuals on parcels of land they had acquired in the vicinity of the school, with a view to eventual sale "as fast as they can pay for it." This practice was to be the basis for establishment of a self-contained, self-reliant community centered on Southland and attuned to its educational, religious, and social message for those who were attempting "to rise above the brutish population around them who care more for whiskey, snuff, tobacco and 'freedom' . . . than civilization."[60]

In light of a continuing struggle against both agricultural incompetence and governmental corruption as well as local temptations of the flesh, Alida cited the "wonder working power of this Institution for good amongst these poor people." At the close of the 1873–74 school term, thirty students had gone out from Southland to aid the state's faltering free schools, teaching 1,800 pupils a day and "bearing within them the knowledge of the Gospel and other instruction given them by . . . messengers of the Lord."[61]

Two of these northern Quaker messengers, Walter Wright and Hettie Graves, both Earlham graduates, were preparing twenty of their students to join the "college course to be added next year." In this regard the *Friends' Review* reprinted an article from the national *Freedmen's Monitor* that listed Southland, with Howard, Hampton, and Fisk, as institutions whose normal programs should be supported by northern benefactors.[62]

Reports from visitors seemed to confirm Southland's rising status and importance. H. E. Merrill, a Cincinnati Friend, reported that many people he had met on the boat trip to Helena were familiar with Southland and spoke highly of it and of the Clarks. "I doubt if two people in the State are better known and more generally liked than they are. . . . None of us need blush for our Arkansas brethren." But Merrill managed to add a note of reality to his enthusiastic message. Given the "disturbed condition" of an area where men went armed to political meetings, it was "no child's play to labor in Arkansas," and, he concluded, anyone who ventured to come South "must have the cause of Christ at heart, and be prepared to overcome many difficulties."[63]

One of those difficulties to be overcome had been inadequate housing for Southland's staff and students, but late in 1874, Mrs. Clark was able to report that faculty were ensconced in a "new and elegant boarding house" along with thirty-seven students, all comfortably sheltered from the "snow, sleet and *zero* winds" of an exceptionally cold winter. Finances, of course, were a continuing challenge but while the institution ran a small deficient ($171.20) for the 1873–74 fiscal year, the missionary board was sufficiently impressed with positive results to support the Chaces' continued missionary activities. For her part, Alida had walked from house to house in the vicinity of the school, spreading the Gospel and delivering five lectures on the futility of water baptism in contrast to saving qualities of Quaker baptism of the spirit.[64]

Mrs. Clark was never devoid of energy nor likely to hide her light under a bushel, and in the mid-1870s she was probably at the height of her evangelistic power in spreading the Southland's message. Late in 1874 she launched a recruiting drive into five northeastern Arkansas counties and then crossed into Coahoma County, Mississippi, describing it as the site of "mobs, riot and bloodshed" where blacks and Republicans were being intimidating, harassed, and attacked. Several of Southland's young teachers in the area, suffering "on account of their peace principles" and temperance advocacy, were later withdrawn from the area because blacks "were likely to be shot down if they were seen collecting together for meetings of any kind."[65]

Given the circumstances facing "these helpless people," Mrs. Clark redoubled her pleas to the American Quaker community for increased financial support, pointing out that Southland educated teachers were needed to join against "the common evils of the day," especially in light of the fact that "all public funds . . . having been squandered . . . there are no [public] schools in operation" anywhere in Arkansas.[66] Because Arkansas public schools seemed to be sliding into oblivion, Southland's managers issued a circular that promised not only quality Christian education in the primary grades and a Normal Department providing "the best methods of teaching classes" but also the prospect of settling near the school where "rich, fertile farming" land could be rented or purchased "on reasonable terms." This flyer also promised commodious accommodations for up to a hundred boarders with the assurance of "mild, but firm" government wherein alcohol, tobacco, snuff, and firearms were prohibited as well as games of cards, checkers, and chess. Tuition and board, including washing and ironing, was three dollars per week, "money paid in advance."[67]

Considering the deplorable state of Arkansas's educational endeavors, the school at Southland was unquestionably performing an invaluable service for black students whose parents or guardians possessed the means to send them there. These fortunate few, in the words of Lydia and Amasa Chace, would "be brought under an influence and discipline which trains them in correct habits, cultivates and refines their tastes and fits them for the duties of life. . . . The aim is not to push rapidly through many studies but thoroughness in training mind and body for future usefulness."[68] The Chaces' description of the changes wrought by the Southland experience was deeply felt and reasonably accurate as far as it went. The school laid claim to sixty teachers already "in the field," training hundreds of children, but their assurances also beg the question of how, beyond elementary instruction, students in the normal department could have received adequate teacher training at an institution whose primary objective was simply to ensure literacy?[69] Perhaps disagreement over that question was the basis for a minute of the missionary board early in 1875 referring to apparently contending letters from the Clarks and teacher E. O. Kennard "in relation to the management of the normal school." After carefully considering this correspondence, the board informed the Clarks of "our earnest desire that all there may work harmoniously together." This was the first hint of difficulty or disagreement over the administration and objectives of the school, though far from the last. The upshot of this incident, beyond the fact that Kennard did not return, was the appointment of Walter Wright, the Earlham graduate who had been teaching at Southland since

1872, as principle of the normal institute while the Clarks agreed to "keep up a good [primary] school with two well-qualified teachers" who would be paid for nine months' work by the board. In exchange, Alida and Calvin as matron and superintendent would have full use of Southland's facilities, discretion in the use of student tuition payments, a thousand-dollar subsidy to pay fees for deserving needy students and an annual six-hundred-dollar payment from the Peabody Fund to support the school's normal and free school classes. The 1875–76 school term began with W. B. Wright, B. S., principal of the college department and professor of languages, bookkeeping, and normal training. His two chief assistants had both been trained exclusively at Southland, and their employment was, no doubt, meant to advertise the school's past academic achievements. Henrietta Kitterall, the orphan raised and adopted by the Clarks, was named principal of the primary and intermediate department, and Chandler Paschal acted as governor and teacher of higher mathematics as well as clerk of Southland Monthly Meeting.[70]

To sustain these advances in organization and instruction on behalf of the education and advancement of "these poor degraded children of Africa. . . . wretched victims of American slavery that 'sum of all villanies,'" Mrs. Clark continued her lobbying activities among wealthy eastern Friends. Late in 1875 she wrote to Hannah W. Richardson and two other prominent female Quakers in Philadelphia pleading for the means to set up a chemistry laboratory for Southland's most advanced students "to wake a new train of thought within those dark minds so long kept dormant . . . not one of [whom] . . . has ever seen any sort of a philosophical experiment performed by apparatus of any kind." Alida was confident that "they can learn and understand many branches of science" if only helpers could be found to make this possible. And, indeed, by August of the following year Mrs. Clark could report that a "complete laboratory for use of chemistry class" had been presented to the school "by three of our Philadelphia friends."[71]

When Elkanah and Irena Beard and two members of the missionary board visited Southland in 1876, they found that students who had advanced beyond the elementary course were being tutored not only in chemistry but in natural history, bookkeeping, German, and Latin as well. Certainly this visit was instrumental in the missionary board's decision in June 1876, "after seeking legal council" and being "fully satisfied that the Yearly Meeting has full power to organize Colleges and issue Diplomas and Certificates," to "establish an institution for the furtherance of . . . literary, moral, religious and educational purposes . . . known and designated as Southland College. . . . to advance their educational and other interests in this part of the State of Arkansas and especially to qualify teachers." The superintendent, matron, and teachers were thus authorized "to organize themselves as a Faculty" and

> those students whose attainments and conduct justify should receive diplomas . . . and thus avoid the necessity of the best class of students going from under our care to other colleges and also to encourage the colored people of that vicinity to aspire after the highest grade of education.[72]

Calvin Clark was designated president of Southland College; Mrs. Clark was to be matron with Walter Wright, Emma Waring, and Henrietta Kitterall appointed as faculty members in whose name "such certificates of scholarship, diploma, degrees, etc." were to be issued. The faculty was also to keep a "Diploma Record," but their power to dispense diplomas would in no way diminish the yearly meeting's "authority or control . . . exercised over said institution." Alida Clark described the commencement exercises on 16 June 1876 as "the great Centennial feast of the colored patrons and friends of Southland College" attended by about five hundred persons, "eager crowds of Africa's long-oppressed, down-trodden, despised and rejected children in their best dress and finest humor." The fact that Southland College's three initial graduates, Henrietta Kitterall, Chandler Paschal, and Emma France, having mastered "the higher branches of mathematics, classics and natural sciences," were all orphans rescued by the Clarks twelve years earlier from the afflictions of war was a source of great pride and satisfaction for Southland's founders.[73] Still, if the moral and intellectual elevation of these formerly helpless and destitute young people could be taken as a sign of how far Southland had come, it also reminded Alida of how far they had yet to go.

> Oh! For more purity of heart, a better state of morals, a higher standard of social life, domestic order and regularity amongst these people and the South generally, less indulgence in intemperance, inordinate affection and licentiousness amongst members of the same families, churches and neighbors, to say nothing of frequent outbreaks of murderous revenge that so often reach our ears.[74]

Chapter 5

Trials and Triumphs

1874–1880

I. Guiding Hands

Where did Southland stand in the wake of its twelfth anniversary celebration? To begin, it was by then obvious that Calvin and Alida Clark had become inexorably melded to the institution and that what began as a missionary endeavor was continuing as a life's work. For Indiana Quakers who knew of the Clarks' labors and of black Arkansans who had benefited from their efforts, Calvin and Alida became Southland embodied. Both the school and the monthly meeting bore the indelible mark of Alida Clark's strong hand and unwavering spirit. Her efforts in nurturing and promoting Southland's dual mission were little short of amazing. Teacher, minister, temperance crusader, and mother-hen, she was also what in later days would be called the "director of development," corresponding with Quaker journals as well as with prominent and wealthy Friends in a never-ending round of public-relations and money-raising activities. In addition to the Clarks' spiritual and pedagogical commitment to Southland, personal motivations and economic investments also helped to hold them in Arkansas. As previously noted, in partnership with their son-in-law Theodore Wright, they gradually acquired considerable land in the vicinity of the institution and, indeed, became planters and entrepreneurs on a considerable scale. From the early 1870s, only Southland teachers received salaries from Indiana Yearly Meeting, and the Clarks worked on an entirely voluntary basis.[1] In the circumstances, Calvin, assisted by Amasa Chace, Daniel Drew, and others, had to give considerable time and effort to farming the family's personal holdings and supervising their other enterprises. In addition, he directed farm work on land connected to the school as well as maintaining Southland's physical plant and keeping its financial records.

Viewed from the Quaker perspective, during the decade of the 1870s both the school and the Friends' meeting connected with it were remarkably successful ventures, growing in size and stature, widely known and greatly respected among the local and regional black population. However, as Radical Reconstruction in Arkansas faded and American Friends became engaged in divisive doctrinal disputes, an objective eye might already have seen the emergence of difficulties, both local and national, that would, in time, disturb this remote Quaker island of peace and tranquility.

II. Matters of Faith: The Southland Meeting and the Changing Face of American Quakerism

After the death of George Fox in 1691, the evangelical fervor of seventeenth-century Friends gradually receded, and their society turned inward seeking purity of worship rather than enlarged membership. Quakerism in both England and North America lapsed into generations of quietism during which Friends, dressing and speaking in peculiar and archaic ways, largely ceased to proselytize among the "world's people." At the same time, many Friends, benefiting from their society's reputation for honesty and fair-dealing, became successful in the world of business, sometimes amassing considerable fortunes. As noted above (Chapter 2), these wealthy Quakers tended to assume leadership positions in their local and yearly meetings if only because they had leisure time to deal with many of the practical problems facing a religious community that lacked regular clergy. The dominate position of the wealthy and weighty in local, monthly, and yearly meetings, sometimes created or exacerbated tensions that reflected social as well as theological differences among Friends. This circumstance was most clearly manifested in the case of the Hicksite Separation that began in Philadelphia in 1828 and quickly spread to the very edge of the western frontier where Hicksite and Orthodox Friends sometimes divided local meetings down the middle amidst un-Quakerly bitterness and ill will.[2] In response to the Hicksite insistence that adherence to Quaker tradition required Friends to recognize the primacy of the "Inward Light" as the chief guide to Quaker belief and practice, Indiana Yearly Meeting reiterated its separate version of orthodoxy by issuing a doctrinal statement emphasizing the divinity of Christ, the centrality of his atoning sacrifice, and the overweening authority of the Bible. Furthermore, in the decade following the Hicksite upheaval, Indiana Friends, inspired by the fire and vision evangelism of the charismatic English minister Joseph John Gurney, "moved significantly closer to the dominant evangelical religious culture of the United States."[3]

Early in 1874 the minutes of Southland Monthly Meeting recorded the reading of the London Yearly Meeting's general epistle "setting before us the great doctrine of the atonement as the foundation of the faith of our religious society."[4] Southland's embracing of the atonement as the "foundation" doctrine of Quakerism, without reference to the inward light of Christ, placed Quakerism's only black monthly meeting in the mainstream of the evangelical "renewal" movement among American Gurneyite Friends. Beyond question this renewal, with its stress on individual initiative and spiritual innovation, breathed new life into Quaker worship services and gave increasing emphasis to social and humanitarian concerns, helping to produce the sort of missionary spirit that inspired devout Friends like the Clarks, the Beards, and the Chaces to come South to give succor to the bodies and souls of long-oppressed black people. Theologically, this same ardent spirit embraced other innovations among midwestern Friends. One of the first of these modifications was the introduction of "First-Day Schools" for the Biblical instruction of young people. Besides the general tendency of these Sunday schools to deemphasize the writings and practices of early Friends, they also promoted, especially among younger Quakers, increasing impatience with silent meeting and with the stilted, sing-song spoken ministry that often prevailed when silence was broken.[5]

In 1860 a group of earnest, evangelistic ministers received permission from Indiana Yearly Meeting to convene a special gathering of young people that became the occasion of sustained emotional outbursts among the thousand or so who attended. This event effectively marked the beginning of an era in which revival-type meetings became a common practice among midwestern Quakers. Within a decade young Friends in Indiana had so far departed from Quaker tradition as to introduce congregational hymn singing into their meetings for worship.[6] Such novel practices reflect the degree to which most Orthodox Quakers west of Philadelphia were being influenced by their evangelical Protestant neighbors. The results of this renewal were impressive, as new converts were drawn into previously diminishing meetings for worship. At the same time, however earnest, most newly convinced Friends had little knowledge of or attachment to traditional Quaker modes of belief and practice such as silent meeting, rejection of paid ministers, and the centrality of the inward light of Christ. The diminishing influence of these distinctive historical practices opened the way for the most radical innovation to spread among American Friends after the Civil War, a dynamic holiness movement embracing the idea of the individual believer undergoing a "new birth" or second experience conversion. This transforming spiritual moment generally occurred in the midst of a revival meeting, centering on the preaching of a single minister, wherein the self-confessed sinner, broken by the realization of past inequities, declared unequivocal belief in Christ's atoning sacrifice and thereby instantaneously gained salvation thorough this single, emotionally driven act of faith. As Thomas Hamm has noted, "nothing more was needed, and nothing less sufficed." Many older, more conservative Friends protested that evangelical revivals, giving rise to such mercurial salvation experiences, bordered on Ranterism, the radical seventeenth-century antinomian movement denounced by Gorge Fox.[7] Nevertheless, during the 1870s and 1880s, a small group of holiness ministers became a significant spiritual force in Indiana and other western yearly meetings. These zealous and charismatic preachers addressed emotionally charged general meetings wherein, often amidst shouting, singing, and speaking in tongues, a considerable harvest of souls was delivered into the Quaker fold. Historian Carol Spencer believes that this holiness revivalism "captivated and energized a new generation of Quakers by providing an outlet for vibrant, activist, reforming spirituality." Thomas Hamm has a somewhat different view, noting that the holiness movement helped to create a sort of elite corps of ministers who claimed that second experience conversion made them answerable only to God. The result, Hamm asserts, was "exalted ministerial standing and . . . prerogatives" within a religious community that had historically maintained "a faithful testimony against a hireling ministry." Given this paradoxical development, it was no great surprise that in 1878 the Indiana Yearly Meeting discarded its long-standing rejection of a paid and professional clergy.[8] In that same year, the Ohio Yearly Meeting, under the commanding influence of radical holiness minister David B. Updegraff, "repudiated the so-called doctrine of the inner light . . . as dangerous, unsound, and unscriptural." Baffled and alarmed by such revolutionary innovations, Barnabas C. Hobbs, the moderate clerk of the Western Yearly Meeting, told a friend in London, "You cannot understand it here. . . . without seeing it. Our meetings were shaken as by a vast whirlwind."[9] Thus, for a time, midwestern Quakerism was overtaken by a spiritual storm created by powerful ministers like David Updegraff, Esther Frame, David Hall, and Dougan Clark who were totally committed to holiness theology and practice.[10] Rejecting two hundred years of Quaker religious peculiarity, they carried midwestern Friends into and even beyond the mainstream of American evangelical Protestantism.

At the same time a considerable body of Quakers, even some who had initially welcomed the evangelical renewal, came to abhor the holiness movement as "facile and deceptive." Traditionally, Friends adhered to the view that recognition of one's sins (justification) did not remove the spiritual damage imposed by sin and that the process of sanctification, that is, freeing oneself from the consequences of sin, was a lifelong struggle. Clashes between conservative and holiness Friends were at times reminiscent of the Hicksite-Orthodox struggles half a century earlier. Elkanah Beard's "Diaries" during this period provide revealing examples of disputes which arose within and between meetings. Early in 1878 Beard visited a troubled congregation at Jericho, Kansas, where "nearly all the old friends," distressed by the growing influence of holiness ideas and practices, had seceded and organized a separate monthly meeting. Beard found this anti-evangelical faction to be "chronic grumblers" who were "sowing the seeds of discord. . . . I suppose the Lord loves them but from the Scripture or a common sense standpoint I cannot see how He admires them."[11]

How then did an idiosyncratic, secluded meeting like Southland respond to such contentious struggles among fellow Quakers? Events would show that, however remote, Southland could no more remain isolated from the trials besetting western Friends than it could avoid the social and political backwash of anti-Reconstruction activities in Phillips County or the state of Arkansas. By the mid-1870s Southland had become a regular, almost required, stopping-off place for both American and British Quakers, evangelical and otherwise, traveling in the ministry who stood on one or another side of the spiritual contest dividing Friends. Elkanah Beard was a frequent visitor, as in the spring of 1877 when Southland minutes credited his "Gospel Ministry" in conjunction with the school's fourteenth anniversary with "strengthening believers [and] . . . awakening sinners." Alida Clark called Beard's visit "the most wonderful revival ever known amongst us," bringing not only conversions from among Southland students but also drawing believers from nearby churches who had tired of their "immoral and drinking ministers."

> We pray fervently that the blessing of the Good Shepard may be so filled and baptized with a Saviour's love . . . that many who now sit in darkness groveling in ignorance and sin may be brought into the ranks of the Lord's army.[12]

Such language evokes the sort of frenetic scenes of religious ardor that were becoming common at holiness revivals, but Mrs. Clark was at pains to describe such meetings as remarkable for the "quiet stillness" that prevailed—"no emotion, no excitement, none at all." This observation seemed to be confirmed in Elkanah Beard's report to Indiana Yearly Meeting that Southland Meeting had been "well sustained, and . . . free from noisy demonstrations" exhibiting "a decided improvement in the manner of those who speak in testimony and prayer." So, while such testimonies seem to suggest that Southland's revival meetings did not resemble the more demonstrative holiness gatherings, other evidence indicates, at the very least, exceptions.[13]

Southland minutes certainly stressed prudent behavior, as in August 1877 when they expressed the need "by example & precept to . . . [practice] simplicity of speech, respectful deportment [and] consistent dress; avoiding the changing & sinful fashions of the world," adding that care should be taken to guard "against reading pernicious books & from corrupt conversation." Thus Mrs. Clark was at pains to make clear that, in contrast to the "depravity, ignorance and wickedness" so common among the masses of the South, both black and white, those who worshiped at Southland Meeting or came out from Southland school were molded in the best Quaker tradition, were "total abstainers from liquors, active Christian and temperance workers . . . haters of tobacco [finding] . . . wide fields of usefulness."[14]

To ensure that members of the meeting continued to uphold these high standards, in 1877 Southland visitor's committee, headed by Daniel Drew, reported on their efforts to "encourage the weak . . . admonish . . . the erring, reclaim those who have backslidden." The committee gave thanks that, "amid the general darkness, there are lights that burn brightly to show forth the blessed truth of Salvation by faith in the blood of Jesus as sufficient to cleanse from sin."[15]

Mrs. Clark made sure that no opportunity for spiritual uplift was neglected, nor unreported, in the Quaker press. Southland Meeting, she observed, drew "encouragement and edification" from the practice of reading the annual London General Epistle as well as the occasional epistolary admonitions from the Women Friends of Indiana Yearly Meeting counseling their Arkansas sisters and brothers to give themselves "wholly, unreservedly to Him who hath bought us with his own precious blood." Alida also invited the inspection of coreligionists, requesting that the missionary board invite "the attendance of such of the Lord's messengers as may by the good spirit be drawn to service." In a letter to the *Friends' Review,* she added:

> Would that we could thoroughly awaken Friends everywhere to the glorious work of rescuing the freedmen from the iron grasp of ignorance entailed upon then by slavery, which rum is riveting more closely, and the Pope binding his deadly embrace of priestly power and superstition.[16]

This particular plea was promptly answered in the form of the "truly acceptable" seventeen-day ministry of English Friends Stanley and Sarah Pumphrey. In the company of Elkanah and Irena Beard, the Pumphreys not only converted thirty souls but caused "backsliders and the lukewarm" to be "reclaimed and stirred up to greater diligence." Naturally, most of these newly sanctified souls immediately applied for membership in Southland Meeting, which by that time had risen to 175.[17] Beyond his soul-saving activities, Stanley Pumphrey also became an eager international spokesman and publicity agent for Southland. In letters to the Quaker press and speeches to Friends' meetings in large eastern and midwestern cities, Pumphrey, citing "false notions" by some Friends of preserving "select respectability," echoed Alida Clark in noting George Fox's conviction that Quakerism was the religion for all humanity. He pleaded with fellow Quakers to extend the "hand of fellowship" to their black brethren. "No missionary work," he said, "was more important in character or fruitful in results."[18]

In the wake of the Pumphreys' visit and its attendant publicity, Alida Clark received a "minute of liberation" from Southland Monthly Meeting to travel "in the love of the Gospel to New York & New England Meetings" with a view to "laboring for the extension of the Redeemer's Kingdom" as well as soliciting material aid for Southland. In conjunction with this fundraising campaign, the Indiana Missionary Board printed six hundred copies of Stanley Pumphrey's letters on behalf of Southland. To the same end, a book containing Pumphrey's speeches, *Missionary Work in Connection with the Society of Friends,* was published by the *Friends' Review.*[19] During Mrs. Clark's subsequent six-months' absence, she traveled about seven thousand miles, attended over four hundred meetings, and collected three thousand dollars to support the work of aiding "a grateful people, helpless in poverty, and steeped in ignorance."[20]

An important aspect of that work was the Southland congregation's continuing missionary activity. Especially through the efforts of Daniel Drew, the preparatory meeting at Hickory Ridge[21] progressed so rapidly that by 1876 the monthly meeting for business was being held there alternatively with Southland.[22] During the next year, however, Southland minutes recorded the need to "extend care very frequently, if not constantly" at this satellite meeting. When, in 1878, Stanley Pumphrey, assisted by Amasa Chace, undertook missionary efforts in the area, he lamented that "colored people . . . were no more disposed to receive us than were the. . . . Samaritans to receive our Master," and the monthly meeting minutes reported that religious services at Hickory Ridge had "not been attended by all that live in a reasonable distance."[23] The undulating fortunes of Hickory Ridge Friends' meeting underlined the importance of the message and methods of those powerful and aggressive evangelical ministers who gathered and held their flocks by the power of their rhetoric and the strength of their wills. So long as Daniel Drew regularly attended first-day meeting at Hickory Ridge and Moses Moore supervised the sabbath school, they could report "growing interest and signs of life" reflecting the meeting's increasingly "more prosperous condition."[24] But in time unfortunate natural and human circumstances would combine to undermine that progress. Soon after "a very destructive tornado" blew down the Friends' meeting house at Hickory Ridge,

Daniel Drew moved from his Southland ministry to the Quaker mission station at Maryville, Tennessee. Without Drew's influence, the Hickory Ridge meeting could not be sustained, and within a few weeks Elkanah Beard reported that the congregation had "quite broken up," most of its members having left the area.[25]

Despite such setbacks, revival waves continued to wash across "the only Friends' Monthly Meeting for colored people in the world." Late in 1880 two female ministers from Great Britain, Mary White and Sarah Sattertherwaite, brought "fervency in prayer . . . loving messages of Gospel Truth . . . [and] social, religious and moral lectures" to the Southland community. This missionary visit was perhaps the inspiration for Lydia Chace's bold assertion that "sinfulness is not much worse here than in New England." The following spring, C. S. Hubbard, a weighty member of the Indiana Missionary Board who attended a series of meetings at Southland in the company of Elkanah Beard, reported that he had "rarely seen a better conducted Sabbath-school anywhere."[26]

As Southland Meeting moved into the decade of the 1880s, its roll of recorded ministers increased to seven with the addition of Amasa Chace and four black preachers, Arthur Crump, Calvin Kerr, Chandler Paschal, and Henrietta Kitterall. At the same time, membership surpassed two hundred, although, as Elkanah Beard reported, members were "very much scattered" with little opportunity for regularly attending worship services or conferring with ministers. Still, Friend Beard believed that all were "conducting themselves creditably . . . [and] walking humbly before their God."[27]

In response to the dispersed condition of the meeting's membership, "our beloved friend Daniel Drew," returned from Tennessee, determined to exercise his gift of ministry by visiting among "the scattered members of this Monthly Meeting in Mississippi" as well as in Arkansas. Alida Clark called Friends' attention to Drew's continued service "in the Gospel of Love" and to the quiet power of newly recorded black minister Morris Brown as examples of Southland's influence "to tone down heathen practices and barbarous traditions, and root out superstitious ignorance and vice." She exalted in the continued "elevation and Christian education of this poor, ignorant, degraded and still oppressed people."[28]

While local conversions continued and an abundance of itinerant northern preachers visited Southland to reinforce local ministerial talent, there were no hints of radical holiness practices in either the Southland minutes or Alida's persistent stream of letters to the Quaker press. During the first half of 1882 Southland was stimulated by the visits of three female ministers, Mary E. Beck of London Yearly Meeting and two eastern Friends, Sarah Goodard and Hannah Wing, who claimed responsibility for the conversion of forty-three souls on a single April day. Their fire and vision had barely cooled when Jesse C. Johnson of Indiana conducted a series of revival meetings wherein another twenty-three were converted, including, according to Mrs. Clark,

> A drunkard, a gambler, a hard-drinking man, and an old grey headed . . . self-righteous man . . . all pleading for mercy . . . under a sense of their lost condition. . . . There was no excitement whatever, but heart-broken sobs.

Young people at Southland, she added, were "*drilled* to give attention, and never to criticize anything said for their instruction and good."[29]

While some might detect a hint of condescension in Mrs. Clark's tone, she went on to make clear that she was "not ashamed nor sorry" to belong to a meeting of 264 souls, all but four of whom were black. Furthermore, she proclaimed that Southland was "*united* in moving upon the *enemy* . . . to undermine superstition ignorance, hypocrisy, drunkenness, and every other crime that has so long stalked abroad unrestricted in this land."[30]

Amidst this struggle to maintain good order in their own meeting as well as to take the fight to the local foes of righteousness, a reminder of the continuing, and growing, doctrinal divisions among American Friends came home to Southland during the Christmas holidays of 1882. Meeting minutes for 27 December noted the visit of Isaac Sharp, a weighty English Friend, and Joel Bean, a minister of San Jose, California, and former clerk of Iowa Yearly Meeting. Alida Clark described their ministry as a great boon to the school and the meeting, eliciting, in the words of Lydia Chace, "an increase of interest in the plan of salvation among the unconverted."[31] The significance of Bean's visit was that by 1882 Bean had become the central figure in the ongoing endeavor of the holiness faction to silence or expel Friends who resisted the imposition of their revolutionary brand of Quakerism.

The story of how Joel Bean and his wife Hannah became the center of a wide-ranging controversy has been clearly set out in previous accounts. Suffice to say that the Beans were highly regarded Friends who settled in Iowa where Joel became clerk of Iowa Yearly Meeting. Initially they were strong supporters of the renewal movement that Joel believed had brought "revival of earnest inquiry, of quickened life, of fresh dedication."[32] By the late 1870s, however, Joel had become deeply concerned about the spreading holiness doctrine of immediate sanctification as well as growing a tendency of holiness Friends to abandon or even disavow traditional Quaker beliefs and practices. For the Beans a turning point came in 1878 when the "Inward Light," the principle which they believed to be the doctrinal rock upon which Quakerism was founded, was condemned by Ohio Yearly Meeting, the stronghold of holiness leader David Updegraff. Joel's forthright denunciation of this action eventually resulted in his removal as clerk by the Iowa Yearly Meeting of Ministers and Elders, an action that amounted to an endorsement of holiness proceedings in Ohio. The fallout from these events not only drove the Beans to leave Iowa for California but also divided Iowa Friends into hostile, feuding camps.[33]

In the wake of these troubling and divisive developments, Joel Bean's visit to Southland, in the company of a moderate evangelical English Friend like Isaac Sharp, seems to indicate that while the "revival wave" continued to sweep over Southland as membership rapidly expanded (reaching 378 in 1884), the extreme holiness faction had been kept at bay. General meetings were still described as "filled to overflowing, many standing in doors and outside" while "gamblers, fiddlers . . . and 'such like' characters prostrated themselves at the altar of prayer" begging to know how to be saved. Alida Clark's answer to their pleas—"Believe in the Lord Jesus Christ and thou shalt be saved"—reflected her policy of steering the middle course, encouraging revivalism without yielding to radical holiness practices. Mrs. Clark also continued to insist that, in contrast to the untrammeled emotions of holiness gatherings, "the greatest quiet & best of order prevailed" at Southland.[34] This stance insinuated Alida's public posture during the next fissure in Quaker ranks initiated by the relentlessly contentious David Updegraff. Under his leadership holiness Friends began to insist that literal adherence to scripture demanded Quakers modify their traditional rejection of outward sacraments or "ordinances" such as water baptism and physical reception of the Lord's supper.[35] In this instance Updegraff went too far. His aggressive actions brought on an "Ordinance

Crisis" that eventually united conservative and moderately evangelical Quakers in opposition to outward sacraments. In the end only Updegraff's stronghold, Ohio Yearly Meeting, held out for incorporating outward ordinances into Quaker religious practice. Southland's official position in the ordinance struggle was framed in Mrs. Clark's words welcoming sixty-four new souls into Southland Meeting in 1884: "We are tired of foolishness and ordinances and ignorant discussions. We want *Jesus*."[36]

During the next year a printed communication from the representative meeting of Indiana Yearly Meeting was inserted into Southland Meeting's minute book warning all members to remain watchful "over the flock lest there may . . . creep into our borders grievous wolves, or rise up from amongst ourselves those who may cause strife . . . & scatter the flock, rather than feed and nourish the lambs." The admonishing document when on to note that "certain individuals, holding the position of Ministers . . . have partaken of the rites of water baptism and of the bread and wine in the so-called Communion of the Lord's Supper." To protect members from such influences, meetings were advised "to refuse to receive as acceptable Ministers . . . those teaching doctrines or practicing rites contrary to the . . . 'Declaration of Faith.'" Shortly thereafter Alida Clark wrote to the *Friends' Review* noting Daniel Drew's passionate rejection of those who practiced "outward rites and ceremonies rather than inward cleansing," adding her reassurance that "ministers calling themselves *Friends*" who preached or practiced such observances would "not be recognized by Southland Monthly Meeting, though composed, with four exceptions, of colored people."[37]

III. The Ignorant Masses of the South

In the early summer of 1877 Alida Clark told of "a most fearful and destructive inundation" that had left crumpled bridges, immobilized railroads, ruined crops, and drowned people and animals in its wake. "Thus it is year after year, that in some way these poor people are deprived of the means of subsistence." A year earlier local blacks had endured the blight of "miniature 'Hamburg' riots . . . upon soil where the guerrillas, bushwhackers, dissenters and the fag-ends of both armies are left tramping about . . . subsisting off industrious and law-abiding citizens" and growing bolder with each political campaign.[38] One manifestation of the increasingly successful counterattack against Reconstruction by "Redeemer" Democrats and the "old Slaveholding Aristocracy" was a law passed by the Arkansas legislature in 1877 reducing the five-mill state school tax to a single mill, retroactive to 1876. An unsurprising result was the drying up of state funds, which from 1869 had supported free summer schools, providing learning possibilities, however brief, for many poor blacks in the Arkansas Delta as well as teaching experience for aspiring Southland students. Furthermore, in 1876, for unspecified reasons, the Peabody Fund withheld its usual six-hundred-dollar donation to assist Southland's teaching mission.[39]

Another foreboding manifestation of the floundering of the Reconstruction regime was an atmosphere of intimidation and the threat of violence graphically depicted in Lydia and Amasa Chace's letter to the *Christian Worker* recounting how they had been terrorized by hostile white men who cut their wagon harness to pieces while they were on a temperance mission in Mississippi. They declared that it was possible to "give but a faint idea of the immorality, poverty, misery and degradation" prevailing among "the ignorant masses of the South," both white and black. This "smothered volcano," they warned, was ready "to break forth at any favorable moment into open war." The Chaces believed that the South faced a stark choice between "education or war" and that, for the sake of the republic itself, northern Friends should take up their share of the burden by supporting institutions like Southland so that the "benefits of Christian influence as well as intellectual culture" might be sustained.[40]

In this spirit, by the summer of 1877 Southland had sent out over a hundred students to teach in rural schools, half of these were members of the Society of Friends, and, for what it was worth, seven were graduates of the institution's college course. These Southland products were serving at least five thousand pupils, teaching not only reading, history, natural sciences, and higher mathematics but also "better ways of living." In 1878 the Phillips County inspector of schools told a visiting Friend, "We should not know what to do without Southland. . . . They turn out the best teachers for the colored people we can get."[41]

Despite Alida's complaint that local newspapers would not carry the school's advertisements, enrollment continued to increase at such a rate that in 1878 an additional unbudgeted teacher had to be hired to cope with the influx of students.[42] Mrs. Clark could not refrain from boasting about such progress. Still, for all present achievement and future promise, Alida warned that if their mission was to be sustained, help was required from every Quaker yearly meeting on both sides of the Atlantic as only a third of Southland's expenditures were covered by the school's annual subsidy from the Indiana Missionary Board. Furthermore, even the diminishing allotment of state and district funds was increasingly unreliable not only because of the above-noted reduction in school tax assessment but also because the value of Arkansas state bonds from which school funds were paid had declined to sixty cents on the dollar. The difference had to be made up from fees, and Southland was forced to impose charges of a dollar a month for day students and three dollars per week for boarders on an already poverty-stricken clientele.[43]

Mrs. Clark pointed out that if bodies like Western Yearly Meeting could add to what Indiana was providing, Southland's fifty boarding students, including "orphans and windows' daughters," might double in number and become "a mighty power for good. . . . Give us these children early and when educated, they will be Friends as readily as they are Catholics under the Pope." There were, for example, seventeen "needy orphans" presently living at the school and from among "these dear helpless girls" would come "the 'women of influence' in their nation, remembering, that it is only as the women of any nation are elevated, that they rise on the scale of civilization as a people." At the same time, Daniel Drew and Lucy Barnett, on behalf of Southland Meeting's committee on education, noted that while some of their meeting's members were teaching in free schools in Mississippi, Tennessee, and Texas as well as Arkansas, it was no easy task "to advance the great work of education on which hangs the character of the church and state" to a people who still had little sense of its value.[44] In her 1878 report to Indiana Yearly Meeting, Alida praised the "untiring and ceaseless" efforts of black Friends to bring their people to "a higher plane of morality, religious integrity . . . and industry. . . . The harvest is coming. . . . Eternity alone will gather all the sheaves." She had faith that in the light of this work the Lord had protected their little community from the scourge of yellow fever—"the pestilence that walketh in darkness and the destruction that wasteth at midday." In submitting his annual financial report to the missionary board, Calvin noted that the "Redeemer" revolution in politics, generally short crops, and the yellow fever quarantine made it necessary for him to wait until the students' parents sold their cotton to collect any part of the nearly $1,300 in schools fees that was owed.[45]

In 1877 Mrs. Clark reported local people had suffered from "a most fearful inundation." The following year worms ravaged the cotton crop, leaving people destitute, while "whiskey dealers . . . [held] mortgages on nearly all live-stock, wagons and other utensils, for supplies already used up."[46] Then, in 1879, another yellow-fever quarantine stopped all business, and a "fearful reign of terror" was imposed by whites emboldened by the political success of anti-Reconstruction forces. Conditions for local blacks were harder than at any time since the war. In addition to the efforts of some lower-class Phillips County whites to "bulldoze" blacks off the land, "unprincipled [black] men" were extorting money from local people to send scouts to "spy out" prospects for the settlement of American blacks in Liberia.[47]

In the circumstances, Mrs. Clark admonished Friends to "wake up still *more* to active, aggressive, evangelistic and proselytizing labors" in the South.[48] Her pleas apparently had some effect. In fiscal 1876–77 private donations amounted to nearly $1,400, including a small gift from Col. Charles Bentzoni who had been instrumental in securing the land upon which the college sat.[49] Still, for all their value in helping to deal with ongoing and unexpected expenses, onetime donations could not permanently sustain the Southland experiment. Mrs. Clark had visions of an endowment that would provide the institution with consistent means to underpin its mission. A small beginning was made in 1878 when an anonymous donor (Benjamin Coates of Philadelphia) sent five hundred dollars to initiate an endowment fund.[50] For a time, Mrs. Clark's greatest hope lay with Elisha Hathaway of Rhode Island, "a benevolent Christian man of feeble health," who had expressed a desire to aid some corporate religious body for "Relief and Elevation of poor people, especially the colored people of the Southern States." Apparently led to Southland by the elderly Levi Coffin, Hathaway spent the winter of 1875 at the school and declared his deep attachment to the work there. His first material contribution was the creation of the "Hathaway Relief Fund" that eventually aided "many aged and helpless widows, orphans" and other poor blacks. Then, early in 1876 Hathaway conveyed assets valued at $34,734, including land in Cincinnati and Chattanooga, to the Indiana Missionary Board. He was to draw the income from this sum until his death, upon which time the principal was to be bequeathed to the missionary board to support its work in the South.[51]

Any benefits arising from this tidy sum were, however, short lived. In

September 1878, Hathaway requested that the twenty-six acres near Chattanooga he had deeded to the missionary board be returned to him, in exchange for which he would make a "liberal contribution" of one thousand dollars towards the construction of a new boys dormitory at Southland, provided Friends raised another two thousand dollars for that purpose. The board agreed to this new arrangement, especially in light of the fact that Hathaway disclaimed any intention of asking for the return of the Cincinnati property.[52] Hathaway did indeed donate one thousand dollars shortly before his death, whereupon Indiana Yearly Meeting was named as the benefactor of his not-inconsiderable estate. In the end, however, Quaker hopes were dashed when the would-be philanthropist's daughter successfully contested the will, including the all the property previously conveyed to the yearly meeting. Indeed, such was the embarrassment of funds arising from this disappointing outcome that the missionary board declined to pay expenses for northern Quaker ministers who wished to attend Southland's fifteenth anniversary celebration.[53]

Undeterred by the board's cautious parsimony or the legal wrangles over the Hathaway legacy, Alida Clark, set about doubling the lately departed benefactor's thousand-dollar contribution by embarking on another fundraising tour among northern Friends. Again traveling over seven thousand miles, she collected, less expenses, two thousand dollars that, when added to the Hathaway donation and six hundred Stanley Pumphrey had raised in England, opened the way for the construction of a dormitory for male students, dedicated in 1880 as Pumphrey Hall.[54] This important addition helped created a physical plant that was increasingly imposing by local standards. The campus, in rough imitation of an English college, was laid out as an open square, the new boy's dormitory forming the north side. A three-storied frame house, with library, office, reception, and living rooms, filled in the southern exposure. The school building was on the west with five classrooms and a large assembly hall that could seat three hundred.[55] These facilities represented a considerable financial investment that Indiana Yearly Meeting could not lightly disregard. But Mrs. Clark remained fearful that officials of the yearly meeting failed to appreciate the vital importance of Southland's mission. As she told missionary board chairman Joseph Dickinson, "Let not Indiana Yearly Meeting flinch now, when victory is in sight."[56]

Despite continuing financial and other concerns, early in 1880 Alida could report that all was harmonious at the school that, in fulfillment of her "long cherished notion," was for the first time staffed by black teachers, all of whom were Southland graduates. By this time Mrs. Clark had concluded that domestic training for female students was "the most important part of their education . . . except for the religion of Jesus."[57] This aspect of the work seemed to be thriving as well.

The Southland Meeting, 174 strong, had recently been addressed by "a remarkable minister," Brother Coleman, a black Friend from Iowa. Alida believed that the spiritual power of the meeting as well as the excellence of the school was convincing even "old *iron-side* Baptists" to give in and send their girls to Southland. Joseph Dickinson, speaking for the board, agreed that the work had been "remarkably blessed" in elevating thousands of young people through Christian education and bringing impressive numbers of these into the Society of Friends.[58]

Still, continued lack of sufficient funding forced Mrs. Clark to listen helplessly to the "pitiful pleadings and tearful entreaties" of widows attempting to protect their daughters from a situation wherein "men of both races were hunting them down from the ages of twelve to eighteen" for criminal purposes or to arrange "improper, early and unhappy marriages," thus thinning the ranks of well-educated young women their race and nation needed so badly. Invoking "the purses and hearts of 'Friends' . . . [to] send us who are in the field money to . . . train and qualify teachers . . . to educate others like themselves to be peaceful, industrious, intelligent . . . and righteous . . . citizens,." Alida could but ask for more.[59]

At times, however, it was not a paucity of funds but the whims of nature and sins of men that conspired to deprive Southland Friends of the fruits of even small victories. In February 1880 shortly after Alida reported on the "very destructive tornado" that knocked down the meeting house at Hickory Ridge, she noted that amidst "scenes of wanton rapine and murder," many people in the vicinity of the ruined meeting house had "fully surrendered to the 'bulldozing party'" and the Ku Klux Klan, meekly voting as their planter employers dictated. Others, seeking to escape such tyranny, had joined in what was becoming a mass exodus out of Arkansas to Kansas where many became hopeless refugees, surviving only on the kindness of strangers. And as sympathetic as Alida was to the suffering of the Kansas Exodusters, she feared that Friends' generosity for those fleeing northward would cause potential donors to forget about those who stayed at Southland to fight the good fight for justice and righteousness.[60]

Whatever the setback, the Clarks soldiered on in the army of the Lord. When in 1880 Elkanah Beard completed another inspection visit to Southland, he reported to the missionary board that the school was "so highly appreciated" that "leading men, white and colored, say 'Southland College is the best Institution of learning in the State.'" With 80 acres of farmland, four substantial buildings, nearly 250 students, and a religious meeting of 200 members, the Quaker mission in Arkansas was, in Friend Beard's view, an exemplary educational, spiritual, and financial resource that should remain "most carefully guarded" by Indiana Yearly Meeting.[61]

Alida Clark sought to enhance Beard's endorsement by pointing to Southland's continued success in putting 130 former students into the field as teachers in Arkansas and surrounding states, "all able to teach the common English branches required by the free schools of the States." Some of these were also instructing students in "higher science, math, Latin and German." Sadly, she might have added that if Southland products were competent, they were among the few proficient teachers employed in Arkansas state schools because the state government consistently depreciated public education, especially for blacks. Thus, only "those of larger worldly means" could come to the rescue of Arkansas's Negro students.[62]

Seeking to find more such worldly means as well as new knowledge and skills, Mrs. Clark along with her prize graduate, teacher, and honorary adopted daughter, Henrietta Kitterall, attended a Quaker-sponsored educational conference at Haverford College near Philadelphia where they mingled "amongst . . . the leading Educators of the country" collecting whatever funds they could gather to enable "colored students . . . to become teachers . . . for the aid of orphans and fatherless children" and "recruits to the Lord's Army."[63]

Still, funds raised by private solicitation always proved inadequate to whatever need was at hand. Donations gathered to pay the fees of indigent boarding students, for example, increased female enrollment to the point of requiring a separate girls' dormitory. As Alida wrote apologetically to British Friends who had already donated considerable sums, "it seems trying to be always presenting our friends such an undesirable and uncomely subject. What shall I do? Quit, or double my diligence as demand for room increases?" Southland students as a body were, she said, "very poor and miserably oppressed" depending upon generous Friends to enable them to strive "against fearful hindrances" and achieve "a higher and better life."[64]

For all Southland's needs, trials, and tribulations, Mrs. Clark ended her state of the mission report with a jubilant question:

> When we look upon our present accommodations and look back to the time when part of the school was taught in a mule stable . . . should not the Mission Board and Indiana Yearly meeting praise the Lord and take courage?[65]

Alida's question was an adjunct to her announcement that Sarah Slade of Fall River, Massachusetts, had donated over $2,000 for the purchase of 135 acres in the area of Southland. This land was, in turn, to be sold in small tracts to local people wishing to live near the college. The proceeds of these sales added to the endowment fund, but more important was fact that those who brought the land, unlike tenants under the crop-lien system, could be assured of the full benefits of their own labor.[66] Then, during the next year it seemed that Alida's dream of a substantial endowment for Southland College was becoming reality. George Sturge, a wealthy English Friend, created a trust of $25,000 the income from which was

> in perpetuity to be laid out in educating such young men and women of the colored race . . . as show an aptitude for teaching, and are willing to employ themselves in the common or district schools of the Southern States . . . after completing their education at Southland College, Arkansas.[67]

The Sturge Fund was a great tribute to the seventeen years of dedicated toil that Calvin and Alida Clark had poured into Southland school and meeting. From the first year it provided a badly needed dividend of four hundred dollars, and indeed the principle remained intact for generations after Southland closed.[68] Still, the expanding endowment provided no miraculous rescue from financial difficulties. Beyond the generosity of benefactors, it was rain or lack thereof, the price of cotton, and the uncertain support of state or local governments (depending upon the constantly shifting political situation) that determined Southland's economic well-being from year to year. Student tuition and boarding fees, meager as these were, continued to compose the school's largest source of income. In the year the Sturge Fund was established Calvin Clark notified the missionary board that a considerable portion of school fees had not been collected on account of "the disastrous wet weather and the low price obtained for damaged cotton." He feared that the next year would be no better.[69]

Indeed, the school sessions of 1880–81 had been marked by extremes, in weather as well as in political and social developments. Mrs. Clark noted that a winter, which was longer and more severe than any they had previously seen in Arkansas, was followed by "a hot, dry and very debilitating" summer ("140–145degrees in sun; 96–100 degrees in shade") that caused local crops to be "nearly worthless" and produced want and misery even among the most thrifty farmers. In the midst of this suffering and wretchedness, local people fought amongst themselves assaulting each other for "the slightest imaginary causes of offense, white men shoot colored and colored white, and it goes on all around us constantly."[70]

For many blacks the instability of their circumstances was made even worse by the bulldozing activities of some poor whites attempting to drive blacks from whatever land they occupied. As noted, these conditions led many local blacks to join with the mass of Exodusters leaving the south for the plains of Kansas. But social conflict in the Arkansas Delta was not only between the lower classes of both races. The exodus of poor black people began to strike fear into the pocketbooks of larger Delta planters who saw the accelerating migration as seriously endangering their cheap labor source. Indeed, from the late 1870s leaders among "Redeemer" Democrats began seeking to placate black farmers and their white Republican supporters. "Consequently," Alida noted with a touch of irony, "such men as my husband and Amasa Chace, and other white and black Republicans were allowed to go to the polls peaceably and deposit . . . their votes—a privilege not allowed to them . . . for three years."[71]

So, for all the difficulties facing the Friends' mission in Arkansas, such an encouraging development was sufficient to convince Alida Clark that her work was more important than ever. After all, Pumphrey Hall, the new boys dormitory, had replaced the "dilapidated, leaky barracks, through which the drifting snow and piercing cold winds whistled." Furthermore, a continuing stream of blacks teachers, over 150 by the early 1880s, had been sent out into Arkansas and surrounding states as agents in the struggle to implant knowledge and virtue among their long-suffering brethren. Surely, she concluded, Southland was "planted in the right place —a beacon light, exposing darkness, vice and corruption, rebuking every phase of crime and teaching how to . . . remedy it."[72] Mary E. Beck, the visiting English Friend, agreed, contrasting the "bright faces" of Southland students with the degradation reflected in the "countenances and habits" of blacks she saw in Helena. "The Institution," she concluded, "is doing great and noble work, and is in every sense worthy of support."[73] Friends would carry on.

Chapter 6

The End of the First Generation

1880–1886

The highest water ever known at Helena and more coming. The distress from water and hunger along the river cannot be told. . . . I have never witnessed as great destitution in all this part of the country as now prevails.

—Calvin Clark to Benjamin Webb, 27 February 1882

I. Flooding In

The optimistic tone that prevailed at the beginning of the school term in 1881 scarcely survived the end of that year. Throughout the late winter and spring of 1882 every dispatch from Southland described "fearful distress, misery and horror" as the Mississippi and its tributaries overflowed their banks and water from broken levees poured into Helena and other towns. A steamer pilot told one Quaker visitor that the river had risen to fifty feet above normal, flooding Helena entirely. Alida Clark reported scenes of horror as crowds of terrified women and children "marched up and down the levee . . . all night long" while their husbands worked to hold back the flood. Another woman, a survivor of slavery, war, the Ku Klux Klan, and cholera, declared that she "never had heard such screaming . . . as rent the air these long, dreary nights."[1] In her annual report to the missionary board at the end of the school term, Mrs. Clark portrayed 1882 as "the most eventful year of distress, suffering and poverty that we have ever experienced." Floods and crop failures threatened the poorest with actual starvation to say nothing of "the frequent and fatal appearance of small pox in various localities." Finally, Alida suffered a personal lost when Lydia Chace was forced to return to Kansas to recover her health. But for all of this, Mrs. Clark could still see "a silver lining, and a smiling providence, over-running all." Generous benefactors had answered her pleas for assistance and provided aid to feed the hungry, minister to the afflicted, comfort the dying, and bury the dead. Furthermore, the school had carried on through every setback and disaster. Enrollment continued to grow, educating young black people to go forth in their turn to train "an army of children . . . several thousand strong" all across the Delta region, spreading literacy and preaching the word of God.[2]

One of the most prominent examples of a Southland graduate who had gone out to teach and preach was George Waltham Bell, a convinced Friend.[3] Some years after he left Southland, Bell spoke at the 1882 conference of the Friends Freedmen's Association in Philadelphia, where he was attending Lincoln University. His emotional address to this gathering, depicting his struggle to obtain an education and his belief that Quakerism was making great strides among "the colored residents of the South,"[4] made a strong impression. Among those impressed was Mary E. Beck, the English Friend who had visited Southland and, convinced that "great and noble work" was being accomplished there, had become one of the institution's most devoted British supporters.[5]

Late in 1882 George W. Bell became the combined focus of Mary Beck's interest in and Alida Clark's ambitions for Southland. Through Beck's good offices Mrs. Clark solicited English Friends for a gift of one thousand pounds to establish an endowed chair to be filled by Bell, who was slated to graduate from Lincoln University the following spring. Alida believed that if Bell could be brought back to his old school, the influence of this eloquent, locally produced black scholar would be "many degrees more impressive" than that of any white man, however distinguished.[6] Mrs. Clark challenging request was apparently not entirely fulfilled. Nevertheless, early in 1884 she was telling English friends how the school's progress was being signally advanced by "our male teacher" George W. Bell who was instructing Southland students in Greek and metaphysics as well as physics and rhetoric.[7]

In the meantime, despite the disastrous events of 1882, both school and meeting continued to thrive. Income from the Sturge Fund provided much needed aid for a growing student population, and "the revival wave" continued to sweep new members into Southland Monthly Meeting.[8] Alida gave particular thanks for the return of Daniel Drew from his ministry in Tennessee. He was, she said, "our main nursing father" who, in imitation of George Fox, traveled the area in evangelical service "refuting the foolishness and *false* doctrine preached amongst his people." Still, the primitive conditions in which this sojourner for truth was forced to live and work were starkly revealed after the death of the horse he depended upon for both his traveling ministry and subsistence farming. As Mrs. Clark noted, he had "not a single dollar" pay for a new animal, being at once the "poorest . . . but the most diligent" of ministers. Since the local meeting had spent its sustenance in paying two hundred dollars toward rebuilding the meeting house in Hickory Ridge, she pleaded for some kind Friend to come to the aid of this courageous and saintly figure who "works hard, lives poor [and] preaches Jesus."[9]

Generous Friends did provide the means for Brother Drew to acquire another horse, enabling him to carry on "extensive Evangelical service." At about the same time, Calvin and Alida Clark embarked on a vacation trip to the West Coast where they hoped "to recuperate the weakened energies of body and mind" after so many years of toilsome service. Indiana Yearly Meeting marked the occasion with a minute praising their "arduous and untiring labors . . . for several years without any pecuniary remuneration. . . . which calls forth our grateful acknowledgment for their self-sacrifice and devotion to this work of the Church."[10] Mrs. Clark declared that they would begin their temporary release from labor secure in the knowledge that Southland "was never in so prosperous condition," following a school year embodying "peace, quiet, and a good degree of prosperity."[11]

When the Clarks returned to Southland, reports continued to indicate the school's progress. Despite a short cotton crop, enrollment was large (over three hundred by spring 1884) with a considerable increase in boarders.[12] There was also the usual parade of visiting Quaker preachers and tourists, most prominently the wealthy octogenarian Irish philanthropist Richard Allen and his wife Mary Anna. The Allens were obviously charmed by what they saw both at the school and in the South in general. Mary

Anna wrote a description of their experiences for British Friends that had the tone of a traveler who had observed an especially arranged folk exhibition on the days and ways of southern black people.[13]

Despite the return of serious flooding to the Arkansas Delta in the spring of 1884, Southland experienced "a season of favor and edification" with religious and temperance meetings leading up to the celebration of the school's twenty-first anniversary.[14] The minutes of Southland Monthly Meeting gave testimony to this outpouring of spiritual fervor. Visiting ministers from Indiana preached revival meetings at the school that resulted in seventeen new applicants for membership with Friends. This resurgence carried over to Hickory Ridge where the meeting house, at long-last rebuilt, was the site of a two-week revival during which "the house was filled to overflowing" and "four score souls of different ages & rank in life" were converted, forty-five of whom, white as well as black, asked to be enrolled in the Society of Friends.[15] Articles in the *Christian Worker* described how a former dance hall was converted into a meeting house after "the chief fiddler and 'banjo picker'" declared for Christ.[16]

Alida's description of the accomplishments and the needs of Indiana Friends' southern mission were echoed by Southland's much admired male teacher George W. Bell. Writing in the *Friends' Review,* Bell recounted his travels in the South during the previous summer where, because of a nearly complete absence of competent teachers, he had witnessed the bulk of black pupils merely advancing "from one stage of ignorance to another." The southern Negro, he said, could only be raised up through the sort of Christian education that was being provided by schools like Southland that were "as a bright light in a dark wilderness" sending forth much needed "teachers and moral leaders" to work among their people. Still, Bell asserted, Southland ought to be training fifty teachers a year rather than the pitiful few the school was presently able to support. He chided "those who have the means to aid in such a cause" for concentrating their support on well-established eastern schools "while we who are in the wilderness crying for the very bread of life are mostly neglected."[17]

As Southland celebrated the conclusion of its twenty-first year, Mrs. Clark supplied readers of the *Christian Worker* with nostalgic recollections on how far those two decades had brought the school and its patrons:

> Since our opening 20 years ago, where and when was heard the fearful tramp of the *war horse*[,] the *muffled* drum and the *dead*

> march, on all sides of us . . . part of our school gathered in an ex-government mule stable, where little black waifs learned their letters, afterward graduated and now teach, govern and carry on this college and other graded and normal schools.[18]

So, by all accounts, Southland seemed to be steadily, if too slowly, advancing and expanding Friends' educational and religious mission in the Arkansas Delta and beyond. In the circumstances, the Clarks, as they entered their third decade of missionary service, would seem to have had every reason for satisfaction with what had become their life's work. Still, amidst what appeared to be favorable developments for the school and the meeting, Alida's letters spoke of new burdens being added to the old difficulties they had invariably faced.

> Dear readers . . . have you the least conception of what *isolation* ours is? Completely ostracized by our own *race* and color, hated and rejected on account of our *business*, that still grows more and more *distasteful* to them. . . .
>
> We are surrounded by *sectarian* prejudices and willfulness; rooted and grounded in ignorance, tradition, hypocrisy and heathen darkness that obstinately repel the light of saving gospel truth. . . .
>
> [We are] poor isolated souls, totally ignored and despised more and more for our work's sake by the pale faces here; and lightly esteemed by the *masses* of the others because we will not lower the standard, and grant certain privileges of familiarity . . . that cannot without serious damage and great risk be taken in any like educational institution.[19]

Causes for this uncharacteristic outburst of glum self-pity were never made explicit, but there are hints. Writing to the *Christian Worker,* Mrs. Clark warned of the need for increased "*vigilance* in this *Southern work*" because "the devourer and he who soweth seeds of discord has been busy, but he has gained less than might have been expected."[20] On the same day these words appeared in print, the minutes of the missionary board noted that its clerk, Joseph Dickinson, had "received private letters from Southland which were difficult to answer" and, after consulting with other board members, he determined to visit the school to investigate whatever questions had been raised. Following his extraordinary mission, Dickinson's report was at pains to make clear that a "thorough and careful examination" of the property, administration and accounts at Southland had revealed "everything in good order . . . carefully and economically managed."[21] The source and content of the obviously accusatory letters was not revealed at the time, but internal evidence and future developments make it reasonable to assume that they were written by George W. Bell, whose employment at Southland, which began with considerable expectation and fanfare, ended abruptly after only one year.[22]

Whatever concerns gave rise to Joseph Dickinson's urgent visit to Southland, there appeared to be no lasting negative effects. The matron's report for 1884 indicated that the school was continuing to flourish, with an enrollment of over 300 including 70 in the collegiate and normal divisions.[23] Furthermore, a third local meeting for worship was being established fifteen miles away at Beaver Bayou where, under a "Brush Arbor," sinners had been "awakened and converted." Ninety new names had been added to the monthly meeting rolls during the year, raising total membership to 386 souls, including 86 at Hickory Ridge and 15 at Beaver Bayou. These heady numbers rivaled those of even the largest North American Friends' meetings and had the effect of reviving Alida Clark's vision of a "Black Quarterly Meeting" spreading the saving gift of Quaker spirituality throughout the Mississippi Delta.[24]

On the temperance front, Mrs. Clark attended the national meeting of the Women's Christian Temperance Union in St. Louis "and experienced a renewed inspiration on that line," vowing never to waver in the cause "till the victory is won or life closes." Certainly, the struggle for sobriety was always near at hand. Alida declared that if Southland Friends had in hand "the whiskey money of any one county along this river for . . . sixty days," they could "fill up the College and make it free." But while the enemies of good order remained strong, the morale of the local Band of Hope was lifted to new heights when Southland's own Lydia Chace, her health restored, was elected president of the Arkansas branch of the Women's Christian Temperance Union. In that regard, a report summarizing the work of the local Band of Hope, inserted into the monthly meeting minutes, proudly announced "an advance . . . of public sentiment in favor of Temperance."[25]

Things continued to look up on the educational side as well. One visiting Friend depicted Southland as a "grand success," expressing particular admiration for "the good order and the religious deportment of scholars and the untiring patience of their teachers," noting especially "the watchful tongue and quick step" of the Clark's beloved "adopted" daughter and recorded minister,[26] Henrietta Kitterall. On the day of Southland's twenty-first anniversary, ground was broken for a new dormitory for forty female boarders, replacing leaky and rotting barracks that were not fit for repair. "Everything prosperous" was Mrs. Clark summation as the school year wound down.[27]

Although Alida suffered "a week's 'breakdown'" at the end of the 1885 school year, she managed to set out a detailed description of the graduation ceremonies, including the perhaps doubtful assertion of a large audience held "spell-bound" for four hours by the proceedings. The major address on that day was delivered by Emma France Landcaster, a Southland graduate, teacher, and Friend who had "come to us . . . a little waif, in 1864." and, recently married, was setting out to establish her own family. Emma Landcaster's speech on "Employment for Women" reflected upon the accomplishments of and possibilities for young women at institutions like Southland. Mrs. Clark (no closet feminist) saw the address as an illustration of the fact that given the opportunity to be raised by education above "the *evils* and *hardships* of . . . marriage . . . to ignorant, cruel and domineering husbands," a larger life could be opened to all women, black and white. Emma's words, she said, should serve as a powerful demonstration "to the men that *women* are their *equals*, and when allowed a chance, their *superiors*. There is no more *needed* lesson to be taught . . . and well rubbed in on them."[28]

II. Burning Out

The bittersweet physical separation of Emma France from the surrogate parents who had for two decades nurtured and prepared her for life in the world marked the beginning of the end for Southland's first generation. But it was not to be a quiet closing. Indeed, commencement ceremonies had scarcely concluded when the minutes of the Indiana Missionary Board revealed "that serious charges have been made by George W. Bell against the management of our institution at Southland." The twice-alarmed board responded immediately by appointing Elkanah Beard and William Hiatt to undertake a second on the spot investigation and by asking the trustees of Indiana Yearly Meeting "to furnish the Board an itemized statement of the condition of our funds."[29]

The men appointed to investigate Bell's charges spent ten days at the school, taking testimony from nearly fifty persons. Upon receiving their report, the board concluded that "after careful and deliberate consideration of this testimony and other information. . . . the Board united in believing that said charges are false and malicious and . . . in continuing the management of the Institution in the hands of the present faculty."[30]

Alida Clark was correct in her initial belief that George Bell would have great influence at Southland, but clearly his influence proved to be less than efficacious for either Bell's would-be benefactors or for their beloved institution. Events, as well as Bell's future activities in Arkansas, would seem to indicate that if he was not entirely honest, he was extremely canny.[31] In retrospect, by the time Bell arrived at Southland, the Clarks had already begun to relinquish their legendary status, becoming at once more vulnerable as well as more sensitive to criticism, especially from younger people in the school, the meeting, and the community. For some of these "Miz Clark" may have seemed more a bossy, righteous old white woman than a fabled friend to the black race. No doubt Bell exploited these feelings when, with whatever motive, he brought charges of irregularity against the Clarks' management. The missionary board found Bell's accusations, whatever they may have been, groundless, but the damage had been done. Mrs. Clark, for one, began to exhibit the classic symptoms of a burnout case. For over two decades she had been teacher, surrogate mother, missionary, minister, matron, and fundraiser with the chief responsibility for maintaining a growing religious congregation and running a large educational institution chronically short of funds and periodically plagued by troubles and complaints that were often out of the hands of the founders and managers. Such a condition was perhaps reflected in Alida's report to Indiana Yearly Meeting at the time when the missionary board's second investigation was still underway. While the school enrollment was still nearly three hundred and the meeting listed almost four hundred members, she warned northern Friends not to "expect too much from these people" who were, after all, only a quarter of a century removed from slavery. "The greatest amount of head knowledge requires greater heart knowledge and years of common sense experience, to be utilized beneficially amongst the masses."[32]

During the following school year there was a dramatic falling off of reports and messages from Southland's venerable, and perhaps deeply wounded, managers.[33] In a letter to a Philadelphia friend and Southland benefactor, Alida commented upon their situation "in the midst of those who *hate our work*, and in their hearts, and any other ways they can, oppose and thwart our success and plans—however pure and virtuous they may be." This combination of bigotry, envy, and ingratitude was, she said, the "last *straw* that broke the camel's back" causing a breakdown in her health.[34] This illness must in part explain the nearly complete absence of Alida's hitherto prodigious epistolary activity. Not until mid-April 1886 was one of Mrs. Clark's typically fervent and newsy letters reprinted in *Friends' Review* commenting on the progress of temperance work at Southland ("a class of ten- and twelve-year-olds studying Mrs. Hunt's *Temperance, Hygiene and Alcohol*") where the entire school continued to resolve itself into a Band of Hope every other Saturday. She also wielded her "begging pen" in pleading for money to finish work on the girls' dormitory that was slowly taking shape.[35] Perhaps this missive was an expression of relief over a decision finally made. Shortly thereafter, the long and perhaps ominous silence that prevailed in communication with Indiana officials was broken when Calvin and Alida Clark informed Joseph Dickinson, chairman of the missionary board, "We now send our resignation as agents and managers at Southland College. To take effect as the School is concerned at the close of the present term of school . . . and all care and work on farm the first of eighth month next."[36]

Given the noticeable chill in its recent relations with the Clarks, the board could not have been deeply shocked or surprised by this announcement. Their subdued and perhaps somewhat embarrassed response was to accept the inevitable "with much reluctance" and to direct the business committee to write expressing "our deep regret and . . . appreciation of their faithful labors during so many years." Alida and Calvin were, with proper Quaker formality, "released . . . after 23 years of most harmonious connection in this labor of love from further charge of the school, and on August 1st proximo . . . from superintendence of the Buildings, farm and finances in every respect."[37]

Despite any lingering resentment the Clarks may have felt about lapses of confidence in their administration, their final report to Indiana Yearly Meeting embodied the generally devout and positive tone of the past. With the help of Indiana Friends and other supporters, they had realized "to a good degree, the fulfillment of our fondly-cherished hopes."

The school, Alida observed, was being handed over "in a healthy and prosperous condition," monthly meetings continued "to be a season of great blessing and spiritual power," and, with Lydia Chace remaining state president of the Women's Christian Temperance Union, there appeared to be "a steady gain for Prohibition." Her only caveat was that "licence" had recently triumphed in their township, leaving only the law forbidding sale of liquor within three miles of a school as a barrier against the ravages of King Alcohol. Calvin's last financial report indicated that the year had ended with a surplus of $371.75 and that work on the young ladies' hall, which he continued to supervise, was well along.[38] There were, however, two unresolved matters left over from the previous year's report. The first of these concerned the nature of the curriculum being offered by Southland. Alida's report in 1885 had mentioned the need for more training in manual as against literary arts, a topic of some resonance for the next generation.[39] Secondly, in both 1885 and 1886 notice was taken that tenants on the "Slade Land," donated as a means of allowing local black farmers to throw off shackles of the vicious crop-lien system, remained deeply in debt to Calvin Clark for supplying them with means for cultivation. The prevalence of short crops, especially in cotton, meant that they were unable to discharge their debt and indeed might have to increase it in order to put in another crop.[40] The question of the degree to which the yearly meeting or its local agents could or should become involved in financing local land sales and leases was another question that would loom large in the future of the Southland community.[41]

Calvin and Alida packed up their earthly possessions to make way for their replacements, the always faithful but aging Elkanah and Irena Beard. Given the physical and mental strain involved in supervising an enterprise as large and stressful as Southland, younger, more resilient successors might have been expected, but, clearly, Quaker couples with young children would be reluctant to undertake the sort of adventurous leap into the unknown that service at Southland required. Certainly, this situation underlined the enormousness of the sacrifice the Clarks had made in giving over their middle years at an isolated southern mission station. The *Friends' Review* printed an appropriately effusion tribute to Southland's founders:

> Few instances . . . in the Society of Friends, showing so signally the value of consecrated energy and individual faithfulness . . . as that

> of the building up, maintenance and extension, of this institution. Artesian wells . . . have by irrigating certain spots in the Sahara, made oases in the midst of desert. Something like this has been the civilizing and Christianizing influence exerted at Southland, in overcoming the effects and tendencies left by slavery, hostile both to civilization and to religion.[42]

Some Friends may have been surprised that the Clarks, upon their removal from Southland, did not return to the more civilized and comfortable climes of southern Indiana from whence they had come. But during two decades their spiritual and material roots had sunk deep into the soil of eastern Arkansas. Besides being local landowners of considerable standing, their connection with Southland and its meeting held them fast. From their retirement cottage, "Hillside Home," barely two miles from the Southland campus and meeting, they could, as Alida noted, look down on the school and remember

> Every beam, post, plank, nail and shingle, on all the buildings. . . . To Him we dedicate it, with all of its interests in the uplifting of the degraded, and only despised *race* of present and future generations, and reckon ourselves "unprofitable servants."[43]

No doubt the Beards and most members of Southland Meeting found the continued local presence of the Clarks a considerable blessing, but events would show that their proximity would not necessarily be appreciated by some future administrators of the College.

In any case, Alida Clark remained as clerk of Southland Meeting and her religious and temperance work proceeded with characteristic determination and enthusiasm. A petition to ensure no saloon could be established within three miles of Southland was circulated and signed by over three hundred local residents. Heartened by this local victory, the temperance committee exhorted Friends to push on to "final victory in the overthrow of the traffic, manufacture, sale or use of the poisonous beverage." Reporting for the Women's Christian Temperance Union, Lydia Chace was encouraged that by the end of 1885 local efforts like Southland's had resulted in twenty-six Arkansas counties voting dry.[44] The Southland Meeting also hosted John A. Clark, a black Quaker minister formerly connected with Wilberforce College in Ohio, who wrote a glowing account of his visit and of the work being accomplished in the meeting and at the school where, under the direction of an all black faculty, John Clark believed that student recitations compared quite favorably to those in northern schools.[45]

However, the Indiana board soon faced more troubling news when, after only a few months service, the Beards asked to be relieved from their duties. But when the school year ended three months later, no replacements had yet been found.[46] Given the circumstances, the Beards, bolstered by a strong vote of confidence in their leadership, agreed stay on until a new superintendent and matron could be recruited.[47]

Reports from Southland in the first year of the post-Clark era were, if not unusual, at least illustrative of both the relentlessly grinding poverty of the region from whence the school drew students and the limited resources available to the missionary board and local administrators attempting to sustain Friends' educational and missionary activities. Elkanah Beard reported a total enrollment of 302, with 55 boarding students. Of these, about 50 had received $1,233.35 in aid from the Sturge Fund, including $75 advanced for "clothing and Books for those too poor to supply themselves."[48] Even then, Beard noted, lack of funds made it necessary to refuse admission to many others "who had neither money nor suitable clothing." In its own report to the yearly meeting, the missionary board commented that because they refused to anticipate income or incur debt, assistance to needy students had to be limited "to the funds at our command."[49]

One anticipated source of income that was seldom realized were the rents to be paid by tenants on the Slade land. Because of this continuing difficulty, the board decided to cease leasing these 138 acres and, instead, to sell small parcels to local black farmers "so as to have them settle around the College." In this way they believed that they might improve the general financial situation for the parents of potential students. This plan was, however, complicated by the fact that Calvin Clark had incurred a considerable debt in advancing funds to the existing tenants for supplies and other necessities. Because the price of cotton remained low, Clark was seldom repaid. So, before they could begin selling Slade lands, the board made a settlement by advancing Calvin five hundred dollars and assigning to him all rents from the land for 1886, 1887, and 1888. Thus, it was not until mid-1889 that the planned sale of the Slade land could be implemented.[50]

Daniel Drew accompanied the Beards to Indiana Yearly Meeting in 1887 and spoke impressively of the Society of Friends as "a church with a definite mission" in Arkansas, a mission he continued to preach to "his people." But Elkanah Beard's report on the state of Southland Monthly Meeting might have caused some Friends to ask just who and where Drew's people were. Beard began with the encouraging news that twelve new convincements had raised Southland's total official membership to over four hundred, but he added, "Most of these do not live within the reach of Friends' Meetings, and many of them we know now little or nothing of, and some have joined other religious societies."[51] In other words, during the Clark era once a name was added to Southland's membership rolls, it apparently remained there in perpetuity unless the individual was disowned or officially transferred. This obviously called into question the actual size of America's only black monthly meeting, although this question was not explicitly raised. Still, one northern Quaker did offer a comment that might also have called into question the reality of Indiana Friends' grasp of the realities of the situation at Southland. Eli Jones, a prominent New England minister, stated, in all earnest innocence, that Liberia would be "a good place for those educated at Southland to go for a field in which to work," as if the Arkansas Delta or the South generally could spare sorely needed teachers for the African mission field.[52]

For all of that, the work at Southland went forward. Elkanah Beard noted that the finishing touches could be put on the new girls' dormitory if generous Friends were able to provide the $1,300 necessary to complete the job. With an eye to raising at least a part of that sum, the *Christian Worker* printed an article by mission board secretary Joseph Dickinson that provided a capsule history of the institution as "a center of religious education and moral training to the colored people." Southland's impact, Dickinson asserted, was symbolized by a large old slave plantation bell that hung in the belfry of the school building "tolling several times each day for twenty years to the old slaveholder that a revolution had taken place and to the colored people to come and embrace the privileges offered."[53]

Ironically, three weeks prior to the appearance of Dickinson's confident and laudatory article, he had received a disconsolate telegram from Elkanah Beard reporting that a fire of unknown origin had destroyed Southland's teachers' residence as well as the kitchen and dining room. Beard, overwhelmed by the disaster, commented, "I fear that the strain on some of us may be more than we can bear up under."[54] Friend Beard's dismay could only have been heightened when he learned that while the buildings that had been destroyed had an assessed value of $9,000, the Indiana Yearly Meeting held only $3,520 in fire insurance.[55]

Shortly after the fire, Lydia Chace wrote in the Quaker press of visiting the school on a "dark . . . cloudy . . . rainy" day to find only "desolate stacks . . . [of] brick and debris" where the buildings had stood. Still, with characteristic Quaker resilience, the president of Arkansas's Women's Christian Temperance Union added that if the fire was discouraging, Friends could take heart in the knowledge that temperance work in the state was most encouraging with "Christian women . . . coming to the front."[56]

Chapter 7

From Miz' Clark to Jim Crow

1888–1892

I. Anxious Times

Because insurance payments for the Southland buildings destroyed by fire covered less that half the estimated replacement cost, the always financially strapped missionary board was again required to take extraordinary measures to raise the funds necessary for rebuilding. A central feature of a newly launched solicitation campaign was a memorial "from the colored people . . . expressing their high appreciation of the Institution and [its] management . . . [and] their hope that new-fire proof building should be built."[1] Calvin and Alida Clark added their own ringing endorsement for "the Christian service needed amongst these people . . . [and] the adaptability of Friends meetings . . . to their conditions."[2] Still, earnest pleas and stirring words did not buy lumber, plaster, or labor, and the total available funds remained $2,500 to $3,000 short of the replacement cost for even one of the burnt-out buildings. Noting their "embarrassed situation," the board made a special appeal to the entire Anglo-American Quaker community for assistance in the "immense work" of educating and elevating black people in Arkansas, making certain that their entreaty was prominently featured in the British Quaker press.[3]

Concurrent with its latest fundraising campaign, the board announced the appointment of Charles W. and Ascenath Osborne as new superintendent and matron at Southland. C. W. Osborne, a successful farmer in Wayne County, Indiana, of unvarnished Quaker heritage, was described as a man in his mid-fifties who was a recorded minister, "a devoted friend of the colored people . . . [and] an earnest and devoted Christian . . . of sterling integrity." The Osbornes were to be paid five hundred dollars, plus traveling expenses for themselves and their twelve-year-old son, during the first year, with the hope they would agree to stay for several more.[4]

As corresponding secretary of the missionary board, Joseph Dickinson obviously felt an obligation to advise and direct Southland's new superintendent in a fashion he would not have dared attempt with the Clarks. Believing that Charles Osborne had "much to learn of his new field of labour," Dickinson's first official letter to him was full of authoritative observations and admonishments that, no doubt, effected more knowledge of the local situation than was warranted given the fact that Dickinson had himself only briefly visited the school. The area, he noted, had been "blighted by the curse of slavery" that could only be overcome if the local folk learned to "fear God & keep his commandments" as in joining the "movement . . . against the use of all alcoholic liquors & . . . desecration of the Sabbath. . . . I have no doubt that the needed grace will be given thee . . . to accomplish great good in the name of the Redeemer."[5] During the course of their brief and troubled tenure at Southland, the Osbornes would be subjected to a steady steam of the sort of condescending guidance from afar that Calvin and Alida Clark would have deeply resented. In any case, Charles Osborne's confidence could not have been bolstered by the degree of long-distance micromanagement imposed upon him.

Arriving at Southland in late May 1888, the Osborne Family were "cordially welcomed" by the Beards and members of the monthly meeting "under a renewed Baptism of fellowship and brotherly love." The gathering of Southland Meeting to greet the new superintendent and matron was doubly significant in that for first time Alida Clark was not presiding clerk, having been replaced by Emma France Lancaster, one of the orphans rescued by the Clarks a quarter century earlier.[6] Among Superintendent Obsborne's first responsibilities was to deal with a series of letters from Joseph Dickinson regarding the rebuilding project which the cautious missionary board finally agreed to support after changing the specifications from a brick to a frame structure for economy's sake. Almost immediately after approving this undertaking, the board became "restless" at delays in hiring a suitable local building contractor. "We have to leave things to your judgment," Dickinson told Osborne, adding emphatically that Southland's new leader should "never delay *what can be done now*."[7]

Because the missionary board had acted in an understandable but un-Quakerly fashion by approving the construction project without money on hand to pay its full cost, Joseph Dickinson pressured the soon-to-be-retired Elkanah Beard to travel to the eastern states on a fundraising tour among wealthy Friends, adding that he hoped Elkanah might "be able to *counteract* some of Alida's statements to some of them."[8] While the nature of Mrs. Clark's statements is not clear, and it is difficult to imagine her discouraging any donations, a continuing undercurrent of tension between Southland's founders and the Indiana Missionary Board seems obvious. Unable to resist the board's entreaties, the long-sacrificing Beard was duly issued a certificate of travel by Indiana Yearly Meeting notifying eastern Friends that this "esteemed minister," recently released from "arduous service" at Southland College, was coming to lay before them "the interests and needs of this Institution."[9]

Joseph Dickinson attempted to smooth Friend Beard's path with letters to wealthy eastern Quakers like Cordelia Hadley describing how the Arkansas blacks, beaten down "almost to brutes" by slave culture, had been raised up and educated "by . . . benevolent people of the North" whose "*missionary station*" had "done *very great good*. Whatever the Lord may move thy heart to do. . . . I hope thou will be faithful."[10] The missionary board was counting on Beard's receiving a favorable reception in the north, but after Elkanah hinted that Phillips County merchants, for whom Southland was a significant customer, might be willing to contribute towards the building fund, Joseph Dickinson began exhorting C. W. Osborne, an uninitiated northern newcomer, to seek five-hundred-dollars' worth of pledges in Helena: "We are *waiting anxiously* for the $500 from Helena Merchants—*push this collection*."[11]

Obviously, the Southland scene was shifting from the sort of on the spot initiative that Alida Clark had established and long maintained to increasingly close direction from afar at the hands earnest men, especially Joseph Dickinson, with an imperfect sense of local conditions. Indeed, Dickinson's pushy approach was likely to have been one source of strained relations between the Indiana leadership and the Clarks. Furthermore, for whatever reason, none of Alida's successors were her equal in extracting money from cautious and frugal Friends. In late July the missionary board minutes reported that while Elkanah Beard had so far collected $490 on his eastern tour, his salary and traveling expenses totaled $855.[12] Eventually, Beard managed to garner a net gain from his efforts, but the missionary board had to borrow money just to meet current operating expenses. In the meantime, costs on the new building continued to mount while Dickinson continued to badger C. W. Osborne about collecting the phantom $500 from Helena businessmen that he described as the "indispensable" key for the board getting out of further debt.[13] Alas, the new superintendent lacked not only Alida Clark's aggressive personality but also any close acquaintance with local white people.

While Osborne was slow to develop contacts among the local white business establishment, he became, perforce, a central figure within the Southland Meeting and its subsidiary branches at Hickory Ridge and Beaver Bayou. In reporting on religious developments, he particularly noted the "continued successful Christian work" being accomplished at Beaver Bayou, an observation in keeping with the monthly meeting's decision to establish an official preparatory meeting there.[14] Southland's Band of Hope also remained active, and Friends were proud of their ability, by means of the Local Option law, to erect and maintain a protective barrier against the inroads of King Alcohol. Northern visitors continued to inspect the Arkansas outpost. Two of these, Clark and Esther Terrell, slipped into enthusiastic Quakerese, describing Gospel services and social relations at Southland and Hickory Ridge as a "brook by the way." Certainly, the meeting had cause to celebrate the marriage of Henrietta Kitterall, school teacher, minister, and the Clarks' adopted daughter, to Benjamin Knox, an elder of the Presbyterian church and former Southland student.[15]

As for the school, which was forced to operate under strait conditions until the rebuilding process was completed, Superintendent Osborne had definite ideas for enhancing its influence. In an area where, according to the monthly meeting's education committee, there was "a manifest lack of interest" in such basic factors as improving teachers, extending school terms and acquiring sufficient text books,[16] Osborne believed that what was most required for black education in the South was a new emphasis on "industrial education." Vocational training, he stressed, was the only means for producing a skilled labor force that could command the wages necessary to allow black people to escape from the cycle of debt and poverty entailed by the crop-lien system under which the majority languished. Osborne observed that, in his experience, "colored people. . . . [were] as industrious as any people I know." What they lacked was the practical education in some trade that, with the vote, would allow them to establish themselves in secure and responsible positions in society.[17]

The answer to questions about the sort of education that could properly prepare black people for life in the South depended on the kind of life educational leaders thought would be adequate for such people. When Charles Osborne began to emphasize the importance of vocational rather than strictly academic education at Southland, he was responding to what was rapidly becoming the prevailing view of philanthropic white northerners concerning the future of black education in the South. This vision would soon sweep through the South and would eventually create controversies into which Southland would be drawn.[18]

As a possible means of ensuring a steadily increasing rate of enrollment at Southland, the missionary board determined to carry through with the idea of selling off small parcels of the 138 acres of land in the vicinity of the school that was owned by Indiana Yearly Meeting. As noted above, the overarching idea for such a use of the so-called Slade land was not primarily to raise additional money but to begin building up a small community of "good reliable educated colored people around the college."[19] By late April 1889 contracts for the sale of four parcels totaling sixty acres had been drawn up. The resulting revenue of $830 was to be added to Southland's endowment. None of the individuals who purchased this property were listed on the monthly meeting's "Record of Membership," although Osborn T. Taylor, an early and active member of the Southland congregation and the first black student to attend Earlham College, had earlier purchased twenty acres in the vicinity of the school.[20] The missionary board also determined that an additional twenty acres of the Slade land was to be occupied by Daniel Drew, half of which he would receive rent free on account of his work in the ministry. Dickinson also urged Charles Osborne to provide Drew with as much lumber and other building materials as he could spare so that Drew might build a dwelling for his family, a sort of parsonage that would remain the property of the missionary board.[21]

In the meantime, a continued embarrassment of funds required that the board once again dispatch Elkanah Beard back East with the hope of his getting increased commitments for annual appropriations from charitable organizations like the Murray Fund and the White Benevolent Fund of Baltimore. Unfortunately, such largess was not forthcoming, and Beard managed only to send back $205 along with a bill of $157.45 for his expenses. Whatever his disappointment at such meager returns, Joseph Dickinson felt obliged to request that Beard return to Southland to assist the Obsornes and possibly to squeeze long-anticipated subscriptions out of the good white citizens of Helena.[22] At the same time, Dickinson continued to maintain a close watch on Osborne, exhorting him, among other things, to imitate Alida Clarke by sending frequent letters and stories to the Quaker press, celebrating local victories and telling "modestly of your needs," including $1,000 for a cooking range large enough to accommodate up to 150 diners. Osborne faithfully carried out these instructions, but when Elkanah Beard, charged with giving "attention to interests that seemed to need care," arrived at Southland early in the New Year, he found an unsettling situation.[23] To begin, enrollment was "much smaller" than in the previous year, and while Beard praised the Osbornes for "working most earnestly," he was also concerned to discover "a *little* feeling of sourness and a disposition . . . of some scholars to positively refuse to do what they were bidden." Elkanah responded to these uncomfortable circumstances by gently urging all and sundry to remain loyal to Southland and to do as they were directed without grumbling. However, Friend Beard was further disquieted by the discovery that Southland Meeting was frequently not attended "by several of our members who live in the neighborhood." He hoped that Daniel Drew's ministry might restore these backsliders, but he did not venture to speculate on why they had ceased to come to meeting.[24]

Not surprisingly, Joseph Dickinson's subsequent letters to Charles Osborne were filled with the sort of instructions a father might send to his son at boarding school, urging him to give "*regular attention* to . . . business be it small or great . . . receive and distribute the mail . . . keep the records required." Despite such admonitions the situation apparently did not improve. A few weeks later Dickinson was raising the question of "some complaint both to the quality and quantity of food at your tables" and reminding the Southland superintendent of the need to "have enough of good healthy provisions" to ensure that no one might have grounds for such complaints. Osborne responded with complaints of his own, noting, for example, that mail was "several times fraudulently taken" from the school office.[25] Obviously, all was not well.

As the end of the school year approached the missionary board's minutes flatly stated that Southland's "educational department does not make so good a showing as formerly." In Quaker parlance such a declaration was the equivalent of meaning "things are in a terrible mess!" The board took note of letters it had received from "some officers of Southland," as well of a report from Elkanah Beard setting out the need "to make the Institution more efficient in its work." In the circumstances, members united in the decision not to renew the Osbornes' contract, while adding, with that devastating Quaker penchant for plain speaking, their "assurance that we have appreciated *to some extent* [my italics] the sacrifice they made to give their time and service to this work."[26]

Even after receiving notification that he had been sacked, Osborne was not let off lightly. Joseph Dickinson upbraided him for failing, as Calvin Clark had done before him, to collect all the tuition money due to the school. Perched at his writing desk in Indiana, the missionary board's secretary opined that because "colored people with their *poor opportunities* & *training* are usually *unreliable*, I think thou should be very industrious in the collection of these accounts."[27] It is not clear if the outgoing superintendent was able to collect debts owed by Southland's mainly poverty-stricken clientele, but his distress and humiliation were unmistakable. When Osborne finally had a face to face meeting with Dickinson in late June, the latter provided a detailed description of this painful confrontation.

> I gave him full opportunity to relieve himself. . . . He knows that parties [at] Southland wrote against him & he's has no opportunity for defense. . . . he said he had no influence or *control* of the *faculty*. . . . He thought it his duty to be civil to C & A Clark whilst some there thought he ought to be at swords' points with them & that Prof. Pretlow was attending to his dentistry prospects & insisted on having a room in expecting to make $100 during the session. . . .[28]
>
> I am sorry that he feels hurt but . . . I still think it may be best that he is relieved. . . . It is an important & difficult place to fill. The management must be fully familiar with the peculiarities of the colored people, an Education man & a missionary.[29]

Those admirable traits were certainly manifest in the unfortunate Osborne's immediate replacement, the long-serving, and to be sure long-suffering, Elkanah Beard who was straightway reminded "to give *constant* & *prompt attention* to our Eastern Contributors." The ever-faithful Elkanah had anticipated the board's directive with a letter in Quaker journals expressing the hope that past benefactors would continue to aid "in the education of many poor but worthy colored children."[30] However, the Beards had scarcely resettled at Southland before another crisis emerged. In August 1889 the missionary board faced the consequences of the collapse of an Indianapolis bank, headed by Quaker Charles Coffin, which took $2,800 of the yearly meeting's funds down with it.[31] The story of the failure of Coffin's bank was a sad chapter for Indiana Yearly Meeting, not least because investigation revealed that serious malfeasance by a supposed pillar of the Quaker community had helped to bring about the demise of his financial institution.[32] For Southland the immediate effect was the reduction of its annual subsidy from yearly meeting from $1,000 to $500 because, as Dickinson lamented, finances had become "*very difficult* . . . & that defeats all the rest." The missionary board's annual report cited a deficit of $183.06 for Southland in 1888–89. Elkanah Beard, of course, vowed to carry on "for the sake of a race long subject to bondage" whatever the setbacks.[33]

With the stalwart Beards back at the helm, enrollment increased substantially during the following school year,[34] and means were found to aid Daniel Drew, "one of the Lord's most humble & . . . efficient servants," in both his ministry and personal finances. Joseph Dickinson assured a potential benefactor that black people were so hungry for the Gospel as preached by Friends that if the means were found to support more evangelists like Drew, "we could have a Yearly meeting in Arkansas in a short time."[35] Dickinson was earnestly overselling his case, but local people did continue to commit themselves to Quakerism. Duncan Freeland, who requested to join Friends around this time, was still an active member of Southland Meeting when it was laid down in 1925.[36]

Amidst the turmoil and difficulties Southland faced at the beginning of the 1890s, there were developments that can only be labeled as quizzical. For example, in January 1890, the report of the missionary board's business committee indicated while the board was "very much embarrassed for lack of money" to cover operating expenses at Southland, Elkanah Beard was directed to purchase eighty acres of timbered land near the College if the price was right.[37] The source of funds for such an enterprise, when the board was desperately pleading poverty, must remain a mystery, perhaps explained by Indiana Quaker farmers' attachment to land as the safest form of investment.

In any case, Southland continued to be a stopping off place for distinguished English visitors like Henry Stanley Newman, a minister and longtime head of the Quaker Men's School at Leonminster.[38] Newman and his wife Marianna stayed at Southland for a fortnight. He praised the school's beneficial influence in providing the only remedy for uplifting black people given that the renewed effort to restrain and repress their social and political rights was "the burning question of the hour in America." Marianna Newman seemed charmed by the place and its students, especially when some of them sang "their old negro melodies, so strange and quaint . . . as they kept time with their feet upon the floor." She even allowed as how "they seem to have hearts like white people."[39]

From the hindsight of a century, such reflections point up the reasons why maintaining a school and mission station like Southland was always a difficult, demanding, and chancy proposition. The minutes of Southland Meeting recorded that the Newmans "preached the Gospel with great clearness and simplicity . . . [with] the power of the Holy Spirit attending all their services" and asked God's continued blessing upon them.[40] Still, with the best will in the world, a two-week stay at Southland for good people like the Newmans was truly an exotic adventure, akin to an African safari or a trek through the Gobi Desert. A brief, close-up experience with unsophisticated, rustic folk in a strange, even alien, environment might serve to enhance the visitors' standing among coreligionists and their comments on and praise for the work being done might bring incidental funds into the school's coffers. But the Quaker mission station in Arkansas was, for most of the Friends who briefly ventured there, part of another world, frightening or inspiring, but never entirely real. All of this makes the dedication and sacrifices of those who stayed in Arkansas, for years or decades, to work for the glory of God and the raising-up of their fellow men all the more impressive. Finally, the most difficult, and rarely accomplished, task for any of them was to somehow close the cultural gap between the selfless giver and artless receiver and for outsiders (northern Friends were always outsiders) to truly believe that those they sought to serve should be equal not only before God but before man as well.

Certainly, Elkanah and Irena Beard had amply demonstrated their faithfulness to Southland and its people, but they were in their late fifties and in delicate health when they again accepted responsibility for the school and the meeting. Henry Stanley Newman and other visitors praised the efficient operation of the school and meeting under their supervision, but also expressed the view that their burden would be eased if the missionary board could engage a well-qualified white man as the school's principal.[41] Such a person was not easy to find, and the board rejected at least one applicant as "too young and inexperienced," before determining, after considerable deliberation, to place William and Sabina Russell of Winchester, Indiana, in charge of the school with the possibility of taking overall direction "after some training under the present heads of the Institution."[42]

II. The March of Jim Crow

The Russells arrived at Southland "to take charge of the educational work" in September 1890 following an especially trying spring term. A storm tore off the tin roof of the girls' hall, and the school's crops were badly damaged in the midst of serious and prolonged flooding during which "many have been drowned by the sudden breaking of the levees." The parents of several students had lost everything in the floods and would require years of toil to restore even their previously precarious circumstances. Furthermore, the economic losses suffered by poor black farmers in the Delta were concurrent with the beginning of the process by which they would also be deprived of hard-won social and political rights earned during the Reconstruction era.[43] Elkanah Beard made oblique reference to the impending political storm in his "Annual Report" to Indiana Yearly Meeting:

> The question is not one of social or political controversy, but shall the Negro be sufficiently educated to cash up his own accounts and manage his own business. If we would have them read the Bible and learn the Law of God, study civil government, and comprehend their relation to it, and in it, we must still render them assistance.[44]

Shortly after arriving at Southland, the Russells were faced with the problem of having to replace a teacher dismissed for unspecified unacceptable conduct.[45] Two weeks later Elkanah Beard recounted another tale of high water, bad crops, and financial dearth requiring that "many poor boys and girls . . . be turned away" for lack of means and even threatening the Southland community with shortages in basic supplies. Beard's gloomy letter stood in odd juxtaposition to the missionary board's report to yearly meeting, published a week later, that Southland had experienced "a prosperous year," but such was the roller coaster ride of life in the Arkansas Delta.[46]

By the end of the calendar year, things seemed to be looking up for the school. Enrollment was at one time as high as 384 students being taught by 6 professors, with 84 enrolled in the vitally important normal course. Early in the spring there was another crucial change in the school's administration when the Beards, citing ill health, surrendered leadership to William and Sabina Russell. In response to the change over, Joseph Dickinson penned an epistle of guidance to the new superintendent and matron urging them to "be of good courage" and to "keep the *religious culture in front*," so that Southland would remain as "an oasis in a desert of degradation, ignorance & every accompanying misery."[47] If misery was indeed the companion of degradation and poverty, at about the time that Friend Dickinson penned his letter, the newly elected Democratic Arkansas legislature was poised set out upon a path that would impose more than a fair share of all of these woes upon the state's black citizens.

In his authoritative account of the triumphant march of Jim Crow in Arkansas, historian John Graves has asserted that "the most dramatic changes in the state's political history" occurred in the early 1890s when nearly all black public officials were removed from both statewide and local office. The chief instruments for this political coup d'état, initiated in 1891, were a new election law concentrating voting machinery in the hands of the state's Democratic Party and a constitutional amendment, approved by statewide referendum in 1892, instituting a poll tax with provisions carefully crafted to reduce or eliminate black voters.[48] By blatantly playing the race card Arkansas Democrats subdued a threat posed by the short-lived Union Labor Party, an alliance of black Republicans and white farmers based on common economic concerns. Presenting their party as the "friend of the white man," the Democrats undermined this brief inter-racial coalition and swept the boards, even in Delta counties with large black majorities. For example, while Phillips County Republicans garnered 1,174 votes (as against 1,221 for Democrats) in the

1892 election during which the poll tax amendment was approved, two years later only 43 ballots among the 1,356 cast in the county were marked Republican. Indeed, after the 1894 election, no black Arkansan served in a statewide office until 1973.[49]

Alida Clark had never hesitated to note and criticize corruption, repression, or violence spawned by Arkansas's chaotic post–Civil War political scene. Alas, after the increasingly aggressive, and successful, efforts to deprive the state's Negro population of all semblance of political power and social dignity were launched during the 1890s, critical commentary from northern Quaker sources about the injustice of such actions was remarkably silent. Arkansas's Separate Coach Law, passed by a legislature dominated by so-called "Redeemer" Democrats, proved a key development in the process of imposing civil disabilities on blacks citizens of the state. Still, it is of considerable interest that two prominent legislative opponents of the bill introduced in 1891 by John N. Tillman, a future president of the University of Arkansas, were listed on the rolls of Southland Monthly Meeting. The first of these was Southland graduate and former teacher, state senator George W. Bell, the same man who had accused the Clarks of misgovernment. Another ex-Southland student and, at least nominal Friend, who entered the debate on Tillman's nefarious proposal was J. N. Donahoo, editor of the *Helena Progress,* who, when the bill's passage became a forgone conclusion, took the sardonic, if somewhat un-Quakerly, stance of welcoming the bill for creating "a solid black race against the white race. . . . that had nothing in common with each other."[50] Donahoo's bitter words may also have reflected his response to the erection of a Confederate memorial in the center of Helena almost simultaneously with the legislative enactments which created a full-blown Jim Crow regime in Arkansas.[51]

Even as the Jim Crow era dawned, Southland veteran and temperance leader Lydia Chase noted that "seventeen years in the south . . . [have] settled my mind that the negro problem can only be solved by the influence of Christian education" that, she added, must be necessarily slow as "raising a race from degradation and ignorance cannot be done in one generation."[52] On the other hand, there was a certain bitter irony in the fact that Alida Clark, one of the postwar generations great champions of justice for Arkansas blacks, faded from the scene just as the seventy-year reign of Jim Crow was being launched.

In March 1892, the Quaker press announced the demise of one of Indiana Yearly Meeting's "oldest and best missionaries." William Russell recounted how on 13 March she had attended Southland Meeting for the first time since Christmas: "Though physically frail, she spoke, with unusual clearness and power, of the depths, heights and fullness of God's love . . . of its expansion to space unbounded." On the next day, "serene with faith and shining with love . . . suddenly yet peacefully, she went from work to rewards."[53]

For a brief period work and play at Southland came to a halt. From as far as Friends Freedmen's Association of Philadelphia to as near as the school's white next-door neighbor, D. C. Gordon, Alida's virtues were recounted and her praises sung. The missionary board appointed a committee to prepare and publish a memorial pamphlet in her honor. Five hundred copies of this tribute were printed, about half of which were shipped to Southland. There was, perhaps, a lingering hint of the latter-day strain between the Clarks and the missionary board in Joseph Dickinson's somewhat abashed expression of gratitude over the fact that "the committee were fully united in this token of respect."[54]

So, Southland's earthly and spiritual mother was gone. Although Calvin Clark, the strong, silent guardian of his wife and the institution they founded, continued to live nearby for several more years, given the turn of events during the next decade, it would be difficult to maintain that Alida's spirit lingered on. Problems and concerns, however, most certainly did.

As always, there were financial exigencies. The schoolhouse erected to replace the two buildings destroyed fire in 1887 was overtaxed from the day it was first occupied. Besides providing administration offices and sleeping rooms for faculty, this Central Hall housed a kitchen and dining hall large enough to serve as many as 150 students and teachers. The cramped and, at times, chaotic conditions created by this situation may have contributed to the complaints of inadequate and unappetizing food that so troubled Charles and Ascenath Osborne's brief tenure at Southland. Obviously, what was needed was a separate kitchen and dinning hall to free up space in the Central Hall as well as to ensure more safe and efficient food preparation. In this instance the ever vigilant Joseph Dickinson managed to conjure up a rescuing angel from New York City who provided $500 to get the project underway. Dickinson was also able to announce what was, for Southland, a minor miracle, that is, that sufficient funds were left over from receipts and donations to undertake vital repairs to other buildings on the campus. Still, in the wake of this cheering news, William Russell had to report that "on account of children being kept in cotton fields," the school year began with a total enrollment of less than fifty.[55]

In his report to the missionary board for 1891, Elkanah Beard had noted that as regards local "colored people" much still needed to be done in the development of "every phase of character building." As an example, he pointed out that despite the best efforts of Daniel Drew, the meeting at Hickory Ridge had suffered loss because of some "members not showing charity to each other in political matters." He added that while twenty-three new conversions had brought the official monthly meeting membership to well over four hundred, "our members are so widely scattered that we have lost all trace of a good many of them."[56] Joseph Dickinson responded to such concerns by lecturing the school's principal, Herbert Charles, on the necessity "that Education be *firmly based* upon *Christian Principles*, that this basis may be the foundation of their after life so that they be as leaven on society wherever they may be." Dickinson also admonished Superintendent Russell to "teach the colored people neatness, *order* & *cleanliness* . . . [so] that the good influences of Southland maybe continuous, reaching . . . far & wide."[57]

Throughout the spring and summer of 1892 William Russell reported that while enrollment was lower than expected, school work was thriving and the "good work" accomplished by Principal Charles and other young teachers from the north had, in the end, made for "a very successful year." In stark contrast, alas, it had been "a hard year for colored people." Once again, the low price of cotton and high price for supplies had left many local farmers without the means acquire necessities, let alone to pay tuition for their children. Beyond these difficulties, progress in local communities was further slowed by "the growing sin of intemperance."[58]

Not all the news was so discouraging. During the summer the missionary board was informed that Sarah H. Henley of Little Rock, "one of the five teachers sent South . . . in 1865," had left bequests of a thousand dollars each to Southland and Earlham Colleges.[59] Southland's bequest was promptly paid and added to the school's endowment fund, the interest from which continued to provide small tuition scholarships for dozens of Southland students. The missionary board was further cheered when Daniel Drew, in Indiana as a Southland delegate to yearly meeting, attended the board meeting in late September to express "heartfelt appreciation of the untiring effort of the Board in behalf of the colored people." Drew assured the board that Southland was scattering "a vast amount of good seed" in sending out well-prepared teachers to different parts of three states to instill "cleanly habits of living" as well as practical knowledge. He also informed the board about Southland Monthly Meeting's renewed efforts to locate and maintain contact with all of the widely scattered members of the meeting. The board was deeply impressed with Drew's visit that the minutes characterized as "timely and highly appreciated as it brought the work so much nearer the hearts of Friends to see a living example of the results of their labors." The final bit of heartening news was a surplus in Southland's budget for the second year running.[60]

Joseph Dickinson told William Russell that Daniel Drew had "helped Southland very much," practically as well as spiritually, when he attended the women's meeting and "came out with his hands *full of money*." Remarking on the changes induced by Friends' Arkansas connection, William Coffin recalled to yearly meeting how two decades earlier Drew, recorded as a minister "in the face of Yearly Meeting," was now greeted as "a consistent Friend and efficient laborer in the master's vineyard." This colored minister, Coffin declared, was a shining example of the fact that Southland was "one of the grandest works in the hands of this Yearly Meeting in actual results and beneficent good to the colored people of the South." Some Friends were so impressed they wanted a "theological chair fixed up at Southland to help educate & train colored preachers & Evangelists."[61]

Emotional enthusiasm was, of course, no substitute for material substance, and theologically-speaking Southland's situation remained humble in the best Quaker tradition, summarized by Sabina Russell's assurances that Southland teachers were "all earnest Christians" who had "begun the year's work with determination to do more for Christ." The institution's spiritual condition as well as its physical appearance may, perhaps, also have been aided by "marked improvements on the chapel" as well as by the 250 to 300 Bibles dispatched to the school by a missionary board anxious to ensure scripturally literate orthodoxy.[62] Still, during the winter of 1893, reports to the board presented a somewhat mixed message. On the one hand, William Russell described the school as "in a prosperous condition financially and educationally with a good degree of religious life amongst the students" and that, overall, "unity and harmony prevail." But Southland's superintendent also gave hints of unspecified, underlying problems: "We often have things to encounter that are unpleasant and things do not come up to our expectations, we see many defects, but. . . . We are here to remedy as many defects as we can"[63] Principal Herbert Charles told Joseph Dickinson that "hard times seem to be getting more oppressive" and that rather than the school filling up, indications were that several students would have to leave in order to work for their families. In March 1893 Elkanah Beard, in the midst of another inspection tour, praised Professor Charles as a "clear headed practical teacher" but added that some local people had taken serious offense at remarks the principal had made in a commencement address at the close of the previous school year, admonishing black people, as a race, to practice "greater diligence, honesty and morality." "Little things grow down here," Beard noted, "sometimes very fast as we have learned from past experience."[64] Perhaps it was one such little thing that, a few days later, inspired William Russell to tell Joseph Dickinson, "We want you to know . . . if our work here is not satisfactory we hope you will have the courage to call us home and commit the charge to other hands. The results fall short of our ideal."[65] And while Russell welcomed the Beards with open arms and hoped they would stay as "somebody to counsel with," some of his work fell short of Elkanah Beard's expectations. For one thing Beard criticized the superintendent's enrollment report, noting that he had failed to specify which students were boarding and which were day pupils: "We can't very well judge of expense or *success without the numbers actually in School are given.*"[66]

Such criticism perhaps helped to inspire a subsequent visit of Charles S. Hubbard "one of oldest members of the Board." But as Hubbard announced himself "much pleased with the condition of things" and feeling the Russells "particularly well adopted" work at Southland, his trip was more likely concerned with the purchase of forty acres of land near the school recommended by both Beard and Russell as "very cheap" (twenty dollars an acre) and necessary "to keep the boys at work and raise our own beef and pork" that "in a few years would really pay . . . in savings for Southland."[67] During his brief visit Charles Hubbard managed to help work out some final details of the land purchase, to organize "twenty-four Bands of Mercy," and to visit several long-standing black Friends of Southland Monthly Meeting. He found that the meeting, with 453 recorded members, remained active and influential in a wide area around the school.[68] The temperance committee had filed another petition to prevent the establishment of a saloon within three miles of the school, and Joseph Coleman, a black Quaker minister from Iowa, held a series of twenty-three revival meetings during which "believers were strengthened and sinners were constrained to seek the Lord." William Russell recounted how, in the midst of Coleman's crusade, a local man asked him, "Why the sinners over here are more spectable and preachable than the church members where I stays?" This was, Russell believed, because black ministers like Brother Coleman and Daniel Drew backed their teaching with "good moral character, a scare article among colored preachers south." The prospects, as Charles Hubbard had remarked with genuine if somewhat premature Quaker optimism, were "full of cheer."[69]

Chapter 8

A Troubled Decade

1893–1903

I. Sharing Hardships, Saving Souls

As the 1892–93 school year wound down, Southland principal Herbert Charles reported that "the quality of school work" has shown "considerable improvement since the first of last year." Students from the normal department who had gone out to teach during the winter months were returning, having "benefited themselves as well as others" by spreading the good work and good news—literacy and the Gospel—throughout the Arkansas Delta and beyond.[1] But while school lessons continued "creditably" and local crops looked good, overabundant spring rains returned the Arkansas Delta to its cyclical crisis mode. By early June William Russell was reporting that "cyclones and storms" had swept through the area "spreading death & destruction" while the overflowing Mississippi brought the highest water that Calvin Clark had seen during his thirty years in Arkansas.[2]

Because Southland was providentially spared from the worst effects of storms and floods, June commencement proceeded as planned. Speakers included two prominent Helena citizens, one black, one white. J. N. Donahoo, editor of the *Helena Progress,* former student, state legislator, and at least nominal member of the monthly meeting, addressed the literary society while Judge Clark, clerk of the U.S. district court, infused the graduating class with "a strong vein of moral and religious teaching." The missionary board, although disappointed by the need to recruit a new principal teacher to replace the well-regarded Professor Charles, seemed sufficiently satisfied with William Russell's performance to promote him from superintendent to president.[3] Four scholars graduated from the normal department, but four others who might have finished were forced to withdraw for lack of funds, another poignant reminder of Southland's persistent fiscal deficiency, additionally reflected in a deficit of nearly $450 for the year. Nonetheless, the board reaffirmed its faith in the mission by establishing a new committee charged with hiring whatever teachers were required and devoting up to $200 to enlist "a suitable person" to launch a recruiting campaign throughout the Mississippi Delta to "solicit students for advanced classes of the college."[4]

For all their hopes, the board's advertising and public relations campaign had only limited effect. Letters of application increased significantly, but the 1893–94 school opened with only a few additional students. At the same time, there was also a considerable rise in the number of necessitous would-be students who could attend Southland only if they were afforded financial assistance. Unfortunately, Joseph Dickinson had to inform President Russell that income from the endowment, the chief source of student aid, would be reduced due to eight hundred dollars from the fund being used to purchase new land.[5] Given the missionary board's fear of Southland's accruing additional debt, Dickinson pressured the Russells to raise additional money by more ardently publicizing their needs in the Quaker press, noting, with a Quaker penchant for hurtful truths, that the institution had "formerly got much more when Alida Clark kept up the agitation."[6]

Financial concerns were exacerbated when Joseph Dickinson, amidst preaching thrift and efficiency to William Russell, allowed insurance policies on the school's fire-prone buildings to expire.[7] Money was not the only problem. Monthly meeting minutes expressed some anxiety that meetings for worship and business were "not as well attended as would be . . . desirable," and meetings for discipline were "somewhat neglected." A faithful few did carry on the spiritual work but most of the hundreds of recorded members remained "widely scattered and . . . seldom get to meeting."[8] As for the school, one of William Russell's innovations was to purchase a small printing press so that students could obtain practical and literary experience producing their own bimonthly *Southland News.* Russell praised the "good moral tone" of the early editions, but in late 1893 Elkanah Beard expressed serious displeasure with the latest number of the school paper that, he believed, brought "no credit to the work or the workers."[9]

No evidence exists to determine how deeply the Russells took such criticism to heart. They did not, in any case, cease their endeavors. Early in the new year the *Christian Worker* published an article by President Russell describing "Emancipation Day" at Southland, a celebration that featured speeches by two successful black men, both of whom had daughters attending the school.[10] Emphasizing the magnetic attraction of the institution as well as its far-reaching positive influence, Russell cited the case of Rebecca Busby, daughter of the black Friend who had purchased land near the school to ensure a quality education for his children. This teenaged member of the normal class had, at the behest of a desperate school director, been dispatched fifty miles down the Mississippi to earn forty dollars a month sharing "the light and knowledge" she had gained at Southland with less fortune children, a signal example of the spreading influence of Friends' mission in the benighted South.[11]

Joseph Dickinson, who never let up in reminding Southland's president of the importance of keeping "the *Institution* & the *needs* of *colored people* before Friends," was pleased with this effort as "just the thing that is needed." For himself, Russell noted that he and his wife, while working for less than a dollar a day, were "ostracized from social life and church affiliation, except with colored people." He pleaded for "some kind Friends . . . [to] share with us in this sacrifice."[12]

Still, however earnestly Russell appealed for assistance to "all who have the means," Southland continued to operate at a loss. Elkanah Beard expressed fear of growing "indebtedness in these hard times" and although the yearly meeting appropriation was increased, the board, that, inexplicably, had not met for nearly a year, still felt "crippled for lack of funds."[13] By the end of the school year, Dickinson consoled Russell with the thought "that thyself & we *are not to blame* in getting in debt" as no one could foresee the economic difficulties that were troubling the entire country. Indeed, Russell was able to report to yearly meeting in 1894 that despite short crops and "stringency in financial matters," Southland's enrollment had increased by fifty students, with five graduates from the normal school as well as one from the college who would teach in the normal department during the following school year. But he also warned that "the usefulness and dignity of the college cannot well be sustained . . . without more means . . . may we not expect larger gifts from Friends?"[14]

For Southland, it seemed a matter of course that whatever money might be forthcoming would prove insufficient for the needs at hand.

During the course of the 1894–95 school year, Russell informed the missionary board that enrollment had decreased on account of a serious decline in cotton prices and that the school's operating deficit would be higher, largely due to the increased cost of salaries for "a good corps of experienced, conscientious teachers" who were "quietly and smoothly" making great progress. The newly reorganized board responded to this usual mixture of bad and good news by sending yet another supplication for increased assistance to all Indiana quarterly meetings.[15]

The news regarding religious work at the school was similarly mixed. Daniel Drew continued his "practical and instructive" work at the Hickory Ridge/Marvel meeting while George Wilburn, an energetic young preacher, received a minute from the monthly meeting to carry on his ministry at Holly Grove as well as a donation of seventy-five dollars to support his efforts. There were, however, distressing tidings from Beaver Bayou where the work was "greatly hindered by the rash conduct of a white man living near the [meeting] house" who had murdered one black farmer, apparently with impunity, and effectively driven most of the meeting's members out of the area. A minute of Southland Monthly Meeting conceded its helplessness in the face of such violent racial hatred, concluding "that no way had opened for further labor at Beaver Bayou."[16]

Another religious development had considerable affect on the spiritual life of the Southland community. Early in 1895 President Russell sent the missionary board an account of his experiences while attending the Arkansas Sabbath School and Christian Endeavor Convention in Little Rock. Russell was much impressed both by the welcome he had received, including an invitation to preach to a local Presbyterian congregation, and by the encouraging progress of Christian work in the state. Deeply moved by the spirit of the convention, he returned to Southland with a strong sense of the need for "more aggressive" Christian endeavor in the school and meeting. In a tone reminiscent of Alida Clark's early ministry, he called for "grand and noble" Quaker mission to plant new meetings among black people with the goal of establishing an Arkansas quarterly meeting of Friends:

> Other churches have been reaping the fruits of the labors of Ind. Y. Meeting here and they stand in the way of progress. I believe that if we should lower the standard of morals here and give up to the Baptists the school would be filled to overflowing in a short

> time. Far be it from us to think of such a thing but I only say this to show what prejudice we have to contend with. There is a good deal of superstitious teaching put into children's heads before they come here [to Southland] and . . . much of it to be overcome before they can accept Christ by simple faith.[17]

In the weeks that followed, President Russell pursued this admonishment nearly to the point of obsession. In early March 1895, he told Joseph Dickinson "that almost every day and every night the Lord is saving some soul amongst us." He noted that on the very evening of his writing, twenty more had come to the "anxious bench" and five had testified "to the goodness and sweetness of the Savior," upon which "one woman jumped up shouting." While assuring Dickinson that their services were free from the usual sort of excitement exhibited by "colored people . . . apt to be demonstrative," he proceeded to paint a picture of a near-hysterical holiness revival:

> We had tonight first a song service then a prayer service, then testimonies after that a call & a response, then prayer and work around the altar then testimony from the seekers.[18]

Throughout the winter and spring of 1895, Russell's letters to the missionary board and the *American Friend* were filled with vivid accounts of gatherings around the "mourners' bench," personal testimonies of blessedness, and miraculous conversions of struggling sinners. When, for example, the greatly anticipated visit of a northern Quaker evangelist was cancelled on short notice, a spontaneous meeting of students and faculty gathered under the ministry of Daniel Drew, and all but one of those in attendance were saved. The minutes of Southland Meeting reported that fifteen persons had asked to join with Friends while others were being brought "under watch-care." Moved by the zealous spirit of the moment, Russell exclaimed:

> The work is heavy, it is growing on our hands but we know that the Lord will not require more than he will give strength to do. . . . The need is great among these people, we yearn to do all the good we can but our arms are too short to reach out very far.[19]

Still, Southland could reach far enough to embrace its own student body, and President Russell obviously succeeded in arousing a fervent atmosphere, ripe for repentance and renewal, among the school's "family." Still, even within the shortest reach, such an emotional ambience could create unintended, and possibly dangerous, consequences, as in the case of one woeful nine-year-old mulatto student. After attending an impassioned religious meeting, this anxious son of a white Mississippi farmer and his black mistress asked God if he would be saved should he die that night. Upon receiving what he perceived to be a distinctly negative reply, the child became so seriously distressed that it took Mrs. Russell's personal intervention to ease his mind, at least temporarily.[20] William Russell related this incident as simply one example of Southland's continuing campaign of Christian endeavor to instill the sort of moral fortitude the school's graduates would require. He feared that if Southland's charges lacked a sufficiently strong spiritual base, the immorality that flourished in "the cold world" beyond the sheltering confines of Friends' influence would "cool their ardor for religious work if not entirely put out the fire from their lives."[21] One wonders, however, if such an emotional fire might not more readily consume rather than warm the soul of a troubled boy, born into racial ambiguity and facing the racially-charged atmosphere of the late-nineteenth-century American South?

Religious fervor aside, Southland carried on its educational mission, hampered, as always, by lack of sufficient funding but also, in the view of William Russell, by the raw material the school had to process. When Russell visited "colored schools" in Little Rock and other parts of Arkansas, he surmised that the pupils there were "much more intelligent than those in Eastern Ark. and Western Miss."[22] Whether by this he meant inherent ability or current level of achievement is not entirely clear, but in the spring of 1895, Edward Bellis and Charles Francisco, two visiting members of the missionary board believed that at least to some extent Southland's progress was deterred by the fact that too many students spent too little time in the classroom. To begin, the designated school year was only eight months rather than nine. This defect was made worse by the fact that many poorer students did not enter school until after the fall cotton harvest and were held out during spring planting. On the other hand, the visiting board members were impressed with both the physical appearance of the Southland campus[23], which stood out from the surrounding flat landscape for a distance of three miles, as well as the diversity and value of the agricultural land in the school's immediate vicinity that was "better & more improved than any we have seen in the State." Obviously this was a reflection of the influence of Calvin Clark's superior farming techniques on the local black people, among whom the visitors found "many sterling characters."[24]

For his part, William Russell celebrated the ministry of his distinguished visitors, who through the "convincing powers of the Holy Spirit" caused forty-three boarding students (all but one) to testify as "to having been born again, or quickened into new life." He contrasted their saving message with local "preaching by ignorant ministers . . . [of] many weird and strange ideas." The visitors responded in kind declaring that they could "not speak more highly" of the efforts of the president, his faculty, and staff in working to fulfill Southland's great potential.[25]

Bellis and Francisco found that there was much about the Arkansas mission of which Indiana Yearly Meeting could be pleased and proud. For while the classrooms might need new desks, the buildings new paint, and the school year another month, these shortcomings, such as they were, paled beside the great work being accomplished for those fortunate enough to be able to attend the school and meeting as well as the residual effects on black people in a widening area in the vicinity of the institution. The visitors were convinced that if all members of the Indiana Yearly Meeting would become "personally acquainted with the work" and personally involved in helping to finance it, Southland could accommodate twice as many pupils as the 132 currently enrolled, and for a mere eighty dollars per student per year.[26]

Bellis and Francisco showed the way for their Quaker brethren by donating most of their traveling expenses to Southland's coffers, but the only other immediate support President Russell reported was a twenty-five dollar gift from the Moral Reform Fund of Philadelphia. In the circumstances, Russell indicated he would soon be greatly in need of considerably more funding to pay teachers salaries as well as his own.[27] It was, alas, an old problem without a new solution. By mid-May, in the wake of the Bellis-Francisco report, the missionary board managed to cobble together only a few hundred dollars with the hope it would see the institution through "for a month or so." A few days later they scrapped the barrel for additional funds ($437) that allowed the President Russell to pay off some of the faculty and the school's cook. Joseph R. Hunt, a teacher who remained unpaid for the time being, had his reward in being chosen as the board's representative to visit various Indiana quarterly meetings on a summer fundraising tour. Russell was naturally thankful for any money he received, but the elemental means at his disposal for coping with the school's indebtedness were reflected in his proudly reporting to Joseph Dickinson that an ice cream social and musical entertainment had garnered $17.50.[28]

Southland's monetary concerns were briefly laid aside in the summer of 1895 with the news of the death of Joseph Dickinson, long the towering presence on the missionary board who had served continuously, "his zeal and earnestness . . . never flagging," since the board's creation as the Committee for Relief of Freedmen in 1864. A number of Friends paid tribute to the memory of this "Joshua . . . fallen from our ranks" with sizeable monetary contributions to Quaker causes. But although Dickinson had been intimately involved with Southland for decades, there was no mention of the Arkansas mission in any of the financial tributes to his memory.[29] Given the fact that Southland's deficit for 1895 alone was over five hundred dollars, surviving board members and their new chairman, Edward Bellis, for all the respect they might have felt for their deceased colleague, could not have been greatly consoled in the knowledge that Joseph Hunt's personal appeal on behalf of the school to seven Indiana quarterly meetings and Wilmington Yearly Meeting had garnered a mere $190.40, out of which, one assumes, Hunt's travel expenses would have had to be paid.[30]

Despite financial concerns, President Russell reported that none of his five years at Southland had "been more freighted with good. . . . Harmony has prevailed and all have a 'mind to work.'" He particularly emphasized "that one of the needs of these people is a better system of primary instruction," adding that if "the colored child" was placed in a similar learning environment to that of the white, "he will not come out very far behind." He believed that their school was close to creating such an environment and therefore hoped that the yearly meeting and the missionary board would not "loosen their hold or slacken their zeal for the extension of the good influences that radiate from Southland College."[31]

Russell's plea may in some part have arisen from his awareness of a growing concern among some Indiana Friends that the financial struggle to maintain the Southland mission was not producing adequate progress among the black population it was intended to serve.[32] In any case, Russell chose this time to revive an educational philosophy, in some ways contradictory to the idea of a better learning environment for black youth, last voiced during the brief, ill-starred tenure of the Charles Osborn, that is, the introduction of "more industrial work connected with the school." The boys were already doing much of the farm work, and the girls had an increasing share in the cooking and laundry. Why not, Russell inquired, formalize these tasks as a part of the school's curriculum? Adding perhaps even a school broom factory might "be a civilizer in the community."[33]

Whether by accident or design, President Russell's bow in the direction of increased industrial education was presented to yearly meeting less than two weeks after Booker T. Washington's seminal speech to the Atlanta Exposition had, in the words of historian James D. Anderson, "set in motion the ideological struggle between industrial philanthropists and black intelligentsia to determine the social purpose of training Afro-American leaders and teachers." For the last three decades of its existence, Southland was, to a greater or lesser extent, involved in this controversy over the future course of education for southern blacks, which, Anderson believes, has until recently been widely ignored by historians of the South.[34]

The most famous southern laboratory for black industrial education was, of course, Booker T. Washington's Tuskegee Institute. The model upon which Washington built his famous school was Hampton Normal and Agricultural Institute, the Virginia school established in 1868 by Samuel Chapman Armstrong, a former Union General, with the assistance of the American Missionary Association (AMA) and the Freedmen's Bureau. According to James D. Anderson, "the theory and method at Hampton were formulated to train an army of Booker T. Washingtons."[35] The son of Hawaiian missionaries, Armstrong believed that centuries of paganism and slavery had left blacks "culturally and morally deficient," lacking, not intelligence, but "foresight, judgment and hard sense." Several generations of the right sort of moral and religious education, Armstrong said, would be necessary to correct these racial deficiencies and prepare black people for full social and political responsibilities. In the late nineteenth century many leading northern philanthropists and southern educational leaders embraced "Negro industrial training" as the surest path to "racial order, political stability and material prosperity to the American South." Historian William Link has noted that aside from its ideological grounding, "industrial schooling served as a smokescreen behind which its white supporters could provide . . . political cover for support among white southerners for minimal black schooling."[36] The John F. Slater Fund, created in 1882 for the purpose of supporting Negro educational and industrial training, embraced this vision as did the General Education Board (GEB), originally endowed by John D. Rockefeller in 1902, which by 1937 had spent $40 million on black schools.[37] Anderson asserts that "white superiority seems to have been one of the few things upon which virtually all of the northern philanthropists and white southerners agreed."[38]

The concept that traditional literary education should be subordinated to industrial training in order to better prepare black students for their proper role as respectable manual laborers flew in the face of the educational and social ideals of those who led the movement for educating freedmen, including Alida Clark, in the early years at Southland.[39] During the 1880s and 1890s black and white critics of the Hampton/Tuskegee model believed that its underlying implication, that all Negroes really needed to know was how to work, crushed the higher aspirations of black students. One black educator called the trend toward industrial training "a miserable fad."[40] Still, whatever its efficacy, one cannot doubt the enthusiasm or the sincerity with which Friends in both Indiana and Arkansas, influenced by national trends, embraced the need for an accelerated course of industrial education at Southland College.

The initial step toward the implementation of this innovative new approach was the missionary board's approval of using up to half of a $1,500 donation from Phoebe Metford for the purchase of land that would provide the school with "added facilities for an Industrial Department."[41] The timing seemed propitious. The rare phenomenon of rising cotton prices led to increased enrollment, and by December President Russell described the school as "better graded, and in fine working order." Soon after the beginning of the new year, forty acres a mile west of the college had been purchased for $800, and the opening of a new industrial and agricultural school headed by Calvin Clark and his son-in-law T. W. Wright was announced, although apparently never implemented.[42] These developments seemed to indicate that the proposed expansion of Southland's agricultural holdings was a harbinger for all-around progress. Soon, however, the buoyant mood was disturbed by reports of more worrisome developments.

To begin, disruptions of the school's household operations early in the new session resulted in the dismissal of a black governess who had apparently caused student dissension towards white teachers and staff. Further difficulty was made manifest by disciplinary problems with female students under the supervision of Mrs. Russell's niece, Mrs. Stata, who was subsequently removed from her post as kitchen manager. These untoward incidents were followed by a more serious report of "some difficulties," followed by "a petition signed [with] 64 names . . . asking for the removal of the present management" being sent to the missionary board. Finally, an even "more serious coloring on the trouble" was indicated by a deeply troubled letter from Southland professor Joseph R. Hunt. Seriously alarmed the board responded by dispatching two of its number, Edward Bellis and William J. Hiatt, to report on the situation.[43]

What the visiting board members discovered was that the major complaints set out in the protesting petition and Joseph Hunt's letter were directly related to the new, and apparently precipitous, emphasis on practical education. To begin, the experiment of having female boarding students do the cooking under the supervision of Mrs. Stata had resulted in a general complaint that the institute's food was "poorly prepared and badly cooked." It was further alleged that Mrs. Russell had created difficulties in the household management department by too often giving hasty directions that subsequently had to be changed, causing additional disciplinary problems with some of the girls she was supervising. When these grievances were brought to President Russell, he responded summarily by calling the complainants liars—an indiscretion for which he later apologized. Members of the faculty told the visitors that some of these difficulties might have been avoided if the administration had regularly consulted with teachers.

Seeking a proper Quaker solution, the visiting board members reported that after they spoke with the Russells about various problems and complaints, the president and matron "accepted our counsel in good spirit" reflecting their continued desire to serve the school and meeting to the best of their ability.[44] On the other hand, Messrs. Bellis and Hiatt found the allegations of petitioners outside the household to be of an "exceedingly frivolous character," perhaps because only one of the complainants was a Friend. Among the accusations was an assertion that William Russell was often away from the school acting as the land agent for "a Northern man."[45] Another complaint, dismissed almost disdainfully as having "but little foundation," did, in fact, speak to the central ideological conflict between advocates of industrial education and those favoring tradition academic emphasis. This involved one father's objection to the fact that his son, sent in his best clothes to a reputed place of learning, was forced to spend part of his time chopping wood in said attire. Board members attributed this and most other complaints to "a spirit of envy and jealousy" setting off a spark that was "fanned into a flame" resulting in "considerable bad feeling." The northern visitors' chief effort at dousing this flame of resentment was to remind the complainants of the sacrifices being made by staff and teachers who had "left good homes and pleasant associations" to undertake missionary work for physical, moral, and spiritual "uplift" of local people who, by implication, should be expressing gratitude rather than dissatisfaction. They reported back to the board that there was "reason to think our visit, investigation, and counsel was salutary."[46]

The underlying tone of condescension in these remarks was perhaps unintended, but such a tone encompassed objections later articulated by W. E. B. Du Bois and others of what they believed was the inappropriate direction the education of black people in the South, and in American generally, was taking.[47] It is not surprising that Southland's directors should take up an educational philosophy that was at the time all the rage with prominent, respectable, and apparently successful professional educators, both black and white.[48] Still, it seems unfortunate that, at the dawning of the Jim Crow era, these Friends seemed to be losing sight of the powerful egalitarian evangelism of Alida Clark and, indeed, of the early Quaker movement, by adopting some of the assumptions that rationalized the relegation of black Americans to a lesser stature in the sight of men and, perhaps, of God as well. For all of that, the minutes of Southland Monthly Meeting declared that the "Christian counsel and advice" of the Edward Bellis and William Hiatt had "greatly comforted and strengthened us."[49]

Some sense of an altered vision about the proper relationship between white Quakers and Arkansas blacks may be perceived from Southland president's report to Indiana Yearly Meeting in 1896. William Russell seemed to have accepted the critical suggestions of the visiting board members with good grace, but a tone of strong, even bitter, resentment towards those students and local people who criticized his administration is readily apparent. Noting the origins of new problems and obstacles being encountered in his attempts to better "the conditions of the colored people," he made clear who he held responsible for the difficulties that had emerged:

> Pray for us, our beloved brethren . . . that in the midst of a crooked and superstitious people . . . our labors may result in the spread of the Master's Kingdom.
>
> It is very apparent to all who have labored with this people that there is a looseness and . . . go as you please manner in nearly all their work. We are convinced there is a great need of industrial training along with the literary.
>
> The financial, moral and religious condition of many of these people is still . . . deplorable . . . it is manifest that if they ever rise to a higher level and become useful citizens to the State and Nation . . . they must still receive help along these lines.[50]

Despite this rash of problems and a continuing deficit (seven hundred dollars for 1895–96), the Indiana Yearly Meeting and the missionary board resolved to maintain their commitment to the new emphasis on industrial training. At the same time, the board looked to balance the school's budget by both reducing teacher pay and ceasing to provide traveling expenses. During the course of the summer retiring Principal Joseph R. Hunt offered suggestions as to how the new program might be more efficiently implemented "so that both boys and girls will be able to make a livelihood at manual labor when they leave school." To begin, the assumption was that all principal teachers should be "from the North," that is, white, and that assistant teachers, including those heading up the various industrial departments—kitchen, laundry, carpentry, farm, etc., should selected from among well-qualified Southland students.[51]

Soon after the start of a new school year, the tireless Elkanah and Irena Beard agreed to visit Booker T. Washington at Tuskegee, the chief source of inspiration for Southland's new industrial programs, and report their finding to the board. In the meantime, William Russell was sending more encouraging accounts of progress under the new, lesser paid staff, including a young married couple, Mary and Edgar Ballard, whose letters to Mary's parents have been preserved in the Earlham College Quaker Collection. Edgar Ballard's early missives reflect both his surprise at grinding the poverty of local people, some of whom lived in "habitations that were hardly fit for humans" and the intellectual limitations of the students who, he felt, generally lacked "reasoning power." Ballard noted that while some did "study fairly well," it would "not do to have to same standard of scholarship here as in our northern white schools." On the whole, he said, Southland students did "not know what it is to work hard either mentally or physically."[52]

Edgar Ballard's ruminations, given after only a few weeks experience at Southland, seem in some way at least to represent preconceived notions about the nature of the people he had come south to serve. Certainly, his appraisal, set out in November, of the reasons why the school had no Christmas break had little to do with personal knowledge. "It is not thought best for these people to have a very long vacation. Their Xmas is usually spent carousing and drinking . . . and from what we gather many of them return all worn out in . . . mind and body as well as purse."[53]

In the course of the school year William Russell praised the efficiency of the Ballards and other new teachers, while especially calling the board's attention to the implementation of an "Industrial plan" wherein residential students were assigned daily, gender-appropriate "industrial" tasks after the close of regular classes. "We believe this people need . . . [industrial] education to help themselves." In the spirit of this continuing emphasis, Russell also recommended that the school's name be changed to "Southland Normal and Industrial Institute" so as to more accurately reflect the future direction of its educational mission.[54]

With characteristic Quakerly caution, the missionary board deferred any decision about a name change, but they did unite in determining that the time had come for a change in the school's management. The board's minutes are not clear regarding the reasons for this decision. It may have been initiated by William Russell's giving notice of his impending resignation or it may have been a response to their frustration over continuing and growing budget deficits and cumulative debt. A covering statement declaring that members had "endeavored in all . . . matters . . . to keep in mind the best interests of the College and to so act as unto the Lord," might indicate that Russell's departure was not of his own volition.[55]

In any case, the board invited Stanley A. Pearson, a Quaker businessman and farmer from Tonganoxie, Kansas, to meet with them so that they might "better determine if it be the right thing to engage him and his wife to take charge of the Institution next fall." Pearson was specifically asked "to express his views of an Industrial school, and the mode of conducting such an Institution." After hearing from Stanley Pearson and receiving several recommendations "as to his business qualifications and earnest Christian character," the board, after much discussion and prayer, determined to employ Pearson and his wife Jennie as president and matron.[56]

If William Russell was indeed dismissed, he seems to have accepted the situation with good grace, expressing confidence in his conviction that the "intellectual, moral and religious tone of the School" had been raised during his tenure. Furthermore, he promised that since he and his wife were retiring to the "immediate vicinity of the college," they would do all in their power to continue to advance its educational and religious mission. For its part, the board offered to recommend the Russells for any work they might undertake in the future.[57]

II. A New Direction?

In October 1897, after only two months at Southland, Stanley Pearson presented a detailed report to Indiana Yearly Meeting on his plan for keeping the school in the front ranks of educational progress. Although expressing surprise at the "magnitude and importance of the work" so far accomplished, Pearson believed that a new approach, mirroring the actions of institutions similar to Southland, was imperative.

> An education for the colored man or woman of to-day, consists . . . being taught to make a living in some useful trade or occupation . . . a respectable and comfortable living, not a mere existence. Some of their leading men . . . of national reputation claim that an education that does not include the industrial education is a positive injury to the colored race, as it tends to create desires they have no means of gratifying; therefore making them discontented and unsettled.

A curriculum embodying carpentry and farm work for boys and cooking, sewing, and laundry for girls would, Pearson believed, allow students to obtain basic education while preparing to become self-supporting adults.[58]

Thus, Stanley Pearson vowed to take the giant steps necessary to transform a Friends institution founded on the premise that freedmen should be provided with means to achieve political, social, and religious equality into an institution reflecting the values and philosophy of schools like

Hampton and Tuskegee, whose primary mission was to assist African Americans to adjust to an apparently permanent subordinate social, political, and economic role in the newly emerging South. Following the Hampton/Tuskegee model, Southland would maintain its normal department, but the emphasis of graduating teachers would not be to inspire aspirations for more advanced learning but rather to inculcate the religious and social discipline that would lead students to make the best of things as they were.[59]

Pearson's assessment of his first full year directing industrial education at Southland was characteristically upbeat. It was surprising, he noted, to see the progress being made by the boys in farming and carpentry and the girls in cooking, washing, ironing, and sewing. In the beginning some students were reluctant "to fall into line," but eventually "they became perfectly willing to derive the double benefit of educational and industrial training" as the means for lifting "themselves, and their race from their present surroundings."[60]

However successful the new industrial programs were deemed to be, continuing financial weakness moved the missionary board to again dispatch one of their number to solicit assistance from "among our eastern Friends."[61] Stringent fiscal circumstances may have influenced the board's uncharacteristic decision to refuse the request of prominent evangelical ministers Nathan and Esther Frame to undertake a missionary visit to Southland, but the explanation set out in the minutes was that "teaching was really more needed than their revival work." Indeed, this deemphasis of outside religious work continued into the next year when the board decided that, in lieu of sending revivalists, two of its own members would travel to Southland "to make observations and encourage workers."[62]

Southland Meeting seemed no worse for lack of evangelical inspiration from the north. Daniel Drew continued to preach to great effect, and in March 1898, after "due consideration," Chandler Paschall, one of Southland's first graduates and a longtime member of the Society of Friends, became the sixth local black man to be recorded as a minister. Late in the same year 563 souls (199 men and 364 women) were listed on the meeting's membership rolls. The Pearsons; the Russells; and Duff Phillips, Southland's new principal, and his wife were among forty-nine new members received into the meeting. There was also a small victory in the temperance committee's continuing to secure the ban on liquor sales within three miles of the college.[63]

Still, early in 1898 an incident in the local area must have served as a stark reminder to Southland Friends of the racial hostility and violent intimidation that had led them to abandon the Beaver Bayou meeting house and that isolated them, white and black, from the mainstream of life in Phillips County. In February rising social tensions set off a new spasm of violence initiated by landless local whites, claiming that they could not rent farms because black people took available land at any price. In February a "gang of hoodlums," called whitecappers, fired into the cabins of some black renters and succeeded in driving many out of their homes. Local white planters, who profited handsomely under the exploitive crop-lien system by renting land to blacks at above-market prices, were outraged by such lawless incidents, but self-defeating racial animosity prevented poor whites and blacks from uniting in a common struggle for economic justice. The triumphant march of Jim Crow continued unabated.[64]

Ironically, there was a sense in which the gentle Friends at Southland may unintentionally have contributed to this unsettling situation. For despite operating with a continuing deficit, which grew to over $1,400 in 1897–98, the lure of land as the best possible investment to secure the future of the school continued to capture the imagination of the missionary board. In this instance the board, at the urging of President Pearson, asked the trustees of Indiana Yearly Meeting for permission to enter into a complicated arrangement whereby they might acquire 170 acres of land near the school to be used for expanded agricultural training. According to this agreement, $1,500 from the Phoebe Metford Fund, plus a $1,000 contribution by yearly meeting, would be used to purchase 120 acres near the school. At the same time Stanley Pearson would donate an additional fifty adjoining acres to the college. As compensation Pearson the would be deeded the 40 acres recently purchased with Metford funds. Thus, yearly meeting would have a net gain of 130 acres for $2,500 (less than $20 an acre). Board members who inspected the land in question believed this would be a salutary arrangement all around if a good farmer could be employed to supervise the enlarged farm. After considerable deliberation the yearly meeting trustees agreed to the proposition with the cautionary proviso that the arrangement would not be renewed unless the missionary board's next annual report reflected a reduction in the current deficit. Duly warned, the board accepted the need for stringent economies, even if meant reducing aid for students and, thus, overall attendance at the college.[65]

The board's confidence and resolve was doubtless strengthened by letters it received from four unidentified individuals living in the vicinity of Southland testifying as to "the benefit it is conferring upon the people for whose treatment the work is being done." In addition, all gave hardy support to the experiment of emphasizing industrial training. Along these lines, President Pearson "was privileged to spend a few days at the Tuskegee conference, especially adapted for imparting information how best to conduct industrial training schools in the South for the betterment of the Negro race." Southland's leader was confident that the methods and ideas he had absorbed would greatly assist him in his work.[66]

Somehow buoyancy and good fortune never seemed destined to last at Southland. In June Pearson reported that a tornado had torn the roofs off the chapel and classroom building, damaged outbuildings and destroyed trees, fences, and growing crops. These damages had scarcely been repaired when word arrived in Indiana that President Pearson, who had only recently described the excellence of his health and abundance of his energy, had died suddenly. The shocked missionary board reflected upon how unceasing devotion to arduous duties had placed an "extra strain upon his sensitive nature" that became "too great . . . to bear." Pearson's death was nearly simultaneous with the passing of missionary board member Caroline Cowgill, whose fatal illness had commenced while she was visiting Southland, a sad omen indeed.[67]

Stanley Pearson's sudden demise of left affairs in considerable disarray, beginning with the "an unsettled condition" of college financial records. Board chairman Edward Bellis had to travel to Southland in an attempt to settle accounts with creditors and the bereaved widow. In addition, there needed to be a complete changeover in administrative personnel. Joseph Hunt was engaged to return as school principal, and, after serious negotiations, the missionary board was able to secure the services of two former teachers, Barclay and Anna Johnson, as superintendent (not President) and matron. Another less advertised modification was the apparent de-emphasis, at least for the nonce, of Pearson's grandiose vision of moving industrial training to the center of Southland's curriculum. After citing an enrollment of sixty-four students in the industrial department in 1899, subsequent reports were silent concerning graduates in cooking or laundry, and after two years the experiment of hiring Henrietta Kitterall's husband Benjamin Knox to direct male students in the operation of the college farm was quietly dropped, with a good part of over two hundred acres of adjunct farmland being rented out to tenants. Apparently Barclay Johnson felt unable or unwilling to continue the much ballyhooed industrial emphasis, although he did ask permission to begin "a short business course of instruction."[68]

With the arrival of the new century, operations at Southland seemed to be returning to normal when events took another ominous turn. On the night of 13 March 1900, fire, apparently set by an arsonist, destroyed the classroom and chapel building. While the insurance carrier honored a three-thousand-dollar claim for the building, the company cancelled policies on all remaining buildings on account of an inordinate fire risk.[69]

Southland did not open as usual in early October 1900. Indeed, this latest in a string of disasters caused some members of the missionary board to question "the wisdom of continuing the work at Southland." The doubters believed that it would be unwise to build any new structures when they could not obtain insurance on fire-prone existing buildings. Others, including Barclay Johnson and Stanley Pearson's widow, argued that the faith and sacrifices of Friends who had sustained the work at Southland required that they should carry on and that the school could not long continue without a new classroom building. In the end this view prevailed, and board determined to begin classes in November, making do in existing space with the expectation of a "new modern schoolhouse in the near future."[70]

While plans for the new structure were formulated, the board determined to illustrate its continuing commitment by sprucing up the college's building and grounds as well as refurnishing both the boys' and girls' dormitories with new beds and bedding. These improvements appear to had have some practical effect. Despite the inconvenience of conducting classes in the dormitory buildings as well as a prolonged drought that cut cotton production by half and an outbreak of anthrax (charbon) that wiped out large numbers of horses, mules, and cows, enrollment increased substantially during the 1901–02 school year. Furthermore, "Southland covered herself with glory" during a tri-county teachers' institute at Marvel (formerly Hickory Ridge) where three-fourths of those in attendance were former Southland students.[71]

Near the end of the 1901–02 school year, Edward Bellis reported to the missionary board on the dedication of the nearly completed new building as a house of worship and a place of learning for the Negro race. In describing this solemn and auspicious occasion, Bellis noted:

> Many testimonies were given of advantage and help in life that had come to one from being a student and receiving the strict moral training and religious instruction that has always been a marked feature of Southland.

Speaking for himself and for the board, Charles Osborne greeted this heartening news by declaring that in overcoming the many trials and tribulations Southland had encountered,

> one of the consolations to us, was the fact that God can and does over-rule our mistakes to His own glory, and whether we make an error of judgment, or whether we are right in all we do, God will see to it, that good comes out of it.[72]

Inspired by the thought that Friends at Southland had persevered through nearly four decades of recurring trouble and strife, the board decided to request that yearly meeting appoint a special committee to write a "history of Southland College from its inception, while those are living who have the facts in their possession." Preserving the record complied by those "acquainted with the first notable work in behalf of the children and wives of the Freedmen" would, they believed, be "an honor to the Church." Thus, in 1905 a committee of weighty and venerable Friends, including Elkanah Bread, Charles Osborne, Samuel Dickinson, Timothy Nicholson, and Eli Jay, oversaw the production of a neatly printed *History of Southland College, Near Helena, Arkansas* (twenty-three pages), complete with photos of Alida and Calvin Clark, Col. Charles Bentzoni, and Joseph Dickinson as well as several college buildings.[73]

Not surprisingly, the pamphlet was filled with unstinting praise for the efforts of Friends on behalf of "the lowly and oppressed," as illustrated by Southland's "excellent fruit in character building, and righteousness." But its publication was, alas, preceded by an incident that, at least temporarily, threw a dark shadow over the entire Southland endeavor. Early in 1902 the *American Friend* published a letter from Southland's late president William Russell, who had become a considerable landowner in the vicinity of the school,[74] noting the "need for a meeting house near Southland College, Ark, for *white people*."[75] What precisely prompted such a potentially explosive announcement is not clear. The fire that destroyed the combination school building and meeting had perhaps, as a minute of the Southland Meeting noted, caused some to become "careless in regards to attending our meetings." Certainly, the congregation suffered a grievous blow when Daniel Drew, so long the ministerial heart and soul of the meeting, requested a certificate of removal to Portland Monthly Meeting in Oregon.[76] Perhaps these developments did influence William Russell's distressing call for a segregated meeting house. More likely, they were the fulfillment of his earlier observations about "crooked and superstitious" people living in the vicinity of the school.[77] In any case, the missionary board and indeed Indiana Yearly Meeting were placed in an extremely embarrassing position. Alida Clark's long epistolary celebration of the common bond of black and white Friends at Southland and even Russell's own lately pronounced vision of an interracial Arkansas quarterly or yearly meeting appeared to have been thrown to the wind, or into the dust.

A few weeks after the appearance of William Russell's notice, Edward Bellis, as corresponding secretary of the missionary board, responded in the *American Friend:*

> We see no cause for the appeal from a Friend to build another meeting house in that locality. Southland College has been a great benefit and blessing to the people for whose benefit it has been so nobly sustained, and no impediment to its good work ought to come from a Friend.[78]

Thus quietly, and properly, chastised within the bounds of established Quaker practice, William and Sabina Russell reacted by approaching Southland Meeting to request that a certificate of removal be sent to the Eighth Street Church in Richmond, Indiana. The meeting's response—"it was thought best not to grant the request at this time"—bespeaks of more than the plain record indicates. However, a committee appointed to consider the petition eventually recommended that a certificate be forwarded to the Methodist Episcopal Church at Lagrange, Arkansas.[79]

The Russells' defection to the Methodists, apparently on racial grounds, seems an unhappy outcome for a Quaker couple long and, for a time, fervently connected with Friends' work in Arkansas. It is not clear if repercussions from this incident were connected with a precipitous decline in Southland's enrollment in 1902, with the lowest total (a hundred pupils) since the school opened nearly forty years before, or with Barclay and Anna Johnson's sudden and "urgent request" to be relieved of further service.[80] In any case, these developments seemed to augur a grim future for Indiana Friends' Arkansas mission station. But at the moment when circumstances seemed to place Southland at a low point in its history, the missionary board announced that the Johnsons' places would be filled by "our dear younger Friends, Harry C. Wolford and wife."[81] This simple announcement was the harbinger of a dramatic turnabout in Southland's fortunes. With the new three-story school and chapel nearly completed and fire insurance procured for all buildings on the campus, Harry and Anna Wolford were poised to preside over a dramatic turnabout for Southland College, leading the school into an exciting and generally prosperous new era of educational engagement and community spirit.

Chapter 9

The Wolford Era

1903–1917

I. Laconic Pragmatism

In his doctoral dissertation on Indiana Friends, John William Buys gave the impression that Southland's enrollment of a mere hundred students in 1902 marked the beginning of a downhill slide from which the school never recovered.[1] In fact, during the 1903–04 school year, Southland began a renaissance that was sustained for a generation under the leadership of Harry C. and Anna B. Wolford, who in their own, very different, way proved worthy successors to Calvin and Alida Clark. Little information about the Wolfords' background or their qualifications to become Southland's new superintendent and matron has survived. At a meeting of the missionary board convened to interview potential candidates for the Southland position, one member, Charles Parker, who had to leave before the prospects were vetted, announced his support for this Westville, Ohio, couple.[2] After the Wolfords were interviewed, the remainder of the board confirmed their absent colleague's choice, with the proviso that Mrs. Wolford, who had a musical background, could not take over the music program that was "already in the hands of a competent teacher."[3]

The following September the minutes of Southland Monthly Meeting recorded acceptance of a certificate of removal from Whitewater Monthly Meeting for Harry C. and Anna B. Wolford. The Wolford's began with certain advantages in that the entire teaching staff from the previous year had been retained and a new hot water heating plant had been recently installed. The staff was naturally delighted by the later development, but, according to Barclay Johnson, the students, "who seemed not to be able to keep warm without seeing fire," were not similarly impressed. In any case, this new creature comfort seemed an excellent investment as nearly all the 125 cords of wood needed to operate the plant could be gathered from college land.[4]

The Wolfords' first year at Southland was mercifully devoid of crises, other than the fact that both the new superintendent and matron contacted malaria, "so prevalent in that section of country," requiring that Anna return to her parents home to recover. Enrollment (155) was up over 50 percent from the low mark in 1902, the budget deficit was under $250, and, perhaps most significantly, Harry Wolford reported "very pleasant" relations with local people, white and black, a harbinger of future developments as regards Southland's interaction with Phillips County neighbors under the Wolfords' leadership.[5]

Despite the closing down of the preparative meeting at Marvel (Hickory Ridge) and the sale of Friends' property there,[6] reports from Southland Meeting seemed encouraging. Harry Wolford reported that members from a number of local land-owning families—the Billingsleys, the Busbys, the Burkes, the Freelands, the Paschals, and others—were "very faithful in the performance of their religious duties . . . and the meetings were all sources of blessing."[7] A series of revivals brought new converts from the surrounding area, and, as Superintendent Wolford noted with pride, "all the students in the dormitories, with the exception of one girl, professed Christianity." Around this same time, however, the general tenor of religious observation within the school took on a more ecumenical flavor as reflected in a minute from 1903 encouraging students "to present statements of their standing in the Church of which they are members" in the hope this "would promote a unity in Christian Fellowship in the school."[8] From this time students who claimed to be Christians and attended Southland Meeting but subsequently moved away were no longer claimed as members unless they actually continued to attend local meetings for worship. Obviously, this practice provided a more realistic assessment of the size and power of Southland Meeting. Indeed, from about 1910, the *Catalogue of Southland College and Normal Institute* was at pains to note that while "under denominational control, Southland is not a sectarian school . . . [but] does what it can to encourage practical Christianity."

Of course, church services and sabbath school gatherings were regularly held in the college chapel with the staff, boarding students, and local Friends in attendance. These consisted of what Quakers call a "programmed meeting," with Bible reading, hymn singing, and a prepared sermon, under the direction of a faculty member or visiting preacher. The minutes of the Southland Monthly Meetings for Business intermittently exhibited flashes of earlier fervor, as under the brief Clerkship of a local black farmer, J. B. Freeland. Responding to the inspiration infused by visiting ministers during the spring and summer of 1904, J. B. Freeland's rhetorical flourishes harkened back to the exalted spiritual exercises of Alida Clark. He recounted how upon hearing

> the word of God in all its purity old soldiers of the cross were revived and their countenances and stammering words revealed a secret that although it were shouted all the intervening time that elapses between here and the successive beats of eternity, yet with truth could we say "the half has never been told." . . . Volunteers enlisted under the blood-stained banner not for one day or two but for the during [*sic*] of the war.[9]

At the same time, Freeland recounted how erring brothers and sisters were approached with "encouraging words" that might loosen the shackles of sin and allow them "with sanctified liberty [to] eat from God's Everlasting Store-house and drink from the never-ceasing fountain head of God's love." These were stirring words but within a month of their having been written there was an unexplained hiatus of nearly two years in the recording of even the most mundane minutes in the Southland meeting book.[10] When word of a meeting for worship and business was again recorded on 20 June 1906, it had reference to the "best way of bettering the condition of the church . . . [and] reviving the ties of brotherhood that bind us into one, good, strong Christian band." There was apparently some success in this regard. In May 1907, the minutes noted that the names of fourteen persons wishing to join the church had been brought forward.[11] So, religious devotions continued to be a integral part of Southland life, but maintenance of most distinctly Quaker spiritual exercises ceased to be a central aspect of worship services. Most meetings for worship at Southland in what was increasingly called the "Friends' Church" were conducted by a revolving series of paid "pastors." (George

Fox would have called them "hireling ministers.") One might almost hear a stirring in Alida Clark's grave.

For all of that, the infant Wolford regime greatly impressed the missionary board by so nearly balancing Southland's budget that Edward Bellis predicted the college would be out of debt by the end of 1904. In his annual report for 1904–05, Harry Wolford noted that while this ideal was not fully realized—a deficit of $130 remained on the books—"the work is progressing . . . in advance of our expectations." In assessing that progress for an educational conference of Friends in the summer of 1905, Superintendent Wolford stated that educational standards had been raised "as the colored people have developed."[12]

By the end of the next school term, Wolford's cautious optimism appeared to be confirmed. While the operating deficit increased by a hundred dollars, enrollment had also substantially increased, allowing "some seed to be sown" in many homes for the first time. Furthermore, the harvest from previous educational and moral plantings was made manifest by the four students who graduated from the college department and the eleven who had successfully completed the normal course in preparation for teaching in common schools throughout the Delta where "Christian education of mind and morals, and industrial training" were badly needed. These points were reinforced by Lillian Jones, one of Southland's black teachers, who addressed Indiana Yearly Meeting on a theme of "advantages and benefits" that the Friends' mission station brought to "the colored people in that part of the country."[13]

The Wolford administration continued to work its apparent magic during the 1906–07 school year, which was prosperous in every account. Enrollment increased to 235, the budget was balanced—with an $8 surplus—16 new members were added to "the church," and, according to Ethel Jones, a white Quaker teacher, students manifested greater interest in the meeting. The missionary board could not have failed to be pleased. However, when Harry Wolford visited with the board in May 1907, they rejected his idea of attaining further savings by using "four colored and two white" teachers the next year (Whites were paid more than blacks and were reimbursed for travel expenses) because members did not think it wise to have a teaching staff more than half colored. (During the Clark era there were years when all the teachers, save Alida, were black.) A month later the board was seriously taken aback when

Mrs. Wolford arrived in Richmond to ask that she and her husband be released from further service. It is not clear if this threatened resignation had anything to do with the recent staffing decision, but "considerable persuasion" was necessary to convince the Wolfords to stay on, if only for one more year.[14]

Amidst a not very promising search for possible replacements, the missionary board encountered another setback when two other white Southland teachers announced their intention to resign in order to enter Earlham College. For a time, the board believed they had secured a replacement in the person of Charles O. Whitely, a Quaker minister from Iowa. Indeed, Whitely was send to Southland to hold a series of religious meetings which Harry Wolford reported as "very acceptable," resulting in over thirty conversions. But when Whitely proposed to take the Southland position for five years, along with his wife, her personal assistant and two children at $90 per month ($20 more than the Wolfords were receiving), the cautious board, operating as ever on a paper thin margin and facing an increased expenditure of $1,200 over the course of the contract as well as the cost of feeding three additional mouths, rejected Whitely's proposal. Growing increasingly nervous, they then offered the position to former superintendent Barclay Johnson; he respectfully declined.[15]

Faced with the real possibility of not securing adequate leadership for the next school year, the board made a final attempt to induce the Wolfords to remain at Southland. Summoned to Indiana, Harry Wolford "spoke freely" in setting out his terms. "After weighting the subject prayerfully," the board agreed to increase the Wolfords' salary to $100 a month, to change his title to president, and to endorse his plan for selling 170 acres of college land in order to finance necessary improvements in the school's infrastructure, including more dormitory space, a better water supply, an electric lighting system, and more and better tools for the somewhat-neglected industrial arts program.[16]

By the time school opened in October 1908, President Wolford had arranged to sell all 170 acres of the so-called Toles land in two parcels on favorable terms, with the proceeds ($4,250) to be used to advance Southland's the physical and educational well-being. Newly recommitted to Friends' Arkansas enterprise, Wolford's report to the yearly meeting set out his vision of Southland's historic mission.

> Its object is to make useful citizens of the American negro, and we . . . are exceedingly encouraged that its mission is being fulfilled. Southland students are called . . . upon to make much self-denial, and the parents still greater sacrifice. . . . done willingly, not grudgingly.

And such sacrifices brought results, Wolford declared. Former or current Southland students taught in nearly every black school in Phillips County and many in adjoining counties. One Baptist minister told him that "without exception" Southland teachers were "doing good work." Indeed, appeals arrived from across the South, from Texas to Florida, pleading for instructors trained at the Quaker academy. Not all such requests were for teachers, the president of one black medical school told Wolford: "Send us more . . . students; they are our very best." By 1908 Southland was overflowing, with 260 students whose hard-earned tuition payments helped create a surplus of over $250. But President Wolford noted with regret that many others, desperately eager to obtain a better education than free schools could provide, had to be turned away because they could not pay and he lacked the means to assist them. These people were willing to make sacrifices. Were, he asked, Friends similarly prepared to meet the challenge by becoming "a part of this service, in His name?"[17]

No great flow of Quaker largess followed President Wolford's plea. There was, however, a development that might have brought hope for an additional source of funding. In the spring of 1908, the missionary board received a communication from Booker T. Washington regarding Southland's possible involvement in the "Fund for Rudimentary Schools for Southern Negroes" established by an elderly Philadelphia Hicksite Quaker, Anna T. Jeanes, of which Washington was a trustee. In October of that same year, Washington briefly visited Helena, although nothing in Southland or other Quaker sources indicates that he met with officers of the school during this stopover.[18] Although no assistance from the Jeanes Fund was immediately forthcoming, another possible source of additional Quaker support emerged about this time.

In 1902 eleven North American Orthodox (Gurneyite) Yearly Meetings endorsed a uniform discipline, largely based upon the theological provisions of the Richmond Declaration of Faith of 1887, and agreed to meet every five years to assess their spiritual condition and progress. Beyond the desire to ensure theological soundness within their ranks, the signatory bodies to this Five Years Meeting set up a number of boards to coordinate evangelical, educational, and peace work, among these was a committee mandated to give special consideration to the welfare of Negroes and American Indians.[19] In 1909 the Five Years Meeting Committee on the Condition and Welfare of the Negroes asked Indiana Yearly Meeting to appoint its own committee to cooperate with the Five Years Meeting in advancing the interest of the Negro race. The Indiana Missionary Board jumped at the opportunity to coordinate activities with the Five Years Meeting, doubtless with the expectation that resources from the combined yearly meetings might be allocated to aid the work at Southland. Alas, three years hence the board sorrowfully noted that appeals for assistance made to the Five Years Meeting "had met with very little success."[20]

Despite the continuing financial pinch, 1908–09 proved to be an "unusually satisfactory" year. Because enrollment was the largest in school history (312), the dinning hall had to be enlarged to accommodate this influx of students. New expenditure was, however, offset by the fact that receipts from tuition payments had doubled during Harry Wolford's tenure. The missionary board also received a glowing report following an inspection tour by Mrs. Edward Bellis, wife of the board's corresponding secretary, praising the excellent work being done by both students and teachers; the Wolfords' accomplishments appeared to be beyond superlatives.[21]

There was, however, one untoward ripple in the wave of propitious news coming from Southland. In September 1909, immediately prior to the opening of a new school year, Southland principal Everett Davis suddenly resigned his position.[22] In responding to this emergency, the missionary board was able to secure the services of O. Herschel Folger, a recent Earlham graduate. Young Folger had no experience as a teacher or administrator, although he grew up in Carthage, Indiana, which, at the time, had a significant black population. Indeed, the 1900 census indicates that the Folger family had black neighbors. Like nearly all Friends who took positions at Southland, Herschel Folger had no knowledge of the South, but he was pleased to have the job as he was unemployed and his family was apparently facing financial difficulties.[23] From a historical perspective Folger's appointment produced another salutary effect. The preservation of letters written by this callow youth to family members in Indiana recounting his early days at Southland provide an always-guileless and often-charming contrast to dry-as-dust official minutes or reports. Folger's open, honest, and more-than-a-little-bemused commentary offers fresh insight into Southland's life and times during the Wolford era.

Folger's early letters are so erratically dated that one might be tempted to say he was either disoriented or so green that he did not even know what day it was. Other evidence indicates that he boarded a train in Indiana on the first day of October 1910 and changed at Wynne, Arkansas, where in the depot he first observed separate black and white waiting rooms. Three hours later the train stopped at the tiny station at Lexa where he was met by Harry Wolford. Herschel's first impression of Southland's president was decidedly positive: "He is nothing like the stern, quiet man I thought, but simple and jolly," although at the time Wolford was suffering from a throat condition that did not allow him to speak above a whisper. One of the first things Folger noticed upon arriving at the school was that there was no bathroom in the house. This seemed to worry him more than the list of duties he ticked off in a letter to his mother:

> As near as I can learn I am to be Pres. of C[hristian] E[ndeavor], teacher in SS [Sunday School], have charge of opening exercises one day a week, take turns with other teachers in preaching. When no one else is here direct a chorus (or Davis did), help with the Literary Society, have charge of study room from 6 on up, & teach 8th Arith., Elementary Agriculture & Spelling, 9th Arith., 10th Alg., Physics, Civil Govt. & Ethics, 11th Alg., 12th Alg. for the Fall term.

As principal, he also directed the efforts of six elementary-school teachers and three others who taught upper-level classes.[24]

Folger's commentary also provides a window into the way in which the school year developed at Southland, with attendance low at the start but growing daily as more and more young people were able to leave work in the cotton fields their families depended upon. During the first week of classes the new principal had only a couple dozen students in his charge, but he was told to expect 150 by Christmas. He taught ten half-hour classes each day and got on "better than I expected . . . with no experience and no time to review old subjects & some entirely new. Am busy as I can be & feeling good."[25]

Like every new teacher Herschel was also feeling his way and having to come to grips with the bugbear that can quickly drive the timid right out of the profession: classroom discipline. "Order still medium," he told his mother, "but I am going to make some changes." At the same time, he was also learning some of the joys that can make teaching so rewarding. "For a while some things worried me but to-day I've not been able to keep my face straight." One student he found particularly amusing was a young Cuban named Dionysio Damos, brought to Southland by a Quaker benefactor a few years earlier. Dionysio spoke in broken English, but he was bright enough to have skipped a grade and "always funny."[26]

Folger was nearly bowled over by the fact that all the black teachers and students but one called him "Professor" and "it is all I can do to keep from laughing. I am certainly in the back woods. No white people, no paper, etc." He found this situation "just a bit lonesome with hens [women] running around & no men." Wolford was " very nice" although due to his throat condition, "he says no more than he is compelled to . . . [but] manages to give me some pretty good advice anyhow. . . . The ladies trust me fine, too." If young Folger had little company, he apparently had plenty to eat. He provided a detailed description of the menu for one meal that included "sausage, liver, sweet potatoes, gravy, peas, biscuits, cornbread, a cross between a squash and custard pie & grapes." The next morning buffalo was served at breakfast![27]

As the weeks passed and enrollment continued to grow, Folger had no difficulty staying busy, and while he thought that discipline had improved and things were going well, he remained uncertain as to "what success I'm having" in the eyes of his superior. In this regard Wolford seemed mainly noncommittal. "Would be glad to hear exactly what H.C.W. thinks." When Herschel told the president of complimentary remarks by students, Wolford only replied, "They spread salve freely." The best Wolford would venture was that things seemed to be going all right, and if he saw anything wrong, he would let Herschel know about it.[28] One of the things the president did not relate to his principal teacher, who had begun to worry about the total depletion of his meager financial resources, was how he would be paid. When Folger finally worked up the nerve to ask, the answer he got provides some insight into the sort of shoestring operation Southland was and would remain. With regard to money Wolford "said he was supposed to do the paying & whenever I wanted any money to ask him but he wouldn't offer it. Said part of the time he would have it & part of the time he wouldn't." As a result, Herschel was on the job six weeks before he was able to send money home, where it was apparently needed. Harry Wolford's reticence, no doubt partly related to his throat condition, even invaded Herschel dreams: "H.C.W. no better I think. Doubt if he ever is. Dreamt the other night he had got so he could talk."[29]

Some sense of the isolation in which Southland's teachers labored is reflected in the fact the Folger did not make his first trip to Helena until he had been at the school for nearly two months. His reaction to what he saw there was what might be expected from a sheltered midwestern Quaker lad and a reflection of why many Friends were so pleased that their school was safely planted in the quiet countryside. Herschel noticed that Helena contained some fine old houses but added that "glimpses I got of some parts gave me a bad opinion. Women smoking cigarettes and drinking." The man who had brought him to town told him Helena was a rough place with someone killed in a fight nearly every week.[30]

Another good reason for the infrequency of nine-mile trips over rough roads to the river port was the work load increasingly imposed upon Folger as more and more pupils arrived at school. By early December there were over 100 boarding students, and a month later Folger reported "as much as 160 in my room. I tell you things are crowded. There are 12 rooms in each dorm & about 70 boys. I don't know how many girls." In February enrollment had finally settled down at 350 students, 175 of whom were boarding in space designated for 100. Principal Folger's charges included 159 pupils in grades six through twelve. Despite crowding in dormitories and classrooms, he continued to be impressed with the quality of meals served from Southland's kitchen: "We have been living high. . . . fine board . . . all of the time." But if the food was good, there seemed to be some uncertainty as to when it might be served. Folger complained that the "worst thing about the management here is the time. . . . You can't tell a thing about meals." A week later he noted that supper had not yet been served at seven o'clock in the evening.[31]

Gradually, Herschel Folger's on-the-job learning experience expanded to include a growing sense of the nature of Southland's influence in Phillips County and beyond. For example, he recounted the visit of an unidentified old Southland graduate, a real-estate broker, who had returned to address students at his alma mater. Folger's cursory assessment was that the fellow possessed "good words and a good opinion of himself." But one must also assume that the preparation he had received at Southland played some part in enabling this alumnus to become one of the wealthiest black men in Arkansas. As one contemporaneous article in the Quaker press noted, Friends were "not satisfied to merely inculcate the theory of 'virtuous energizing' but are anxious too that our students learn to do something practical . . . that has market value because it is useful to the world at large." Southland's leaders often spoke with pride about its success in training young men and women for success. Most often they pointed to the scores and even hundreds of teachers sent forth from Southland to help prepare black children to cope with the realities of a generally hostile wider world. Another reality of this situation was that many of those dispatched from Southland to the common schools of the Delta were but children themselves whose leaving often had more to do with economic necessity than adequate preparation. In the middle of the 1909–10 school year, Folger told his sister of how "one of our very best girls *had* to go teach school a week or two ago. I did hate to see her go and she almost cried when I told her good-bye."[32]

Still, if individual cases might be less auspicious than met the distance eye, Friends continued to be encouraged by the larger picture that seemed to be developing at Southland and were often supported in their optimism by outside authorities. Near the end of Herschel Folger's first year, Southland received a distinguished visitor, the Rev. Robert C. Bedford of Belliot, Wisconsin, secretary to the Tuskegee Institute's board of trustees. While the school was only beginning to reemphasize the Tuskegee-type industrial education that had languished after the sudden death of Stanley Pearson, Reverend Bedford was "More than pleased with what I saw there." Bedford was particularly happy about Southland's rural setting where a "minimum of temptation . . . is more largely realized . . . than in any other place I know," while the school was also close enough to Helena to be favorably influenced by the town's growing economy. He found the Wolfords to be "plain, unassuming people" who were providing an excellent example to students and local people and complimented the young female Quaker teachers as "above the average of white teachers that work in the South." He was also impressed by male students who seemed to be "nice fellows . . . and . . . very obedient."[33]

While fulsome in his praise of the moral flavor and human effort at

Southland, Reverend Bedford also made clear that the school was seriously overcrowded, with some classrooms having ninety pupils under the supervision of a single teacher. Students were jammed to overflowing in the dormitories, where, he was told, "three slept in nearly every bed." Such testimony from a highly esteemed witness gave added currency to Harry Wolford's warning that while religious meetings had sparked "interest and enthusiasm" and the entire "boarding family" had been blessed with good health, the overcrowded living conditions needed to be corrected before they became a serious handicap to the moral training that was so central to Southland's mission.[34]

Clearly heartened by the encouraging report from Reverend Bedford and cheered by expectations that the "prospect for another year's work was never better," the missionary board determined to ensure continued progress by offering the apparently peerless Wolfords an unprecedented three-year contract. The board also received the approval of yearly meeting trustees to add an annex to the college classroom building. Finally, yearly meeting approved of a request to use Phoebe Metford funds to begin construction on a sizeable addition to the girls' dormitory. These new expenditures were agreed to in the face of what, for Southland, had been a huge deficit of over $1,700 during the previous year. But the board concluded its report to the yearly meeting by noting that they were

> Fully persuaded that as Friends became better informed of the good work that is being done in the formation of manly and womanly character at this Mission Station, they will the more readily and cheerfully give their help.

Had not the secretary of the Tuskegee trustees concluded that Friends had "every reason to be proud" and that he was certain "you will find Tuskegee . . . glad to render any assistance"?[35] Time, of course, would tell.

II. Friend of the Oppressed or Lord of the Manor?

By 1910 Harry Wolford had, with good reason, earned a sterling reputation among Friends involved with or interested in the continued development of Southland College. Beyond his status as the long-serving president of an institution that could offer superior educational possibilities for the area's black children, there was another dimension of President Wolford's capacity to please that might be discerned from a perusal of the Southland College catalog for 1911–12. This substantial publication listed not only the names of the missionary board and faculty but also of every pupil enrolled during the previous school year as well as every graduate of the college and normal departments since 1879. There was also a detailed account of the curriculum at every grade level. Perhaps the most surprising aspect of the catalog was that its final fourteen pages were filled up with advertisements by many of Helena's most prominent merchants.[36] This sort of patronage from the local white business community appears to represent a sea change from previous attitudes. Historically, northern Quakers at Southland had, with but few exceptions, remained isolated from local white people. The open hostility of the early years had largely been replaced by a live-and-let-live approach, but white people in the area generally showed little interest in lending more than nominal support for the school. Given the fact that this catalog was fairly widely distributed among the local black population, there were sound economic reasons for businessmen to attempt to attract black consumers as well as to maintain the school's not-insubstantial custom. Probably a more important reason for this surprising development was the fact that of all the Quaker emigrants to Arkansas, the Wolfords became the most completely assimilated into the culture and society of the Delta. Their relations with local people, black and white, were consistently "very pleasant" because their approach was thoroughly accommodationist. Harry Wolford especially exhibited a unusual ability to befriend and cultivate business owners and other members of the local white establishment while remaining a highly respected figure among black people.

Wolford seems to have impressed the white community as a solid, no-nonsense man who paid his bills, minded his business, and kept Southland blacks deferential and out of trouble. Perhaps just as important was the fact that from about 1909 Wolford became an important player in the local real-estate market. In this he could be said to be following an established practice of previous representatives of Indiana Yearly Meeting, selling land to black families who wished to farm in the vicinity of a school that could offer substantial advantages to their children. The difference with Wolford was a matter of scale. During a quarter century's residence in the area, he was involved in over two hundred landed transactions. He brought and sold some land of his own, but the vast bulk of his real-estate ventures involved in taking up deeds of trust from local black people for the purpose of advancing them, at interest, the means for putting in a crop, buying additional land, or paying off debts.[37]

A prominent example of a black farmer benefiting from Wolford's activities was the case of Frank Roden, who in about 1906 moved his large family from near Huntsville, Alabama, to Southland for the express purpose of being near the school. Harry Wolford arranged for Roden to buy land within a half mile of the campus, which was still occupied by his descendants half a century after any trace of Southland had disappeared.[38] Phillips County deed records confirm the recollection of one local farmer and former Southland student that "lots of twenties and forties 'round here . . . [were] purchased from Mr. Wolford."[39]

Wolford also assumed the role of unofficial, and unlicensed, banker to people in and around the Southland community. Because local financial institutions seldom considered lending money to blacks, when families in the vicinity of the school needed money to put in a crop or meet some other emergency, they could seek a loan from Southland's president. Such loans were not interest free, and, indeed, the question would later emerge as to whether Wolford's entrepreneurial instincts eventually got the better of his benevolence.[40] This is not an easy question to refute or confirm. There are no extant records of the terms upon which Wolford offered these loans to local people, but when his will was probated in Phillips County, the inventory of his estate indicated that the bulk of his personal property was represented by mortgage indebtedness of local individuals as well as rent and loan payments due the estate.[41] In the 1920s some northern Quakers were deeply shocked by Wolford's financial activities, even accusing him of comporting himself like "the lord of the manor" in and around Southland.[42] On the other hand, local black people generally remembered him as a true friend and benefactor to the their community. Surviving students universally attested to the respect in which Mr. Wolford was held because he, in his own words, helped them "to live kindly and honestly" and to build "a community . . . which stands for ambition and energy and peace." Overwhelmingly, local people believed that the Wolfords "did right" by them, and, as a former student recalled, when Wolford admonished two boys for fighting, he told them, "We want you to do what's right, too."[43] Conflicting interpretations of

Harry Wolford's ways and days are, unfortunately, indicative of some of the difficulties that troubled Southland during its last few years.[44]

Future problems aside, things continued to look up as Southland entered the second decade of the twentieth century. In February 1911 the missionary board received a most encouraging report from one of its members, Mary A. J. Ballard, after her inspection tour of the school. Recent improvements, she said, especially the new addition to the girls' dormitory, had greatly added to the appearance of the place. More significantly, new techniques in the study of chemistry and agricultural science were being implemented. At Indiana Yearly Meeting in September 1911 a Southland teacher, Zona Williams, spoke with great passion about the students' eagerness to learn and the resulting competence and good character of those who were able to complete the course of studies. No Southland graduate had "ever been arrested for disobeying the law," she noted with pride.[45]

Travel to the school was greatly enhanced when the Missouri and North Arkansas Railroad established a new station, called Southland, about a mile east of the campus. With these positive developments and an enrollment nearing four hundred, the missionary board concluded that the 1910–11 school year had been "the best the institution has known." But every success brought new concerns. The most pressing of these was the boys' dormitory where physical deterioration and overcrowding made renovation of and addition to that facility an urgent necessity. As Wolford's report to the yearly meeting put it, "we must soon heed their piteous cry for more room." But from whence would come the money for this considerable project? Receipts from tuition—a dollar a month for day students, seven dollars for boarders who worked, and nine dollars for those who did not—had markedly increased and were the single largest source of revenue, but there had been an operating deficit of nearly $1,000 in 1910–11 that, when added to a note due the Dickinson Trust in Indiana, made for a total liability of $1,953.41. As always, Southland would have to depend on the generosity of Friends and other outside sources.[46]

Despite the existing deficit, the missionary board reluctantly decided that it was imperative to borrow an additional $5,000 to remodel and enlarge the boys' dormitory. They were seriously jolted when the trustees of Indiana Yearly Meeting announced that "they could not legally loan the College the money on the present security."[47] Then, in the very nick of time, a bequest in the will of an Indiana Friend, Luzena Thornburgh, allowed work on the boys' dorm, including the installation of a steam-heating unit, to go forward. The project was completed in December 1911 at a cost of over $4,000. The board celebrated this development as "a great blessing to the boys" while simultaneously reporting that the immediate outlook for Southland was "not very encouraging." A precipitous drop in cotton prices following hard upon a ruinous boll weevil infestation meant that many black families could not afford even a dollar a month for their children's education, a reflection of the stark economic realities of rural life in the Arkansas Delta. Enrollment fell from 400 to 300 and revenue with it. Early in 1912 the board reported it had only $58.50 at hand as against indebtedness of nearly $1,200, and Wolford was cautioned not to take in any new boarders without clear assurance they could pay.[48]

In the spring of 1912 Mary McVicker, a Quaker minister from Farmland, Indiana, held a series of revival meetings at Southland and personally reported to the missionary board on the high level of spiritual interest that produced a considerable, if temporary, increase the membership of Southland Meeting. She was much impressed with the fact that "everything was in such good condition, clean and neat." But during the same meeting the board heard woeful tidings from Harry Wolford that the school's laundry and resident farmer's quarters had been destroyed by a fire that, in Wolford's view, might have been contained if the school had possessed a proper water plant.[49]

The board, no doubt grim faced and frustrated, once again girded up its loins and voted to borrow additional money to rebuild the laundry and install a water plant. President Wolford also proposed, in light of the local economic crisis, to reduce the school's boarding costs to four dollars a month for students who worked (Nonworking students would still pay extra.) This potential lost in revenue was partially offset by the Wolford's promise to pay $100 towards construction of a new wash house and, in addition, to bear the cost of materials for a new, two-story carpenter shop to be build by student labor. In the face of this "trying year," the board borrowed $2,600 from a Richmond bank and asked yearly meeting trustees for an increased appropriation of $1,200. So, by the beginning of the next school year, Southland, ever deeper in debt, sported a new laundry and carpenter shop, with a water plant that supported nine strategically placed fire hydrants.[50] Worn but still determined, the missionary board continued on their southern roller coaster ride.

> The institution is as worthy a one as Indiana Yearly Meeting has the privilege of owning; and is doing great work for the betterment of the Negro race. We realize more forcibly than ever that the endowment fund is not large enough for present needs. In order to keep the institution and the instruction it furnishes up to a reasonable standard . . . Friends should see to it that Southland College is properly equipped for the work she is striving to accomplish.[51]

III. Are Friends Truly Serious in Their Mission?

Southland's financial situation remained perpetually shaky, and the missionary board, holding fast to its belief in the importance and, indeed, the necessity of their mission, was in dire need of new sources of revenue. An article in the *American Friend* by the board's chairman and corresponding secretary Edward Bellis again sought to touch the hearts and consciences of the national Quaker community. Celebrating the school's past accomplishments and future prospects, Bellis emphasized, to begin, that Southland was providing a "good common school education" not otherwise available to local people. Still, he added, its primary mission was not scholarship nor labor nor even ethical training. Rather, the school's greatest gift to southern blacks was "character-building" and the production of "sober and industrious" graduates "working steadily at some successful occupation." Much had been and was being accomplished, Bellis asserted, but a great deal more might be done if a new band of benevolent Friends, ready to sacrifice on behalf of an ill-used and necessitous people, would emerge.[52]

A perusal of the school's financial statements for 1913 did not reflect any new outpouring of assistance in response to such earnest solicitation. Still, President Wolford's annual report celebrated "an exceedingly successful year." Although classes had begun with an air of grave concern about the miserable circumstances facing most black farmers in the Delta, the school year had proceeded in a "very encouraging" fashion. Enrollment climbed back to near four hundred with the result that tuition payments accounted for more than half of the school's revenue of over ten thousand dollars. All told, there was even a small surplus.[53]

The Wolfords had, somehow, done it again. The missionary board noted that for all the looming problems of the previous year, dedicated and efficient management had put "our child . . . in better condition . . . than ever before." The teachers, including graduates of Earlham and Penn colleges, were the most qualified in school history, and industrial training had been revived in a small way. As Southland approached her fiftieth anniversary, the board determined "to make appropriate allusion to . . . the Yearly Meeting showing the growth from 30 acres with a few small buildings to the present efficiently equipped college home where much has been and is being done for the uplifting of the colored race."[54]

Early in 1914 Harry Wolford received a letter from Leo M. Favrot, associate supervisor of Arkansas rural schools,[55] describing his recent visit to Southland as "so delightful in every way that I must write and tell you of my appreciation of the valuable work being done by you and your faculty. I know of no school in the State that is doing more genuine work." Favrot's earlier note to the director of the Anna T. Jeanes Fund was even more effusive. Southland, he said, was "the best Negro school I have seen." The school's faculty, he said, was "very superior" and the students' "respect, obedience and good manners" were exemplary.[56] Leo Favrot's visit and subsequent complimentary assessment not only marked the beginning of Southland's official connection with the Arkansas Department of Education but also his own decade-long personal involvement as an advocate of and advisor to the school.[57] Favrot was part of what educational historian William A. Link calls an "infant bureaucracy" that grew in Arkansas and other southern states during the early twentieth century. According to Link, such administrative growth did not necessarily augur well for black schools that, on the whole, continued to be ignored while education for white Arkansans gradually expanded. Favrot, however, remained deeply involved in Negro education, and with Southland, as state agent for black schools from 1916 to 1923 and later as a southern field agent for the Rockefeller Foundation's General Education Board.[58]

Surprisingly, the missionary board made no mention of Leo Favrot's extravagant praise in their annual report to Indiana Yearly Meeting, but they did make clear that Southland was providing Friends with extremely good value for money under the Wolfords' management. In the decade since their appointment, the school's enrollment had more than doubled (155 to 400) while the percentage of revenue from tuition payments had risen from about one-third in 1904 to over one-half in 1914. Thus, while per capita expense had been considerably reduced, both a "larger opportunity of benefit to the student body and . . . a wider filed of labor for the gospel of right living" had been achieved.[59] The Wolfords' self-effacing response emphasized that Southland had made its "most creditable showing," with both work and conduct reaching "a higher plane than they had ever known," due to the spirit of "co-operation and sympathy" embraced by students, parents, and teachers.[60]

Prospects could scarcely have been more encouraging, but before the next school year began, the guns of August, blazing thousands of miles away on European frontiers, had immediate and devastating effects on economic life in the Arkansas Delta. In a letter to the *American Friend* in late 1914, Harry Wolford declared, "No one in the United States has been hurt so much as a colored man of the South by the conflict in Europe." Dislocations in international markets caused cotton prices to fall by more than half, and black farmers had to sell at any price just to buy food on increasingly inflated terms.[61] Massive unemployment added to the general misery as hundreds of local men were laid off by railroads, mills, and factories. For Southland the major effect was a rapidly declining enrollment. Wolford recounted heartrending stories of young girls, "crying bitterly," being removed from school by their desperate fathers to help rescue their families from starvation by earning some pittance as migratory field hands. The school tried to help with scholarship funds, but, at most, it could only "diminish a little the interminable tale of suffering." In the circumstances Southland's president pleaded with Friends to "give freely and promptly" as each twenty-five dollars he received might rescue one child from "the frost and wet" of wintertime fields. In her own letter to the missionary board, Anna Wolford described the "pitiful plight" of respectable, hardworking men and women who appeared at Southland's doorstep asking for food. Certainly, it was to the Wolfords' credit that in the hardest of times, local people looked upon the school as a place that offered hope and even sustenance, but their needs were greater than the means available to relieve them.[62]

As the European war entered its second year, Harry Wolford reported to the yearly meeting that the "outlook for the coming year, while not one of discouragement is *certainly one of concern.*" Their work, he said, was "somewhat handicapped" by the economic crisis gripping the rural South. Still, crisis or no, Wolford apparently retained the confidence and support of at least a dozen white business owners who placed paid advertisements in the 1915–16 Southland catalog.[63] Significantly, whatever economic dislocations troubled the Arkansas Delta, for Wolford personally the war years were a period of accelerated activity in his land-trading activities. From late 1914 to the end of the conflict in Europe, Southland's president was involved in dozens of real-estate transactions recorded at the Phillips County courthouse. Most of those who brought, sold, or traded land with Wolford were black farmers, a few of whom can be found on the membership rolls of Southland Monthly Meeting.[64] But Wolford was also involved in sizeable ventures with the wealthy and powerful. In October 1916 Arkansas congressman and future senator Thaddeus Caraway and his wife Hattie (who succeeded her deceased husband in the senate) sold Southland's president twelve thousand dollars' worth of land that he proceeded to sell off to local people in a several small parcels at prices that would have earned him only a small profit.[65] It is impossible to discern whether the motive for these transactions was strictly business or an attempt to help local families. As noted above, surviving evidence indicates that the black farmers in and around the Southland community trusted and respected Harry Wolford. But within a few years some Indiana Quakers would seriously question the ethical soundness of Wolford's business practices.

The 1915–16 school year began with a new principal as Herschel Folger was replaced by Russell Ratliff, an Earlham graduate who had acted as assistant principal for the previous two years. Over sixty years later Ratliff recalled Southland as "a garden spot," with well-maintained grounds and freshly painted buildings amidst a poverty-stricken landscape. Ratliff also found students to be generally respectful toward teachers and discipline never a serious problem. On the other hand, he observed that many students were not well prepared for the grade levels to which they were assigned and expressed some sympathy for Wolford who, because of irregular attendance especially by boys, could only estimate the class into which students seemed most likely to fit. Illness forced Russell Ratliff to return to Indiana in fall 1916, but he came back to Southland three years later when he met and eventually married a fellow teacher Tressie Thomas.[66] Mrs. Ratliff remembered with some amusement that on first hearing students speaking in the distinctive local dialect, she could not understand a word and momentarily panicked for fear she would be sent home for inability to communicate. Overall, the Ratliffs' recollections of their time at Southland were extremely positive. Local whites would have little or nothing to do with them, but they did not feel terribly isolated because relations among the integrated faculty (a rarity anywhere in early-twentieth-century America) were cordial and even warm. They also came to admire the sterling qualities of people in the local community who were members of Southland Meeting. Tressie Ratliff fondly recalled weekend walks to Crowley's Ridge for picnics as well as the students' love for the music they sang and played to entertain the faculty and local people.[67] During the Wolford era Southland apparently became a magnet for black people in Phillips County and beyond. An article in the *American Friend* described "a gala day" in May 1916 when a crowd of nearly two thousand of "the best colored people" attended festivities on Southland's fortieth Graduation Day, "without incident or accident . . . to mar its joyousness."[68]

This celebration marked the end of a much-improved school year. Tuition revenues increased as enrollment again climbed to nearly four hundred, but food prices remained high and a trouble-plagued engine in the school's much-vaunted electric lighting plant had to be replaced at considerable cost. The missionary board also agreed to the purchase of the Southland's first automobile, a five-passenger Ford that, according to Harry Wolford, "proved its worth every day," running mainly on dirt, or mud, roads for six thousand miles with little cost in maintenance or repairs. Such added expenses totaled nearly a thousand dollars and helped to create an overall budget deficit.[69] The missionary board responded by organizing "Southland Day," a fundraising event to be celebrated by every local Friends meeting in Indiana on the third Sunday in May 1916. The underlying idea was that young white Quakers should attempt to recreate the ambiance of their Society's southern mission station. A special flyer was sent to every Bible school attached to Indiana Yearly Meeting, including Portland and Puget Sound quarterly meetings on the West Coast, outlining a suggested "Program for Southland Day" that might include the singing of Negro spirituals or recitation of James Weldon Johnson's poem "O Southland" or original plays depicting their perceptions of southern Negro life staged amidst cardboard mockups of Southland campus buildings. The Southland Day guide did note that it was "not necessary for those taking part in this program to darken their hands or faces." The culmination of the event would be the taking up of a special Southland collection.[70] This earnest effort in over 130 Bible schools, a manifestation of Quaker heartfelt goodwill and innocent ignorance, raised, obviously in nickels and dimes, $439.48—not quite enough to offset Southland's overall budget deficit for 1915–16. Unfortunately, the Southland Day collection may at least partially explain a coincidental decline in other donations from other northern Friends and benefactors.[71]

In his annual report for 1915–16, Harry Wolford noted that while student prospects for the coming year were promising, "the real concern to us is how best to properly care for them . . . limited as the work is financially." The missionary board echoed the president's anxiety in a special report by board member Harlow Lindley[72] emphasizing that lack of sufficient funds made it impossible "to measure up with the needs of the school as listed by an expert examiner of schools for colored people." The best the board could do was to ask the trustees of Indiana Yearly Meeting for an increased appropriation to ensure, first and foremost, the advanced purchase of sufficient staple food supplies for the coming year.[73]

By the middle of 1916 the distress and dislocation inflicted on the rural South by the European war had abated as prices for farm commodities, including cotton, climbed to record levels. Economic improvement brought on by what historian George Tindall described as "ubiquitous war prosperity" aided even the poorest southern farmers.[74] This economic boom was certainly reflected in Southland's enrollment, which climbed to nearly five hundred during the 1916–17 school year. Harry Wolford also continued his efforts to convince influential local white people that the school was a great asset to the surrounding area, producing better educated but peaceful graduates who represented no threat to the social, political, and racial status quo. He boasted that Helena merchants told him they could always spot a Southland student and were happy to have such well-behaved youngsters in their stores. In the fall of 1916 the *Helena World* published a story noting how local people were surprised and impressed by the "exceedingly good" Southland College exhibits at the Phillips County Fair. Indeed, the president of the fair board told Wolford that the school's exhibits were "the best on the grounds, and have done more good for Southland than any other thing that it has ever done."[75]

In the spring of 1917 Charles E. Tebbetts, a Quaker minister, wrote in the *American Friend* about his visit to Southland. Following the usual compliments about the dedication of the Wolfords and good work of the students, Tebbetts introduced a topic that had seemingly been largely forgotten or ignored for some time, that is, the condition of Southland Monthly Meeting. By 1917 the misleading recording of students as permanent members of the meeting had long since been discontinued, and the much-reduced list of members was largely limited to black families who lived in the vicinity of the school.[76] Why, Tebbetts asked, did so many of those who joined the congregation "go out . . . to other churches"? Why, he continued, in a tone reminiscent of Alida Clark,

> would not colored people make as good Friends in this country as they do in Jamaica . . . ? Is it because Friends do not regard the gospel as we hold it suited for all races? Early Friends did not think so. If it is not suited to all races, it is not suited to any.[77]

Russell Ratliff noted that students were "'Quakers' while they were at school," and Tressie Ratliff said that she felt like a missionary when she was assigned to lead services on Sunday morning, but Mrs. Clark's idea of establishing a great chain of black Quaker meetings throughout the Delta had obviously been abandoned.[78] Indeed, the answer to Charles Tebbetts question was that while Indiana Friends had retained an admirable commitment to the continuance of educational and religious work at Southland, attitudes had moved some distance from Mrs. Clark's vision of, at least, spiritual equality. In contrast to the views of Southland's founders, many northern Friends had come to believe that the school's primary role was to prepare southern blacks for decent, useful lives within the constrains of southern racial attitudes rather than to draw them onto the peculiar and difficult Quaker path to heaven. To be sure, midwestern Friends had drawn closer to mainstream American evangelical Protestantism, but they also maintained some of the residual elitism from the earlier years of their Religious Society. The fact was that many Indiana Quakers who genuinely wished to "raise up" southern black people could not entirely overcome a certain reluctance to worship with them as equals in the sight of man or God. Russell and Tressie Ratliff related how during the early 1920s when a black member of Southland Meeting came to Richmond to work in a local Quaker household, some members of the local meeting protested her presence at their worship services.[79]

It would be unfair to imply that this sort of prejudicial behavior represented all or even most Quaker attitudes. Southland's integrated faculty, a rare exception to established practices almost anywhere in early-twentieth-century America, lived and worked in the closest proximity. White teachers like the Ratliffs made a point of dealing with their black colleagues on terms of absolute equality, establishing friendships that were lifelong. Strong disapproval of this sort of race mixing was an important reason why most local white people would have little to do with Southland's Yankee teachers. Still, northern Quakers living at a distance from the realities of the southern mission station, were, however generous and well intentioned, not immune from the racial predilections and social limitations of their time and place.

At one time or another during the 1916–17 school year nearly five hundred students from five states were enrolled at Southland. In their fourteenth annual report to the missionary board, the president and matron were pleased to note that this record number had provided "a splendid opportunity for a broad field of useful work" that proved to be "signally blessed."[80] But if there was an aura of celebration in this encouraging account, the atmosphere was also ripe for impending change. To begin, with their report, the Wolfords announced their intention to retire and seek rest after their many years of arduous and successful service. Another significant transformation meant that the Wolfords' carefully chosen successors, John A. and Mildred J. Baldwin, would take charge not of Southland College but of the newly and officially designated Southland Institute, a name more accurately reflecting the level of educational training at the school. Southland's administrative structure was altered along with its new title. John Baldwin would be addressed as director rather than president, and he would report to a newly created board of trustees that incorporated members of the executive committee of the missionary board.[81] The final alternation of Southland's situation was the fact that the Friends' Five Years Meeting's Committee on the Condition and Welfare of the Negroes[1] began for the first time to become closely involved in efforts to shape the school's future development. This national board was responding to a study by the Department of Interior's Bureau of Education stating that "no religious group has surpassed the Friends, either in financial contribution or personal endeavor for the education of Negroes." The Five Years Meeting board concluded that among the eight schools for blacks operated by the Society of Friends, Southland, more than any other school, had "made itself known and beloved among the negroes." While the board's own financial resources were limited, they believed that, given the Quakers' reputation for dedication in advancing black education, they might be successful in approaching officials of the various national organizations established to aid Negro education to provide increased financial assistance for Southland. For, despite a banner year, the school had added nearly nine hundred dollars to its existing indebtedness, largely because, for the sake of a generally impoverished clientele, the school's tuition rates had not been raised for ten years even to offset war-induced inflation.[82]

In this encouraging and hopeful environment, Harry and Anna Wolford handed the torch to the Baldwins and delivered their farewell address to the "useful and honorable" students and parents who had so loyally supported their beloved school.

> You have learned to live kindly and honestly and helpfully with your neighbors. You have built up a community, around the school, which stands for ambition and energy and peace.[83]

Thus, as the fifty-year era of Southland College gave way to newly established Southland Institute, so would Harry and Anna Wolford take a richly deserved place of honor among those "Friends of Indiana" who had "given a noble gift to the negroes" of the Arkansas Delta, standing just below the founders, Alida and Calvin Clark, in the pantheon of Southland's educational and moral heroes. Or so it seemed.[84]

1. The founders. *Courtesy of Special Collections, University of Arkansas Libraries, Fayetteville.*

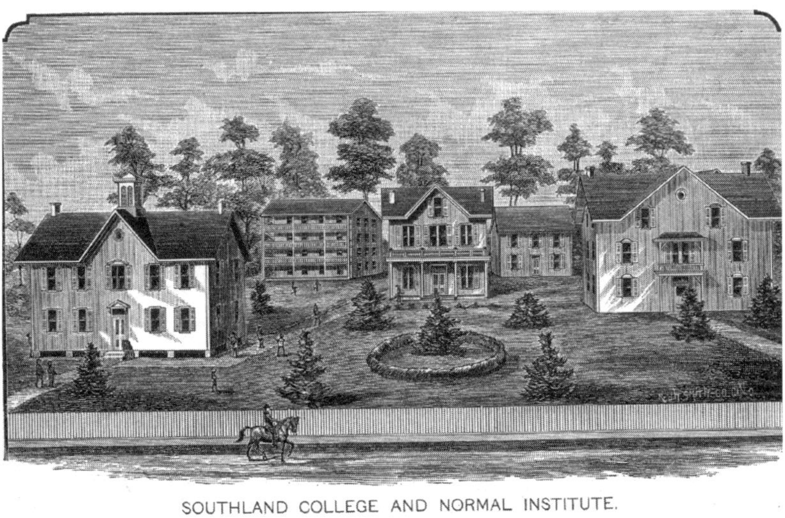

2. An idealized vision, circa 1885. *Courtesy of Special Collections, University of Arkansas Libraries, Fayetteville.*

All images within this book appear courtesy of Southland College Papers (MC 577), boxes 23 and 24. Special Collections, University of Arkansas Libraries, Fayetteville.

3. Chapel and school building. *Courtesy of Special Collections, University of Arkansas Libraries, Fayetteville.*

4. Pumphrey Hall, boys' dormitory. *Courtesy of Special Collections, University of Arkansas Libraries, Fayetteville.*

5. Girls' dormitory. *Courtesy of Special Collections, University of Arkansas Libraries, Fayetteville.*

6. Panoramic view of campus. *Courtesy of Special Collections, University of Arkansas Libraries, Fayetteville.*

7. Assembly Hall. *Courtesy of Special Collections, University of Arkansas Libraries, Fayetteville.*

8. Dining room, Central Hall. *Courtesy of Special Collections, University of Arkansas Libraries, Fayetteville.*

9. Student body assembled. *Courtesy of Special Collections, University of Arkansas Libraries, Fayetteville.*

10. Harry C. Wolford. *Courtesy of Special Collections, University of Arkansas Libraries, Fayetteville.*

11. Anna B. Wolford. *Courtesy of Special Collections, University of Arkansas Libraries, Fayetteville.*

12. Aspiring Southland student. *Courtesy of Special Collections, University of Arkansas Libraries, Fayetteville.*

13. After the Southland experience. *Courtesy of Special Collections, University of Arkansas Libraries, Fayetteville.*

14. Girls playing croquet in front of Central Hall. *Courtesy of Special Collections, University of Arkansas Libraries, Fayetteville.*

15. Students posing on lawn. *Courtesy of Special Collections, University of Arkansas Libraries, Fayetteville.*

16. Duncan Freeland, Staltwart friend. *Courtesy of Special Collections, University of Arkansas Libraries, Fayetteville.*

17. Wolfords and faculty, 1920–1921. *Courtesy of Special Collections, University of Arkansas Libraries, Fayetteville.*

18. Young student in school uniform. *Courtesy of Special Collections, University of Arkansas Libraries, Fayetteville.*

19. Visitors with Wolfords: T. J. Wooster, J. A. Presson, Jackson Davis, Harlow Lindley, Anna Wolford, Ruthanna Simms, Harry Wolford, Leo M. Favrot. *Courtesy of Special Collections, University of Arkansas Libraries, Fayetteville.*

20. Missionary board delegation: Charles A. Reeve, Harlow Lindley, Walter C. Woodward, J. Willis Beede. *Courtesy of Special Collections, University of Arkansas Libraries, Fayetteville.*

21. Raymond and Cecilia Jenkins. *Courtesy of Special Collections, University of Arkansas Libraries, Fayetteville.*

22. Faculty with Raymond Jenkins, 1923. *Courtesy of Special Collections, University of Arkansas Libraries, Fayetteville.*

23. Road past Southland. *Courtesy of Special Collections, University of Arkansas Libraries, Fayetteville.*

24. Gathering place, Martin's store. *Courtesy of Special Collections, University of Arkansas Libraries, Fayetteville.*

25. Catherine Penny and a friend, circa 1923. *Courtesy of Special Collections, University of Arkansas Libraries, Fayetteville.*

Chapter 10

New Beginnings and Unhappy Endings

1917–1922

I. A Searching Test of Democratic Ideals

The first catalog of newly christened Southland Institute described the school as located in "a beautiful and healthful neighborhood of industrious, intelligent people . . . away from noise, temptations and distractions of a city, drinking fully of the wholesome air and pure sunshine." This message came, perhaps, a year too late for Friend Arthur Stoffensham who in 1916 had withdrawn his application for a Southland teaching position "on account of fear of malaria."[1]

A more significant and more accurate point of emphasis in the catalog was that since the school's founding over five hundred teachers had been trained and sent forth as educational and moral leaders among their people for whom nothing was "more desirable . . . than intelligent and enlightened teaching and training." Above all else, the catalog concluded, was Southland's Christian influence, since "no amount of intellectual training, without morality, virtue and religion, can fit young people for usefulness in the world." No less an agency than the U.S. Bureau of Education seconded this assertion in paying homage to "the high moral aspect" of the service rendered by Southland and other Friends' schools for black people.[2]

Such high praise coincided with the vision of the newly energized Five Years Meeting on the importance of the Society of Friends role in advancing Negro education.

> Never was there a more searching test of democratic ideals than the present necessity of a wise adjustment of the hopes and aspirations

of 10,000,000 black people and the standards and principles of 90,000,000 white people in the United States.[3]

The 1917–18 school year at Southland began under new management, but retired president Harry Wolford maintained his connection by volunteering to give the missionary board the benefit of his long experience, providing advice on financial and managerial affairs while also aiding with the process of recording the articles of incorporation that would insure Southland's legal status as a degree-granting institution.[4] It seemed an auspicious new beginning, but, too soon, the board discovered that "owing largely to change in management, high cost of food stuffs, incomplete condition of incorporation," and overdue loans, Southland had been placed in a "peculiar embarrassing condition financially." Hard, cold figures made that condition clear.

> With an average of 66% increase in the cost of living, 40 percent in teachers' salaries and 50% decrease in attendance, with 6% on borrowed funds, and increased insurance rates, it is simply impossible to keep the institution in successful operation.

Faced with this daunting prospect, the board was, at least for the moment, relieved to know that until the legal incorporation of Southland Institute was completed, Indiana Yearly Meeting would be responsible "for all needed expenditures made by the Missionary Board Committee."[5]

These new complications signaled the need for an emergency conference of the missionary board executive committee and yearly meeting trustees wherein steps were taken to ensure Southland's continued operation through new loans and measures to consolidate outstanding debts. Because yearly meeting retained responsibility for the Institute's fiscal condition, the joint meeting determined to delay the recording of Southland's new articles of incorporation until the entire yearly meeting could be consulted at its annual late-summer gathering. In the meantime, the missionary board decided that a portion of the borrowed funds should be devoted to a long-range plan for making Southland more self-sufficient through increased agricultural production, thus offsetting the growing problem of inflationary food costs. Such a policy would, they believed, have the added advantage providing practical agricultural training for male students who would help to work the land. Unfortunately, before this plan could be set in motion Southland was visited by a new series of vicissitudes, beginning with the onset of what proved to be the coldest Arkansas winter on record. In a series of reports Director John Baldwin "very forcibly portrayed the severe struggle . . . to hold on . . . during the extreme cold which dropped to 11 below zero at one time & for 3 weeks touched 0 degree mark each morning." As a result of these severe conditions, the heating plant in the chapel building froze solid and a section of the wall in the girls' dormitory was fractured by freezing water pipes. Amidst these demoralizing setbacks, the wife of the farm supervisor died, causing all outside work on school property to fall to John Baldwin who had, in the meantime, run a nail through his foot that required him to go about on crutches for a week. Only by working twelve to eighteen hours a day was the beleaguered new director able to hold things together and, among other feats, "save 35 young pigs from freezing." Not surprisingly, Southland's operating deficit continued to soar while the board wrestled with the continuing fiscal crisis. Then, a crowning blow struck when fire destroyed the school's barn and other outbuildings with the loss of contents valued at a thousand dollars. In the circumstances, the very existence of Southland seemed to be threatened. Dr. W. C. Cox, chairman of the missionary board's executive committee, was moved to ask his colleagues, "Shall we borrow funds, build a new barn, etc. and go forward with the work or succumb to the unfortunate situation?"[6]

On 13 March 1918 what was now designated as the permanent board for Southland Institute met to discuss Dr. Cox's question. In the midst of these somber deliberations Southland director John Baldwin appeared "very unexpectedly" and "in a short but wonderfully impressive talk . . . made his hearers more clearly than ever-before understand and realize the worth . . . of the Missionary work done at Southland." Inspired by Baldwin's oration, the board voted to raise an additional six thousand dollars for rebuilding the barn and other damaged structures. Also in keeping with Baldwin's recommendations, it was decided to end the school year in early April in order to save money and to make a head start in the rebuilding process. Finally, seeking every possible source of additional financial assistance, the board not only made a special plea to all Indiana Friends' meetings for extraordinary contributions but also drew up "plans for endeavoring to interest Helena Business Men in the welfare of Southland."[7]

So, following Southland's early closing, the missionary board wrote to the Helena Chamber of Commerce "to arrange for J. A. Baldwin to have a hearing . . . on the needs of the Institute and . . . its value as a commercial asset to the city." But while Director Baldwin, finally in receipt of required funds, dutifully paid off the school's debts to Helena merchants, the board, even several weeks after sending its letter, had received no reply from the city's chamber of commerce.[8] This incident was perhaps an unfortunate reflection of the board's naivety in believing that a corporate body of southern white men might be willing to make at least some small sacrifice on behalf of the children of their black neighbors. It was also a harbinger of future difficulties that would illustrate that even so unthreatening an institution as Southland was not immune the bitter racial animosity that so virulently infected the American South during the early twentieth century.

The missionary board's deliberations produced another development of considerable significance for Southland's future. At a meeting on 13 March Atwood Jenkins, an "expert Fire Insurance Agent," was appointed a member of the board. This decision seemed appropriate given Southland's history of trial by fire; it also brought Richmond's prominent Jenkins family into direct association with subsequent developments at the Arkansas mission station, an association that would have profound consequences during the final years of Southland's existence.[9]

In the midst of its emergency fundraising activities, the missionary board received a notice that was more significant and more surprising than their being snubbed by the Helena business community. Edgar Hiatt, the Quaker president of the Dickinson Trust of Richmond, Southland's chief creditor, informed the board that while Dickinson Trust would supply Southland with whatever operating funds it needed until Indiana Yearly Meeting assembled in 1918; after that time the bank would cease to advance additional funds, and, furthermore, it would expect all the institute's outstanding debts to be paid in full. This action, with which all bank officials were in "hearty accord," was being taken at the request of the U.S. government "to the end that all money now employed in non-essential channels may be made available for the successful prosecution of the war."[10] Such a declaration, effectively establishing the American war effort as a priority over educational and missionary activities, seems strange coming from an institution controlled by members of religious body heretofore notable for its historic peace testimony. Certainly, such obeisance to government war policy stands in stark contrast to the actions and statements of Quaker coreligionists in London Yearly Meeting, which fully supported those, who for conscience sake, refused to serve in any capacity that advanced the British war effort.[11]

In any case, this looming financial crisis soon merged with a new dilemma. During the summer of 1918 John Baldwin gave every indication that he would continue to serve as Southland's director. He remained on the campus, supervising building projects and consulting with the board about teaching staff for the coming school year as well as planting nearly a hundred acres in sundry crops and clearing new land for fall planting. Then, perhaps on account of his wife's illness or because the drought-induced failure of most of the school's crops was the final blow to his psyche, Baldwin suddenly resigned as director a few weeks before the beginning of the new school year, leaving a scene of some disorder behind him.[12] One new teacher, arriving at the school shortly before classes were to begin, found the barn "a black, gaping hole in the ground . . . electric wires . . . down on the ground being run over by the wagon" and things generally in a state of disrepair.[13] Thus, barely a month before classes were scheduled to resume, Southland was without a leader on the ground. To make matters even worse, Southland principal Russell Ratliff had been inducted into the military. In the circumstances, the missionary board offered a contract to the sole applicant for the vacant principal's position despite some concern that he was "not up to the efficiency in all particulars." Then, two weeks before the opening of the school year, this individual backed out of his commitment, fearing a change in his own draft status.[14]

At this dark moment, the quiet white knight and his lady again came galloping to the rescue. As one Southland teacher put it:

> Harry and Anna Wolford had been hurriedly recalled from their Ohio home. . . . They could not resist the call and came at once and very able they were, respected by Negroes all over the county. Nobody could have met the situation as well as they, somehow, did.[15]

In the meantime, the relieved and grateful yearly meeting trustees agreed to the Wolfords' terms that the school's current indebtedness be paid off and that necessary repairs, amounting to approximately $13,000, be completed as soon as possible. A special ad hoc "Committee to Consider the Future of Southland Institute" also recommended that all midwestern yearly meetings "be invited to co-operate in the future management of Southland Institute, through the Home Mission Board of the Five Years Meeting." Thus, while Southland was blessed by the providential return of its longtime director, the institution's future direction was placed in the hands of an ambitious but inexperienced body of trustees who, from afar, would, in time, carve out a different and ultimately incompatible vision from that of the much-praised Harry Wolford.[16]

Still, for the time being, Wolford seemed something of a miracle worker. Arriving on short notice without a school principal or other male teacher available and conditions in a state of considerable disorder, he and his wife managed to open the school in early September as usual. Among the teaching staff of six females, the three black women who handled the primary grades all had considerable experience, but the three young northern white women were new to the classroom as well as the South. Despite these apparently untoward circumstances, one of these neophyte instructors, Mildred White, left a remarkably positive account of the ensuing school year.

> We three new teachers were dismayed, but we divided up the classes . . . and carried on. . . . I had . . . history, English, physiology, and even a class on teacher training for which I had no training whatever. We all taught every period of the school day. . . . I had ten classes in the big school room for I had to supervise the study room at the same time.[17]

Such a regimen might be expected to draw a chorus of complaints, comparisons of Wolford to a slave driver or depictions of him as a sort of latter-day Mr. Squeers. Much to the contrary, Ms. White gave an wholly enthusiastic assessment of the veteran director's leadership, praising, for example, the decisive and effective but noncorporal punishment he imposed upon an older student who had been impertinent to her. After this object lesson, she noted, "I had no more open disobedience or disrespect."[18]

Although Mildred White noted that the hard-put staff had little chance for outside recreation other than weekend walks on Crowley's Ridge or the occasional train ride to Helena for a few hours shopping and lunch in the drugstore, her depiction of Southland life during an arduous and stressful school year seems almost idyllic.[19] Indeed, many faculty and students of the Wolford era looked back upon the school with respect and affection. It was, as Russell Ratliff recalled, a "garden spot" of Phillips county to which young Friends came for service and adventure and from which many earnest, respectable students launched full and useful careers. The integrated faculty lived, worked, and played together on terms of friendship and equality—a rarity in the South (or anywhere else in America) at the time. As one former student said, "We didn't know the difference. . . . They [northern whites] . . . settled themselves in here . . . and acted just like colored people."[20]

Mildred White remembered sitting down to eat "good southern food together in a cheerful dinning room" with her black colleagues and recalled their kind and gentle ways. She was especially fond of Marylee Moore and Blanche Hudson, two Southland graduates, who "helped the white teachers and shielded us from mistakes whenever they could." Sunday religious meetings, attended by all the boarders and a few local people, were held in the school assembly room where, in keeping with a long Quaker tradition of female ministry, Mrs. Wolford and the white teachers took turns leading the service. White was touched by the way local black Friends, when moved by a speaker's message, would "all pat their feet on the floor gently making a soft rumbling noise" rather than shouting out "Amen."[21]

Often, in good weather, there were evening "socials" with popcorn for refreshment. "The children were very merry and easy to entertain. . . . They always wound up singing." Evangelical Indiana Friends had long since put aside early Quaker prohibitions against hymn singing, and Mildred White had what can only be called lyrical recollections of the ubiquitous presence of music on the Southland campus.

> In the evenings we all sang hymns with the Negro teachers taking the main lead. . . . What a volume of harmony would ring in that old school room as the music teacher played the organ. All the children . . . loved music. In a school body of 350, there was not one monotone. . . . On week nights after supper the boarders would sit out on the steps of their dormitories and sing spirituals and old plantation songs. They had some sweet solo voices. Sometimes they sang antiphonally across the campus.[22]

In the midst of that school year, the dreaded and deadly Spanish flu ravished the South, but Southland, fortified by a self-imposed quarantine with only Mr. Wolford leaving campus for supplies, "escaped wonderfully" with the exception of Mildred White herself. "I had no doctor but Mrs. Wolford pulled me through with aspirin, care and reassurance." After the quarantine was lifted, Ward Avery, who replaced the original music teacher in the middle of the year, drew upon the school's musical talent to produce a "wonderful operetta for parents and patrons . . . [that] put heart and enthusiasm into us all."[23]

When classes ended in May, Mildred White left for Indiana and graduate school, without ever returning to Southland, but her brief memoir is both charming in its descriptions of school life and illuminating for its sense of accomplishment. Despite a daunting work load, nearly complete isolation, and a possibly life-threatening illness, what stands out is her considerable pride in having helped fill a genuine need.

> With all the limited resources and constant pinching of funds we met there, we could still see what a great thing for the south Southland Institute was. . . . Many of our students had never done anything but chop cotton and hoe corn. . . . Yet they learned many refinements there and most of all they got a steady, consistent character training.[24]

Equally important, at least in a historical sense, is young Mildred White's deep and abiding respect for and admiration of Anna and Harry Wolford. Obviously, they were as much surrogate parents to her as they were to the students she lived with and taught. Still, her unmitigated praise for the Wolfords' self-sacrificing kindness and unmatched competence stands in stark contrast to the distressing circumstances and troubling accusations that marked the end of their tenure at Southland. Did this celebrated pair of Quaker missionaries and educators undergo some mental or moral sea change during the three years between Mildred White's departure and their own contentious removal from service? Or did the most fundamental changes occur in the minds of earnest men and women meeting at some distance from the blistering cotton fields and dusty, rut-filled roads of the poverty-stricken Arkansas Delta? These are hard questions, but Southland's fate was inexorably intertwined with differing visions of what the school had been, what it was, and what it should become.

By any measure the war years had been an exceedingly difficult time for Southland, but the war's ending brought new beginnings for the Friends' Arkansas mission. The school year that ended in May 1919 was lauded as "remarkably successful," especially considering the cloud of gloom under which it had begun. In the view of the missionary board, this dazzling recovery was a product of "good management" by the amazing Wolfords and a generous special appropriation from Indiana Yearly Meeting. Enrollment had climbed to 350, the institute's debt had been reduced by nearly three thousand dollars, and the year ended with a cash balance of eight hundred dollars in the hands of the board's treasurer.[25]

The warm glow of optimism that exuded from the missionary board's report to Indiana Yearly Meeting 1919 burst into a bright flame of expectations when that meeting agreed to turn over the work at Southland to "the newly organized Home Mission Board of the Five Years Meeting." Thus, a process that had begun when Edward Bellis recommended that the Indiana board attempt to interest other midwestern yearly meetings in aiding Southland ended when, after a remarkably Byzantine progression of committee meetings and conferences, the home mission board of the Five Years Meeting agreed to assume primary responsibility for the school and meeting.[26] In anticipation of transferring its responsibilities to the Five Years Meeting, the Indiana Missionary Board expressed its high hopes for the beneficial effects of this change in administration:

> It seems to us that if the Friends of America through the Home Mission Board of the Five Years Meeting, want to make a notable contribution to the . . . Negro race, the opportunity is offered at Southland. The physical property is there, we have the management, the faculty and the reputation and it is located in . . . a county that is 85 per cent. negro, and 70 per cent. rural, and where the need is great. With the entire Five Years Meeting supporting the work, it should move forward to greater usefulness and . . . grasp the opportunities at its door.[27]

The idea that Southland's financial well-being and educational standard might be significantly raised through its access to the resources of all the yearly meetings that formed a part of the Five Years Meeting seemed simplicity itself. Still, the corollary to the availability of increased aid was the introduction of more vigorous, careful, and critical supervision by a body whose members were largely unfamiliar with conditions in the South generally or the circumstances that had shaped Southland Institute in particular. Seasoned veterans of Southland's struggles, like Harry and Anna Wolford, might not, for a number of reasons, appreciate a flood of new suggestions or orders from distance and inexperienced overseers, however idealistic or well intentioned.

II. To Awaken More American Christians to God's Call for Service

In December 1919 the Home Missions Board of the Five Years Meeting was legally incorporated and prepared to take charge of the current administration and future direction of Southland Institute. This task was to be undertaken by a committee composed of three home mission board members and three members of the former Indiana Southland board.[28] A office was set up at Friends central headquarters in Richmond under the direction of an acting executive secretary, Ruthanna M. Simms, who would remain singularly devoted to Southland during its final difficult years. With the beginning of a new decade, the newly incorporated board assumed the self-defined mission of offering a channel of communication and cooperation for thirteen American yearly meetings in order to

> win more American homes to a knowledge of an ever-present Heavenly Father, to waken more American Christians to God's call for service, [and] to draw capitalist and worker, Indian, Negro and alien into one Christian brotherhood.[29]

While these gentle Friends prepared their plan for advancing human brotherhood, in Phillips County, Arkansas, not far from the educational institute where their grand design was to be initiated, an ominous illustration of the corrosive racial climate of the American South was tragically unfolding. Only a few days after Southland Institute peacefully commenced another school year, a murderous series of events erupted in and around the tiny town of Elaine. Between 30 September and 9 October 1919, five white men and at least twenty-five blacks were killed in armed clashes. The initial violence involved black members of the Progressive Farmers and Household Union and county law-enforcement officers,[30] but fighting spread to include other local black citizens, hundreds of white vigilantes and a contingent of U.S. Army troops from Camp Pike near Little Rock.[31] By early November dozens of black men had been convicted for involvement in a supposed plot to murder local planters on evidence provided by a single questionable witness. Twelve of those convicted received death sentences.[32] While these horrific events took place within twenty miles of the Southland campus and must have had terrifying affect on local people, nothing in the Southland papers or the official records of either Indiana Yearly Meeting or the Home Missions Board reveals even a hint of the Elaine tragedy. In late 1919, however, an article entitled "Slavery in Arkansas" appeared in the *American Friend,* via the *Chicago Daily News,* that provided some background on the attempt to form a branch of the Progressive Farmers and Household Union in the Arkansas Delta, refuting the popular insurrection theory upon which the black defendants were convicted. Indeed, the article quoted one local white man who "laughingly said, 'If the niggers had gotten all that they had earned, they would own the Delta by now.'" John Miller, the attorney who prosecuted the black men accused of murder in the Elaine disaster (no whites were tried), later commented that there was no "question but the sharecroppers were being defrauded" by planters and that conditions in Phillips County at the time "came as near a feudal state as ever existed."[33]

It strains credulity to believe that Southland was somehow impervious to the effects of the race hatred and murderous horror that raged so close at hand, but from available evidence the casual observer would be led to believe that the school year progressed steadily without a whisper of the sort of natural or economic calamity that had so troubled Southland's recent past, let alone the terrible tragedy so near at hand. An increase in boarding students meant that enrollment topped the previous year's mark of 350, but day-student attendance was lower because the local free school had extended its term to a full six months and because unusually heavy fall rains had made most roads "nearly impassable." An increased appropriation from Indiana Yearly Meeting and the sale of farm produce had enabled Director Wolford to balance the budget and even emerge with a small cash balance.[34]

In its report to Indiana Yearly Meeting, the Home Missions Board made clear that the bulk of the eight thousand dollars appropriated for work among Negroes from the Five Years Meeting's "Forward Movement"[35] budget would be spent for Southland because that institution offered "to Friends of every Yearly meeting an opportunity to influence in a vital and far-reaching way the Negro problem in the United States." An important initial step in making use of these funds would be "a careful and systematic survey" to be undertaken as a joint venture of the Home Missions Board, the Rockefeller Foundation's General Education Board, the Phelps-Stokes Fund for Negro Education, and the supervisor of Negro schools in Arkansas.

> Upon the results of this survey the future development of Southland will be based, including undoubtedly a very greatly enlarged industrial training department, in which the boys may be taught brick laying, carpentry, farming, dairying, etc., and the girls sewing, cooking and household management.[36]

What the new board obviously envisioned for Southland, even before the completion of the survey, was a reemphasis on the sort of industrial training program that had been attempted, with limited success, in the 1890s before the untimely death of its chief advocate, former Southland president Stanley Pearson.[37] This reemphasis is understandable, given the fact that the three charitable agencies offering gratis assistance in support of the "Forward Movement" all enthusiastically advocated industrial training as a major component in Negro education. In an article summarizing the board's new thrust, the *Friends Missionary Advocate* asked, "Why not make Southland the second Tuskegee?" This seemed a worthy ambition but one that seemed in danger of giving rise to an ominous sort of racial stereotyping. In announcing its enthusiastic support to the Home Missions Board's exalted vision of Southland's future, the *Friends Missionary Advocate* commented, "Negroes like all backward races seem to belong to soil."[38] Was Southland's role, then, to help make young black Americans more prosperous and more content while adjusting themselves to the subaltern positions to which they had been permanently assigned?

School opened in September 1920 in an atmosphere of high hopes and promising expectations. An article in the *American Friend* noted that most observers "seemed impressed with the system and efficient management of the Home Mission Board" in carrying forward the "Negro work" at Southland.[39] The Wolfords were beginning their seventeenth year of service, assisted by principal Lawrence Scott and former principal Russell Ratliff as a high school teacher. Also returning after several years absence was Tressie Thomas, veteran domestic science teacher, soon to become

Mrs. Russell Ratliff. There were five black teachers that year, Blanche Hudson, Mary Maxey, and Mary Moore, who taught the primary grades, as well as Will Thorpe, the manual training instructor. The other black teacher was Joseph C. Penn, a Wilberforce graduate who had earned high praise the previous year for the "exceedingly good service" he had given as governor of the boys' dormitory. Penn was a mainstay at Southland during the next few years, for better or for worse.[40]

Despite the additional funds the Home Missions Board had contributed and the small cash balance that Harry Wolford had managed to squeeze out of the 1919–20 operating balance, finances remained a serious problem.[41] Even with a much increased budget of $14,300 for the new year, money, as always, remained in short supply.[42] Aided by advice from various philanthropic organizations as well as Tuskegee Institute, the Home Missions Board worked long and hard to determine not just what would be needed to keep Southland afloat but to make it a national center for Negro education. Obviously, more private donations were required, and a series of articles in the *American Friend,* illustrating the vital importance of Southland to the downtrodden of the Arkansas Delta, attempted a national appeal to Quakers with tender consciences and deep pockets. One of these articles told the story of Betty, an abused mixed-race girl from a dysfunctional family who arrived at Southland at age ten and left fourteen years later a convinced Friend and experienced teacher with great prospects for the future. Betty was one of Southland's success stories, but her deliverance stood in tragic contrast to her younger brother, "a homely freckle faced fellow" who, for lack of a fifty-dollars-per-year, remained trapped in a miserable hovel with his "poor, ignorant and superstitious" drunken and abusive father. The lesson was clear: for every child rescued by Southland, many more were denied refuge for lack of funds. While this was obviously a touching and compelling story, there was no evidence of greatly increased private donations despite the broadened base of solicitation. [43]

In late January 1921 the much-anticipated survey was conducted by the Home Mission Board and cooperating agencies at time of the school year when enrollment was usually at its height. On 27 January a distinguished team of experts in the field of Negro education, accompanied by Harlow Lindley and Ruthanna Simms of the Home Missions Board, arrived at Southland. Jackson Davis was general field agent for the

Rockefeller General Education Board; T. J. Woofter Jr. represented the Phelps-Stokes Fund, T. J. Presson was supervisor of Arkansas's Negro schools, and Leo M. Favrot supervised rural schools in Louisiana. In 1917 Davis and Favrot had been selected by the General Education Board to establish a model curriculum for black training schools. They devised a curriculum fairly evenly divided between the three Rs and basic industrial and agricultural training for the elementary grades, with secondary courses that emphasized principles of teaching, class, and school management.[44] Obviously, the views of such experts would carry considerable weight. The inspection team stayed for three days studying "the present courses of study and opportunities for industrial training, in light of the needs of the Negro and Arkansas public school standards."[45] Their conclusions were published in the First Annual Report of Board of Home Missions (1921).

The visiting committee began its report by noting that while Southland was a "well-managed rural school," it was, overall, "not quite up to modern school standards." The school did exert considerable influence in the local black farming community, largely, the committee believed, because it had "inculcated some of the white man's standards of work in the class room," but this influence could "be broadened and still more directly related to the life of the people if greater emphasis were placed on higher standards in agriculture and industry."[46] Teachers were praised for their "sterling work under adverse conditions," but the committee felt that the teaching loads of all the staff were "too heavy to allow them to do the good work of which they are capable." Obviously, additional staff would be necessary "to adequately develop the academic, industrial, agricultural, and boarding department activities necessary in a school of the importance of Southland." To begin, the committee's recommendations aimed at establishing guidelines for academic standards equal to those the best public high schools. Staff deficiencies also meant that industrial work, especially for boys, was sorely lacking while classroom work on the principles of agriculture was inadequate given the availability of a 167-acre farm whereon practical training could be related to class presentations. To accomplish this goal, the committee suggested that Southland employ an instructor of agriculture who could "carry out practical demonstrations" of important skills such as "simple iron work" and proper care of farm implements.[47]

Touching on Southland's historical role of providing teachers for black primary schools in the Arkansas Delta, the committee agreed that "the greatest need of surrounding colored groups is for trained teachers." In this regard, they believed that insufficient attention was being given teaching theory and practice teaching, including the employment of a critic teacher as overall supervisor of the teacher-training department. Of course, the bulk of Southland students went out to teach after graduating from high school, a situation that said more about the general condition of Arkansas's black public schools than it did about the quality of teacher training at Southland Institute.[48]

The visiting committee concluded by recommending two new general policies that would, in their view, eventually transform the nature of the institution. First, they believed Southland's vital contributions to the surrounding black community might be better served if the school would "eventually rid itself of all save two or three of the upper elementary grades and concentrate its energies on adequate training of pupils in subjects of higher grade than those offered in rural public schools." Secondly, they envisioned Southland becoming "a center for the life of the Negroes of the northern portion of Phillips county," fostering agricultural fairs and farmers' institutes as well as "short courses for teachers and preachers."[49] In other words, Southland should strive to become for the Arkansas Delta what Tuskegee was for the deep South and Hampton for tidewater Virginia—a local institution making a substantial contribution to the solution of the national "Negro problem" by aiding a larger segment of the southern black population to fit comfortably into the roles assigned to them by the realities of southern life.

Home Missions Board secretary Ruthanna Simms noted that all those involved with the survey team had highest praise for what the Wolfords had achieved in spite of the handicaps under which they labored, concluding that

> The foundation which they have laid will make possible the development of Southland Institute into a school which may exert a nation-wide influence. . . . Southland offers a wide-open door of opportunity to the Society of Friends to give invaluable help to the Negro race and also to the United States in its efforts to adjust race relationships.[50]

For all their studied praise, high hopes and admirable intentions, the Home Missions Board and its advisory committee had unknowingly set themselves on a collision course with historical and cultural realities pressing upon Southland Institute. To begin, their sense of what Southland was and could become was at some odds with Harry Wolford's more humble perception. After nearly two decades of service at the school, Wolford, by making extraordinary use of the extremely limited resources available to him, had transformed Southland from a postabolitionist, Quaker-centered missionary settlement into a regional teacher-training academy for a fortunate few black inhabitants of the Mississippi Delta as well as a primary school for the children of local residents, demonstrably superior to the miserable and neglected black primary schools in the vicinity. Mildred White had described one of these schools as set on piles over a muddy pond so that the ground all around could be planted in cotton and not wasted for a mere school for black children. Indeed, Ruthanna Simms related that upon investigation of a district public school on one cold day, she and a colleague found "a young teacher with 25 or 30 pupils huddled about a stove in one end of the school." The teacher in question had been hired out of Southland by local educational authorities upon completing the sixth grade.[51]

Beyond question, Southland offered possibilities for moral and intellectual development that surpassed anything otherwise available to black people within the range of its influence. At the same time, after the primary grades, what Southland could provide was, by national standards, a barely acceptable minimum. Reasons for these limitations were obvious. Students arrived at the school when their economic and familial circumstances allowed. In some years, when cotton was fetching a decent price and no other family crisis loomed, a substantial number of children might be ready to begin classes when the school opened its doors in mid-September. This was especially true of boarding students from somewhat better-off families, including the mixed-race children of wealthy white planters. Students who began school on time were also the most likely to be present at Southland's May graduation ceremonies, having acquired, usually under the direction of dedicated if not always fully qualified teachers, a very good education by local standards. But a more likely scenario for the majority of Southland day students would have been late enrollment, beginning in October and continuing through the weeks to a postholiday high point when four hundred or more pupils sat in overcrowded classrooms and boys were assigned two or three each to a bed in the dormitory. As spring advanced the number of day students and boarders might have started to diminish because money for tuition was running short or because children were withdrawn to help put in the crop upon which their family's meager fortunes depended. Even for students who attended every day, the school was open for less than eight months a year.

How in these circumstances were grade levels to be determined or meaningful progress assessed? The answer was that Harry Wolford made educated guesses as to which classes late-arriving students should be placed in. As a result, lessons were given and grades assigned to pupils whose aptitudes and preparedness ranged from excellent to pitiful. Still, even if the education most Southland students received was in no way equivalent to that of contemporary northern public schools, there was little doubt that even the least prepared and shortest-term pupils were in a learning environment superior to that of the miserable, so-called free schools grudgingly offered for a few months a year to blacks in Phillips and surrounding counties.

The Wolfords appear to have made peace with this arrangement, determined to influence the largest number of students for the longest amount of time. In the circumstances, quality might take a back seat to quantity, but the more students who were introduced to the lessons and values Southland had to teach, the more possibilities were created for decent and useful lives in a society where even such fundamental goals were made exceedingly difficult for black citizens. Most local parents recognized this condition, and many were willing to make special sacrifices to afford the dollar a month to give their children the advantages Southland offered. It was "their school," and Wolford was prepared to cut corners, take tuition payments in kind, or sometimes defray payment altogether in order to ensure that as many children as possible could attend.[52]

In addition, during the Wolford era a Southland education remained value laden but less distinctly Quaker. Alida Clark had wished to use Southland as the base for creating a great southern black Quaker movement, combining firm evangelical belief with traditional Quaker practice. Less intense but perhaps more realistic, the Wolfords maintained contact with and influence among the diminishing Southland Friends community but made no real attempt to enlist students on the Quaker meeting's membership rolls or to proselytize in the surrounding area. Sunday worship as well as daily living emphasized the need to "live right" in peace and harmony with oneself, one's neighbors, and the world by adhering to broad Christian principles rather than particular Quaker beliefs or practices.

Long experience shaped the Wolfords' vision of the role that Southland should play in advancing the interests of the black population in the Arkansas Delta. Two factors arising from this experience helped them to achieve some success in their endeavors. First, they determined that they as individuals and Southland as an institution would be better served by not challenging racial attitudes that prevailed among the dominant white population. Because they were willing to accommodate the local social, economic, and political power structure, the Wolfords avoided being labeled as the sort of "outside agitators" who might attempt to subvert or undermine the racial status quo. At the same time, Harry Wolford became a person of considerable standing among local blacks in an economic as well as educational sense. Beyond the respect accorded him as president and director of a school that generously offered valuable educational and cultural possibilities to local people and their children, many blacks also looked upon Wolford as a friend and benefactor who sold and leased land on fair terms and lent money to those who could not hope to qualify for a bank loan. As time passed, Wolford became more and more comfortable as both an educational and business leader among black people and as a conduit between the black and white communities. As members of the Home Missions Board looked to advance Southland beyond its status as a local school serving a limited constituency, Harry Wolford's tight little world was about to be challenged.

III. Are Other Pastures Greener?

About the time students were starting home for summer vacation, the Home Missions Board under its new chairman, Earlham professor Harlow Lindley, gathered for long and intense meeting, largely devoted to Southland's future development. After consideration of the visiting committee's survey, the board agreed "to proceed immediately to develop the agricultural training department" beginning with the erection of a new barn at a cost of $2,500. The board also decided that the Southland committee should add three new members "without the limitation of color," while also noting that it "seemed impractical to secure three [or any] Negro members" at that time.[53] Apparently, no individuals in the Southland community, not even black Quaker members of Southland Monthly Meeting with long-standing and intimate knowledge of the school and the area, were considered fit for such a position.

On the other hand, the board, in its effort to build a "better, bigger, and more efficient school . . . [and] secure greater interest in farm life, more intelligent farmers and more successful producers," was pleased to announce the appointment of a black faculty member who seemed an ideal agent for fulfilling their ambitious new goals for Southland. Indeed, as the board noted, John W. Moses, appointed as special director of agriculture, had "expert training for this task" based on eight years' experience in southern agriculture as well as impressive educational attributes: AB, Oxford; MA, Cornell; and two years special study and teaching at Tuskegee Institute. By all account the board had managed to engage a rising black superstar.[54]

Obviously, the board was confident that a man with Moses's impressive credentials could turn Southland's farm into an economically profitable as well as educationally useful operation. When members of the board visited the school in November 1921, they were duly impressed with this proud, handsome, articulate young man of apparently sincere religious convictions.[55] In the year that followed John W. Moses's name continually reappeared in the pages of the *American Friend* and other Quaker publications as a sort of black Renaissance man who not only trained students and local farmers in advanced agricultural techniques but also taught classes in "physiology, general science, geometry and Latin" and played the violin at various school functions. Universally popular with Southland students, Moses was unanimously selected as commencement speaker by the class of 1922. Much to the delight of the missions board, he also wrote articles about Southland for the *American Friend.* In the first of these, Moses observed that members of his race who became "despondent and doubtful" about their situation should recall the work being done by Friends at Southland that was "being developed each year . . . to inculcate the principles of right living and Christian service." In another piece he described various joyful activities connected with Southland's Thanksgiving celebration.[56]

The innocent fun depicted in Moses's account took place within a few days of another horrific incident of racial hatred and violence that occurred a short distance from the school. Just before Thanksgiving Will Turner, "an 18-year-old hard working negro lad," was arrested in Helena after being accused of attempting to rape a white girl. Somewhere on the road that ran by Southland, Turner was forcibly taken from the custody of deputy sheriffs and shot to pieces by a "frenzied mob" that then dragged his body back to Helena where it was burned in the city square.[57]

This appalling atrocity in Arkansas may be contrasted with earnest efforts of the Home Missions Board to overcome the practical problems standing in the path of transforming Southland in keeping with their exalted vision of its contribution to the solution of the "Negro problem." Money, of course, was still at the root of their difficulty. Because the consortium of yearly meetings associated with the Five Years Meeting had supported the Home Missions Board's declaration that Southland would be the focus of American Friends' endeavors to make a positive contribution to racial harmony in America, the board counted upon members of their religious Society to provide the means for carrying on this work. In November 1921, however, the board issued a statement noting that it had received only about 80 percent of the money pledged for the previous fiscal year (1920–21), and of its projected budget of $56,500 for 1921–22, a grand total of $3,000 had been paid in. As newlywed Southland teachers Wilbur and Lois Kamp pointed out in the *American Friend,* Southland was "only a drop in the bucket when one considers the great need of the Southern Negro for the education of both the mind and the heart."[58] Could not Friends represented by the Five Years Meeting be moved to provide that drop for black people in the Arkansas Delta? Why they were holding back?[59]

The immediate response to this question was somewhat disheartening. In February 1922 the *American Friend* commented that "Southland teachers are waiting for part of their December salaries" while an undischarged debt of three thousand dollars was still being carried. Obviously, Friends needed to step forward if they were serious about helping to provide "leadership for Negro Americans in their day of big racial problems." From Southland John W. Moses seconded the board's plea for a more generous and comprehensive response from Friends with a passionate article in the *American Friend.* Southland, Moses noted, had shaped the lives and rescued the souls of thousands who might otherwise have sunk into the educational poverty that wracked their "oppressed, mobbed, [and] lynched" race. "Our Southland," he concluded, stood apart from "all other work of the Society of Friends. . . . It is the Quaker's living monument for his love of justice, fair play, progress and life."[60]

By the time the school year ended, pledges apparently had improved sufficiently to allow for a cash balance in the institute's annual operating budget. Whether or not this represented a response to John W. Moses's emotional appeal, he received high praise in the missions board's annual report. As Southland's director of agriculture, the report noted, Moses was putting the school's farm to better use and teaching agricultural classes both to students and local farmers while inspiring the Southland community and the board itself with his energy and oratory. In hopes of sustaining the momentum he apparently had helped to create, the missions board invited Moses to deliver a series of lectures to Ohio and Indiana Friends outlining Southland's past triumphs, current achievements, and future needs.[61]

In addition to the missions board's enthusiastic response to the charismatic presence and pedagogical achievements of Southland's director of agriculture, the second annual report ticked off what, in spite of continued fiscal problems, seemed an impressive list of accomplishments in the course of the just completed school year: enrollment had increased, interest in industrial training had grown, community influence had widened, and, not least, the long-needed new barn had been built to support the renewed emphasis on agricultural education.[62] But for all the apparent progress in implementing the recommendations of the 1921 visitation committee, there were warning signs of possible trouble just beneath the surface. For one thing, members of the board felt more and more strongly that educational conditions in Phillips County, around Arkansas, and throughout the South made it imperative that Southland "become more than a local school." Much obviously needed to be done before such an ambitious goal could be achieved. For example, some northern Friends visiting Southland for the first time were amazed at the primitive conditions at the school and general lethargy that seemed endemic to the surrounding area. One visitor recounted, with a combination of surprise and revulsion, that Southland had "no bath tubs, no lavatories, no toilets, no, not even in the teachers quarters." Such shameful conditions, he said, were not a reflection on those running the school, as they were "probably" doing their best with limited resources. But how, the author asked, could students be taught a "better way of life" without "modern sanitary conditions"?[63]

To their credit, most members of the board looked beyond new plumbing to the essential educational and moral training elements that they believed required reemphasis. They concluded that this emphasis could best be supplied by a new breed of efficient and energetic young white teachers able to make the most of "opportunities for expression of good will and racial cooperation" while working to fulfill the Home Missions Board's long-range goals for Southland Institute. The individual especially recruited to furnish this sort of dynamic leadership during the 1922–23 school year was twenty-five-year-old Francis Raymond Jenkins, son of a prominent Richmond Quaker family and a recent Earlham graduate who had made a "special study of Negro education" during a just-completed year at Hampton Institute and a summer internship at the Peabody School in Tennessee. With Raymond Jenkins installed as Southland's new principal, the board expected that "the academic standards of the school will be gradually raised."[64] A new era was about to begin at Southland Institute that would see the enactment of a substantial portion of the board's ambitious agenda resulting in the emergence of other unintended, unexpected, and undesired consequences.

Chapter 11

An Avenue of Great Service

I. Home Missions Take Command

Walter C. Woodward, executive secretary of the Five Years Meeting, recalled that of all the many problems and trials facing the Home Missions Board "none . . . required so many hours of time and so much weariness of body and mind" as Southland Institute. The vision of Southland becoming as important and influential in Negro education as Tuskegee or Hampton caught the imagination of many Friends in positions of responsibility. The board met "almost continuously" during the summer of 1922, and most of its business revolved around making preparations to achieve their exalted goal.[1] Expectations were high, but, as usual, available resources remained inadequate for expanding needs. During the past year Indiana Yearly Meeting, the largest contributor to Southland's budget, had accumulated a budget deficit of over $3,000 on expenditures of $45,311 and could not increase its regular appropriation of $2,000. Minimum estimates for expenditures for the 1922–23 school year were around $11,000, including the salary of an additional high school teacher and funds for a series of evangelical meetings. Thus, no provisions could be made for the considerable list of improvements required to fulfill the board's plan to raise academic standards and improve a deteriorating physical plant. Money for these necessary changes would have to come from concerned Friends willing to shoulder some part of the schools' financial burden. Harlow Lindley, chairman of the board's Southland committee, seeking to touch the hearts or consciences of his fellow Quakers, spoke of the "wonderful opportunity" open to them for making a significant contribution to the advancement of racial harmony in American.[2] For its own part, the Home Missions Board undertook another effort to raise the consciousness of Friends regarding their responsibility to support the Society's most ambitious and costly missionary endeavor. Throughout the summer of 1922 John W. Moses, Southland's charismatic director of agriculture, stumped through Friends' meetings in Ohio and Indiana delivering emotional pleas for financial support. In New England, former Southland teacher and principal Herschel Folger was enlisted to present a series of stereoptican lectures on Southland to local meetings. The Quaker press was mobilized to advance the school's challenging agenda; a total of eighteen separate articles on Southland's past accomplishments and future needs appeared in the *American Friend, Friends Missionary Advocate,* and *Home Field News.*[3]

Given the magnitude of the Home Missions Board's commitment to Southland's transformation, it seems a bit puzzling that the weight of personal responsibility for lifting Southland from a well-run local school to a institution of national standing was placed on the shoulders twenty-five-year-old Francis Raymond Jenkins. When young Jenkins arrived at Southland in the late summer of 1922 as the school's new principal, he brought, as noted, impeccable Quaker credentials; an Earlham degree; a year's experience at Hampton institute; a new wife Cecilia, who had also taught at Hampton; a black Hampton colleague, Walter Webb; and a burning desire to make a meaningful contribution to the resolution of the "Negro problem." For all his youth and lack of experience in or knowledge of the Deep South, Jenkins possessed the hardheaded vigor of a man determined to overcome every obstacle and the confidence that he had the means to do so. This confidence arose, in large part, from his brief educational experiences at Hampton and from the assurances given by members of the board's Southland committee that he would have a free hand in his efforts to improve academic and other standards at the school.[4]

Not surprisingly, Harry and Anna Wolford did not look upon Raymond Jenkins's arrival as their day of deliverance. Tensions were immediately apparent as the aggressive new principal wasted little time in passing out criticism in broad strokes and pronouncing Southland utterly unfit for the opening of classes in mid-September. Jenkins's negative evaluation of nearly every aspect of the school's operation—and Walter Webb's questions about the farming methods and other activities of that seeming paragon John W. Moses—quickly reached the ears of the Southland committee. In response to reports of "turbulent" problems among the staff, in late September a delegation of four weighty Friends, headed by Five Years Meeting general secretary Walter Woodward, journeyed to Arkansas "charged with responsibility of making some important adjustments in the work and administration of the school."[5] The conclusions eventually reached by this delegation and actions taken as a result would bring about a sea change in the affairs and administration of Southland Institute.

After the delegation's arrival at Southland, one of its first actions was to "release" John W. Moses from further service. Because the deputation's subsequent report to the Home Missions Board has apparently been lost, or, perhaps, suppressed, the reasons for Moses's discharge remain murky. The board's own subsequent report, reflecting the Quaker propensity to back and fill in order to put the best face on untoward or embarrassing situations, noted that

> Not withstanding . . . earnest efforts made to carry out under the former management, the new program of development and reorganization agreed upon by the Board, it became evident immediately after the opening of school that this could not be done.

Walter Woodward's biographer was more blunt, observing that the delegation's report, filling nineteen typed pages, gave "a much more truthful idea of the seriousness of the problems faced" that centered on the operation of the school's farm "and the personnel of the faculty."[6] Such evidence as is extant indicates that Moses's firing was related to accusations by Jenkins and Walter Webb that many of Moses's activities were not entirely above board.[7] In any case, neither Moses's dismissal nor the visitors' efforts "to bring order out of emotional and mental chaos" were sufficient to usher in a new reign of peace and goodwill to the Southland campus. The delegates stayed longer than they had intended in attempting to smooth over the difficulties between the Wolfords and Raymond Jenkins, but they had "hardly reached home when telegrams arrived to report more serious discord."[8]

A second delegation was duly dispatched with the result that "Harry and Anna Wolford withdrew from all official connection with Southland on October 8th." The thoroughly Quaker official explanation for the resignation of the Wolfords was that they had

> not found it possible to appreciate the need for certain changes in policy agreed upon by the Home Mission Board as necessary, and have experienced great difficulty in carrying out plans for the larger development of the school.[9]

For the general Quaker reader these dramatic developments were summarized in an article by Walter C. Woodward with the retrospectively embarrassing title, "Down Among the Cotton and the Pickaninnies: A Visit to Southland."[10] Woodward's article is important because it unintentionally reveals the duality of some Quaker attitudes toward black Americans, toward the "Negro problem" and toward Southland as a vehicle for helping to resolve that problem. *Webster's Twentieth Century Dictionary* (2nd ed.) defines *pickaninny* as "a patronizing or contemptuous term." Walter Woodward surely did not intend to convey such an attitude, but his usage of the term and his humorous asides at the expense of southern blacks reflect the fact that not even the best intentioned Quaker could remain entirely free from the propensity of early-twentieth-century northern whites to accept the validity of southern white stereotypes about black people.[11] The article also provides clues as to why and how the Home Missions Board's lofty ambitions for Southland clashed with the more mundane vision of Harry Wolford who, having thoroughly assimilated local culture, both black and white, determined to adjust his personal and administrative activities to satisfy the wishes as well as the needs of local black people without unduly raising the suspicions or fears among local whites.

However earnest and well-intended, Walter Woodward's article gives the impression that he and his weighty Quaker compatriots had undertaken a rescue mission into that "flat, unalluring country" filled with "ragged little towns," "dilapidated country-side hovels," and only "the fleck of a white face here and there amidst 'the rising tide of color." Compared with such a "drab, dreary landscape," Southland presented "much the appearance of a prosperous Indiana farm" with the local black community and its people showing the beneficent effects of the school's influence. But for all of that, Woodward concluded, that Southland had "been made too subservient to the general administration and . . . lacked force and identity." Woodward's impressions certainly reflected the Home Missions Board's steadfast belief that the time had come for Southland to make "a larger and more comprehensive contribution to the colored life of the South," beginning with the strengthening of the school's educational base and the raising of academic standards. Despite the problems that arose from the abrupt change of administration, the board was convinced that new leadership applying more up-to-date educational methods could, in Woodward's words, make Southland an "avenue of great service in the solution of one of the gravest domestic problems that ever faced any country."[12]

The Southland committee visitors admitted that members of the local community had at first been "troubled" by the change in management but judged their subsequent response to be "very encouraging" as the neighboring black people "pledged loyalty to the new administration in daily increasing numbers" and school enrollment remained steady. Furthermore, they were convinced when, once the immediate effects of the sudden transition had passed, student discipline remained "splendid" and, most auspiciously, there were signs of awakening spiritual life at the school. Young faculty members, led by American Friends Service Committee volunteer Irene Utter, were seeking to revive Southland Monthly Meeting, which under the Wolfords had gradually lapsed into nondescript worship services.[13]

With the departure of the Wolfords, Raymond and Cecilia Jenkins were appointed as Southland's acting director and matron. Raymond was determined to take aggressive action in dealing with the shortcomings he saw everywhere around him. Ironically, this activism had the effect of increasing the Home Missions Board's tendency to micromanage affairs at the school. But while the board was generous with advice, they were never able to provide the financial wherewithal necessary to accomplish the improvements they envisioned. As for the Jenkins administration, youth was its most apparent aspect. Most black members of the staff had considerable teaching experience, but all of the white faculty were new to Southland and to the Arkansas Delta. Still, lack of local knowledge and experience was no deterrent for Southland's new director who assumed his responsibilities with great confidence and high energy. Raymond Jenkins had arrived at Southland with a mandate to effect fundamental changes, with or without Harry Wolford's cooperation, and, beyond question, he had played an important role in securing Wolford's eventual removal.[14] Jenkins had expected to find lax administration and low academic standards under the Wolford regime, but he was truly shocked to discover

Wolford's activities as land broker and money lender ("at high rates of interest") to the local community and deeply upset by what he perceived as the veteran director's attempts to arouse animosity against him from the moment he arrived on the campus. Hostility between Wolford and Jenkins accelerated when, after the dismissal of the locally popular John W. Moses, Jenkins secured the appointment of his former Hampton colleague Walter Webb as Southland's new director of agriculture. At that point, some members of the community, no doubt encouraged by Wolford, called for the removal, first of Webb, then of Jenkins, from the staff.[15] This demand provoked the crisis that brought the second delegation from the Southland board that led to the Wolfords' removal from the position they had held for nearly twenty years.[16] With Harry Wolford gone from the scene, the Home Missions Board promised Raymond Jenkins "a clear field" to "do some real work in Arkansas." And, as a former Hampton colleague noted, "From all that I have heard of the schools of that state, there seems plenty of room for a lot of hard work."[17]

If hard work alone could raise Southland to new heights of excellence, Raymond Jenkins was the man for the job. His energy and dedication are impressive by any standard, possibly challenging even Alida Clark's capacity for labor. The range of his activities was enormous, and his correspondence accounts for about half the volume of the collected Southland Papers. One of his first acts as director was to institute regular faculty meetings to solicit teachers' opinions, organize various faculty committees, and ensure conformity and consistency in the application of new, more stringent academic and disciplinary standards. To begin, a merit-demerit system for students was established to be overseen by a faculty discipline committee. Certainly, the occasion for demerits was considerably widened by the implementation of a broad set of regulations covering items ranging from forbidding gum chewing in school and chapel to limiting visits to the community store. The playing of ragtime and other popular music was forbidden on Sundays, and "the music termed 'Blues' . . . left off entirely." Students were encouraged to organize social activities but a faculty committee was appointed "to act as a board of censorship for plans for all student socials." On the academic side, teachers were instructed to encourage the use of "proper English" and to maintain as nearly as possible "grading standards equal to accredited schools . . . giving work similar to ours." When this more demanding regimen immediately resulted in a high percentage of failures, these results were attributed to "the irregularity of attendance and the low scholastic standards that have prevailed formerly in the school."[18]

Under the previous administration, all matters covered by established rules of governance would have been handled personally in ad hoc fashion by Harry Wolford. So, without question, Raymond Jenkins had installed a more democratic, orderly, and exacting system. His first few letters to officials in Indiana (he usually wrote at least twice a week) would seem to indicate that his efforts had begun to pay dividends. From mid to late October he reported that things were "going along very nicely" and that they seemed to be on the way to "a much better year that it looked for awhile."[19] He soon discovered, however, that the gulf between establishing regulations and enforcing them would be difficult to bridge. To begin, because of "certain unrest among students" some individuals, that is, parents or neighbors considered to be agitators, were banned from the campus. This sanction did not prevent the boarding students, "led by a certain few," from boycotting breakfast due to complaints about the food. Furthermore, following Wolford's dismissal, Jenkins began to receive letters from concerned parents that reflected stories and gossip circulating among local people. For example, Mrs. Fannie Buford of Helena wrote demanding her daughter be sent home because of rumors that Southland girls were "going around by them selfs." The new director could only reply that girls were closely supervised and that "everything is going smoothly at the school." He added that recent negative stories about Southland were false and were being spread by individuals wishing to damage the school.[20]

Jenkins became convinced that the chief source of these damaging rumors and innuendoes was none other than Harry Wolford, who had taken residence in a Helena hotel from whence he continued to act as personal banker and land agent for numerous black families in the area around Southland.[21] Routine correspondence that passed between Wolford and Jenkins was correct if not amicable.[22] But Jenkins received reports that the former director was organizing meetings among local people, many of whom had purchased land or borrowed money from him and remained in his debt, and he became convinced that Wolford was attempting to orchestrate the formation of a coalition to oppose his leadership. Quaker families like the Freelands, Busbys, and Rodens insisted that things were "getting along splendidly," but Jenkins remained suspicious "that Mr. Wolford or someone or perhaps several are still doing their best to wreck the school." Indeed, events would reveal that his concerns about Wolford's possibly subversive activities were not entirely misplaced.[23]

Whatever slanders Wolford or others were spreading, grim realties were soon more than sufficient to cause serious consternation. Following the new acting director's early and unequivocal pronouncement that "any immoral relation or absolute disregard for the rules" would result in the guilty party being "immediately barred from school," Jenkins was, in early December, forced to report a near "epidemic" of "immoral relations" that had occurred "off and on ever since the very beginning of school." But while Jenkins was deeply chagrined by such shocking behavior, he determined that the students involved suffered from a "terrible lack of knowledge" about the possible consequences of their actions. This situation, he admitted, was at least partially the result of the faculty's failure to impart the necessary warnings about the effects of sexual immorality.[24] Jenkins believed that "constructive work along these lines is in many cases opposed by heredity and environment, much being due to environment." He resolved to strike back against this "moral looseness" by requiring physical examinations for older students and by instituting a series of "frank talks" on sexual purity. At the same time he pleaded for the funds that were needed to place a full-time, live-in matron, "with the proper training, the proper racial attitude and with a love for that kind of work," in the girls' dormitory where most of the illicit acts had occurred.[25] Given Southland's precarious financial situation, this request proved to be superfluous, not to say unrealistic, and the girls' dormitory remained without a regular chaperone.[26]

Such untoward events only increased the volume of letters from concerned or dissatisfied parents requesting that their children be sent home. In addition, there were complaints from those who believed that the new director was overburdening the students who were working to offset tuition charges or not living up to arrangements parents had previously made with Wolford.[27] Adding to the flow of dropouts were students leaving to attend the local short-term "free" (public) school. Many of these made application to return to Southland when the free school closed. This had apparently been a common practice when Wolford was director, but Raymond Jenkins believed that it was not fair to other students or to teachers to readmit such on-again-off-again pupils. However reasonable from a pedagogical standpoint, this decision was, to say the least, not locally popular. Taken together, the consequences of student defection on enrollment figures gave considerable cause for concern. Early in 1923 Jenkins reported to the faculty that 69 of a total of 270 students, or one-fourth, had withdrawn from school.[28]

Beyond having to deal with problems left over from Harry Wolford's more casual, or more tolerant, regime, Jenkins, from first week he assumed his duties, was faced with a surfeit of debts and a nearly empty cashbox. Just before Thanksgiving he told Ruthanna Simms that while a check from the Five Years Meeting had arrived in the nick of time to cover bills incurred in August, he was still "in quite hard straits to make ends meet" because another five hundred dollars was needed immediately to pay other delinquent accounts and provide for teachers' salaries.[29] In nearly every one of Jenkins's frequent letters to Ruthanna Simms or other board members, he cited some old, or new, unmet obligation. But regardless of the Home Missions Board's persistent pleas for donations and Jenkins's personal efforts to solicit support from wealthy individuals,[30] Southland's operating deficit continued to grow month by frustrating month.

While the board remained unable to ensure a regular supply of funds for operating expenses, it did seek to relieve some of Jenkins's burden by securing the volunteer services of a midwestern Quaker couple, Jesse and Mary Overman. At first, the Overmans appeared to be invaluable addition to the Southland staff; he as a jack-of-all-trades making whatever repairs and improvements he could manage, and she as a nurse and kitchen manager. But if the Overmans' labors saved the school considerable expense, their personal eccentricities eventually created tensions among the staff that became a serious distraction for the acting director. Meanwhile, the overall financial picture remained bleak. Jenkins's parents used the occasion of a Christmas visit to issue a plea in the *American Friend* urging Friends, in the spirit of the season, to help to put Southland "in a position to be no small factor in the solution of the Race problem" through its educational mission. Another article soliciting monetary aid noted that Southland stood for "the finest type of Negro education" offering simple, practical courses to aid the Negro as he seeks to adjust himself to an ever . . . advancing civilization."[31] Little substantial help arrived.

Early in 1923 Jenkins told Ruthanna Simms that he had been forced to advance faculty members twenty dollars each from his petty-cash box so that they could have at least something for Christmas, as they had not been paid for either November or December. He noted, with masterful understatement, that "regular salary payments tend to make a contented faculty."[32] Despite such urgent supplications, by the end of January 1923 faculty members had received only about half what was due them, and Ruthanna Simms confessed that the missions board had no resources to send other than fifty dollars from an emergency fund.[33] Nonpayment of faculty salaries was only part of the problem. Local merchants and other creditors were constantly pressing Jenkins for their arrears. In early February, for example, the local wholesale grocer presented a two-month bill for $476, and was less than enthusiastic when Jenkins responded with a check for $89.70.[34]

The financial struggles that troubled Southland in its last years can in considerable part be explained by some basic statistical analysis that speaks volumes concerning how the Five Years Meeting's enlarged and ambitious vision accelerated the downward journey to the school's eventual demise. When Raymond Jenkins approached Mary M. Crossand, a wealthy Indiana Friend, about the possibility of a financial contribution, he noted that the fourteen faculty teaching about two hundred students were all overwhelmed with work and that two or three additional teachers were needed to do a proper job. Given that Southland was offering twenty separate classes in 1922–23, no doubt Jenkins's statement had merit. But only four years earlier the Wolfords, Mildred White, and five other teachers handled a student population of 350 and completed the school year with a small budget surplus. Certainly, the standard of work under the Wolford administration was lower than Raymond Jenkins would have found acceptable, but unless Mildred White's description of the cooperative, almost joyous atmosphere of the school was completely fictitious, both the patrons and the faculty, operating under much more stringent conditions, seem to have felt that a great deal had been accomplished in the course of that 1918–19 school year.[35] Obviously, then, for those involved, Southland's successes or failures were very much a matter of perception. Local people liked "their" school under Mr. Wolford's direction because it served their needs and fulfilled their vision of what a school should be. The fact that the Home Missions Board and Raymond Jenkins imagined a very different Southland from the one most of its patrons had known reflected a cultural gap that was difficult if not impossible to bridge.

Still, for all his financial woes and his constantly being "head over heels with work"—Jenkins's day usually began at six in the morning and ended at nine at night—the young director remained "well and happy" and ready to take up every challenge.[36] But other, more delicate Southland workers from the north did not remain as physically and mentally fit as Jenkins seemed to be. Indeed, the new year brought a series of personnel problems that reflected the difficult and primitive conditions under which the school's faculty had to toil. In January 1923, Jenkins was forced to spend his last available reserve funds to send Nell Vore, the music teacher who had become seriously ill, home for an operation. Six weeks later Jenkins telegraphed Harlow Lindley with the news that another white teacher, Mabel Martin, had suffered a nervous breakdown at about the same time that Leigh Barrett's visiting sister had to undergo emergency surgery. All of this transpired at a time when Southland teachers' salaries were still over a thousand dollars in arrears and the school was unable to purchase additional supplies because the wholesale grocer was still owed more than three hundred dollars.[37]

Jenkins was given leave to float a short-term loan to carry Southland through the immediate crisis, and sufficient funds were eventually cobbled together to keep the school afloat through the spring term. Of course, precious little of that money came from the Southland's black patrons who struggled to pay monthly tuition of one or two dollars for day students and eight to fourteen dollars for boarders, depending on the amount of work they performed.[38] The Southland Papers are dotted with letters from nearly illiterate parents or guardians pleading for partial or complete respite from payment of school fees. On the one hand, such missives are sad revelations of the poverty and confusion of their authors, but they are also touching and even inspiring reminders of the depths of sacrifice the school's patrons were willing to make in hopes of securing a decent education, otherwise unavailable, for their children. For example on 20 February 1923 Mrs. Caroline Cooper wrote, "Hear is your money. I am sick and are in Bead so hear is $2.00 and owe you 14 cents moore. . . . Send me a receat." A month later a letter from Will Edwards informed "Mr. Gankis" that he had been sick but "I am goin to Send you this monts money this week and I wont you to let Garland still go on. . . . I Show means to treat you rite."[39] Generally speaking, Southland carried delinquent accounts for some time, but Jenkins believed that patrons should make at least token contributions to the school's maintenance. On occasion, he would notify parents that "unless some move is made to settle this account . . . we shall have to ask your children to stop school."[40] Such ultimatums did not further endear the young director to those in the community who remembered Harry Wolford's tendency to ignore the unpaid bills, especially those incurred by families who lived in the neighborhood of the school.

In contrast to events on the ground, articles in the *American Friend,* reminding readers that Southland was Friends' "only channel . . . touching unitedly the race problem," painted a fairly rosy picture of the school's progress. One of these emphasized that despite early difficulties after Harry Wolford resigned, the community was "gaining confidence in the present administration and beginning to express satisfaction with the work which Raymond Jenkins and his helpers are trying to accomplish."[41] At the same time, Jenkins himself had begun to express concern over rumors spreading through the school and community that Southland might close and that, if it did, Wolford had promised local people he would buy the property and reopen the school. Some local people might welcome such a development, but black Quakers like Duncan Freeland and the Busbys told Jenkins that they would rather the school close down than see the Wolfords regain control. For his part, Jenkins was confident that the board would never allow Wolford to regain control of Southland.

II. The Deep Concern in Many of Our Hearts

Despite the desperate shortage of funds available to maintain Southland's educational mission, the home missions board had made provision for a series of revival meetings to be held during the 1922–23 school year. This evangelistic effort was an expression of one of the spiritual goals on the board's ambitious agenda, that is, the attempt to resuscitate of Southland's moribund monthly meeting. As noted, the school had maintained a regular nondenominational Sunday service for boarding students and local people, generally organized and ministered to by Quaker staff, but midweek gatherings of Southland Monthly Meeting for business and worship had apparently been abandoned. Prior to the board's mandate to restore a specifically Quaker worship service in August 1922, no entry had been made in the Southland Monthly Meeting minute book since September 1919 when a statistical report indicated an active membership of fifty souls, with an additional thirty-five nonresidential members. The first manifestation of a revival effort in the minute book began on 22 August 1922 under Wolford's leadership, with a brief comment on a midweek devotional service. The following week, with John W. Moses acting as clerk for the day, a longer entry emphasized the meeting's need to reach out to the local community, including regular correspondence with nonresidential members.[42] This effort to maintain regular meetings for business was short-lived. The final entry in the Southland's minute book was made in late October 1922 by volunteer teacher Irene Utter, clerk for the day.

> It being the deep concern in many of our hearts that this Monthly Meeting be revived, a group of members of this meeting gathered to consider steps toward its re-organization. . . . It was urged that everyone present make a special effort to secure a full attendance at the next meeting, and to invite those who are not now members to join us if they desire to do so.[43]

For whatever reason the proffered invitations seem not to have been taken up. In late January 1923 Jenkins told Ruthanna Simms that "only about 5 or 6 persons come anyways near regularly" from the community.[44] These could be ticked off on the fingers of one hand: the Freelands, the Busbys, the Rodens, Lucille Bone, perhaps the Burkes. It seemed a forlorn end to Alida Clark's hopes for a black quarterly meeting reaching out from Southland into the entire Mississippi valley and beyond.[45]

But if the monthly meeting was only a pitiful remnant of past days, Southland was still a Quaker school with a Christian mission, and Raymond Jenkins worked manfully to ensure that it stood, as always, "for the spiritual development of the students as well as the mental and physical." To this end he organized a series of special religious meetings in February that, he believed, would do "much to win the community back . . . and . . . also put a new spirit into the school."[46] In the meantime, dates for the long-awaited evangelistic meetings were established. Charles O. Whitely, a member of the Home Missions Board executive committee and the general superintendent of the Iowa Yearly Meeting, was to preach a series of revival meetings from the eighth to the eighteenth of March. In preparation for Whitely's arrival, Jenkins told the faculty that "there should be singing every evening after supper" because Friend Whitely would "need the best of singing in the services."[47]

Charles Whitely's preaching certainly did cause a stir. The minister discovered that while students were willing to talk about religious matters, many of them, "hindered by past training," were "so superstitious and so ignorant of spiritual truths that it was difficult to make clear to them even the first steps in Christian experience." Every day brought some incident that illustrated the need for "a more concerted effort along religious lines." Still, in the end, "new life seemed to manifest itself throughout the school . . . and in the community." More than sixty "took some definite stand" to follow Jesus Christ and the missions board received more than twenty letters from students recounting how the revival had changed their lives. A minute of Indiana Yearly Meeting described the "spiritual awakening" that resulted from Whitely's revival efforts as of "more value than any other forward step taken at Southland this year."[48]

The apparently efficacious results of Charles Whitely's evangelism brought Raymond Jenkins's buoyant optimism to the fore. In late March he told correspondents that "the community is coming around slowly. . . . Mr. Freeland and Mrs. Busby feel that things are in a very good shape."[49] As the school year wound down, things did indeed seem to be looking up. Increased donations had made possible the installation of a water heater and bathing facilities in the teachers' quarters in Central Hall. Important steps were made to improve student morale with special privileges for the senior class: chaperoned picnics, unchaperoned walks, and a separate dinning table as well as Southland's participation in a "colored field day" sponsored by Helena public schools.[50] Thus, by early May, regardless of the unpaid grocery bill for $583.52 still sitting on his desk, Jenkins told the faculty that "in spite of a bad beginning, the school has made very definite strides. . . . All look forward to an even better year next Fall."[51]

Within a week of Jenkins's hopeful assessment of the school's generally improving condition, a petition signed by over a hundred school patrons and members of the Southland community was dispatched to the Home Missions Board in Richmond, asserting that under Raymond

Jenkins's leadership "their" school's operation had been "the most unsatisfactory in many years" and requesting "that the management be changed and that Mr. and Mrs. H. C. Wolford be re-employed as managing heads of the Institution."[52] As if this petition, apparently representing a consensus of local opinion (but obviously bearing marks of Harry Wolford's personal intervention), were not sufficiently disheartening, within a few days Raymond Jenkins was obliged to come to grips with still another shocking incident bringing the school year to a distressing and dismal conclusion.

The problem in question had begun the previous November when Jenkins had attempted to counsel Catherine Penney, a bright, attractive but "sassy" girl of seventeen who had become a disciplinary problem. Jenkins was immediately "taken to task" for his treatment of the girl by one of the black teachers, Joseph C. Penn, a Wilberforce graduate who had taught at Southland for several years. Soon afterwards Jenkins was approached by a group of local men who told of rumors spreading through the community that the principal had been "too familiar" in his actions toward Catherine Penney. Shocked by this attack on his integrity, Jenkins made clear that there had been no impropriety as his wife Cecilia had also been involved in the counseling sessions.[53] That particular storm had apparently blown over, but the acting director's difficulties with regard to Catherine Penney had barely begun.

Shortly after the school year ended in 1923, Jenkins wrote to Florence Jamison, the Southland teacher and Hampton graduate who had earlier recommended a live-in matron at the girls' dormitory, to disclose some "unpleasant facts" concerning Joseph Penn, once described in the *American Friend* as "a bright, capable young man" whose "good influence in the [boys'] dormitory was not lacking."[54] Jenkins eventually learned to his dismay that Penn had considerable influence in the girls' dormitory as well. Tipped-off by an informer, Jenkins discovered through the tear-filled testimony of Catherine Penney that Penn had "been having immoral relations" with her since early in the just-completed school year when, according to her account, after several unsuccessful attempts, he finally "overpowered her and committed the deed." These alleged assaults continued until Penn left for the summer and the facts were revealed. Furthermore, Catherine admitted that, spurred on by Penn and another black teacher, Mary Lee Moore, she had circulated a letter in the community that had resulted in the earlier accusatory visit from members of the community.[55] Jenkins was deeply affected by Catherine's story: "Poor girl, she was broken-hearted. . . . She tried so hard to keep away from him. . . . The girl is almost in a daze." When Catherine, pleading fear of family reprisals if her secret was discovered, asked to stay on at school during the summer, Jenkins acceded to her request. On the other hand, beyond vowing that Penn would never again darken Southland's door, the director took no immediate action, legal or otherwise, against him. Jenkins even put off a letter informing Penn that his nefarious acts had been discovered until after he traveled north to consult with the Home Missions Board.[56]

In this instance Raymond Jenkins's reluctance to bring charges or otherwise confront Joseph Penn probably saved him, the school, and the Home Missions Board from additional embarrassment. When Jenkins left for Indiana to confer with the board, one of the Quaker teachers, Leigh Barrett, offered to take charge through the quiet summer months for little more than his living expenses. Barrett got a good bit more than he bargained for. Among other things, he discovered that Catherine Penney's subsequent behavior belied her self-created image as a violated innocent. In late July Barrett reported on the outrageous behavior of Catherine and another female summer boarding student, Sam Judah Wells. Not only had these girls stolen items from teachers' rooms and remained insolent when detected, they had at least twice slipped away with boys for most of the night, bragged to other students about their escapades, and "told all kinds of stories in the community." As a final blow, Barrett discovered that Catherine was carrying on a regular, and romantic, correspondence with her supposed ravisher Joseph Penn, sending him letters under an assumed name.[57]

This distressing series of events ended with both Catherine and Sam Judah being dismissed from school and Joseph Penn disappearing from the scene.[58] Raymond Jenkins emerged from the episode a sadder and warier young man, considerably less sure about whom he could trust.[59]

In the meantime, Jenkins meetings with the Southland committee centered, as always, on financial considerations. With the help of special donations like a $1,900 bequest from the estate of Levi Jessup,[60] the committee had managed to keep Southland operating from week to week, but no funds were available even to begin making necessary repairs to a physical plant that had been allowed to deteriorate to the point where some buildings were unsafe. That was only the tip of the iceberg:

> Some rooms are already not habitable. The electric light plant and heating plant demand overhauling before use another year. Students' bedsprings in many cases are so broken as to tear the mattress to pieces. There are not enough chairs or dishes to go around. Water could not be served on the table last spring for lack of glasses or cups in which to serve it.[61]

In light of this gloomy discussion of Southland's deteriorating physical condition and the discouraging lack of response by the national Quaker community to the board's pleas for support, some members of the mission board's executive committee seriously considered the possibility of closing the school down. But at the moment when things appeared most discouraging, the committee was "moved almost to cheers by a stirring message from Raymond Jenkins" urging them to carry on despite any difficulties. Moved by Jenkins's emotional appeal, the board determined to borrow sufficient money from White's Institute[62] to meet immediate needs and continue operations for 1923–24 school year. In addition, the committee resolved to approach the Five Years Meeting with a new plan for raising twelve thousand dollars earmarked for the renovation of Southland's physical plant. These developments allowed Jenkins to dash off an excited telegram to Leigh Barrett: "Will run next year. All jobs safe. . . . clear the deck for action." Again, hopes were high, but the board felt compelled to add an ominous but realistic warning that if Southland failed to gain "adequate support . . . by June 1924, it will be necessary to close."[63]

Because Jenkins had come to believe he could best serve Southland as an educator rather than full-time administrator, he convinced the Home Missions Board to begin a search for

> some Friend and his wife, of mature years, wide experience, business ability, and spiritual power, with practical knowledge of farming, if possible, for at least two years of service in directing Southland through its readjustment period . . . with Raymond Jenkins as principal of the school.[64]

Not surprisingly, the paragons of ability and virtue set out in this job description never emerged from the ranks of American Quakerism. Ultimately, the board was, by necessity, compelled to fall back on Raymond and Cecilia Jenkins. They responded, as befit their youth, with renewed confidence, dedication and energy, but the mold for Southland shaped by Friends like the Clarks, the Chaces, and the Beards had been broken and could not be restored. Harry Wolford had spent most of two decades reshaping Southland in his own image, which eventually proved incompatible with the vision of northern Friends who paid most of the bills. Raymond Jenkins and the Southland committee believed, correctly as events would show, that Wolford, using his financial "hold" on local people, was largely responsible for organizing opposition to the new administration in hopes of forcing the Home Missions Board to restore the school to his control.[65] In addition, many potential Southland patrons, unlike earlier generations of freedmen, were not prepared passively to accept a newly minted version of "their" school, apparently formed out of whole cloth by distance white Quakers who seemed disinterested in local peoples' advice and consul. Given time and mutual forbearance, cultural gaps might have been sufficiently bridged to make Southland's survival a viable possibility, but, at the end of the day, money, or the lack of it, would be the final arbiter.

Certainly, Southland's shoestring finances were a glaring reality during that summer of 1923. What Leigh Barrett discovered immediately after he volunteered to "run the ranch " out of "a great love of Southland" was that the ranch was "running on the ragged edge." Two days after Jenkins left for Indiana, Barrett sent out a urgent plea that Ruthanna Simms "get us some money from some place" as the school creditors had begun "to talk of turning our accounts over to the Credit Association." The mission board's harassed secretary could only respond by sending stop-gap sums that were insufficient to cover even regular expenses. When a grocery bill of over five hundred dollars remained unpaid, the exasperated Helena wholesaler complained, "We never have found you people as derelict in the payment of your account."[66]

By tapping a variety of sources, Simms was able to scrounge up enough cash to allow Barrett to settle most accounts in Helena and pay the arrears owed several faculty members, although the considerable bill for an early shipment of winter coal could not be covered.[67] At the same time, Raymond Jenkins was writing to and visiting various well-to-do Friends and prominent black educators in an effort to get new pledges of support. Among those he contacted was Dr. James H. Dillard, president of the John F. Slater Fund, who responded with a promise of five hundred dollars and expressed an interest in providing future support.[68]

Amidst this scratching and clawing for a few hundred dollars here or there, the Southland committee determined to seek the assistance of one of their religious Society's most nationally prominent members, L. Hollingsworth Wood of New York. Pacifist leader, civil rights lawyer, and humanitarian activist, Wood was a founding member of the American Civil Liberties Union, the American Friends Service Committee, and the National Urban League, of which he was president from 1915 to 1941. He was also active in black education as a trustee of Fisk University and supporter of other Negro schools.[69] The committee believed that because of Wood's national reputation and influential connections he could be a pivotal fundraiser, able to tap into the resources of wealthy eastern Friends as well as to bring Southland to the attention of philanthropic organizations like the Rockefeller-funded General Education Board. Indeed, the enlistment of Hollingsworth Wood as Southland's chief East Coast advocate added a new dimension in the struggle to revive and renew Friends' educational mission in Arkansas, making Southland, for the first time, a truly national Quaker cause.[70]

While representative boards and committees of the Five Years Meeting sought to launch their largest and most aggressive campaign in Southland's behalf, the front-line struggle was still being fought on the ragged fields of the Arkansas Delta. When Raymond Jenkins returned to the campus, he was immediately faced with a lingering personnel crisis. After discovering the role that longtime Southland primary teacher Mary Lee Moore had played in spreading rumors about him and in helping organize the petition drive to remove him and bring back the Wolfords, Jenkins, feeling betrayed, determined not to reemploy her. As he told Ruthanna Simms "under the present circumstances it would be most unfortunate to have Miss Moore anywhere on the place." For her part, Moore appeared to be completely flabbergasted by the nonrenewal of her contract, which Jenkins, somewhat disingenuously, blamed on a shortage of funds. Eventually, after an unsuccessful attempt to reassume her position despite Jenkins's refusal to take her back, Moore threatened legal action and the Southland committee, after considering various ploys to put her off, agreed to an out of court settlement.[71]

The unpleasantness over the dismissal of Mary Lee Moore was only one aspect of the personnel problems facing Raymond Jenkins. For while he had told Moore that the fiscal situation necessitated staff cutbacks, the fact was that throughout the month of August Jenkins and various members of the Southland committee scrambled hither and yon seeking to fill the positions Jenkins felt were needed to ensure the improvements he envisioned.[72] Among the black faculty, Jenkins most admired his former Hampton colleague Walter Webb, but he was deeply shocked and surprised when, six weeks before school was to begin, Webb informed him that he was resigning his post as director of agricultural studies to take a similar post at Arkansas AM&N College in Pine Bluff. Webb later explained while he appreciated all Jenkins was trying to do, ill-will toward him in the Southland community "tore my mind all to pieces."[73] Jenkins was able to retain the services of two other experienced black teachers, Florence Jamison and Blanche Hudson, and eventually to hire a Georgia women, Sarah Neal, to complete the faculty for the primary grades of the newly titled Edward Bellis Training School.[74] In the end, the Southland catalog for 1923–24, reissued with high hopes after a hiatus of six years, listed a faculty of twelve as well as five staff members.[75] All but three of these were northern white Quakers, five of whom were volunteers working for ten dollars a month or simply room and board.[76] No replacement was found for Walter Webb, and agricultural teaching had to be spread among the academic staff. For all the difficulties and disappointments during the troublesome summer of 1923, the new catalog boldly declared that "the educational policy of the school has been strengthened, the standard of work raised and new courses added." As always, Southland stood "ready to do all it can to help Negro boys and girls to make the most of themselves in order that they may contribute their part to the welfare of this State and Nation."[77] So, as Southland entered its sixtieth year, the call to intellectual and moral uplift again rang out to the black citizens of Phillips County and the Arkansas Delta. How would they respond?

Chapter 12

The Guard Changes

1923–1924

I. A School That Has Slipped Down

When Raymond Jenkins wrote to thank Dr. J. H. Dillard for his assistance in helping Southland secure a five-hundred-dollar grant from the Slater Fund, he remarked on difficulties he was encountering in his struggle "to build up a school which has slipped down."[1] Jenkins was not exaggerating. Less than six weeks before classes were to begin, both he and the Southland committee were still frantically recruiting teachers. Even more daunting was the condition of the school's physical plant which on close inspection he found to be "even much worse than I had feared." In the course of his tour, Jenkins compiled a fourteen-page property inventory that, with characteristic thoroughness, listed every knife, fork, mop, and watering can on the campus.[2] He also discovered that the school's heating plant was close to collapse, the water pressure nearly nonexistent, and the dormitories structurally unsound. The latter were also in a filthy condition, largely owing to fact that the mattresses Wolford had bought were too large for the beds, resulting in serious damage to both. Every building on the grounds seemed to be overrun with bugs and bats. The entire plant was, in short, "rapidly going to pieces" and a good bit of money would be needed just to halt further deterioration.[3]

Human conditions, both within and beyond Southland's physical plant, also needed to be addressed. Most serious of these was the need to respond to the petition, signed by over a hundred local people and sent to the Home Missions Board at the close of the school year, again demanding Jenkins's removal and the reappointment of the Wolfords. The Southland committee drafted a response in early August, but before this was mailed to the signers the original version had been considerably amended. Three sentences were added in the final draft, two of which were of paeans of praise for the highly educated and sincerely dedicated Raymond Jenkins "whose whole aim in life is to be of help to the Negro" and whose pleas on Southland's behalf were the chief reason why the school had not already closed down.[4] These changes had, in fact, been inserted by Raymond's father, Atwood Jenkins.[5] The elder Jenkins's ringing defense of his son is understandable and, indeed, admirable, but it did not really speak to the causes or possible cures of alienation within the Southland community. The fact that the elder Jenkins had been permitted, even urged, to add his bit said more about the closely ordered hierarchy within Indiana Quaker circles than it did about efforts to placate local black people.[6] Their concerns were not about Raymond Jenkins's educational background, his efforts to improve standards, or even his sincere desire to be of service to American Negroes. Rather, the petitioners wanted "their" school to be operated in a way that they understood and approved. From past experience they were confident that Harry Wolford would run it that way. The fact that honest, generous, and large-hearted Quakers failed to understand this view was sad but not really surprising. In any case, such failures in communication certainly contributed to Southland eventual demise.

Before the committee's response to the dissenting petition arrived at Southland, Raymond Jenkins surmised that the situation in the community was not nearly so bad as he had feared. To begin, Blanche Hudson, one of Southland's veteran black teachers, told of resisting Harry Wolford's attempts to lure her away from the school and also expressed the view that Wolford's "money strings" on local people was the only reason many of them to agree to sign the petition. Jenkins also had a conversation with a local man whose name appeared on the petition, but who denied ever having signed such a document. This, of course, raised the question of how many local people had actually signed. In any case, Southland's beleaguered but optimistic young principal saw signs that support for Wolford was "dying out" as local people came to understand they had to "choose between him and the school"[7] For his part, Jenkins remained determined that "our standard . . . must be put in force this year," regardless of the possible effect on enrollment, because the sooner they broke free from "old ideas" the better.[8]

When the school opened in late September, Jenkins remarked that, in marked contrast to the previous year, there had been "no disorder or irregularities." There were also very few students, a mere forty when classes began. As usual, he put the best face on the situation, noting that new standards and regulations had eliminated the most troublesome pupils and that financial stringency arising from a poor cotton crop had probably caused many to wait until October to enroll. Alas, no last minute rush occurred and when registration closed on the first of November, only ninety-six students were attending classes, the lowest enrollment on record. Still, Jenkins insisted that this was largely because only those really interested in education had signed up. Overall, he said, "the grade of work . . . is much improved' and student "discipline, morals and religion" were on a higher level.[9]

Still, even the remarkably sanguine Raymond Jenkins had discouraging moments. For all his efforts, many problems with Southland's deteriorating physical plant remained unresolved and many bills remained unpaid. From her distant perch in Indiana, Ruthanna Simms, noting that Raymond had received nearly four thousand dollars during a six-week period, asked how it was possible for him to spend so much money? She even suggested that money matters might improve if he abandoned his advanced new accounting system and reverted to the simpler scheme that Harry Wolford had always used. Such questions and comments, coming amidst a sea of troubles, must have been at least annoying. Still, however wounded or irritated, the harassed Jenkins soldiered on, patiently explaining why his new accounting system was more accurate, why the old heating system was a complete disaster, and why, even with him and three other men working constantly, they could not "get caught up with the things that must be done to save this plant"—all of which, of course, cost money that he almost never had.[10]

Ruthanna Simms concerns were understandable. As executive secretary for both the mission board and its Southland committee, she was at the leading, and often jagged, edge of attempts to raise money and to deal with the queries and complaints from those who might provide financial assistance. For all of that, her letters often give the impression that her major concern was to keep every contributing Friend happy, whether they offered a substantial donation or a mere pittance. Thus, while Jenkins waited for money to pay the grocery bill, Simms gave him detailed instructions on how best to spend five- and ten-dollar donations and where to send miniature models of Southland's buildings for Sunday school class demonstrations.[11] For his part, Southland's principal made the point that while any money was welcome, they did not need knick-knacks or treats sent South by well-meaning Friends; better to sell these and send him the money.[12]

In his instructions to the mainly new Southland faculty, Raymond Jenkins emphasized the need, especially for white teachers, to ensure that by word and deed they rejected racial prejudice of any kind and used their influence to help overcome the "Race problem." At the same time, he reminded them that the school might close the next year "unless better cooperation existed in the community." There was some irony in the fact that some of Jenkins's own decisions, arising from his sense that a number of local people were still supporting Wolford's attempts to undermine his authority, helped to increase tensions in that community. For example, Martin's store near the campus had become an after-school gathering place for students seeking candy, soda pop, and gossip. Because he suspected that Mr. and Mrs. Martin were in collusion with Harry Wolford, Jenkins declared the Martins' store off-limits and established an on-campus shop, "for convenience only . . . not competition," to be used by students and staff. Students caught making purchases at Martins' store while out walking on Sundays "would forfeit their privilege to leave the grounds on Sunday."[13] However Jenkins justified such an action, it could scarcely be construed as a good-will gesture. Still, he remained baffled at the community's lack of appreciation for having a school like Southland close at hand.

Despite Jenkins's earlier sense that community relations had improved, by mid-October low enrollment and evidence of continued wide support for the Wolfords' return had soured him considerably. "The character of this community as a whole," he told Ruthanna Simms, "is lower than I ever realized. Rotten is almost too good a word in many ways." He remarked that Southland's veteran black teachers and local Quakers like the Busbys and Freelands had "lost all respect for the average person around here." While he believed that his reformation in rules and curriculum had helped rid the school of "a very undesirable class of students," he concluded that only a small beginning had been made in replacing these with a better class.[14]

In the meantime, there was no abatement to Southland's financial woes. Normal operating expenses immediately devoured whatever contributions were received from whatever source. When the trustees of Indiana Yearly Meeting sent a special allocation of $1,124, with instructions indicating what improvements their donation should cover, Jenkins eventually reported that expenses for basic maintenance of mechanical equipment were more than double what the Indiana Friends had provided.[15] Obviously, new sources needed to be tapped if Southland was to survive. The Southland committee had placed its hopes on the promise of Hollingsworth Wood to head up the special campaign to raise the twelve thousand dollars for necessary improvements to the school's physical plant and farming operations. Wood was indeed the sort of experienced, resourceful, well-connected, no-nonsense Quaker man of the world who might get the job done. After committing himself to work for this development, Wood determined to combine a long-planned trip to a conference in Kansas City with a visit to Southland in order to discover at first hand the strengths and weaknesses of the institute he was attempting to save. He was encouraged in this effort by Dr. James Dillard, head of the Slater Fund, who believed that the school was indeed "well worth developing."[16]

The Southland committee was delighted by the prospect of Wood's inspection tour, but before he could render an opinion on what he found in Arkansas, another challenge to Southland's survival emerged from within the ranks of American Quakerism. In late October the *American Friend* published a letter from Alden Knight, a Quaker minister from Iowa, that was severely critical of the mission board's inordinate financial commitment "to an institution that has in fifty years brought no visible results" in missionary terms. As much as some might take comfort in their Society's "fine sentiments" and "traditional friendliness to the Negro," Knight continued, spending dollars on Southland that "get us nowhere with the Negro" was "a suicidal policy" of no practical advantage to the Society of Friends. Southland, he concluded, should be placed in proper perspective, that is, closed down.[17] Ruthanna Simms, who had already expressed fears that Southland's low enrollment and large staff might be "difficult to justify to many Friends," wondered how Jenkins or the board or both should respond to Knight's attack. For his part, Southland's principal, aglow in the wake Hollingsworth Wood's just-completed visit, demurred, noting that he had larger concerns in working to establish a "real constructive program at the school."[18] Wood himself was "greatly pleased with what he found at Southland," especially the quality of teaching he had observed. He concluded that the school was the "only bright spot in a . . . depressed country" on the bottom rung of the social and economic ladder. In such circumstances, the "need of a really first-class industrial school with proper ideals of education. . . . cannot be over-estimated."[19]

Hollingsworth Wood's enthusiastic endorsement of the new and exalted vision of Southland's future prospects immediately broadened the base of the mission board's fundraising activities. His connections with weighty and wealthy eastern Friends as well as with the leaders of educational and philanthropic organizations supporting attempts to improve educational possibilities for black Americans seemed to augur well for that future. Wood quickly set to work, reminding D. Elton Trueblood, a rising young Quaker star, of the diminution of their Society's historic role in aiding oppressed black people and of Southland's potential as the vehicle for restoring Quakerism's place of honor in the struggle for human freedom and dignity. Trueblood, for one, noted that he had previously failed to grasp the opportunity Southland might provide in allowing their Society to "find its soul in regard to the Negro."[20] But for all Wood's rousing appeal to the consciences of wealthy and important Friends, no great surge of Quaker donations poured into the nearly dried-up coffers of the Home Missions Board.[21]

The first prominent non-Friend Wood approached regarding Southland was fellow New Yorker Jackson Davis, general field agent for the General Education Board (GEB). Davis had visited Southland in 1921 as a part of the inspection team that had set in motion the mission board's efforts to upgrade the school's educational standards and infrastructure, which eventually led to Harry Wolford's forced resignation in 1922. Thus, Davis was familiar with the school and believed it was "situated in a needy field, where it can exert a fine influence," but he did not believe that such a small, local institution "would need any assistance from our Board for maintenance."[22]

While Hollingsworth Wood set about the task of convincing Jackson Davis and the General Education Board that the Five Years Meeting was determined that Southland should indeed become the sort of nationally significant school that the GEB was created to support, Raymond Jenkins was seeking assistance closer at hand. In late October he requested that J. A. Presson, supervisor of Negro schools in Arkansas, conduct a critical inspection of Southland, especially its normal program. Presson, who had recently completed a report of educational activities in Negro schools, was a strong advocate of a Tuskegee-Hampton-type program, stressing the three Rs plus the sort of industrial and agricultural training that would "prepare the girls and boys for more efficient work" at home and on the farm.[23] When he visited Southland in late November 1923, he was sufficiently impressed to grant the school's normal graduates two-year state teaching certificates without examination.[24] This encouraging development was quickly followed by a letter to Jenkins from Leo M. Favrot, field agent for the GEB and former state supervisor for Arkansas's black education who had also been part of the 1921 inspection team. Favrot's letter, promising a visit in December to gain some idea of the school's most important needs, seemed a direct respond to Hollingsworth Wood's recent pleas to the GEB on Southland's behalf. Favrot, like his former colleague Presson, was also deeply influenced by the Tuskegee-Hampton model for black education that Raymond Jenkins was attempting to emulate at Southland.[25]

Despite terrible road conditions, Favrot managed to spend a few hours at Southland shortly before Christmas, and he submitted a fairly detailed report of his observations. While he took note of the serious problems facing the school, especially its crumbling infrastructure and the lost of confidence among many local residents, Favrot was "most strongly" impressed with "the youth, energy, capacity for organization, competence and enthusiasm of the new principal, Mr. Raymond Jenkins." Given Jenkins's "capacity and determination," the support of his committed staff, the more rigorous standards being imposed, and "the splendid field in which Southland Institute has to work, there is no reason why it should not grow into an institution of tremendous influence and importance in that section of the South."[26]

Southland could best reach this potential, Favrot believed, by working in tandem with an institution like a new Rosenwald school[27] that would assume responsibility for primary instruction while the Quaker academy addressed the upper grades, including a two-year teacher-training program whose students would have a ready venue for practice teaching in the associated primary school. Favrot concluded with a note of caution, emphasizing that no significant expansion should be attempted until local people's confidence in the school was restored, educational reforms were fully implemented, and sufficient improvements were made to ensure efficient service for its patrons. Still, in a separate note to Raymond Jenkins, Favrot praised the young principal's "eager desire to do the right thing" as reflecting a spirit that should "measure up to a high standard of success."[28]

Favrot's comments seemed guaranteed to warm the hearts of the Southland committee and mission board, offering a ringing endorsement of both their grand plan for the school's future and their choice of Raymond Jenkins to implement it. As for restoring the confidence of local people, developments were a bit less promising. In his efforts to win back the community, Jenkins inaugurated a free night school offering a variety of practical and academic classes, but found the response disappointing because of "a general lack of interest in anything for the betterment of the community." Furthermore, he surmised that Harry Wolford had conspired with local individuals to prevent Southland from getting a post office on campus, and, apparently for security purposes, Jenkins advised Friends to send mail to Lexa rather than to the post office at Martins' store.[29] An even more telling illustration of the continuing difficulty in bridging the gap between northern Quaker sensibilities and local standards was a letter from Southland teacher Clay Treadway to the Phillips County District Attorney asking him to put a stop to events like the Christmas Day shooting match in front of Martins' store, using live geese and turkeys. Treadway indignantly suggested that, even in the absence of specific laws against mistreatment of animals, "these colored brethren be asked to find some better form of amusement than unnecessary cruelty to dumb and harmless geese and turkeys."[30] There is no record of any action being taken; indeed, one can imagine the district attorney shaking his head and wondering what that fool Yankee was babbling about.

Raymond Jenkins was not on hand to observe the turkey shoot. He had returned to Indiana for a meeting with representatives of the mission board. Despite the positive aspects of the Favrot report, they were forced to wrestle with "some pretty hard problems," nearly all of which had to do with finances. These gloomy consultations were dramatically recounted in an article in the *American Friend* by the Five Years Meeting general secretary Walter Woodward.[31] Discussion centered around three vital objectives established by the Southland committee: 1) efficient management, 2) revamping the physical plant, and 3) "a sound, progressive policy for meeting new demands for Negro betterment." Those present agreed that Jenkins's "aggressive new regime" had effectively replaced the "easy going, benevolent" arrangements of the Wolford era. However, the remaining two goals could only be solved with dollars that, despite their best efforts, had not been forthcoming. Such "cold, depressing facts" again seemed to point, inevitably, to closing down the school. At this crucial juncture, two representatives of the Board of Young Friends were admitted to the meeting and the tenor of deliberations was immediately transformed. These Young Friends had come "gripped with a sense of the call of God through Southland." They believed that a concerted effort to save Southland might rouse their entire religious society from its apparent complacency. As the executive secretary of the Young Friends put it, "so many Quakers . . . don't seem to have a great deal of . . . religion," let alone a proper concern with regard to America's racial crisis. Moved by these earnest supplications, the board decided it could not close Southland's doors without "giving youth its chance" to make Southland "a symbol and embodiment of the ideal of Quaker service." Thus, a final decision was put off until early March 1924 in hopes that the Young Friends movement might unite American Quakers for the first time since the Civil War in a truly national effort to do their part in the struggle for racial justice and harmony.[32]

This crucial meeting was indeed followed by an outpouring of youthful enthusiasm and idealism. Young Friends from across the country promised to throw themselves into the fight: "O, how dare we as Friends just now of all times, abandon our even feeble testimony that black men in America are . . . truly our brothers"; "It seems impossible to me that Friends can *let go*"; abandoning Southland "would be a tragic mistake, almost traitorous in character"; "I promise to give eight dollars a year for the next three years." Their heartfelt messages reached across a century of sometimes-bitter division to draw young Hicksite Friends into the struggle to save this Orthodox academy.[33]

Young Friends, "deeply stirred," possessed the will but, alas, lacked the means to carry out a successful rescue operation. Most of the "unpleasant things" that Raymond Jenkins reported on after his return to Southland could only be saved with cold, hard cash. More than a few wealthy, and generous, older Quakers would be required to replace the furnaces that had broken down in the school building and the boys' dormitory during the coldest week of the winter.[34] Upon hearing news of this latest disaster, Ruthanna Simms offered her admiration for Raymond's courage and endurance in facing difficulties, but rather than money, she promised to publish an article about the frozen campus in the next *American Friend* with hopes it would bring in sizeable sympathetic contributions.[35]

By return mail Jenkins reported a fire in the school's electrical power plant that left the entire campus temporarily without heat or light. At one point, classes had to be dismissed when a new wave of cold air had sent everyone looking for a warm place. Furthermore, such constant breakdowns did nothing to improve the school's standing with real or potential patrons. Jenkins concluded that the choices were either to close down or spend at least $25,000 to put things right.[36] Such a figure was certainly in keeping with Jenkins's vision of the sort of Tuskegee-Hampton model he had in mind, but Simms had to point out that some people with experience in operating schools "have said very frankly that the budget is larger than it ought to be." Jenkins, seeking the means to pay the grocery bill, indignantly replied that people who thought the budget was excessive should be told that there was "a job down here . . . when ever they want it." So far as he was concerned, something "definite and tangible" had to be done regarding finances, and if nothing changed, "the Board need not . . . consider me as an applicant for . . . next year" even if the school was still open.[37]

Jenkins followed this outburst by submitting his budget estimates for the next year, optimistically based on student populations of 150 to 200. He assumed that revenue from tuition, board, and other sources would cover only half the operating expenses, excluding teachers' salaries and insurance. The balance of over $35,000, including $25,000 for necessary new equipment, would have to come from donations provided by Quaker or other outside sources.[38]

While it is not difficult to see why even committed Friends might find this excessive, Jenkins and his advocates desperately hoped that the combination of Leo Favrot's favorable report and Hollingsworth Wood's powerful influence would convince the General Education Board to become the *deus ex machina* needed to rescue Southland. Officials at the GEB had, in fact, begun to consider the school's plight and that board's initial response revealed a good deal about Southland, past and present. After studying Favrot's report, GEB director H. J. Thorkelson wrote to Hollingsworth Wood setting out a comparison between the school's size and operating expenses in 1923 and a decade earlier. Under H. C. Wolford's direction in 1913 Southland had 352 students with a yearly income from all sources of $4,115; a decade later with a student population of 95, its total income was $21,750. Such figures gave strong indication that Wolford had operated, however primitively, within the limits of resources available to him.[39] Jenkins, on the other hand, earnestly believed that Southland's budget needed to reflect his exalted ideal of what the school should become.

At least for the moment, Raymond Jenkins's vision won the day. The "Southland Emergency Campaign" projected an annual operating budget of $20,500 for three years, of which $16,500 was to come "from the North." However, this plan would be implemented only if "funds were in sight . . . to pay the bills and operate the School in a creditable manner" by the 5 March deadline.[40] With less than a month to meet this target date, the Southland emergency campaign swung into action by imploring 175 Friends designated as "Southland Multipliers" to send money and pledges and to ask relatives and friends to follow suit. If hundreds of Friends rather than dozens sacrificed in the school's behalf, the necessary funds could easily be raised.[41]

One new and innovative aspect of the emergency campaign was an attempt to enlist Southland alumni, especially those living in large urban centers like Chicago, Detroit, and Washington DC in the fundraising effort. To this end, Jenkins approached one of Southland's most distinguished graduates, Anna M. Paschal Strong, principal of Robert R. Moton High School in Marianna, Arkansas,[42] to write a letter of solicitation to all alumni whose addresses were known.[43] Strong responded with a heartfelt plea for all former students to join in the effort to the prevent the "terrible tragedy" threatening their beloved alma mater. Her letter brought an immediate and often emotional wave of response.[44] As a result of this initiative, Southland alumni in Chicago sent $115 in cash and a group of about twenty Detroit alumni set a goal of raising $2,000.[45] Eventually a Southland Alumni Exchange was established, which coordinated correspondence among groups or individuals in Washington DC, St. Louis, Cleveland, and other cities. Alumni in nine states and the

District of Columbia contributed over $2,000, $1,500 from the Chicago group alone.[46] This effort was gratifying, but however impressively Southland's former students had prospered, their contributions were merely a symbolic witness to American Friends of how important the school had been and how much more might be accomplished if, at a time when philanthropic bodies were expressing real interest in Southland, they threw their combined weight into ensuring the school's survival.

Ruthanna Simms, Hollingsworth Wood, and others continued to press wealthy and influential Friends "to pull together in connection with Southland . . . and the whole question of the Negro in our midst." Contributions were forthcoming but most were small, and by the end of February only about $1,000 in cash and pledges had been raised toward the first year's $12,000 emergency fund. Still, Ruthanna Simms believed that with the awakening of alumni loyalty and Young Friends' deepening concern, it was not time to contemplate surrender.[47] Hollingsworth Wood expected his proselytizing efforts among eastern Friends would eventually result in "some thousands" in new donations. But both he and the mission board were pinning their hopes on substantial help from the General Education Board, particularly since the Southland emergency fund made no provision for infrastructure repair. In this regard, Leo Favrot of the GEB had estimated that $10,000 would provide for necessary improvements in heating, lighting, water, and sewerage, but Raymond Jenkins own estimates, which seemed to grow exponentially, eventually reached close to $40,000, part of which he envisioned as being offset by volunteer Quaker and student labor. His view was that since the GEB had, so far, never "done anything" for Southland, they should be prepared to offer "real aid" in the present circumstances.[48]

For Jenkins, the present circumstances continued to be extremely trying. To begin, he had to report another case of immorality involving "two of our best boys and girls" who had to be removed from school on account of one of the girls being pregnant. Furthermore, the child's parents not only refused to take her back but threatened to sue him for what had occurred while she was in his charge. Jenkins managed to place the girl with an aunt who lived nearby, but Southland's local reputation suffered another blow as a result.[49] Rumors also continued to spread that Harry Wolford was poised to buy the school and reopen it under his direction. This was more than Jenkins could bear. He told Ruthanna

Simms that he would rather see the place "rot to the ground" than allow Wolford to regain control.[50]

Simms assured Jenkins that the school was safe from Wolford's wiles, although she had to add that Hollingsworth Wood had discovered that the General Education Board's budget for the current year was "entirely full" and, thus, no grant for Southland could be forthcoming until the next fiscal year. Wood had, however, extracted a promise that GEB officials would visit the school that spring, and he was confident that "a pretty substantial sum for improvements" could be expected from the board during the next year. These developments were bitterly disappointing to Simms who felt crushed between the fact that last minute contributions had nearly met the mission board's $12,000 emergency-fund goal and the knowledge that the board's narrow focus on Southland meant that its budget for other Quaker causes was floundering.[51] In a moment of un-Quakerly frustration and exasperation she told Wood

> you do not appreciate how *many* Friends know practically nothing of business methods. Already they think we are embezzling funds here at the Central Office. If we close Southland even though the $12,000 is raised, they will accuse us of not keeping our promise, regardless of the fact that we never made one. I am much discouraged today.[52]

However downcast, Simms felt a spark of hope in Wood's assurances that the GEB would eventually come through. Would it be possible, she inquired of Jenkins, for the school to operate for one more year without the without new heating and lighting plants? After consulting with the Southland staff, Jenkins telegraphed an emphatic "NO." Without improvements there would be nothing to attract students and operating costs would outweigh educational returns.[53] Surely this was conclusive. But the day before the Southland committee gathered to decide the school's fate, Ruthanna Simms, rebounding from her recent slough of despond, telegraphed Jenkins to say that support for Southland was running so strong that she feared "friction" if the school closed for even one year. What, she asked, would be the minimum operating budget?[54]

In a dramatic four-hour session on 5 March, the Southland committee determined to carry on, having become convinced that closing, even temporarily, would "jeopardize the rising tide of interest and support."

"No surrender" messages and donations had been received from a hundred people, including one from a wealthy Friend who promised to pay up any unpledged balance to the $12,000 emergency fund. Young Friends had sent in over 200 letters and $750 to keep the Southland dream alive through its symbolically important sixtieth-anniversary year. With provisions for a reduced staff and sizeable increases in tuition and board fees, the committee projected an operating budget of over $28,000, with the addition of $4,000 from the emergency fund to provide for stop-gap improvements while awaiting the expected large commitment from the GEB.[55]

The decision to keep the school open was obviously popular move, but, however bold, it did not really address a multiple of problems that still needed to be considered, most significantly raising the money necessary to met relentlessly daunting budgetary projections. Her confidence restored, Ruthanna Simms set out to meet that challenge. One of her first steps was to approach Sarah Swift, the elderly eastern Friend who had saved the day by giving nearly $2,000 to put the emergency fund over the top, and, like Oliver Twist, to ask for more, $5,000 more. Obviously touched by Southland's plight, Swift gave nearly that much more, insisting, in the best Quaker spirit, only on anonymity.[56]

On the ground in Arkansas, Jenkins and his staff, while pleased with the decision to stay afloat, had serious difficulty with committee's recommendation to increase school fees. They feared that, given both the economic circumstances of most of the school's patrons and staff's efforts to regain the confidence of local people, "to increase tuition at the present time would be ruinous." Furthermore, Jenkins believed the mission board was not facing up to the fact that Southland could not "*be operated . . . next year without these repairs and equipment.*" While used equipment and voluntary labor might significantly reduce costs, so far as he was concerned, the board had to find some way to pay for the necessary improvements.[57]

II. Not to Slump Back into a Minor Place

In the meantime, the immediate focus of Jenkins's attempts to restore harmonious relations with the community was a banquet intended both to celebrate Southland's sixtieth anniversary and to recognize local people who had given steadfast support to the school. Jenkins was able to enlist the much-admired Anna P. Strong as featured speaker for the "Booster-Anniversary" gala, which he deemed "a grand success," reflecting a spirit that promised "more cooperation and good feeling from the rest of the Community."[58]

But if Southland's principal was pleased by the prospect of improved relations with the school's neighbors, he remained unhappy about both the slow academic progress and general deportment of many students. "The student body has got away from us," he told Ruthanna Simms, and he did not believe things would improve until sufficient physical and education changes were made to draw the sort of student body needed to make Southland the school it ought to be.[59] As fervently as Jenkins might wish for a better class of student, he was required to deal with ones who were on hand. At times, this was a distinctly unpleasant duty as when, a few days after the successful banquet, he had to report new "trouble about immorality." In this instance, ten students (more than the 10 percent of the student body) were expelled as a result of elicit activities in the girls' dormitory. Among these was one of the school's most charming, and troublesome, pupils, Derric Sylva.[60] The bright and articulate son of a Cuban clergyman, Derric had caught the eye of several visiting Friends who believed him to be a lad of considerable promise, perhaps even in religious work. For Jenkins, however, young Sylva had been no end of trouble, challenging his teachers, leaving campus without permission, once for several months, and, shortly before his expulsion, attempting to obtain money from a Quaker school in Jamaica under false pretenses.[61]

As if this latest scandal was not a sufficient distraction, Southland's embattled principal was simultaneously confronted with serious complaints and accusations by Harry Patten, a disaffected staff member. According to Jenkins, Patten was a poor worker and disruptive influence. Not only had his ill-tempered outbursts nearly "caused student riots," but he had also made abusive comments about black colleagues. After verbally assaulting Jenkins as "weak and a poor manager," Patten resigned and demanded money for travel to Indiana. When Jenkins refused, Patten "let loose about my personal religious life" and stormed off the campus in the company of Leigh Barrett, who appeared sympathetic to the recusant's plight. Indeed, after Barrett returned from taking Patten to the railway station, Jenkins was shocked to see him in the company of Will Newsome, a local Wolford loyalist Jenkins considered to be "*our arch enemy,*" spreading false and misleading rumors in the community.[62]

In fact, this unseemly and distinctly un-Quakerly incident added a new and disturbing dimension to the Southland saga. From Arkansas Patten immediately headed for Richmond where he was closeted for several hours with members of the Southland committee. The upshot, as Ruthanna Simms told Hollingsworth Wood, was that Patten might cause "considerable trouble" for their cause. In addition to his theological mud slinging at Jenkins and "half the staff," Patten was circulating a letter, written by Leigh Barrett, advising Kansas Friends "to withhold further support from the school" because Jenkins and some other members of the staff were "not orthodox." This onslaught of internal discord and negative publicity convinced Simms that Raymond Jenkins was correct in seeing the nefarious influence of Harry Wolford at the root of nearly every difficulty. In contrast, Wood responded to this unfolding drama with considerable impatience. To begin, he said, incessant harping on Wolford's misdeeds reminded him of that "school of religious thought . . . always pinning things on the devil personally." As for the theological criticism, it merely confirmed his low opinion of Leigh Barrett and reaffirmed his belief that low-paid volunteers needed to be replaced by professionally trained individuals whose first priority was education rather than some personal vision of Quaker orthodoxy.[63]

For all his annoyance with recent developments, Wood also had encouraging news. Citing Jackson Davis's comments to a recent professional gathering that Southland was "going to be one of the first-class Quaker schools," he believed that Davis, the key man in GEB decision-making, had become a strong supporter of their cause. Wood also learned that Davis and Leo Favrot were planning another visit to Southland. He saw this as an opportunity "to keep before the General Education Board an idea of something better than a patched-up school" and to show that Friends had "both vigor and vision."[64]

Raymond Jenkins could not have agreed more. His view remained that if Southland was "not to slump back into a minor place," the mission board should pull out all stops and request the sort of assistance that could make the school's drive for first-class status a reality.[65] In the meantime, he would have to make do with two thousand dollars, extracted from Sarah Swift's recent largess, that the Southland committee made available for essential repairs. But even this relatively trifling sum was put on hold pending the visit of Jackson Davis and his associates.[66] Davis duly arrived on 9 April accompanied by a considerable entourage, including Leo Favrot and representatives of the Rosenwald and the Jeanes-Slater funds as well as Arkansas's state superintendent of schools.

After guiding these influential visitors through an all-day inspection tour of Southland's facilities, Raymond Jenkins was convinced that they were, as a body, "vitally interested" in the school and in full agreement with his view that its survival depended on immediate revitalization of the physical plant as well as improved academic standards. He was particularly impressed by Jackson Davis's enthusiasm about the school's future promise and was so sure of Davis's support that he recommended the Southland committee up the ante by asking the GEB to provide the entire $40,000 needed to implement improvements and repairs: "I firmly believe that these Boards are ready to believe in us if we can show we believe in ourselves."[67]

Buoyed up by Jenkins's report and urged on by Hollingsworth Wood's assurances of GEB support, the Southland committee determined to seize the moment. Arrangements were made to send Howard Gluys, an Earlham engineering professor, to ascertain precisely what needed to be fixed and how much might be saved if volunteer labor and government surplus equipment could be secured. The committee also made efforts to recruit J. A. Henley, former physical plant manager at Guilford College, to assume control of Southland farming operations. In the meantime, Wood kept close watch on deliberations at the GEB, pushing Jackson Davis for estimates on the amount of support Southland might expect.[68]

Encouraged by this burst of activity, Jenkins was also happy to report that "the feeling between the community and the school is the best I have seen it." Other local considerations, chiefly financial, were less pleasing. Holding, among other obligations, an unpaid bill of over four hundred dollars from the long-suffering wholesale grocer, he was "almost afraid to go to Helena to buy anything." Teachers salaries were also considerably in arrears.[69] While the need for operating funds was an enduring problem, there were other difficulties, newly evolved and more serious. For one, the Southland committee seemed puzzled by the negative reaction by Jenkins and his staff to the committee's plan to increase revenue by raising fees for patrons who were enjoying the benefits of the school but paying only a minuscule part of the cost of operations. Jenkins acknowledged that local people might not be paying enough, but asserted that, in the circumstances, they could see no reason to pay more: "School to them is just school," he said, and until Southland could offer something better than it currently did, raising fees would be seriously ill-advised. He added, with considerable pique, that given the pace at which the mission board was moving to acquire needed equipment, "I feel confident that we will not have a one single thing here before school is out to show . . . that we mean business."[70] Apparently impressed by this outburst, the Southland committee did not, at least, increase school fees.

A potentially even more contentious issue was bound up in the theological criticisms voiced by dissident members of the Southland staff. Some of these, including Leigh Barrett and his wife, were refusing to attend chapel services that they considered inappropriate or unorthodox.[71] Jenkins had responded to theological criticisms in what Ruthanna Simms described as a "fine long letter" to the Home Missions Board. Nonetheless, she warned Hollingsworth Wood that the situation was "pretty bad" and some members of the Southland committee felt it was "not possible to continue Raymond another year as Director of the school." Wood replied with undisguised revulsion: "As to the theological problem, I think it is next to suicide to change principals on any such basis." Jenkins had more knowledge of the situation than any possible replacement and GEB officials would not understand why a change was being made at such a crucial time. "Frankly," he concluded, "I cannot see myself bothering about the school at all if this sort of thing is contemplated."[72]

Despite Wood's vehemence, Simms replied that the questions surrounding Jenkins's continued tenure as principal were "so important" and had "so many angles" that it was impossible to avoid a showdown at the next committee meeting. Wood replied that since the GEB's interest in Southland was largely based on "Jackson's Davis' appreciation of and confidence in Raymond," their cause would be "considerably jeopardized" by any change in the school's leadership.[73] This view was overwhelmingly confirmed by a letter from Davis's right-hand man Leo Favrot, which concluded with a ringing endorsement of Raymond Jenkins:

> His whole soul is wrapped up in trying to improve the school. He has a clear vision of what the school needs, and in the judgment of

> the men who have seen him work, he needs a free hand . . . and the wholehearted support of the Society of Friends. . . . He is genuine, sincere, full of energy, and understands the physical needs of the school. . . . Except for the faith, buoyancy and determination of Mr. Jenkins, I should be inclined to advise that it be left to die. With Raymond Jenkins in charge, however, I believe it can be revived.[74]

Favrot's letter, apparently representing the GEB's position, was undoubtedly decisive. In the end, the Southland committee voted "unanimously" to retain Jenkins as principal and to support his policies despite his "apparent inability to win the loyalty . . . of his staff." Serious criticisms in this regard, Simms related to Wood, had come even from those sympathetic with his theological stance, but the committee decided that he deserved the chance, for once, to work with the sort of " properly qualified . . . workers" they planned to hire for the next school year.[75]

Within a week of the decision to retain Jenkins as principal, Hollingsworth Wood learned that the General Education Board had voted to appropriate twenty thousand dollars, half the sum needed for Southland's improvements, if Friends could raise the other half by October 1924.[76]

Had the stone finally been rolled to the top of the hill?

Chapter 13

Last Days

1924–1925

Southland had survived its sixtieth year and, in anticipation of the largess of the General Education Board, seemed assured a sixty-first. Yet, only the funds provided by 309 Quaker contributors, ranging from $1 to $4000, had made it possible for the school to remain open. And the Home Missions Board would have to depend on the continued generosity of Friends to take full advantage of the GEB's $20,000 offer. In making their case for such help, the board described Southland as "a channel of Christian service"; Raymond Jenkins added that the school presented American Friends with "a God-given opportunity. . . in working out the question of race relations"; Hollingsworth Wood represented the Arkansas mission as "the hand of the Society of Friends in the place where such a hand is most needed, where our white civilization is failing most outrageously to meet the need of the Negro."[1]

The school year had closed on a high note with a student production of the operetta "Pocahontas" attended by a large crowd, including ten white citizens of Helena, one of whom was a bank president. Soon thereafter, a student "Fair and Exhibit" brought the president of the Helena Chamber of Commerce to the Southland campus where he volunteered "very helpful" advice and encouragement.[2] Bolstered by recent developments and determined to secure a larger enrollment and a better class of students, over the summer Raymond Jenkins sent out 1,800 letters to black high schools in Arkansas and surrounding states inviting applications. At the same time, he attempted to negate Harry Wolford's continued harmful influence. In a letter addressed to two prominent recent visitors to Southland, S. L. Smith of the Rosenwald Fund and Arkansas superintendent of schools A. B. Hill, Jenkins complained that Wolford had exerted his "strong financial hold" on local people to have himself elected a director of Phillips County Public School District 16. From this position Wolford had manipulated a meeting to ensure the passage of provisions that excluded Southland from plans for future expansion of district schools. Jenkins claimed that these actions were illegal because Wolford was not resident in the school district he purported to represent. While this complaint was endorsed by Arkansas state school officials, it is not clear if Wolford was ever removed from his position.[3] In any case, Jenkins soon had the satisfaction of knowing that his preoccupation with Harry Wolford as Southland's bête noire was not simply a distracting obsession.

To begin, during the summer of 1924, a question emerged as to authenticity of Harry Wolford's claim to membership in the Society of Friends. Suspicions were raised after it was discovered that his name did not appear on the membership list of the New Westville Monthly Meeting that Wolford claimed as his meeting of origin. As it turned out, this was a false alarm.[4] Shortly thereafter, however, Jenkins received a letter from Charlotte Hawkins Brown, principal of the Palmer Memorial Institute in Sedalia, North Carolina, seeking information about her husband, John William Moses, late of Southland, who was listed as business manager on Palmer Institute stationary. Why, she asked, had Moses been dismissed from Southland and why, in light of his dismissal, had the Wolfords provided him with a superlative recommendation when he sought employment at her school? Discreetly avoiding personal comment, Jenkins referred Hawkins Brown to Walter C. Woodward, executive secretary of the Five Years Meeting. Hawkins Brown's letters to Woodward related how she had employed John W. Moses on the basis of outstanding recommendations from the Wolfords and Tuskegee Institute as well as his impressive educational credentials. Obviously swept off her feet by his charm as well his "splendid work," Hawkins Brown married Moses after a whirlwind courtship, only to discover a few months later that he was "a fraud and a swindler" whose academic credentials were forged and whose friendship with Mrs. Wolford was "of a criminal nature."[5] Seeking to expose the dubious character of the man she accused of carrying out "one of the greatest frauds ever perpetrated upon my race," Hawkins Brown enclosed an undated letter from H. C. Wolford to John W. Moses that set out a plan of campaign against Southland and Raymond Jenkins:

> The object with us is to *keep away* students, *keep away* donations, and to *irritate Jenkins* and the *Board* by criticizing the *management* and Board—but to say or do nothing they can use to advantage in their own cause.[6]

In response, Woodward put as much distance as possible between John W. Moses and any agency of the Society of Friends, noting the Home Missions Board had determined that Moses's "attitude and bearing" had produced damaging consequences for Southland. He added that any recommendation from individuals connected with the school must have come from the Wolfords and emphasized that the only recommendation from Southland's management committee was that Moses "leave the institution" immediately. Woodward also suggested Hawkins Brown contact A. M. Gardner, a lawyer and member of the Southland committee, as someone who might aid her in pursuing a legal case against her former husband. It was Gardener, Woodward said, who had "finally succeeded in getting Mr. Moses to depart from Southland."[7]

While much about the life and activities of John W. Moses remains unclear, Charlotte Hawkins Brown's biographers have uncovered some useful evidence. They describe Moses as "a very handsome" ladies man, "smooth-talking . . . with much charisma" and mental agility who was born in British Guiana. Before he was hired at Southland, he did attend Tuskegee but left without taking a degree. Less than a year after he married Hawkins Brown, she ended the marriage upon discovering evidence of his infidelity and duplicity. He may also have made off with funds entrusted to him as the Palmer Institute's business manager. There is no extant record of further contact between Moses and the Wolfords, but sources have traced him to New York City where Mrs. Wolford lived, apart from her husband, for some time after leaving Southland.[8]

Whatever sense of justification Raymond Jenkins may have felt as a result of these startling and scandalous revelations concerning Wolford's deceitful protégé, Southland's financial circumstances, pending the hoped for influx of GEB funds, remained precarious. At the end of the school year, half of Sarah Swift's four-thousand-dollar donation, first fruits of the projected twenty thousand needed to match the General Education Board's grant, had to be used to pay outstanding bills and teachers' salaries. The Southland committee felt able to use the money in this way because they had been informed through Hollingsworth Wood that the GEB would, at intervals, begin making pro rata payments to match the donations that flowed into Southland's emergency fund.[9] Ruthanna Simms was pleased to note that, in the wake of the GEB's pledge, even the Home Missions Board's two "most conservative members were quite won over to the conviction that Southland is really going ahead." She suggested that Jenkins use the occasion of Southland's pending commencement to assure patrons that adequate light, heat, and water would be provided during the next school year. In this atmosphere of great expectations, the first round of repairs to school buildings was authorized, and a Quaker engineer and surveyor were scheduled to be dispatched from Indiana to take charge of installing the necessary mechanical equipment and constructing a new drainage system. The Southland committee also confirmed the employment of Jesse Henley and his family to take charge of the Southland farm and physical plant, with the expectation that they would eventually be housed in one of the "cottage homes" to be built on the campus for them and for Raymond and Celicia Jenkins.[10] No mention was made of how this ambitious new building project would be financed; perhaps there was a perception that, once engaged, the General Education Board would continue open-ended support for what Jackson Davis had, after all, called "your splendid work."[11]

By mid-June, Jenkins reported the preliminary painting and carpentry work was "going along nicely," although the school's bank account was overdrawn and the workmen remained unpaid. He was only half joking when he pleaded for enough money to ensure that "we will not yet get put in jail," but he was deadly serious in asking Hollingsworth Wood if he could not "place a bomb under somebody" on the mission board in order to "get things started."[12]

While Hollingsworth Wood and other weighty Friends attempted to clear the decks for the arrival of GEB matching funds, Jenkins got only a few hundred dollars operating money and the mission board floated a new bank loan to carry Southland through the summer.[13] Then, suddenly, at the end of June, a new and formidable barrier arose to block the path to Southland's progress. While completing requisition forms for the GEB's first matching payment, Ruthanna Simms noticed a declaration requiring affirmation that Southland had "no outstanding debts." Did this mean, she asked, that the $6,700 in notes the mission board held for Southland had to be paid off before they could obtain any of the promised $20,000? Unfortunately, much to their chagrin, the board discovered that the GEB's agreement did require Southland to be debt free before any matching funds were dispatched. This meant that the $3,000 already spent on repairs and equipment would not be matched by the GEB and that all Southland's debts would have to be discharged before any matching funds were received. Leo Favrot tacked on a final bit of bad news when he reminded Jenkins that the agreement with the GEB specified that matching funds had to be raised by October 1924.[14]

Hollingsworth Wood was able to avert an immediate crisis by securing an extension for fundraising efforts, but the mission board's cupboard was still bare and its new solicitation campaign barely underway. At this point, the Jenkinses, son and father, added an ambitious new dimension to plans for Southland's future progress. The elder Jenkins had accompanied Jesse Henley, the new farm manager, to Southland in response to Raymond's request that his father inspect a piece of land located a few miles south and east of Southland on the main road from Helena to Little Rock. As soon as Raymond spied this hundred-acre site situated on "a beautiful knoll, surrounded by woodland" with good drainage, he began to envision moving the school to this "near ideal" setting. Both Atwood Jenkins and Jesse Henley quickly joined in the chorus for transplanting Southland. Indeed, the elder Jenkins immediately approached the landowner and "found him friendly to the Negro and . . . not opposed to selling for a Negro school." Within a few days, the Jenkins had, on their own, signed an option to purchase "not less than one hundred acres . . . at price not to exceed $90 per acre."[15]

The initial reaction from northern Friends about the possibility of moving to a new location was less than enthusiastic. Hollingsworth Wood was opposed to the idea, although Ruthanna Simms was willing to call a meeting of the Southland committee to discuss the proposition. In the meantime, Atwood Jenkins composed a long letter to Simms incorporating his view of why it would be "bad judgment" to spend forty to fifty thousand dollars throwing good money after bad at the current location where poor drainage could not be corrected and most buildings would have to be replaced within a few years. Because no member of the mission board or Southland committee could personally come to inspect the new site, the elder Jenkins proposed sending Raymond and Cecilia to Richmond bearing photographs of the projected new location to assist the committee its deliberations. Simultaneously, Raymond Jenkins wrote to both Leo Favrot and Jackson Davis to seek their advice. As he told Favrot,

> The Society of Friends are undertaking so many things, that I feel that we will have to lay plans for a broader solicitation. . . . I feel that I need some good advice . . . from such persons as you and Mr. Davis, as I feel that a large part of this burden is going to rest on me.[16]

Favrot and Davis were both impressed by Raymond Jenkins's arguments, supplemented by photographs of the proposed new location. Indeed, Jackson Davis agreed, site unseen, that there were "strong reasons in favour of the new site" and hoped the mission board would give the question serious consideration. Favrot noted that improved facilities in the new setting would offer "a great field of opportunity . . . to provide for Negro youth in that section of the South." But for all his apparent enthusiasm, Favrot, at least, did wonder about funding such an undertaking.[17] Indeed, given the state of the Southland's finances, it is surprising that money seemed not to be the chief concern of the majority of those who attended a meeting of the Southland committee to consider this bold new initiative. Still, the Iowa Friend Charles O. Whitely, who had made several evangelical visits to the school, injected a cautionary tone in observing that for all the good reasons to recommend moving, this would be impossible without prior sale of the current property. After the introduction of this note of hard reality, it was determined, in great tradition of Quaker backing and filling, to establish two subcommittees, one to deal with organizational structure for a new school and the other to study "practical considerations" attendant upon moving the institution.[18] This episode points up one of the striking ironies of the struggle to save Southland, that is, the more desperate the financial situation became, the more grandiose Quaker rescue plans became. Raymond Jenkins sincerely believed that the proposed change of location would produce a "bigger and better school," although he did acknowledge that the plan presented "quite a problem," requiring that Friends receive a considerable new infusion of "financial and spiritual" assistance.[19]

Following the meeting of the Southland committee wherein the possibility of moving was discussed, a pensive Walter C. Woodward set out his thoughts on the matter to Hollingsworth Wood who had hitherto opposed the move. This bold new plan, Woodward said, required "the most statesman-like thought," but even more crucial, he thought, was the question of changing the school's management "so as to make Southland an all American Friends enterprise." Apparently, Woodward and other members of the mission board had come to believe that Raymond Jenkins's theological views and leadership style had not only created divisions among Southland's staff and contributed to difficulties in the local community but also might be hindering financial support from evangelical midwestern Friends. Wood's wise counsel, he said, would be needed in dealing with these weighty issues.[20]

As it happened, a potentially damaging incident casting light on Jenkins's diplomatic shortcomings occurred during this crucial period. During the summer Anna Paschal Strong, the Marianna High School principal who had led the campaign to raise funds from Southland alumni, wrote to Jenkins asking him to forward her transcripts to Hampton Institute where, at great personal sacrifice, she was beginning the process of seeking an advanced degree.[21] In response, while he praised Strong as "a splendid woman" and "outstanding graduate," Jenkins provided Hampton officials with only a general assessment that indicated that Strong's graduation in 1903 was "equivalent to the High School course or perhaps slightly above." Shortly, thereafter he received a blistering letter from Strong, no shrinking violet, noting that her record should be the "equivalent to an accredited second year college course" and expressing deep disappointment at receiving such a shoddy recommendation from her beloved alma mater.[22] Somewhat shaken by the realization of how this apparent insult to a highly respected local figure might cause serious difficulties with potential school patrons, Jenkins, digging deeper into old grade records and catalogs, wrote back apologetically acknowledging that Strong should, indeed, have academic credit for two years beyond high school.[23]

Whether northern Friends were aware of this incident, certain weighty individuals were, in fact, conferring on the means to satisfy dissident elements in Arkansas and the wider Quaker community by easing Raymond Jenkins away from Southland while still retaining the vital support of GEB representatives like Jackson Davis and Leo Favrot. While no written evidence is extant, internal evidence would seem to indicate that the mission board contrived a Solomon-like resolution to Southland's looming leadership crisis.

In the midst of the board's vigorous fundraising efforts on behalf of the Arkansas mission, L. Willard Reynolds, a young evangelical Iowa minister, had, like fellow Iowan Alden Knight before him, written to question increasing expenditure on Southland given the fact that the missionary effort there had produced so few converts to the Society of Friends. Ruthanna Simms felt compelled to respond at considerable length, informing Reynolds of Southland Monthly Meeting's historically impressive membership among black Arkansans. The fact that Southland Monthly Meeting had more recently lost its power, she said, "has been due in the last twenty years [the Wolford era], more to lack of oversight and interest on the part of Northern Friends than to anything else." What Southland needed, she said, was a permanent pastor like Reynolds who could attract new black members into the Friends Church. Apparently moved by Simms's admonitions, Reynolds answered the call and was subsequently appointed vice-principal of the school and pastor of Southland Monthly Meeting. This appointment allowed the mission board to call Raymond Jenkins back to Indiana to engage in full-time fundraising activities while also possibly quieting some midwestern opposition to the mission board's concentration of its time and money on Southland.[24]

In the meantime, Jenkins, always the young man in a hurry, while thanking his GEB patrons, Favrot and Davis, for their "deep interest in us and our work," hinted that they might be even more helpful by putting more pressure on the mission board to "move faster or catch a bigger vision of the work to be done."[25] Jenkins was also hard at work on another publicity campaign to recruit students of the "right sort" by mailing letters addressed simply to "The Pastor of the Negro Church" to select post offices in Arkansas, Mississippi, and neighboring states. He also sought to enlist more Phillips County students by purchasing the subscription list of the *Helena World*, a black-owned newspaper, to advertise Southland as a school that would provide a healthy environment with good food, religious training, and cultural possibilities in a "carefully guarded" social setting. It was an ambitious plan but hindered by the fact there was no money for envelopes or stamps. Indeed, barely a month before the new school year was to begin, Jenkins informed the Richmond office that he had only ten dollars at hand and numerous outstanding bills. In the circumstances, as he told Walter Woodward, even though many things had to be done to "put this school into usable condition," he did not feel justified in contracting further renovations until he paid for the work that had been completed.[26]

A week later Jenkins, still without funds, told Ruthanna Simms that expenses incurred in May had still not been paid and that the school could not open unless other essential repairs were made. In the days that followed Jenkins went on to report a serious accident in the lighting plant as well as the breakdown of the school's only automobile. "I suppose to some of you in the North it seems that we have one calamity after another," he wrote.[27] So it seemed.

In response to Jenkins latest desperate plea, Ruthanna Simms sent the remaining balance from both the building and special maintenance funds, leaving the Southland committee "without any reserve" with which to pay accumulated bills of over three thousand dollars for equipment and repairs. Nothing further could be done, she said, until they received hoped for contributions as a result of still another special request for assistance in the *American Friend*. The only immediate possibility for significant aid was a promise from the board of White's Institute[28] to visit Southland to ascertain if they might provide support for the plan to refurbish the school.[29]

There was also another sudden, somewhat bizarre, development. In early September Simms queried both Jenkins and Hollingsworth Wood concerning a suggestion from Jackson Davis that the mission board turn Southland, lock, stock and barrel, over to the state of Arkansas and take responsibility for Calhoun Institute in Lowndes County, Alabama, with Jenkins as director.[30] James E. Gregg, principal at Hampton Institute, also weighted in on the issue, relating to Hollingsworth Wood that Calhoun's founder and director Charlotte Thorn, suffering from poor health, favored the idea as a means of ensuring her school's survival under competent leadership. At first glance, it seems amazing that, as Simms told Wood, the mission board actually seemed willing even to consider this idea. Perhaps, given Southland's financial situation, some members of the board simply wished to be rid of their perpetual burden in Arkansas, even if it meant taking on a fresh charge in Alabama.[31] Wood, at least, kept a clear head, informing Dr. Gregg that he opposed the idea not only because of the obvious complications involved but also, adding an historical perspective, because "due to the internecine strife in the Society of Friends in 1828, it would be impossible to stir up a real interest in Calhoun on the part of the Society." Gregg probably did not grasp the subtle nuance of Wood's implication that after nearly a century, Calhoun benefactors who were mainly Hicksite Friends might be seriously disturbed if that school were to be placed in the hands of the Orthodox Five Years Meeting.[32]

Jenkins relayed his personal communications with Jackson Davis concerning the Calhoun proposition to Simms, but this startling proposal died aborning. Davis did visit Southland in early September to discuss Calhoun as well as look at the proposed new site, but apparently his chief interest was to entice Jenkins to leave Southland in order to take charge of the floundering Alabama school.[33]

In the meantime, despite the worsening financial crisis, Raymond Jenkins expressed great optimism about the forthcoming school year. Listing the largely new staff of seventeen (nine white, eight black), Jenkins believed that, finally, "we have workers qualified to do what they came to do. . . . We are getting on our feet here and the problem now . . . is to get support for our work in the north." In his initial meeting with the Southland staff, Jenkins emphasized that their first priority should be "teaching the students to lead a bigger and better Christian life," especially by their example of living and working together with good will and racial harmony.[34]

As he prepared to leave Arkansas to take charge of fundraising in Indiana, Jenkins remained upbeat, noting that school began with a 30 percent increase in enrollment over the previous year. He was also pleased to report that upon seeing the proposed new site, Jackson Davis had announced his support for moving, "provided the Friends really got behind Southland." Davis also told Hollingsworth Wood that the new site was "an admirable one" that "presented a fine opportunity for service in the whole cause of Negro education."[35]

By this time the most members of the Southland committee had cautiously embraced the idea of moving the school, although the executive committee of the mission board had made no firm decision. Such an undertaking would take at least two years, and, in the meantime, the board to would have to raise sufficient funds to pay off bank notes of $6,700 before beginning to replenish the special Southland fund to provide a dollar-for-dollar match to the General Education Board's grant. Ruthanna Simms, having pronounced September as Southland's "Golden Month," set out her plan for accomplishing this monumental task in "the immediate future." According to her scheme, which was incorporated into a letter soliciting aid from a select group of wealthy Friends, if $12,150 could be raised by the end of October (only $750 had so far been promised), the Home Missions Board could discharge the existing $6,700 debt and add the remaining $4,550 to the $5,450 already collected (and spent). This $10,000 would then be matched by the GEB (which, as noted, had agreed to a year's extension for fundraising efforts). With these matching funds, all outstanding bills for heat, light, water, and repairs would be paid, thus seeing the school safely through the winter. The remainder of Simms's rescue plan rested on the thin thread of her conviction that the board of White's Institute, whose members were preparing to visit Southland, would, upon seeing the need, agree to provide a gift of $10,000 to 20,000. In any case, she wanted Jenkins to ensure that Leo Favrot would also be on hand to greet representatives of White's Institute and help convince them that any investment made in Southland would be educationally sound as well morally uplifting.[36]

Given that the mission board had barely managed to raise $12,000 during the entire past year, one might question the plausibility of projecting contributions of the same amount in one month's time through letter writing and articles in the *American Friend.* Such skepticism was implied in Hollingsworth Wood's somewhat puzzled response to Simms's elaborate plan, which seemed to indicate that he should henceforth concentrate his efforts on raising funds for Southland's operating expenses while she negotiated with White's Institute to supply matching money for the GEB grant. Wood's own idea was personally to approach wealthy New England Friends with the vision of their having a role in the emergence of a great new Quaker institution representing the combined contributions of all American Friends (Orthodox, Hicksite, Wilburite) to racial justice and harmony. Did, Wood asked, Simms really believe that his time would be best spent pleading with a theologically diverse group for funds in order that the evangelically dominated mission board of the Five Years Meeting could paint buildings, dig drains, and repair window panes?[37]

Taken aback by Wood's skeptical response, Simms, in a "long and rambling" reply, assured him that she was not asking him to raise money for day-to-day expenses but only wished to ensure that any money he collected could be used to help pay off existing debts. She insisted that the situation would be clarified once a definite decision had been made regarding the projected move, which was now favored by the entire Southland committee. If, as she expected, the mission board's executive committee concurred in this opinion, Raymond Jenkins, having returned to Richmond as publicity chairman and fundraiser, could begin to make personal solicitations on basis of the plan for moving the school to a superior location. Simms had apparently convinced herself that with Raymond working full-time, it might be possible to raise as much as eighty thousand dollars, provided the General Education Board would be willing to double the existing grant.[38]

While Simms's explanation may not have entirely resolved Wood's concerns about the feasibility of the new fundraising scheme, he remained a good soldier in Southland's cause, perhaps because the Arkansas mission was the Society of Friends' only truly national effort on behalf of American Negroes, whose welfare and advancement he had worked long and hard to secure. The cornerstone of Wood's renewed plea to wealthy prospective donors was a three-page message outlining Southland's history and current crisis. There was, he concluded, "every reason to believe" that the combination of a better location and the dedicated service of young Friends like Raymond Jenkins would allow Southland to "grow into an institution of tremendous influence and importance in that section of the south where . . . the need is so terribly great."[39]

Contributions did begin to trickle in. By late October Wood had collected several hundred dollars from eastern Friends, although no contribution was larger than five hundred.[40] Wood also met with officers of the General Education Board to try to convince them, on the basis of the mission board's decision to move to a more favorable location, to "make an additional grant of $20,000 toward this increased and more intelligent expenditure."[41]

Ruthanna Simms expressed her thanks for Wood's work as well as her poignant hope that some "good soul" would step forward to deliver the money needed to purchase the land to which the school was supposed to move.[42] So, the mission board was asking for tens of thousands of dollars to create a major Quaker institution out of an historic but troubled school on land they did not own or yet have the means to purchase. Whether one perceives this as an admirable expression of deep faith or an example of ironic naivety, Simms and her colleagues could only wait and anxiously check the mail. It was, as they might have said, "all in God's hands now."[43]

Waiting for the fulfillment of these future hopes, or dreams, Southland, for all its deteriorating infrastructure and diminished enrollment,[44] was still a functioning educational institution, boasting, somewhat incongruously, the largest staff in its sixty-year history. After Raymond Jenkins returned to Indiana in late September, assistant principal and chaplain L. Willard Reynolds was left to deal with day-to-day developments. Reynolds had been pastor of a Friends Church in Iowa, but he had never lived in the South and had no previous experience directing a school. Obviously he had a lot to learn and his on the job training began very quickly. In early October Jenkins wrote to inform the staff that because contributions were coming in slowly, payment of salaries would have to be delayed. This letter crossed one from Reynolds with news that the light plant had again broken down and that repairs to keep the school's Dodge truck running had taken a large chunk out of available operating funds. There were also discipline problems, especially with long time boarding student Alfred Barnes who "talks back to everyone [and was] most too saucy for a boy in a place of this kind."[45]

Day by day, as problems mounted, Willard Reynolds was learning more than he wished to know about the kind of place he had become responsible for operating. Beyond coping with a shortage of funds to pay bills or provide for teacher's salaries, Reynolds also had to report that farm produce was poor, that two wells on the campus had dried up, and that the cook, Mrs. Kamp, was serving mainly unsatisfactory cold suppers. Furthermore, the old bugaboo, immorality, appeared to have again raised its ugly head when one of the female boarding students was reported, erroneously as it turned out, to be pregnant.[46]

Jenkins sympathized with Reynolds's difficulties, but he advised him to be firm in his relations with both erring students and dissident locals. He also provided precise instructions on how the acting principal should conduct the crucial visit of the representatives of White's Institute who were coming to inspect the school and assess the possible new location prior to advising their board about what sort of contribution White's should make to the Southland emergency fund.[47]

In addition to offering copious advice to the inexperienced Reynolds and attempting to squeeze money from potential contributors through face-to-face contacts, Raymond Jenkins published weekly essays in the *American Friend* offering examples of Southland's efforts to "climb higher and higher carrying its message of Christian education and interracial good will." He emphasized the sacrifices being made by poverty-stricken local people in the effort to save "their" school, including the story about one older man who gave all the money he had except for the two dollars he needed to buy a pair of pants. Given such dedication and the fact that struggling parents of students paid enough in tuition and board to offset at least a portion of the school's budget, could not, he asked, American Friends dig deep enough to ensure that Southland would continue to serve as an example of their religious society's historic commitment to the welfare of America's oppressed people of color? Jenkins efforts were clearly heartfelt, but the outcome continued to be disappointing.[48]

In light of generally meager results, the Home Missions Board was depending heavily on a saving contribution from the board of White's Institute following the visit of their representatives to Southland in late October. But several weeks passed without word concerning any help White's might provide. And despite Jenkins assuring Willard Reynolds that things were "slowly getting into shape," such contributions as were being received continued to prove insufficient even to support ordinary operating expenses. Reynolds was thankful for a six-hundred-dollar check just before Thanksgiving, but he rather timidly reminded Ruthanna Simms that beyond the thousands they owed for various bills, members of the staff were "very anxious to have their pay promptly."[49]

Jenkins responded to Reynolds complaints with a request for a list of all current accounts payable as of 1 December. In return he received an account list showing nearly $3,700 in debts, about a third of which represented arrears for unpaid salaries.[50] There is no evidence that the school's staff got any special allocation for back pay as a result, but one communication Reynolds did receive was a letter from the Arkansas state health officer regarding a "probable investigation" based on complaints he had received concerning "immoral and venereally infected pupils" at Southland. There can be little doubt that this potentially damaging inquiry represented another of Harry Wolford's efforts to undermine Southland's administration and reputation. Just before Christmas, however, Reynolds was able to report that, after examination by local health officials of ninety-eight pupils aged twelve and over, no venereal disease had been discovered.[51]

This incident occurred nearly simultaneously with the General Education Board's assigning field agent Leo Favrot to undertake an investigation of "the antagonism stirred up in the community by Wolford." Hollingsworth Wood thought that their case might be aided if Raymond Jenkins provided chapter and verse to the GEB concerning Wolford's continuing attempts to turn local people against the new Southland. After spending some time interviewing people in the neighborhood, Favrot concluded that Wolford had indeed been busy "stirring up" antagonism toward the school among both black and white residents in Phillips County but that these efforts had had only limited success. He also recommended that Raymond Jenkins return to Arkansas to give Southland the benefit of the sort of "active, personal interest . . . and enthusiasm" that only he could provide.[52] No doubt Favrot's confirmation of his dedication and Wolford's misconduct gave Jenkins some sense of satisfaction, but it brought no appreciable increase of contributions to the mission board's coffers.

There was, however, one significant, though bittersweet, development in the fundraising effort. The trustees of White's Institute at long last decided that the extent of their support would be limited to the cancellation of the mission board's two-thousand-dollar debt as well as a gift in the same amount toward the purchase of the proposed new site, after Southland's remaining debt had been discharged. Given that this otherwise-significant contribution represented only a fraction of what the Southland committee had hoped to receive, their abject disappointment was reflected in Jenkins's warning to Willard Reynolds not to make any new plans or start any new programs since "at times we do not see how we can run even next year."[53]

On the ground at Southland, the inexperienced Reynolds seemed slowly to be acclimating himself to local surroundings. In a story for the *American Friend* on "Christian Education At Southland," the acting principal expressed his thanks for the moral support and religious devotion of a number of "faithful stand-bys in the community." Through the example of their personal lives and unbending loyalty, he said, families like the Freelands, the Busbys, the Rodens, and others had made and continued to make invaluable contributions to the school. But this story of inspiring faith and good will appeared along side the description of a tragic accident a few days before Christmas when the two-year-old son of a Southland cook burned to death after overturning an oil lamp onto his bedclothes.[54]

Then, on Christmas Day, an incident occurred that served as a grim reminder that financial difficulties and physical deterioration were not all that militated against a reasonable education for young blacks in the Arkansas Delta. On Christmas afternoon, Joseph Moses, Southland's black governor of boys (no relation to the departed John W. Moses), was driving a group of boarding students to a free movie in Helena when he collided with a car driven by a young white woman. No one was injured, and the damages were not extensive. However, two young women in the other automobile began verbally assaulting Moses and physically threatening him with a tire iron. Finally, they snatched the keys from the school's vehicle and drove into town. When Moses followed on foot and attempted to retrieve the keys, they called the county sheriff who, before Moses could get back to the accident scene, moved the school's vehicle to the county courthouse. The bewildered Moses then sought out Willard Reynolds in Helena with another group of students. When they went together to speak to the sheriff, he ordered his deputy to "lock the nigger up." When Reynolds attempted to intervene, he was told that he should be in court the following Tuesday (five days later) until which time Moses would presumably remain incarcerated even though no charges had been filed against him and no investigation had been conducted to establish fault for the accident. Reynolds was only able to secure his colleague's release when Southland's banker agreed to guarantee the court appearance of a school representative. After Moses was released, Reynolds was advised by sympathetic local whites not to contest the case as "the evidence would probably go against Moses" since he was a black man and his adversary was a white woman. The idea of racially assumed guilt was troublesome enough for an Iowa Quaker, but, as Reynolds related to Raymond Jenkins, what truly shocked him was the conduct of the thoroughly respectable young woman in the other car whom he described as a

> type of rabid nigger hater such as I scarcely suppose existed. She seemed to resent the "nigger's impudence" much more than the damage to the car. She told us that she ought to have killed him and would if she had had a gun. "I would not think any more of killing a nigger than a dog," she said.[55]

Reynolds concluded his troubled and troubling letter with an addendum referring to a less profound but equally persistent difficulty. "Most of the teachers," he noted, "are far behind in their salaries" and that some of Southland's creditors were becoming unpleasantly insistent.[56] Vice-principal Reynolds's on-the-job training was proceeding apace.

While Willard Reynolds faced the New Year with a plethora of problems, including an emergency tonsillectomy which laid him low for several days,[57] a meeting of the mission board's executive committee and Friends interested in the future of Southland was convened in Richmond. Among the weighty Friends in attendance was Wilbur K. Thomas, head of the American Friends Service Committee (AFSC), who opened the meeting by noting that the mission board could not go on supporting the Arkansas school "without additional help from all Friends in America." The purpose of the gathering, therefore, was to discover from those closely involved with Southland how the AFSC might be of assistance. To this end, Raymond Jenkins took the lead in describing the school's current condition and future hopes. In his presentation, Jenkins continued what appeared to be the trend among Southland's would-be rescuers, that is, the more desperate the financial situation, the higher the stakes should be raised. To develop Southland "along industrial lines . . . as a unique school for interracial work," at a better site with a new physical plant built to accommodate 150 boarders and 150 to 200 day students, would, he said, require $104,000.[58]

After hearing Raymond Jenkins report, Wilbur Thomas, speaking for the AFSC, said that it would be "utterly impossible" for the service committee, which was chiefly involved in emergency relief, to secure the finances necessary to do what the mission board seemed to be requesting. Still, he said, some way should be found to save the school. To accomplish this, Thomas suggested the appointment of a self-perpetuating committee of Friends "vitally interested in the Negro problem" who would take over the assets and liabilities of Southland to work out a rescue plan.[59] So, full of good will but bereft of resources, another group of weighty and earnest Friends, including Wilbur Thomas, made the thoroughly Quaker decision to form still another committee.

Meanwhile, on the ground in Arkansas, events were following a familiar pattern. Reynolds attempted to dole out whatever money he received as judiciously as possible, but with some creditors becoming "pretty insistent," he worried that continued failure to meet obligations might "bring an unsavory reputation upon the Quaker name." Just as unsavory but closer to home were the chronically unpaid salaries of an increasing penurious staff. Raymond Jenkins told the acting principal that money was coming in "slightly better," but while Reynolds realized that the mission board could not send money it did not possess, it would help, he noted, "to keep up a better feeling here if we could have at least some information from time to time along this line."[60]

Amidst such trying circumstances, Jenkins cast-off remark in a letter to Reynolds that if things got too bad they might "just abdicate the throne" effectively became a prophecy. Within a few days Hollingsworth Wood broke the news that officials of the General Education Board had "advised me of the decision . . . that they thought Southland ought to be abandoned and consequently were withdrawing their support." In the circumstances, Wood concluded, "we had better look the facts in the face" and admit the withdrawal of GEB funds marked the coup de grâce for Southland's hopes.[61]

This news left Ruthanna Simms crestfallen. Why, she wondered would the General Education Board suddenly abandon Southland at the moment it was primed to make great strides toward advancing Negro education in the Arkansas Delta? Simms still believed "that every advancement . . . made at Southland in the past two years has been decidedly worthwhile," but she had to agree that without GEB support "we cannot hope to frame our new program. . . . There seems nothing can be done but to take steps towards closing the school in a dignified way as soon as possible."[62]

Responding to Simms's query about the reasons for the GEB's defection from the ranks of Southland supporters, Hollingsworth Wood surmised that the board's decision was apparently traceable to the recent report of the school's erstwhile champion, Leo Favrot. In this document, which Wood characterized as "not . . . very illuminating," Favrot cited both local white hostility toward Southland's "practice of social democracy as eating together is called" and "latent antagonism" among black people in the community based on unfortunate events in the past and probably unfounded rumors concerning recent developments. Given these apparently broad-based attitudes, the GEB had determined that the ends of Negro education in Arkansas would be better served by allocating its funds to superintendents in black school districts than to risk further ill-felling by concentrating its support on Southland. Noting that his past success in gaining support from the GEB was based on his asking them to do what he knew they were willing to do, Wood felt that the Board had raised a bar against Southland, "and I am not willing to jeopardize my happy influence by hacking at that bar." It was, nonetheless, "very painful to be the harbinger of this ill news."[63]

However disheartening and apparently final, the distressing tidings were not communicated immediately neither to the Southland's national Quaker constituency nor to those on the ground in Arkansas. Raymond Jenkins did admit to Willard Reynolds that things "do not look very bright," and Ruthanna Simms confessed to Southland's principal that she felt "wicked *all* the time" in view of the strain he faced in dealing with a continuing multiple of problems, including the latest, a breakdown of Southland's plumbing system. This meant that all water for cooking and drinking had to be hand-carried seventy-five yards to Central Hall.[64] The only succor she could offer, other than the occasional small check, was the assurance that he and his staff were earnestly remembered in prayer at every meeting she attended.[65] As much as Reynolds may have appreciated those prayers, he probably was more deeply effected by a visit from Southland's neighbor Mrs. Maggie Busby who served as a poignant reminder both of why he and other Friends had come to the South in Christian service and of the heroic spirit of some of those he had come to serve. What Mrs. Busby brought was a hard-won ten-dollar contribution from her ever-faithful family. Surely, most middle-class northern Friends would have to give many times that amount to make an equivalent sacrifice. But interest among those who collectively might have at least temporarily rescued the school continued to flag, and the perilous state of Southland's finances was reflected in the fact that the Busbys' humble gift was immediately added to Southland's shrunken fund for paying day-to-day expenses.[66]

Then, in early February, two weeks after the General Education Board had seemingly slammed the door to Southland's future, a small glimmer of hope emerged. After Hollingsworth Wood remonstrated with Jackson Davis and Leo Favrot about their sudden desertion of Southland, they agreed to sit down with Wood and Raymond Jenkins to reconsider the GEB's recent decision.[67] But when the Southland committee convened at Earlham College two days after receiving Wood's hopeful message, they at long last admitted that enough was indeed enough. With uncharacteristic speed, they drafted three emphatic decisions: 1) that they would have no further dealings with the General Education Board, 2) that they would "bring to a close the work carried on at Southland," and 3) that they would attempt "to secure money to pay outstanding accounts" (about $12,000), possibly through the use of the school's endowment fund.[68] All this seemed clear enough: Southland would, in Quaker parlance, be laid down. Still, the meeting closed with an expression of

> the unanimous feeling that an earnest effort be put forth to see if a group of Friends could be gotten together who would undertake the management of a school in the region of the present location of Southland Institute.

The idea, as Jenkins explained to Hollingsworth Wood, was to investigate the possibility of some new but unidentified board undertaking Friends' educational work on behalf of black people at a new location, perhaps in conjunction with the American Friends Service Committee. This idea was explicitly endorsed by at a subsequent meeting of the Southland committee when that body determined that as soon as outstanding debts were paid, Raymond Jenkins should "turn his attention to investigating the possibilities of a new organization to carry on the work of Southland under new management and on a new site."[69]

This new and, it would seem, chimerical vision explains Raymond Jenkins's instructions to Willard Reynolds to obtain as much information as he could about the Rosenwald School that was scheduled to open in the vicinity of Southland. Obviously, if Friends were really going to maintain an educational interest in the area, the future role of this philanthropic venture would be important to their planning, especially in light of the persistent, though groundless, rumor that Harry Wolford would be appointed principal of the new Rosenwald school.[70] But if

Reynolds was a conduit for information from Arkansas, he heard little enough about Southland's fate, other than admonitions not to undertake new financial obligations and promises that he would soon be fully apprised of future plans. The moment of truth for Southland's staff came when one of them, Grace Camelin, asked to be released from her contract in order to take another position. Feeling unable in good conscience to prevent Ms. Camelin from acquiring alternate gainful employment, the mission board decided that notice of the impending closing should finally be released, though, in the beginning, only to Willard Reynolds and Grace Camelin. In a long and detailed letter, Jenkins explained that the board did not wish to announce the closing until all outstanding accounts had been settled lest there be a "run on the bank" when creditors, including the staff, discovered the school was shutting down. Ms. Camelin's request had forced them into action before all the bills had been paid, but sufficient money could be forwarded to cover unpaid faculty and staff salaries. With his letter to Reynolds, Jenkins also a sent an official notice of the school's closing for the teachers and another for the students and community, advising Reynolds to inform each group when he thought best and in easy stages, for example, at a staff meeting on Saturday, at the worship service on Sunday, and to a student assembly on Monday. Both notices emphasized the need to complete Southland's final year with heads held high and "colors flying." Reynolds pragmatically decided to defer the fateful announcements "until we get the next monthly tuition and board in."[71]

Finally, in early April 1925, the Home Missions Board released "A Statement Concerning Southland Institute," written by Walter C. Woodward as executive secretary of the Five Years Meeting, setting out a brief narrative of that board's efforts to save Southland since they had, in 1920, assumed responsibility for a school. In the end, he said, their best efforts "had ceased to breathe the spirit that would reflect Friendly ideals of service," and school's physical plant "represented little more than a shell."[72] So, after five years of attempting to make Southland the sort of high-class institution they had hoped to create, the mission board and Southland committee had concluded that while there was "a distinct contribution for Friends to make toward this great interracial problem which confronts our nation . . . the school . . . on the present basis is not an adequate expression of that contribution." The Five Years Meeting had, for a time, believed that there was still "a great open door" for Friends to establish the sort of school that, in a new location, would "enable us to apply ourselves to the greater task." But after undertaking "an heroic venture of faith" and leaving "no stone unturned that would . . . bring us nearer the goal of our hopes," they had realized that they could not secure the necessary financial resources "to go forward with this greater task." Still, while Southland was being discontinued and not replaced, the Home Missions Board believed that Friends could continue to render some as yet undetermined service "toward better interracial relations in our country."[73]

This earnest, artless, and, in some ways, naive statement was issued almost simultaneously with a letter received by Principal Reynolds that stood as an agonizing expression of the need Southland would no longer be able to fulfill.

> I Know I am behind in with children schoolng Paying I ben down sick three week. . . . I had to Bye medison. . . . I Will send it in Sunday or Monday it has ben hard by me bein sick[74]

This message was both a heart rendering expression of the desperate hopes of a functionally illiterate women trying to ensure her children would not remain sunk in the mire of nearly hopeless poverty and an outrageous example of what Southern race hatred and oppression could do to poor, rural black people. Racism was not really a crucial element in the demise of Southland Institute, it was simply a fact of life. But for some black Arkansans, the closing down of even so humble a place as Southland deprived them of yet another tool that might in a small way help a few young men and women to cope more effectively with life in a racist society, South and North. As one Southland alumnus declared on hearing that the school was to be shut down, "The shock to me was equally a greast as the Elain riot. . . . Lelain cryed all night. Will you kindly advise me what the trouble is? I lived there when the school was going through some of it hardest storms I thought, and . . . hoped the storms had passed."[75]

When Raymond Jenkins and Clarence Pickett traveled to Southland in late March to discuss the inevitable closing with the students and the community, there were no storms, only shock and sorrow. "There was hardly a dry eye," Jenkins recounted. "Mr. Freeland spoke at the end and broke down. . . . Everyone here is heart broken. . . . Everything is black and they see no light. It is terrible. If there is anything we can do, we must do it. . . . For me personally one of the hardest times was at supper . . . when the students in the other dinning-room broke out with the Southland song:"

Dear old Southland, our dear old Southland
Dear old Southland, we're all for you
We will fight for the white and yellow,
For the glory of old S.I.
Never daunted, we cannot falter
In the battle tried and true,
Dear old Southland, our dear old Southland
Dear old Southland, we're all for you.[76]

But if a death sentence had been imposed, it had not been executed. For few more weeks there were students to be taught, including a sudden influx of pupils from the new Rosenwald School after its premature closing.[77] Indeed, the faculty had determined that Southland would close in style. So, Nell Vore produced and directed the spring operetta, "Miss Cherry Blossom," the Henleys and Joseph Moses organized the annual May agricultural fair and exhibition, and a student musical recital was followed by the senior-class play performed two days before the Baccalaureate Service leading up to the final Commencement exercises.[78] There was even one last "investigation of possibilities of creating a new Board to take over the management," including the issuing of a pamphlet soliciting new sources of funding, "our last effort to put the thing across," as Jenkins related to Willard Reynolds.[79]

The Home Missions Board was deeply moved by the "real pathos" with which members of the Southland community led by Duncan Freeland pleaded that Friends find some way to keep the school open. Ruthanna Simms and Clarence Pickett drafted a statement proposing the two or three workers, including a married couple, remain at Southland, seeking "to discover channels for inter-racial service" that still might be possible at the Arkansas mission station. Hollingsworth Wood, having invested considerable time and effort to the cause, expressed the view that American Friends ought to be "bending all our energy in selling the buildings and purchasing the new site." Wood even agreed to attempt to extract money from the philanthropist Leopold Scheep, whom he called "a weak-minded millionaire." Finally, he held out hope that the General Education Board might contribute to some sort of fresh venture, but, in the end, nothing came of the idea.[80] This time no *deus ex machina* appeared to rescue Southland, bereft of students and staff, from the dust of the rutted, unpaved road that ran by its soon-to-be deserted buildings.

The Home Missions Board issued a sad farewell to its attempts "to Christianize race relations through Southland," while admonishing all Friends to take personal responsibility for promoting interracial harmony and good will.[81]

Finally, in September, a conference of interested Friends meeting at Earlham determined that until the property was sold, John and Luetta Henley would look after the buildings and farm while Lester T. Perisho, a former Southland teacher, would keep up religious activities in the Southland Meeting and Sunday school as well as conferring with a few "most regretful" local people who had offered to support one or two teachers who might reopen the school on a small scale.

Lester Perisho remained at Southland for several months, meeting with the remnant of black Quakers and teaching a small Sunday school class.[82] Writing from his lonely mission station, Perisho proved to be a thoughtful, and at times even incisive, observer. Remarking upon how the few students he was tutoring seemed almost resentful when he attempted to impose strict standards, he added:

> Sometimes I don't wonder that the people held to Wolford so. I believe that he was giving them the kind of school they wanted and still want. Of course some really see the need for a different sort, but I am not sure but nearly all appreciated the opportunity he gave them to be in school just when they wanted to, and stay out when it suited. . . . Everything was just as was convenient, even the payment of tuition. I don't consider such a school any kindness to the people, and I don't believe the Friends will ever be willing to put their united effort into supporting such.[83]

Perisho had put his finger on both the reasons why Harry Wolford proved an inadequate director for the sort of school the Five Years Meeting and Home Missions Board wished Southland to be and why many local people deeply resented his being forced to leave. Wolford came to terms with the situation he found at Southland, but the subsequent inability of northern Friends, despite their unimpeachably genuine goodwill, to effectively communicate the need for change to the majority of local patrons proved fatal to the school. These were two incompatible visions of Southland and, ultimately, neither could be sustained.

So, long after the last boarding students had left the campus and the last faint echoes of quarrels and strife that had troubled some of Southland's final days faded away, Lester Pershio attempted to put a sad situation into some manageable perspective:

> We are pretty much alone down here . . . there is a certain restfulness about it, for we are free from annoying controversy and high-pitched argument. . . . One is led to think that, though controversy is perhaps justifiable at time, it robs us of the prayerful, unselfish interest we would do well to have in each other.[84]

Prayerful, unselfish interest may be a rarer commodity than controversy even, alas, among Quakers, but at Southland not a few gentle Friends had exhibited such an interest long enough to keep an improbable school and impossible dream alive and to permit future generations to see in their not ignoble story a true, if distant, "Light in the Lord."

Epilogue

The experiment of having Lester Perisho stay on at Southland to continue the religious meeting for Southland Quakers and conduct a Sunday school for local young people while Jesse and Luella Henley operated the farm did not prove successful. While Perisho enjoyed his Sunday school class, he also had the sense that some of the students whom he was privately tutoring "resented" his attempts to maintain high standards. John Henley was considered a very efficient farmer, but even the help of Perisho and local hired hands, the farm proved to be a losing proposition, and the Home Mission Board soon gave up any attempt to make it pay.[1]

Among the major players in Southland's final drama, only Harry Wolford stayed in Arkansas, looking after his real estate and other business interests; he never again became involved in education and died in Helena in 1938. Raymond Jenkins was appointed a member of the Friends service committee of Indiana Yearly Meeting in 1925 and later received a scholarship from the Rockefeller General Education Board. He eventually returned to Hampton Institute where he taught for many years before coming back to Richmond to take charge of the family insurance business that he directed well into his eighties. He had mixed memories about his three eventful years in Arkansas, but for all the difficulties, frustrations, and disappointments that venture brought him, he still believed that the Home Missions Board's attempt to revitalize Southland had been a noble mission.[2]

Ruthanna Simms remained executive secretary of the Home Missions Board for many years, and Hollingsworth Wood returned to his practice as a civil rights lawyer, working for justice and equality for African American citizens in private practice and as president of the National Urban League and a trustee of Fisk University.[3]

After attempts to maintain some Quaker presence at Southland Arkansas proved unsuccessful, the Home Missions Board determined to sell its Arkansas holdings as quickly as possible. Early on, a white Helena congregation, the River Grant Episcopalian Church, was granted an option to purchase the Southland property and physical plant for twenty thousand dollars. However, after this option expired on 15 July 1926, the property remained unoccupied until 1929 when it was purchased by the Sovereign Grand Lodge of Arkansas Free and Accepted Free Masons for eleven thousand. This organization briefly reopened a school at the site, but in 1935 sold the premises at a loss to Walters Institute of the Arkansas Conference of the AME Zion Church.[4] This Methodist group subsequently sold much of the original Southland property but from 1936 until at least the late 1940s operated a school called Southland-Walters Institute at the site that, according to one account, "flourished" for a time. A number of new structures were erected, including a substantial brick classroom building.[5] Eventually, however, lawsuits involving the AME Zion Church's ownership of the property caused the school to shut down. After Southland-Walters closed, a local historian visited the site in 1962 and found "the administration building in almost ruin due to neglect." She also inspected the girls' dormitory, which was in similar condition with a local family apparently squatting in the best preserved area of the building.[6] In the late 1960s the main Walters-Southland building was accidentally destroyed during a salvage operation.[7]

In the last report the Home Missions Board would receive from Southland before it closed down, acting principal Willard Reynolds reflected on the dignified proceedings of school's final commencement ceremony and the lamentable consequences of its demise.

> It is with sadness that we contemplate that this little garden which we have been cultivating . . . must be plowed up and its plants gathered far and near. Some will survive the transplanting and go on to flower and fruit under others' care. Some may not be able to take root in strange soil. But that must be left in the hands of the Great Gardener.[8]

Today, one may drive north along the highway from West Helena toward Lexa past the former site of Southland school and meeting without observing any material trace of the community's Quaker heritage. But at least some former Southland students were able to take root in strange soil. A number of these were meeting together for an annual reunion picnic of the Southland College Club at Dan Ryan Woods in Chicago well into the 1960s.[9] A few, like Alfred L. Billingsley[10] and Emma Roden Young stayed on in the community to which this anomalous Quaker academy had given birth, raising children and crops on the land their forebears had purchased to ensure the possibility of a decent education for them. All of these surviving Southlanders looked upon the closing of "their" school as an inexplicable tragedy. "We never did understand what happened in Indiana," said one. Another remembered the school's irreplaceable influence on the community:

> It seemed to motivate a lot of people to go into higher education. There have been some doctors and some very famous people.[11] . . . The Quakers brought a lot of culture here. . . . People just seemed to solve a lot of their problems. We were proud of that.[12]

For her part, Emma Roden Young recalled the closing down of Southland Monthly Meeting as a stinging blow to the remaining Quaker families in the area:

> We never went to no other church but there. That's the onliest church we went to. . . . We would sing. I remember Mr. Freeland. You remember how he would sing bass?[13]

Her memories were perhaps the last surviving remnants of Quakerism's first predominantly black monthly meeting. For the collective memory of American Friends, Southland was poignantly recorded as "the Lost Negro Meeting in Arkansas."[14]

Southland was finally "laid down," as Quakers say, because the Friends' Five Years Meeting could simply not afford to operate it in accordance with their exalted vision of the sort of school it should become. They took some consolation, or perhaps only cold comfort, in the fact that more educational opportunities for black children were beginning to emerge, even in Phillips County, Arkansas.[15] For all of that Southland deserves to be remembered not for its final failure to achieve an exalted status modeled on Hampton or Tuskegee but for the long, selfless service it performed for a small body of truly needy human beings and for the generous spirit that impelled that service. Southland pioneer Lydia B. Chace spoke for each of the "messengers of the Lord in Arkansas":

> It seems to us so vastly important to our stability as a nation that the ignorant should be taught and the degraded uplifted and enlightened, and we surely . . . owe a debt to this long downtrodden people that will not be paid in our lifetime.[16]

Perhaps that debt has yet to be paid, but one small, dedicated band of American Quakers should no longer be held accountable.

Appendix A

Southland Leaders

DATES	SUPERINTENDENT/ PRESIDENT/DIRECTOR	MATRON
1864–1886	Calvin Clark	Alida Clark
1886–1888	Elkanah Beard	Irena Beard
1888–1889	Charles W. Osborne	Mrs. C. Osborne
1889–1891	Elkanah Beard	Irena Beard
1891–1897	William Russell	R. Sabina Russell
1897–1899	Stanley A. Pearson (died in office)	Jennie L. Pearson
1899–1903	Barclay Johnson	S. Anna Johnson
1903–1917	Harry C. Wolford	Anna B. Wolford
1917–1918	John A. Baldwin	Mildred J. Baldwin
1918–1922	Harry C. Wolford	Anna B. Wolford
1922–1924	L. Raymond Jenkins	Cecelia C. Jenkins
1924–1925	L. Willard Reynolds (acting)	

Appendix B

Sample Southland Budgets

YEAR	RECEIPTS	EXPENSES	BALANCE
1874	$5,252.71	$5,423.91	-$171.20
1879	$1,047.33	$1,025.61	+$22.72
1881	$1,259.26	$1,231.38	+$27.88
1886	$4,216.46	$3,844.71	+$371.75
1889	$6,378.74	$6,561.80	-$183.06
1892	$6,437.70	$6,106.13	+$331.57
1894	$6,458.10	$7,318.68	-$860.58
1900	$3,084.26	$3,544.66	-$460.40
1904	$4,149.33	$4,397.33	-$248.00
1907	$6,415.46	$6,407.46	+$8.00
1911	$9,721.77	$10,675.18	-$953.41
1917	$12,848.26	$13,739.63	-$891.27
1918	$14,195.98	$14,273.86	-$77.88
1920	$15,348.68	$15,319.12	+$29.56
1922	$16,767.17	$16,606.77	+$160.40

Source: Minutes of Indiana Yearly Meeting, 1864–1920, Second Annual Report of Board of Home Missions, 1922

Appendix C

Southland Enrollment

YEAR	TOTAL	BOARDERS	YEAR	TOTAL	BOARDERS
1869	216		1901	158	
1870	?		1902	100	
1871	136		1903	130	
1873	186	37	1904	155	
1874	155		1905	168	
1877	154	41	1906	225	
1878	200+	51	1907	235	
1879	177		1908	260	
1880	300	88	1909	300	160
1881	213	76	1910	385	
1882	277	52	1911	403	
1883	273	73	1912	300	
1885	286		1913	~390	
1886	274	40	1914	400+	
1887	302	55	1915	~300	
1888	?	103	1916	380	
1889	189	62	1917	~490	
1890	224	102	1918	375	
1894	171	58	1919	350	
1896	233	76	1921	200	
1897	173		1922	300	
1898	184	37	1923	172	
1899	135		1924	96	
1900	127		1925	130	

Source: Minutes of the Indiana Yearly Meeting

*These figures give the highest attendance figure in any given year; average daily attendance was often much lower.

Notes

Preface

1. Dale P. Kirkman, "Southland College," *Phillips County Historical Quarterly* (hereafter as *PCHQ*) 3, no. 1 (September 1964): 30–33.

2. Russell and Tressie Ratliff and F. Raymond Jenkins, interview by the author, 19 June 1981.

3. Thomas C. Kennedy, "Southland College: The Society of Friends and Black Education in Arkansas," *Arkansas Historical Quarterly* (hereafter as *AHQ*) 42, no. 3 (Autumn 1983): 207–38.

4. Thomas C. Kennedy, "The Last Days at Southland," *The Southern Friend* 7, no. 2 (Spring 1986): 3–19; "'To Raise This People Up': The Early Years at Southland College," *Reflections* 12, no. 2 (Spring 1987): 1, 7–9; "The Rise and Decline of a Black Monthly Meeting, Southland, Arkansas," *AHQ* 50, no. 2 (Summer 1991): 115–39. Reprinted in *The Southern Friend* 19, no. 2 (Autumn 1997): 5–29, and *The Carillon* 6, nos. 1–2 (January–February 2008); "Another Kind of Emigrant: Quakers in the Arkansas Delta, 1864–1825," *AHQ* 55, no. 2 (Summer 1996): 199–220.

5. Thomas C. Kennedy, *British Quakerism: The Transformation of a Religious Community, 1860–1920* (Oxford: Oxford University Press, 2001).

1.

1. According to William M. Lytle, comp., *Merchant Steam Vessels of the United States, 1807–1868* (Mystic, CT: Steamship Historical Society of America, 1952), 11, the *Argyle* was built in 1853 at Freedom, PA, and lost, place unrecorded, in 1867. Quaker sources referred to the steamer as the *Duke of Argyle,* but Lytle lists no vessel of that name.

2. Ruthana M. Sims (hereafter as RMS) to F. Raymond Jenkins (hereafter as FRJ), 3 June 1924, quoting from the *Christian Worker,* n.d., box 6, Southland Papers (hereafter as SP), Special Collections Department, Mullins Library, University of Arkansas, Fayetteville. The *Argyle* left Cincinnati on 26 March and obviously stopped at Fort Pillow several days before 13 April 1864 when a Confederate force under Gen. Nathan Bedford Forrest captured the fort. Subsequently, members of Forrest's command massacred, in cold blood, large numbers of the surrendered garrison, most of whom were members of a "colored" Tennessee artillery unit.

3. Maria R. Mann quoted in Louis S. Gerteis, *From Contraband to Freedmen: Federal Policy Toward Southern Blacks, 1861–1865* (Westport, CT: Greenwood Press, 1973), 121; Carl H. Moneyhon, *The Impact of the Civil War and Reconstruction in Arkansas: Persistence in the Midst of Ruin* (Baton Rogue: Louisiana State University Press, 1994), 139–40. See also Margaret E. Breckinridge, "Adventures on a Hospital Boat in the Mississippi," *PCHQ* 1, no. 2 (December 1982): 35–36.

4. As early as May 1861 Gen. Benjamin F. Butler, later commander of Union forces at New Orleans, was seizing slaves working for the Confederate Army in Virginia as contraband enemy property. See Moneyhon, *Impact of the Civil War,* 137.

5. John Eaton, *Grant, Lincoln and the Freedmen* (New York: Longman, Green & Co., 1907), 22, 24. There were at least a few sympathetic soldiers. Seventeen-year-old Chauncey H. Cooke of Wisconsin told his mother, "The boys have their laugh at me for helping the blacks. . . . I won't side with the boys that are abusing them." "Wisconsin Troops in Helena: XI," *PCHQ* 15, no. 3 (June 1977): 10, 14.

6. Breckinridge, "Adventures," 36; Charles W. Johnson, "Minnesota Troops at Helena: Narrative of the Sixth Regiment," *PCHQ* 24, nos. 3–4 (June-September 1986): 5; Bobby Roberts, "'Desolation Itself': The Impact of Civil War," in *The Arkansas Delta: Land of Paradox,* ed. Jeannie Whayne and Willard B. Gatewood (Fayetteville: University of Arkansas Press, 1993): 76. Authorities estimated that 25 percent of Helena's earliest contrabands died from exposure and disease. See Bobby Lovett, "African Americans, Civil War and Aftermath in Arkansas," *AHQ* 54, no. 3 (Autumn 1995): 314.

7. For the origins and structure of Quaker relief work, see chapter 2, below.

8. *Elkanah Beard's Journal* (hereafter as *EB's Journal),* 24 April 1864, in Daniel J. Salemson, ed., "'to spend some time as a missionary among colored people': The Civil War Writings of an Indiana Quaker," *Southern Friend* (hereafter as *SF*) 10, no. 1 (Spring 1998): 46–47. Guerilla raids around Helena were so frequent in the spring and summer of 1864 that one Union commander asserted it was "hardly safe to go out of our lines a mile." Quoted in Roberts, "Desolation Itself," 88. See also Gerteis, *From Contraband to Freedmen,* 158.

9. *EB's Journal,* 7 March 1864, 43–44.

10. Ibid; *Friends' Review* (hereafter as *FR*), 17 September 1864, 38; Lydia W. Hinshaw to brother and sister, 6 November 1864, "Negro-related activities," F PG III, Earlham College Quaker Collection (hereafter as ECQC); Minutes of Indiana Yearly Meeting, (hereafter as MIYM, with year), 1864, "Report of the Executive Committee on Freedmen," MIYM, 1864, 19; H. S. Newman, "Southland College, Arkansas," *The Friend* (London) (hereafter as *TF*) (1 March 1890): 67.

11. MIYM, 1864, 19; *EB's Journal,* 18, 25 March 1864, 44–45.

12. *Christian Worker,* quoted in RMS to FRJ, 3 June 1924, box 6, SP. One assumes the military heeded Elkanah Beard's admonition "to have a large bathing tub and plenty of towel crash" available for bathing the children. *EB's Journal,* 3 March 1864, 45.

13. The Clarks had apparently been in touch with a soldier stationed at Helena, Capt. Theodore Wright, their future son-in-law and business partner, concerning the abundance of good and cheap farm land available in the Arkansas Delta. See chapter 3 below.

14. For accounts of extensive clearing timber by girdling, deadening and burning in Wayne County, see Henry Clay Fox, ed., *Memoirs of Wayne County* (Madison, IN: Western Historical Association, 1912), 2:30–31; Andrew W. Young, *History of Wayne County, Indiana* (Cincinnati: Robert Clarke, 1872), 38. Henry Morton Stanley left "a vivid and informative account of hewing cotton fields from Arkansas forests" just before the Civil War. See Orville Taylor, *Negro Slavery in Arkansas* (Durham, NC: Duke University Press, 1958), 94–95.

15. See William Johnson, "Prelude to the Missouri Compromise," *AHQ* 14, no.1 (Spring 1965): 47–66.

16. U.S. Census Bureau, *Fourth Census of the United States: 1820,* Washington DC, 1820, 41, listed 145 slaves in Phillips County. See also Carl H. Moneyhon, "Economic

Democracy in Antebellum Arkansas, Phillips County, 1850–180," *AHQ* 40, no. 2 (Summer 1981): 158.

17. An informative discussion of Crowley's Ridge and other geographical features in the Delta area is Thomas J. Foti, "The River's Gifts and Curses," in Whayne and Gatewood, *Arkansas Delta,* 30–51.

18. For early economic development, see Moneyhon, "Economic Democracy," 154–72; Donald Holley, "The Plantation Heritage: Agriculture in the Arkansas Delta," in Whayne and Gatewood, *Arkansas Delta,* 238–71.

19. Donald P. McNeilly, *The Old South Frontier: Cotton Plantations and the Formation of Arkansas Society, 1819–1861* (Fayetteville: University of Arkansas Press, 2000), 126, 132–33, 167–68; Ted Worley, "Helena on the Mississippi," *AHQ* 13 (Spring 1954): 1–15; Moneyhon, "Economic Democracy," 159.

20. Taylor, *Slavery in Arkansas,* 52, 60; Holley, "Plantation Heritage," 244; Moneyhon, "Economic Democracy," 159–64; Moneyhon, *Civil War Arkansas,* 106–8. See also Moneyhon, "The Impact of the Civil War in Arkansas: The Mississippi River Plantation Counties," *AHQ* 51, no. 2 (Summer 1992): 106–8.

21. McNeilly, *Old South Frontier,* 10, 57, 121 209; Carl Moneyhon, "Impact . . . Plantation Counties," 107–8. Planters, large and small, controlled 40 percent of improved land, 65 percent of all land, and 57 percent of the slaves. See Moneyhon, "Economic Democracy," 168.

22. Moneyhon, "Economic Democracy," 161–62, 172.

23. G. H. Hackett, ed., "Diaries and Letters of Rev. Otis Hackett," *PCHQ* 1, no. 1 (Summer 1962): 29.

24. McNeilly, *Old South Frontier,* 167–68.

25. Two standard histories of Wayne County are Andrew W. Young, *History of Wayne County, Indiana* and Fox, *Memoirs of Wayne County.*

26. Bernhard Knollenberg, *Pioneer Sketches of the Upper Whitewater Valley: Quaker Stronghold of the West,* quoted in Richard P. Ratcliff, *Our Special Heritage: Sesquincential History of Indiana Yearly Meeting of Friends, 1821–1871* (New Castle, IN: Community Printing Co., 1970), 13.

27. Young, *Wayne County,* 26–29; Fox, *Memoirs of Wayne County,* 27–29, 89–92; Salemson, "among colored people," 9; Jacquelyn Nelson, *Indiana Quakers Confront the Civil War* (Indianapolis: Indiana Historical Society, 1991), 3, 7.

28. John T. Plummer, *Richmond* (1857), quoted in Fox, *Wayne County,* 503.

29. Fox, *Wayne County,* 465.

30. Taylor, *Slavery,* 98; Moneyhon, "Economic Democracy," 159; U.S. Census Bureau, *Seventh Census of the United States: 1850,* Washington DC, 1853, 535, 556; ibid., *Eighth Census of the United States: 1860,* Washington DC, 1864, 1:18, 2:2, 7.

31. Harlow Lindley, "A Century of Indiana Yearly Meeting," *Bulletin of Friends' Historical Association* 12, no. 1 (1923): 3–7.

32. Quaker monthly meetings, wherein representatives of two or more local or particular meetings for worship met every month to consider both practical and spiritual concerns, were largely autonomous administrative bodies, responsible for matters of membership, finance, property, discipline and the resolution of disputes as well as the solemnization of marriages. Several monthly meetings generally formed a quarterly meeting that gathered four times a year for purposes of fellowship and communication. Indiana Yearly Meeting (hereafter as IYM), formed in 1821, incorporated five

quarterly meetings and embodied the final constitutional authority for the all members of the Society of Friends within its purview.

33. Lindley, "Century," 11–13; Thornburg, *Whitewater,* 9.

34. Lindley, "Century," 15.

35. Quotations are from Walter Edgerton, *A History of the Separation in Indiana Yearly Meeting in the Winter of 1842 and 1843 on the Anti-Slavery Question* (Cincinnati: Achilles Pugh, 1856), 136–37 and from a handwritten "History of Southland College Near Helena, Arkansas," 4–5, Lilly Library Quaker Collection, Earlham College, Richmond, Indiana (hereafter as "Southland History"). In 1901 the yearly meeting appointed a committee to prepare a history of Southland. See also MIYM, 1901, 47. This document, largely written by Eli Jay, is probably the draft presented to Indiana Yearly Meeting in 1905. See MIYM, 1905, 57.

36. Rufus M. Jones, *The Later Periods of Quakerism* (London: Macmillan, 1921), 2:584.

37. Jean R. Soderlund, *Quakers and Slavery: A Divided Spirit* (Princeton: Princeton University Press, 1985), 4, 17, 32. Soderlund's highly critical account is the definitive work on the mixed legacy of eastern Friends' struggle with of slavery and racial prejudice. For a more positive view regarding midwestern Friends see Thomas D. Hamm et al, "'A Great and Good People': Midwestern Quakers and the Struggle Against Slavery," *Indiana Magazine of History* 100, no. 1 (March 2004): 3–25.

38. Soderland, *Quakers and Slavery,* 26–27. Woolman's gentle but spiritually riveting persuasion had been preceded by the sometimes unruly protests of Benjamin Lay and others. See ibid., 15–21, 47. See also Edgerton, *Separation,* 13.

39. Friends who still owned slaves in 1776 were not disowned unless they refused "to execute suitable instruments for their liberation." See Edgerton, *Separation,* 21.

40. Soderlund, *Quakers and Slavery,* 177, 184, 187. For a different view see Hamm, "A Great and Good People," and *The Transformation of American Quakerism: Orthodox Friends, 1800–1907* (Bloomington: Indiana University Press, 1988), 10. Friends, Hamm says, attacked slavery for the inhumanity of the institution as well as for the fulfillment of their spiritual responsibilities; thus, they engaged in antislavery activities not only to ensure their "growth in holiness" but also because, as the Quaker writer Thomas Arnett noted, slavery deprived its human victims of the ability to live out their lives according to the light within them.

41. "Southland History," 5.

42. Ibid., 4–5, and Fox, *Memoirs of Wayne County,* 1:147–65. *The Reminiscences of Levi Coffin* (Cincinnati: Robert Clark & Co., 1880) discusses both his experiences with the Underground Railroad and the bitter separation of antislavery Friends from the Indiana Yearly Meeting. *Reminiscences* was reprinted by Arno Press in 1968 and by Friends United Press in 1991.

43. See Edgerton, *Separation,* 44–47 for the full text of this declaration.

44. Minute by William Talbert, Clerk of the Committee on the Concerns of the People of Color, 1837, reprinted in Ratcliff, *Our Special Heritage,* 73. Edgerton, *Separation,* 34–37 quotes from a series of yearly meeting documents of the late 1830s exhorting Friends to promote "immediate and unconditional emancipation."

45. Edgerton, *Separation,* 38, 40–41; Jones, *Later Periods,* 1:589.

46. Edgerton, *Separation,* 39; Stephen B. Weeks, *Southern Quakers and Slavery: A Study in Institutional History* (Baltimore:[4], 1896), 232–33.

47. Meeting for Sufferings originated in seventeenth-century England. At a time when Quakers were still enduring considerable persecution, a body of influential Friends was created to make pleas on behalf of their suffering brethren to Assize Judges meeting in London. In time, this body, meeting on the first Friday of each month, evolved into the operating executive committee of London Yearly Meeting. Friends in American yearly meetings generally followed the example of their English brethren.

48. Ratcliff, *Our Special Heritage,* 21, 68. An good recent study of the separation of antislavery Friends is Ryan Jordan, "The Indiana Separation of 1842 and the Limits of Quaker Anti-Slavery," *Quaker History* 89, no. 1 (Spring 2000): 1–27. For an contemporary antislavery version of the Henry Clay incident, see Edgerton, *Separation,* 84–86.

49. Jordan, "Indiana Separation," 1–3; Ratcliff, *Our Special Heritage,* 69; Edgerton, *Separation,* 58–60, 88–92.

50. Edgerton, *Separation,* 62–66, 68, 88–92, 119.

51. Jacquelyn Nelson, *Indiana Quakers . . . Civil War,* 5, names only eleven antislavery monthly meetings; Jordan's list of twelve includes monthly meetings in Michigan and Iowa as well as Indiana. See Jordan, "Indiana Separation," 15.

52. Ratcliff, *Our Special Heritage,* 68. Edgerton's study is notable for his reprinting of nearly every document or declaration issued by either side during this ideological and social struggle. See Edgerton, *Separation,* 100–327.

53. For the various addresses, epistles, and pleas from London Yearly Meeting, including those of a visiting delegation of weighty British Friends, see Edgerton, *Separation,* 304–52. Also see Rufus Jones, *Later Periods,* 590–94.

54. Jones, *Later Periods,* 594; Edgerton, *Separation,* 99; Jordan, "Indiana Separation," 19–21.

55. See Jordan, "Indiana Separation," 20.

56. Hamm et al, "A Great and Good People," 7–9.

57. Jordan, "Indiana Separation," 21–23; Salemson, "among colored people," 9; Thornburg, *Whitewater,* 8; Hamm, *Transformation,* 61.

58. Moneyhon, "Impact . . . Plantation Counties," 108–12, 118–19; "The 28th Wisconsin Infantry Regiment at Helena," pt. 4, *PCHQ* 13, no. 2 (March 1975) 23; ibid., pt. 5, *PCHQ,* 13, no. 4 (September 1975): 15; ibid., pt. 7, PCHQ, 14, no. 2 (June 1979): 30–40. See also Bobby Roberts, "'Desolation Itself': The Impact of Civil War," in Whayne and Gatewood, *Arkansas Delta,* 70–94

59. Young, *Wayne County,* 138

60. Nelson, *Indiana Quakers . . . Civil War,* 20–21, 37–38, 81–89, 94; Richard Wood, "Evangelical Quaker Acculturation in the Upper Mississippi Valley," *Quaker History* (hereafter as *QH*) 76, no. 2 (Fall 1987): 141; Thomas D. Hamm, Gretchen Kleinhen, Margaret Marconi, and Benjamin Whitman, "The Decline of Quaker Pacifism in the Twentieth Century: Indiana Yearly Meeting of Friends as a Case Study," *Indiana Magazine of History* 96, no. 1 (March 2000): 48.

61. *FR* 27, no. 21 (3 January 1864): 324–25. The conscientious objector clause passed by Congress in January 1864 was reprinted in ibid. 28, nos. 26, 27 (February 1864). Also see Ratcliff, *Our Special Heritage,* 73.

62. MIYM, 1863, 28–29; *FR* 27, nos. 11, 14 (November 1863): 166; "History of Southland College," 8–10; Nelson, *Indiana Quakers . . . Civil War,* 97.

63. MIYM, 1863, 28–29; *FR* 27, nos. 11, 14 (November 1863): 166; Salemson, "among colored people," 10; *Friends Intelligencer* 21 (July 1864): 217.

2.

1. In July 1862 Congress had passed the Confiscation Act that declared that slaves held by masters in rebellion against the federal government were henceforth free.

2. John Eaton, *Grant, Lincoln and the Freedmen* (New York: Longmans, Green & Co., 1907), 2, 19, 125–26.

3. Eaton to Coffin, 27 March 1863, quoted in Gerteis, *Contraband to Freedmen,* 121–22; Eaton to Coffin, 5 July 1864, quoted in Eaton, *Grant, Lincoln and the Freedmen,* 133–34; Job Hadley, "Reminiscences, 1883," ECQC, 6–16; Christopher B. Coleman, "A Contraband Camp," *Indiana History Bulletin* 1, nos. 11–12 (September 1924): 138–40; *FR* 17, no. 10 (7 November 1863): 152.

4. Because of early English Friends' devotion to spiritual equality, Quakers traditionally rejected the idea of a separate, trained, privileged, and paid clergy. Still, the special gift of vocal ministry was always recognized and, from the early eighteenth century, inspired preachers, both male and female, were acknowledged and "recorded" by their monthly meetings. The practice continued into nineteenth century but following the evangelical revival among midwestern Friends in the 1870s, many yearly meetings, including Indiana's, replaced the original practice of recognized but unpaid ministers with a system of paid "pastors" presiding over "programmed" meetings that increasingly resembled the services in most evangelical Protestant denominations. See Hamm, *Transformation,* 124–27 and chapter 5 below.

5. Salemson, "among colored people," 10–11, 13; *EB's Journal,* 1 June 1863, 21–22; ibid., 21 June 1863, 22; ibid., 28 June 1863, 22–25. The school Elkanah Beard visited in Helena was probably being taught by a representative of the American Missionary Association. See Carl Moneyhon, *Impact of the Civil War,* 151 and Larry Wesley Pearce "The American Missionary Association and the Freedmen in Arkansas, 1863–1878," *AHQ* 30, no. 2 (Summer 1971): 123–44.

6. A few weeks after Samuel Shipley's visit another observer found people in Camp Wood near Helena, "suffering extremely for want of clothing, shoes and bedding." David Worcester to Major Sargeant, 23 February 1864, quoted in Randy Finley, "In War's Wake: Health Care and Arkansas Freedmen, 1863–1868," *AHQ* 51, no. 2 (Summer 1992): 137. Beard told a prominent eastern Quaker that "several thousands" of refugees in camps in the interior of Arkansas who were even "more destitute . . . than any on the river." Beard to J. Wister Evans, 24 December 1863, quoted in *FR* 17, nos. 21, 23 (January 1864): 323.

7. Salemson, "among colored people," 11; Beard, *FR* 17, no. 16 (19 December 1863): 250–51; S. Shipley to J. Wistar Evans, 22 December 1863, quoted in *FR* 17, no. 22 (30 January 1864): 347; Beard to Samuel Rhoads, 8 January 1864, quoted in *FR* 17, no. 23 (6 February 1864): 362; MIYM, 1864, 26.

8. *FR* 17, no. 16 (19 December 1863): 250–51; ibid. 17, no. 22 (30 January 1864): 348; ibid. 17, no. 23 (6 February 1864): 362–63; *American Friend* (hereafter as *AF*), 16 March 1905, 182–83; Eaton, *Grant, Lincoln and Freedmen,* 202; Report of Indiana Yearly Meeting's Executive Committee for the Relief of Colored Freedmen, Richmond, IN, 1864, 4–7, quoted in Linda B. Selleck, *Gentle Invaders: Quaker Women Educators and Racial Issues During the Civil War and Reconstruction* (Richmond: Friends United Press, 1995), 98.

9. Eaton, *Grant, Lincoln and the Freedmen,* 201; Beard to Indiana Executive

Committee, Report of Indiana Yearly Meeting's Executive Committee for the Relief of Colored Freedmen, 33, quoted in Salemson, "among colored people," 44; *EB's Journal,* 8 March 1864; Hadley, "Reminiscences, 1883," 14–15.

10. *FR* 18, no. 4 (24 September 1864): 53.

11. I am grateful to Dr. Lori Bogel for sharing this information, and much of what follows concerning the Clarks, with me.

12. The family picture and a single photo of Alida appeared in a story about her family in the *Richmond Palladium,* 29, September 1940, a copy of which is in F PG VI, ECQC.

13. *FR* 17, no. 6 (10 October 1863): 82; Hamm, *Transformation,* 48–52. Hamm's discussion of "The Renewal Movement, 1850–1870," ibid., 37–73, provides a clear, concise, and evocative portrait of changing nature of Quaker religious and social thought in the American Midwest. See also chapter 5 below.

14. Richard E. Wood, "Evangelical Quakers Acculturation in the Upper Mississippi Valley," *QH* 76, no. 2 (Fall 1987): 128–29, 140.

15. John Henry Douglas to *FR* 19, no. 14 (December 1865): 4. See also Dale P. Kirkman, "Southland College," *PCHQ* 3, no. 1 (September. 1964): 30 and Lori Bogel, "Carpetbaggers of Souls," unpublished paper.

16. *FR* 17, no. 38 (21 May 1864): 603; ibid. 17, no. 42 (8 June 1864): 667; ibid. 17, no. 46 (16 July 1864): 730; ibid. 18, no. 4 (24 September 1864): 53; Locke to Eaton, July 1864, microfilm roll 6, Freedmen's Bureau Records (hereafter as FBR), Mullins Library, University of Arkansas; John Eaton, Report of the General Superintendent of Freedmen, Department of Tennessee and the State of Arkansas for 1864, Memphis, TN, 1865, 72; A. McD. McCook to Rev. J. H. Nixon, 26 March 1865, FBR.

17. Lydia and Nathaniel Hinshaw, John L. Roberts, Susan Horney, Joanne Moore, and William Penn Hunnicutt were mentioned at one time or another in Quaker sources as having charge at Helena in the Clarks' absence. See MIYM, 1865, 18, 41–43; *FR* 18, no. 13 (26 November 1864): 203; Lydia W. Hinshaw to brother and sister, 6 November 1864, ECQC. Also see Eaton, *Grant, Lincoln and Freedmen,* 200.

18. *EB's Journal,* 1 September 1865, 52.

19. *FR* 18, no. 19 (7 January 1865): 294; ibid. 19, no. 13 (25 November 1865): 203; Minutes of the Indiana Yearly Meeting Committee for Freedmen, 30 September 1864, 13 October 1864, 22 November 1864, F PG I, ECQC; MIYM, 1865, 44–46.

20. MIYM, 1865, 42–44; *AF* 1, no. 1 (January 1867): 2; "Diaries of Rev. Otis Hackett, 1 Jan. 1866," *PCHQ* 1, no. 1 (Summer 1962): 37; "Report of the Superintendent of Freedmen," Henry Sweeney, 30 June 1865, quoted in *PCHQ* 16, no. 3 (1978): 14; MIYM, 1865, 45; *FR* 19, no. 13 (5 November 1865): 203; ibid. 19, no. 14 (2 December 1865): 218; "Letter to the Senate . . .," 14 December 1865, quoted by Selleck, *Gentle Invaders,* 132–33 and Eaton, *Grant, Lincoln and Freedmen,* 207.

21. MIYM, *1865,* 47; *FR,* 19/14, December 1865, 218–19; and MIYM, 1866, 36.

22. *FR* 19, no. 44 (30 June 1866): 700; ibid. 19, no. 14 (2 December 1865): 218; ibid. 19, no. 19 (6 January 1866): 300; Sweeney Report, 13 October 1865, quoted in Finley, "In War's Wake,"" 155; Cornelia Hancock quoted in Deborah K. Day, "'The Magic Awakening Touch': The Interplay Between Spirituality and Public Activism: Quaker Women and Education in the South, 1865–1901," *Southern Friend* (Fall 1996): 9–10; Ruth Emily Edwards's Diary, 12 January 1866, SC 21, ECQC. I am grateful to Thomas Hamm for identifying the author of this diary.

23. Sweeney to Sargent, 31 January 1865, Sweeney to McCook, 21 April 1865, Sweeney to Palmer, 10 October 1866, and Sweeney to Tyler, 26 April 1867, quoted in Finley, "In War's Wake," 137, 145; "Dairies of Rev. Otis Hackett," 1 January 1866, 38; C. H. Watson to Father, 18 July 1864, quoted in "Wisconsin Troops at Helena," *PCHQ* 15, no. 3 (June 1977): 8.

24. Freedmen's Record I, December 1865, 4, 7, Richmond, IN; ibid., March 1866, 9. The origins of Southland College confirm Carl Moneyhon's assertion that "the Union Army was a major force determining the structure of postbellum life." Moneyhon, *Impact of the Civil War,* 142.

25. *AF* 1, no. 1 (January 1867): 2; ibid. 1, no. 1 (February 1867): 29; Minutes, Missionary Board of Indiana Yearly Meeting, (hereafter as Min., MB, with year), SP, 358; Alida Clark (hereafter as AC), "Normal Institute and Orphans Home," 9 June 1871, ECQC; "Southland History," 12; Kirkman, "Southland College," 30–31.

26. Heather Andrea Williams, *self-taught: African American Education in Slavery and Freedom* (Chapel Hill: University of North Carolina Press, 2005), 62–63. The Fifty-Sixth Regiment was formed in St. Louis and Arkansas in August 1863, and its members were part of the more than five thousand black troops raised in Arkansas. *AF* 1, no. 1 (January 1867): 28; Bobby L. Lovett, "African Americans, Civil War and Aftermath in Arkansas," *AHQ* 56, no. 3 (Autumn 1995): 35; Moneyhon, *Impact of the Civil War,* 138. For an account of the Fifty-Sixth Regiment's stalwart conduct under fire, see Brian K. Robertson, "'Will They Fight? Ask the Enemy': United States Colored Troops at Big Creek, Arkansas, July 26, 1864," *AHQ* 66, no. 3 (Autumn 2007): 320–32. Indiana Quakers, who seemed compulsively interested in the monetary value of everything, estimated that the Fifty-Sixth Colored Regiment had donated a total of $4,166.75 to the yearly meeting. MIYM, 1866, 40–41.

27. Williams, *self-taught,* 63; AC, "Normal Institute and Orphans Home," ECQC; MIYM, 1866, 32–35; *FR* 20, no. 16 (15 December 1866): 251–52; *AF* 1, no. 1 (January 1867): 28; Kirkman, "Southland College," 31.

28. Calvin Clark to *FR,* July 1866, 6. The original site was described as "comparatively level, productive . . . parts of it somewhat wet." "Southland History," 17. For a description of the original school compound, see "Report of Joseph Dickinson and Timothy Harrison," Freemen's Record I, September 1866, Richmond, IN, 11.

29. The asylum was originally called Swarthmore after the home (Swarthmoor) of Margaret Fell, a pioneer of English Quakerism who, as a widow, married Quaker founder George Fox. No doubt Alida Clark felt a strong attraction to this able and dynamic early female Friend, but the name was changed because Swarthmore was also the name given to the college in Pennsylvania established by Hicksite Friends in 1869 who, amidst a bitter theological and social clash within the Philadelphia Yearly Meeting during 1828–29, had separated from their Orthodox brethren. Thereafter, Orthodox or Gurneyite Friends like those in the Indiana Yearly Meeting refused to acknowledge Hicksites as true Quakers. See H. Larry Ingle, *Quakers in Conflict: The Hicksite Reformation* (Knoxville: University of Tennessee Press, 1986).

30. There are brief biographical sketches of the Clarks in the *Dictionary of Quaker Biography* (*DQB*) in the Haverford College Quaker Collection (HCQC) and in *Biographical and Historical Memoirs of Eastern Arkansas* (Chicago, 1890), 756–7. Lori Bogle has written a biographical essay on Alida Clark for *Arkansas Biography,* ed. Nancy A. Williams (Fayetteville: University of Arkansas Press, 2000), 61–62, and her

obituary is in *FR* 45 (1892): 605. For Calvin see *AF* (14 February 1908): 108. For addition information see Selleck, *Gentle Invaders,* 191–223.

31. Quoted in Irene Utter, "A Thanksgiving Guest at Southland," *AF* (November 1923): 860; *The Friend* (London) (1 July 1884): 186; *CW* 8, no. 20 (15 May 1878): 231; "Southland History," 44–46.

32. *CW* 17, no. 51 (2 December 1887): 609; Emily [Ruth] Edwards's "Diary"; MIYM, 1866, 35; *The Friend* 41, 230.

33. *FR,* 20, no. 20 (12 January 1867): 316; Minutes, Freedmen's Relief Committee, 31 May 1867, ECQC; MIYM, 1866, 32; ibid., 1869, 60–61; Salemson, "among colored people," 13–14.

34. Moneyhon, *Impact of the Civil War,* 236; Diaries of Judge James Millinder Hanks, 1865–69, 24 January and 23 April 1866, Special Collections, Mullins Library, University of Arkansas (hereafter as Hanks Diaries); Diaries of Rev. Otis Hackett, 38.

35. Lovett, "African Americans," 316; David Biron Davis, *The Problem of Slavery in Western Culture* (Ithaca, NY: Cornell University Press, 1966), 254; Ronald G. Butchart, *Northern Schools, Southern Blacks, and Reconstruction: Freedmen's Education, 1862–1875* (Westport, CT: Greenwood Press, 1980), 99; Jeannie M. Whayne, Thomas A. DeBlack, George Sabo III, and Morris S. Arnold, *Arkansas: A Narrative History (*Fayetteville: University of Arkansas Press, 2002), 208–12; John W. Graves, *Town and Country: Race Relations in an Urban-Rural Context, Arkansas, 1895–1905* (Fayetteville: University of Arkansas Press, 1990), 9–10; Thomas DeBlack, *With Fire and Sword: Arkansas, 1861–1874* (Fayetteville: University of Arkansas Press, 2003), 155–56.

36. *FR* 20, no. 20 (12 January 1867): 316; *AF* 1, no. 2 (February 1867): 30; ibid. 1, no. 7 (July 1967). See also Finley, "In War's Wake," 152, 154.

37. *FR* 20, no. 20 (12 January 1867): 316; *AF* 1, no. 1 (January 1867): 1–2; Sweeney to IYM, quoted in *AF* 1, no. 6 (June 1867): 144–45; ibid. 1, no. 9 (September 1867): 213; AC, Normal Institute and Orphans Home, 29 June 1871, ECQC.

38. Whayne et al, *Arkansas,* 206–8; Fred Berry and John Novak, *The History of Arkansas* (Little Rock: Rose, 1997), 111; Col. Willoughby Williams to Powell Clayton, quoted in DeBlack, *With Fire and Sword,* 146.

3.

1. AC to *FR* 26, no. 44 (21 June 1873): 702.

2. Ibid. 21, no. 25 (15 February 1868): 397.

3. *AF* 1, no. 5 (May 1867): 173; ibid. 1, no. 7 (July 1867): 165–67; ibid. 1, no. 8 (August 1867): 189; *FR* 20, no. 45 (6 July 1867): 715. For descriptions of the 1867 flood and its effects, see "Diaries of Rev. Otis Hackett," 1 April 1867, 41, and W. Colby to Col. C. H. Smith, 13 April 1867, reel 28, FBR.

4. *FR* 21, no. 25 (15 February 1868): 397–98.

5. Butchart, *Northern Schools, Southern Blacks,* xiii, 8, 16, 41, 59, 94, 161, 213n.

6. Ibid., 10, 16–17, 25, 41, 59, 166.

7. Hamm, *American Quakerism,* 69; Butchart (83) does indicate that Quakers did not entirely speak with one voice by noting the split between the strongly evangelical Western Freedman's Aid Commission (WFAC) and the Committee for Relief of Colored Freedman (CRCF). Some Friends believed Levi Coffin, who accused the CRCF of being composed of "Hicksites and Infidels," seemed more interested in

denouncing that organization than acting "for relief to the sufferers." George Evans to A. M. Taylor, 26 March 1863, Henry Rowntree to Taylor, 20 May 1863, A. M. Taylor Papers, HCQC.

8. Hamm, *Transformation,* 69–70.

9. *FR* 27, no. 21 (23 January 1864): 35; Salemson, *EB's Journal,* 1 November 1864, 5, 51; Freedmen's Record, 1 December 1865, 5. In March 1867 Douglas noted that "Providence has opened a great field in which we may easily manifest our love for Christ by caring for his helpless children." *AF* 1, no. 5 (May 1867): 114.

10. For the view that Quakers "shared many of the attitudes expressed by Evangelicals about the quality of Christian life," see Donald G. Matthews, *Religion in the Old South* (Chicago: University of Chicago Press, 1977), 135–36. For evangelical influences on slave religion, see Milton C. Sernett, *Black Religion and American Evangelicalism* (Metuchen, NJ: Scarecrow Press, 1975) and Albert J. Raboteau, "The Black Experience in American Evangelicalism: The Meaning of Slavery," in *African American Religion,* Timothy E. Fullop and Albert J Raboteau, eds. (New York: Routledge, 1997), 89–106.

11. Freedmen's Record, 1 June 1866, 7; "History of Southland," 23–5; Walter T. Carpenter to *AF* 1, no. 1 (January 1867): 2; ibid. 1, no. 3 (March 1867): 57; *FR* 20, no. 20 (12 January 1867): 316.

12. *FR* 20, no. 30 (23 March 1867): 473, 475 (emphasis in original).

13. *AF* 1, no. 4 (April 1867): 87; MIYM, 1867, 78; Calvin and Alida Clark to Missionary Board, IYM, 11 March 1868, ECQC. For Drew, see *The Friend* (1 December 1869): 277 and Selleck, *Gentle Invaders,* 205–9.

14. *AF* 2. no. 6 (June 1868): 146–47, ibid. 2, no. 7 (July 1868): 161. See also MIYM, 1869, 38, and Elkanah Beard Diaries, 11 February 1869, 24 February 1869, ECQC, noting his support for eight additional Southland blacks who had applied for membership. By this time Beard had apparently disposed of any lingering doubts about the suitability of blacks Quakers.

15. *FR* 22, no. 40 (29 May 1869): 636; ibid. 22, no. 51 (14 August 1869): 810–11; ibid. 24, no. 10 (28 October 1870): 155.

16. MIYM, 1870, 9; *FR* 24, no.10 (29 October 1870): 155; ibid. 24, no. 12 (12 November 1870): 185.

17. *AR* 2, no. 4 (April 1868): 76; *FR* 22, no. 48 (29 May 1869): 636; ibid. 24, no. 10 (29 October 1870): 155.

18. Joseph Moore, "Visit to Helena, Ark.," *CW* 1, no. 4 (15 May 1871): 68–69; MIYM, 1869, 45; and *British Friend* (February 1871): 45.

19. Reprinted in *FR* 24, no.48 (22 July 1871): 759–60, 763. The general tone of Philadelphia Yearly Meeting was conservative or "Wilburite," stressing the need to hold fast to traditional Quaker forms of worship and discipline.

20. *The Friend*): (Nov 1869), 252–53; *AF* 2, no. 6 (June 1868): 147.

21. *FR* 24, no. 13 (5 November 1870): 171; ibid. 24, no. 21 (14 January 1871): 331.

22. *AF* 1, no. 6 (June 1867): 141; ibid. 1, no. 10 (October 1867): 237–38.

23. Box XII, Enoch K. Miller Papers, Small Manuscript Collections, Arkansas History Commission, Little Rock; Miller to Wm. Colby, 13 May 1867, FBR, quoted in Larry Wesley Pearse, "Enoch K. Miller and the Freedmen's Schools," *AHQ* 31, no. 4 (Winter 1972): 321; Colby to C. H. Smith, 1 April 1868, FBR, roll 28, 140–41; *AF* 2, no. 12 (February 1868): 48.

24. MIYM, 1867, 9–10.

25. *AF* 1, no.11 (November 1867): 261; Elkanah Beard, "Diaries," 9 January 1868, ECQC. Calvin Clark reported farm produce had yielded over three hundred dollars in sales, and he expected the next year to be even better. Southland's assets were estimated at over $9,400. MIYM, 1867, 11.

26. Even prior to the Civil War Arkansas had only twenty-five publicly financed schools. See Graves, *Town and Country,* 33.

27. Graves, *Town and Country,* 9–10, 33; Larry Wesley Pearce, "The American Missionary Association and the Freedmen's Bureau in Arkansas, 1866–1868," *AHQ* 31, no. 3 (Autumn 1972): 243–45; *The 1868 Report: A Collection of Historical Documents From Arkansas' First Land Commissioner* (Little Rock: Commissioner of State Lands, 2002), 171–73. Also see Robert E. Waterman and Thomas Rothrock, eds., "The Earle-Buchanan Letters of 1861–1876," *AHQ* 33, no. 2 (Summer 1974): 159–60.

28. *FR* 21, no. 25 (15 February 1868): 398; *AF* 1, no. 12 (December 1867): 302.

29. *AF* 2, no. 2 (February 1868): 48; ibid. 2, no. 3 (March 1868): 51–52; Alida to Friend Miller, February 1868, box 7, E. K. Miller Papers, Arkansas History Commission, Little Rock; Colby to Smith, 1 March 1868, reel 28, 122–24, FBR.

30. *AR* 2, no. 7 (July 1868): 161; ibid. 2, no. 9 (September 1868): 223. Eventually, nineteen children were chosen for teacher training. MIYM, 1869, 39.

31. Alvord to Colby, 26 February 1869, quoted in Larry Wesley Pearce, "AMA and Freedmen's Bureau in Arkansas," 248–49; MIYM, 1869, 36, 38, 42.

32. "Southland College" (1895), F PG II, ECQC, 5; *AF* 1, no. 1 (January 1867): 2; James D. Anderson, *The Education of Blacks in the South, 1860–1935* (Chapel Hill: University of North Carolina Press, 1988), 25; Moneyhon, *Civil War in Arkansas,* 117; James M. Hanks's "Diaries," 9 April 1867, Mullins Library, Special Collections.

33. Butchart, *Northern Schools, Southern Blacks,* 117–8; Report of 2 March 1868, roll 32, FBR. Elkanah Beard recorded the story of a black man searching for a stray cow who was shot, without provocation, by two whites. Elkanah Beard, "Diaries," 5 April 1868.

34. Fon Louise Gordon, "From Slavery to Uncertain Freedom: Blacks in the Delta," in Whayne and Gatewood, *Arkansas Delta,* 103; *American Annual Cyclopedia,* 1867, D. Appleton & Co., 7:53.

35. Graves, *Town and Country,* 14, 24; DeBlack, *With Fire and Sword,* 161; Whayne et al, *Arkansas,* 213–15; "Hanks Diaries," 4 and 10 August and 27 September 1867, MLSC.

36. Graves, *Town and Country,* 25, 30; Berry and Novak, *History of Arkansas,* 112; DeBlack, *With Fire and Sword,* 169–73.

37. "The Asylum," *AF* 2, no. 4 (April 1868): 76.

38. *FR* 22, no. 10 (31 October 1868): 157. The Ku Klux Klan attempted to intimidate blacks in rural areas in 1868 but was largely driven underground by the firm response of newly elected governor Powell Clayton, a northern Republican "carpetbagger" who lived in Helena. Governor Clayton mobilized the mainly black state militia in restoring law and order. Graves, *Town and Country,* 24–27, 37 and Whayne et al, *Arkansas,* 216–18.

39. J. W. Alvord to Wm. Colby, 26 February 1869, FBR, quoted in Larry Wesley Pearce, "AMA and Freedmen's Bureau," 248–49 and MIYM, 1869, 38–39, 42, 44.

40. MIYM, 1869, 43; *The Friend* (November 1869): 252.

41. *Arkansas Senate Journal, 1866–67,* 217–18, cited by Robert E. Waterman and Thomas Rothrock, eds., "The Earle-Buchanan Letters of 1861–1876," *AHQ* 33, no. 2 (Summer 1974): 159–60; Pearce, "AMA and Freedmen's Bureau, 1866–68," 243–47.; Fon Louise Gordon, *Caste and Class: The Black Experience in Arkansas, 1880–1920* (Athens: University of Georgia Press, 1995), 9; *FR* 22, no. 40 (29 May 1869): 635.

42. MIYM, 1869, 42; MIYM, 1870, 9–12; "History of Southland College," 18; Joseph Moore, "Visit to Helena, Ark.," *CW* 1, no. 4 (15 May 1871): 69.

43. *EB's Journal,* 11 February 1869, "to spend some time," 63.

4.

1. Letter from AC, *FR* 26, no. 27 (22 February 1873): 426.

2. MIYM, 1870, 9; DeBlack, *With Fire and Sword,* 203. For a discussion of the difficulties of Powell Clayton's administration and the ensuing split within the Republican Party, see Whayne et al, *Arkansas,* 223–31 and Graves, *Town and Country,* 46–50.

3. Henry Page to Calvin Clark, 23 August 1873, roll 2, 114, FRB and MIYM, 1870, 10–12.

4. Elkanah Beard in *CW* 8, no. 20 (15 May 1878): 231; *I*1872, 11; Dale Kirkman, "Southland College," *PCHQ* 3, no. 1 (September 1964): 30–33.

5. "Visit to Helena, Ark.," Joseph Moore, *CW* 1, no. 4, (15 May 1871): 68–69 and MIYM, 1871, 12

6. *FR* 26, no. 13 (5 November 1870): 171; ibid. 26, no. 7 (5 October 1872): 108; ibid. 26, no. 10 (26 October 1872): 155; Minutes, Missionary Board of Indiana Yearly Meeting (hereafter as MB), 28 September 1872, box 11, Southland Papers (SP), Mullins Library, Special Collections, 3; *CW* 2, no. 16 (15 October 1872): 191.

7. MIYM, 1872, 6; *FR* 26, no. 17 (14 December 1872): 264.

8. MIYM, 1873, 16; Minutes, MB, 16 September 1873, 19; *FR* 27, no. 8 (11 October 1873): 120; *CW* 3, no. 20 (15 October 1873): 308; and Minutes, Southland Monthly Meeting (hereafter as SMM), 17 December 1873, box 12, SP, 3.

9. *CW* 4, no. 2 (15 January 1874): 21. For an informed and lucid discussion of the ideas and impact of the renewal and holiness movements on American Quakerism, see Hamm, *Transformation,* 36–97.

10. *FR* 27, no. 8 (11 October 1873): 120; ibid. 27, no. 9 (18 October 1873): 137. So-called "threshing" meetings organized by seventeenth-century Friends to attract Seekers provided an historical precedent for such evangelically inspired general meetings. See W. C. Braithwaite, *The Beginnings of Quakerism,* 2nd ed. (Cambridge: Cambridge University Press, 1955), 134, 160, 167.

11. Minutes, MB, 18 March 1873, 8; ibid., 17 June 1873, 11–13; ibid., 28 July 1873, 14–15; ibid., 30 September 1873, 20. See Hamm, *Transformation,* 71–72 for the impact of general meetings.

12. *FR* 25, no. 31 (23 March 1872): 493; ibid. 30, no. 41 (26 May 1877): 651; ibid. 35, no. 42 (27 May 1882): 660.

13. For discussion of Mrs. Clark's fundraising activities, see chapter 5 below.

14. On 18 March 1874, for example, the Southland minutes contain a copy of London Yearly Meeting's general epistle "setting before us most freely the *great doctrine of the atonement as the foundation of the faith of our religious society*" (emphasis in origi-

nal). Minutes, SMM, 10–11. See also ibid., 17 October 1877, 16 and ibid., 15 January 1879, 93 and Hamm, *Transformation,* 49.

15. Minutes, SMM, 17 December 1873, 3. Hamm, *Transformation,* 26, notes that by the 1860s "First Day Schools for Scriptural Instruction . . . had become a fixture in most Friends meetings."

16. Minutes, SMM, 21 January 1874, 6–7.

17. Ibid., February 1874, 9. For an example of the "Queries" regularly sent out to monthly meetings by Indiana Yearly Meeting, see MIYM, 1872, 7–8.

18. Minutes, SMM, 19 July 1876, 54.

19. Ibid., February 1874, 9.

20. See Circular Letter of William Colby, Superintendent of Education, Arkansas, 13 January 1868, quoted in Butchart, *Northern Schools, Southern Blacks,* 163; MIYM, 1870, 10–11; *FR* 24, no. 30 (18 March 1871): 474; ibid. 25, no. 31 (23 March 1872): 493.

21. MIYM, 1871, Minute 18, Report of Calvin and Alida Clark, 15 September 1871, 17; *FR* 25, nos. 31 (23 March 1872): 493.

22. *FR,* 25, no. 31 (23 March 1872): 492; ibid. 24, no. 30 (18 March 1871): 475; MIYM, 1870, 10–11; ibid., 1871, 16–17.

23. MIYM, 1871, 17; ibid., 1874, 13.

24. Quaker Heritage Press, s.v. *The Autobiography of Lydia Meader Chace,* www.qhpress.org/quakerpages/qwhp/lydiachace.htm (accessed 14 February 2003).

25. MIYM, 1873, 9–10; AC to *FR* 27, no. 3 (6 September 1873): 42–3; ibid. 28, no. 26 (15 February 1875): 413. See also Lydia Chace's obituary in *AF* (22 June 1916): 477. Both Lydia and Amasa Chace (sometimes *Chase*) (1823–1888) are included in the *DQB,* HCQC.

26. Lydia M. Chase, "The Freedmen Again," *FR* 27, no. 6 (27 September 1873): 93.

27. *CW* 4, no. 16 (15 August 1874): 250–52; *FR* 27, no. 52 (15 August 1874): 826–28; MIYM, 1874, 11; Minutes, SMM, 20 May 1874, box 12, SP, 17.; Minutes, MB, 7 October 1874, 64; ibid., 6 October 1874, box 11, SP, 65–66; *The Autobiography of Lydia Meader Chace,* 12; Biographical sketch of Amasa Chase, *DQB,* HCQC.

28. See chapter 5 below for Alida's 1874 funding raising mission.

29. MIYM, 1875, 14–15, 17–18; Lydia Chace to Daniel Hill, 21 May 1875, reprinted in *CW* 5, no. 15 (1 August 1875): 236–38; *FR* 28, no. 52 (14 August 1875): 827–28; *American Missionary,* May 1875, 107–15. The penchant for numerical summaries seems to have been a ubiquitous aspect of late-nineteenth-century Quaker reporting on religious activities.

30. Minutes, SMM, 20 January 1875, 26; ibid., 15 July 1874, 18; ibid., 19 August 1874, 20; *FR* 8, no. 7 (3 October 1874): 106; ibid., 29, no. 10 (23 October 1875): 157; *CW* 5, no. 7 (15 April 1875): 107.

31. *CW*5, no. 15 (1 August 1875): 238; MIYM, 1875, 14–15; Yardley Warner to the *Maryville Monitor,* quoted in *FR* 26, no. 36 (26 April 1873): 575. For these Friends, conversion to the Church of Rome apparently seemed a worse fate than remaining entirely unchurched.

32. *FR* 30, no. 38 (5 May 1877): 652; Minutes, SMM, 18 March 1874, 12–13; ibid., 21 March 1877; MIYM, 1877, 36.

33. Minutes, SMM, 20 June 1877, 68. Southland's first overseers were Morris Brown, Calvin Clark, Angeline Gant, Evaline Hall Ivy, Jacob J. Johnson, Henrietta Kitterall, and James T. Walton. See ibid., 21 January 1874, 6.

34. Southland minutes and record of membership indicate that at least fifteen members were disowned between 1876 and 1883 and only four thereafter, the last in 1912. The names of five others were brought before the meeting by overseers, but these were returned to good standing after they admitted guilt and asked forgiveness.

35. Minutes, MB, 27 April 1874, 43.

36. *FR* 30, no. 23 (20 January 1877): 362.

37. AC to Rev. M. E. Streiby, 2 March 1877, American Missionary Association Archives, Microfilm, Arkansas History Commission, Little Rock. See also Minutes, SMM, 21 February 1877, box 12, SP, 61.

38. *FR* 29, no. 8 (9 October 1875): 124; ibid. 29, no. 14 (20 November 1875): 222.

39. Early on Southland Quakers had emphasized the biracial nature of Hickory Ridge Meeting. Not surprisingly, this seems to have been a fairly short-lived phenomenon.

40. *FR*29, no. 32 (25 March 1876): 505–6; Minutes, MB, 15 August. 1876, 100–101; and Minutes, SMM, 19 April 1876, 45–46, 48.

41. Minutes, MB, 28 August 1876, 112; Lydia Chace to *FR* 29, no. 29 (4 March 1876): 458; Lydia Chace to *CW* 6, no. 5 (1 March 1876): 67.

42. MIYM, 1876, 33; AC to *FR* 29, no. 45 (24 June 1876): 715–16.

43. Amasa and Lydia Chace to *CW* 4, no. 16 (15 August 1874): 250–51.

44. Joseph Moore to *CW* 1, no. 4, (15 May 1871): 69.

45. MIYM, 1871, 12–13; AC to *FR* 24, no. 48 (22 July 1871): 763.

46. MIYM, 1871, 12; *CW* 1, no. 8 (15 September 1871): 158; *FR* 25, no. 31 (23 March 1872): 492.

47. *CW* 1, no. 9 (15 October 1871): 171; FR 25, no. 31 (23 March 1872): 493; ibid. 26, no. 37 (8 May 1873): 588. With regard to "profligacy in dress," Elkanah Beard remarked that the clothing of many local blacks was better suited to "a drawing room than a cotton field." MIYM, 1872, 12–13.

48. MIYM, 1872, 10–13

49. In March 1873, Alida Clark, with Prof. M. W. Martin of Pine Bluff, appeared before the board of trustees of the new University of Arkansas depreciating the lack of facilities for training black teachers and asking that "a normal school for the education . . . of persons as colored teachers" be established. Acting upon this testimony, the board recommended the legislation that established the Branch Normal School at Pine Bluff (now UA–Pine Bluff). See Thomas Rothrock, "Joseph Carter Corbin and Negro Education in the University of Arkansas," *AHQ* 30, no. 4 (Winter 1971): 281–84.

50. AC to *FR* 26, no. 27 (22 February 1873): 426.

51. Minutes, MB, 28 October 1872, 5; ibid., 18 March 1873, 7; ibid., 8 April 1873, 9; *FR* 26, no. 37 (3 May 1873): 588; ibid. 26, no. 44 (21 June 1873): 701–2.

52. Minutes, MB, 16 September 1873, 18–19; *CW* 3, no. 20 (15 October 1873): 308.

53. MIYM, 1874, 14; AC to *FR* 28, no. 7 (3 October 1874): 106; *CW* 4, no. 16 (15 August 1874): 256.

54. For brief accounts of the so-called Brooks-Baxter War and its effects, see DeBlack, *With Fire and Sword,* 216–24; Whayne et al, *Arkansas,* 229–33; and Berry and Novak, *History of Arkansas,* 119–22. In 1875 the Democratic legislature passed what opponents called the "peonage act," giving landlord's lien for rents precedence over laborer's lien for crops. See Graves, *Town and Country,* 59–61.

55. MIYM, 1874, 11–12; AC to *FR* 28, no. 26 (13 February 1875): 413.

56. Graves, *Town and Country,* 46–47. Graves (67) cites Phillips County as "an outstanding example" of open political violence during this period.

57. AC to *FR* 28, no. 26 (13 February 1875): 413; MIYM, 1874, 14; "Annual Report of the U.S. Commissioner on Education for 1873,"quoted in *FR* 28, no. 21 (9 January 1875): 327; Graves, *Town and Country,* 57.

58. Yardley Warner to *FR* 26, no. 36, (25 April 1873): 574–75.

59. Joseph Moore, "Visit to Helena, Ark.," *CW* 1, no. 4 (15 May 1871): 68.

60. AC to *FR* 25, no. 31 (23 March 1872): 493; ibid. 27, no. 26 (15 February 1875): 413.

61. AC to *FR*26, no. 44 (21 June 1873): 701; MIYM, 1874, 11–12.

62. AC to *FR* 26, no. 44 (21 June 1873): 702; ibid. 28, no. 22 (16 January 1875): 343–44.

63. H. E. Merrill to *CW* 4, no. 20 (15 October 1874): 317–20.

64. MIYM, 1874, 13–15; *FR* 26, no. 26 (13 February 1875): 413; Minutes, MB, 7 October 1874, 26 October 1874, 64–66; MIYM, 1875, 17–18. For subsequent Quaker controversy over water baptism, see chapter 6 below.

65. AC to *FR* 27, no. 26 (13 February 1875): 413; ibid. 29, no. 14 (20 November 1875): 222. Mrs. Clark was not exaggerating about the situation in Coahoma County. In October 1874 a white mob led by Mississippi ex-governor James Alcorn, a "reformed' scalawag, broke up a black political meeting there. The resulting melee ended with the deaths of six blacks and at least two white men. Subsequent failure of the federal government to respond to Republican governor Ames's plea for assistance in halting such violence effectively ended Radical Reconstruction in Mississippi. See Eric Foner, *Reconstruction: America's Unfinished Revolution, 1863–1877* (New York: Harper & Row, 1988), 560–61; Nicholas Lemann, *The Promised Land: the Great Black Migration and How it Changed America* (New York: A. A. Knopf, 1991), 12–14.

66. *FR* 29, no. 8 (9 October 1875): 124–25; ibid. 29, no. 10 (23 October 1875): 157; Minutes, SMM, 10November; MIYM, 1876, 35.

67. *FR* 29, no. 15 (27 November 1875): 235.

68. Amasa and Lydia Chace to *CW* 4, no. 6 (15 August 1874): 250–51.

69. H. E. Merrill to *CW* 4, no. 20, 15 October 1874, 318.

70. Minutes, MB, 16 January 1875, 67; ibid., 26 July 1875, 70–71; *FR* 29, no. 15 (27 November 1875): 235.

71. AC to H. W. Richardson, 11 December 1875, HCQC; MIYM, 1876, 37.

72. Minutes, MB, 31 July 1876, 94–96; MIYM, 1876, 34.

73. Minutes, MB, 31 July 1876, 94–96; *The Friend* (1 November 1876): 288–89; *FR* 30, no. 5 (16 September 1876): 74.

74. *FR* 30, no. 15 (16 September 1876): 75.

5.

1. See AC to Rebecca Collins, 7 September 1878, quoted in *FR* 32, no. 6 (21 September 1878): 92; Joseph Dickinson to *FR* 33, no. 127 (14 February 1880): 423.

2. The most informative study of the Hicksite Separation is H. Larry Ingle, *Quakers in Conflict: The Hicksite Reformation.*

3. Hamm, *Transformation,* 18–20; Opal Thornburg, *Whitewater: Indiana's First Monthly Meeting of Friends, 1809–1959* (Richmond: Earlham College, 1963), 6.

4. Minutes, SMM, 18 March 1874, 10–11.

5. In 1859 the Indiana Yearly Meeting deemphasized the "Inward Light" by officially resolving that holy scripture was "the only outward standard of soundness." Thornburg, *Whitewater,* 10. What follows owes much to Thomas Hamm's seminal account of *The Transformation of American Quakerism,* 36–120.

6. Thornburg, *Whitewater,* 10; Richard P. Ratcliff, *Our Special Heritage,* 26–27. Changing attitudes towards singing as a part of Quaker worship services were reflected in Elkanah Beard's "Diaries." On 1 March 1868 Beard "cried unto the Lord to save me from singing"; ten years later (25 January 1878) he remarked approvingly: "We have some singing in nearly all our meetings." Beard "Diaries," ECQC.

7. Early Quakers were widely accused of Ranterism by their detractors, but Fox denounced Ranter practices as "dry and barren." See *Journal of George Fox,* John Nickalls, ed. (London: Religious Society of Friends, 1986), 79–81, 181–83. See also Thornburg, *Whitewater,* 10; Hamm, *Transformation,* 85; Pamela Calvert, "'How Blessed It Is for the Sisters to Meet': Historical Roots of the Pacific Northwest Quaker Women's Theology Conference," *QH* 92, no 2 (Fall 2003): 25.

8. Thornburg, *Whitewater,* 10–11; Carol Spencer, "The American Holiness Movement: Why Did It Captivate Nineteenth Century Quakers?," *Quaker Religious Thought,* 28, 4, no. 90 (January 1998): 29; Calvert, "'How Blessed It Is,'" 25; Hamm, *Transformation,* 63, 78, 97: "Joel Bean and the Revival in Iowa," *QH,* 76, no. 1 (Spring 1987): 40. As late as August 1874 Southland Monthly Meeting had confirmed its "testimony against Priests and Ministers wages." See Minutes, SMM, 19 August. 1874, 19.

9. Minutes, Ohio Yearly Meeting (hereafter as OYM), 1879, 28–29, quoted in Hamm, *Transformation,* 123;"London Yearly Meeting," *British Friend* (1 June 1878): 140; Calvert, "'How Blessed It Is,'" 27–28.

10. The popularity and influence of the new brand of Quaker ministers was, no doubt, reflected in one of Alida Clark's pleas for traveling preachers when she specifically asked why individuals like David Updegraff, Dougan Clark, and Donald Hall were not coming to Southland. See A. Clark to *CW* 5, no. 7 (15 April 1875): 107–8.

11. Elkanah Beard, "Diaries," 17 January 1878. Beard also noted of the Jericho dissenters that "from the contour of their visages I conclude they think it meritorious to be of a sad countenance."

12. Minutes, SMM, 18 April 1877, 65l; AC to *FR* 30, no. 41 (26 May 1877) 651.

13. AC to *FR* 30, no. 41 (26 May 1877): 651; MIYM, 1877, 34–35; *FR* 31, no. 10 (20 October 1877): 153. For example, judicious deportment was apparently absent from meetings at Holly Grove where, Beard commented, "at times my voice was completely drowned" by the "noisy demonstrations" of some six hundred in attendance. Also, in his report to yearly meeting in 1878, Beard seems to have somewhat revised his assessment of Southland's demeanor, noting "encouraging" signs that meetings there were "not quite so emotional" as previously. MIYM, 1878, 32–33.

14. Minutes, SMM, 15 August 1877, 70; ibid., 21 August 1878, 87–88; *FR* 30, no. 5 (16 September 1876): 74–75; MIYM, 1874, 13; *CW* 8, no. 42 (17 October 1878): 495.

15. Minutes, SMM, 17 October 1877, 76.

16. Ibid., 23 January 1878; ibid., 20 February 1878, 79–80; ibid., 20 March 1878, 81; ibid., 15 January 1879, 93. See also *FR* 31, no. 35 (13 April 1878): 554.

17. MIYM, 1878, 39; Minutes, SMM, 17 April 1878, 82; ibid., 22 May 1878, 84–85. In a letter to *FR* 31, no. 41 (25 May 1878): 643–44, Stanley Pumphrey exulted in the fact that on one occasion Christian students at Southland school "rose at two and continued prayer to four for their unconverted comrades."

18. "History of Southland College," handwritten manuscript, ca. 1905, ECQC, 29–30; CW 8, no. 19 (8 May 1878): 218.

19. Minutes, MB, 29 July 1878, 141–42; *FR* 31, no. 39 (11 May 1878): 614–16; *Missionary Work in Connection with the Society of Friends* (Philadelphia: Friends' Review, 1879).

20. Minutes, SMM, 22 May 1878, 85; ibid., 19 February 1879, 95; *CW* 8, no. 23 (6 June 1878): 266; ibid. 9, no. 10 (6 March 1879): 110; MIYM, 1874, 13.

21. The Helena *Clarion,* 22 March 1873, described Hickory Ridge as "a right lively town" where stores and houses were springing up "like magic." Quoted in *PCHQ* 2, no. 3 (February 1964): 8. See also *FR* 29, no. 32 (25 March 1876): 505.

22. See chapter 4; MIYM, 1874, 11; ibid., 1876, 33; Minutes, SMM, 19 July 1876, 52; *FR* 29, no. 45 (24 June 1876): 715.

23. *FR* 31, no. 41 (25 May 1878): 643; Minutes, SMM, 21 August 1878, 90.

24. AC to Stanley Pumphrey, 4 March 1879, quoted in *CW* 9, no. 16 (17 April 1879): 185; AC to Stanley Pumphrey, 1 September 1879, quoted in *FR* 33, no. 12 (3 November 1879): 189.

25. Minutes, SMM, 18 February 1880, 107; ibid., 17 March 1880, 109–10; *FR* 33, no. 40 (15 May 1880).

26. *FR* 33, no. 48 (10 July 1880), 765; Minutes, SMM, 15 December 1880, 121; *CW* 10, no. 52 (23 December 1880): 629–30; ibid. 11, no. 20 (19 May 1881): 238; FR 34, no. 39 (7 May 1881): 615; MIYM, 1881, 21.

27. *FR* 31, no. 40 (15 May 1880): 637–38; ibid. 33, no. 48 (10 July 1880): 764–65.

28. Minutes, SMM, 13 April 1881, 126; ibid., 15 June 1881, 130–33; MIYM, 1881, 22.

29. Minutes, SMM, 18 January 1882, 136; ibid., 17 May 1882, 141–42; MIYM, 1882, 8–9; AC to *FR* 35, no. 42 (27 May 1882): 669–70; ibid. 36, no. 26 (3 February 1883): 412. Among the May 1882 converts were five members of the Busby Family who lived in the vicinity of the school. They and their descendants would remain pillars of Southland Meeting until it was laid down in 1925. Minutes, SMM, 17 May 1882, 142–43.

30. AC to *FR* 36, no. 20 (23 December 1882): 316; MIYM, 1882, 14–15.

31. Minutes, SMM, 12 December 1882, 156–57; AC to *FR* 36, no. 26 (3 February 1883): 412; Lydia Chace to Daniel Hill, n.d., quoted in *CW* 8, no. 14 (5 April 1883): 161; "Joel Bean's Visit to Southland College," *British Friend* 41, no. 2 (1 February 1883).

32. Hamm, *Transformation,* 117; "Joel Bean and the Revival in Iowa," *QH* 76, no. 1 (Spring 1987): 38, 40–41; Calvert, "'How Blessed it is,'" 24–25.

33. Hamm, "Joel Bean," 41–49; Calvert, "'How Blessed it is,'" 28–30. See also Joel Bean, "The Issue," *BF* 39, no. 3 (1 March 1881): 49–51. By 1883 the Bean's antiholiness allies in West Branch Meeting took the lead in forming the Iowa Yearly Meeting of Conservative Friends which remains a bastion of traditional Quaker belief and practice.

34. MIYM, 1884, 9; AC to *CW* 12, no. 13 (29 March 1883): 149; ibid. 14, no. 23 (5 June 1884): 355; Minutes, SMM, 24 May 1884, 183. Joel Bean noted the employment of "singing and music" at Southland but also commented on "the dignity of the

proceedings . . . and force of the remarks" in the conduct of the meeting. See "Joel Bean's Visit," *BF* 41, no. 2 (1 February 1883).

35. In the manner of early Friends, Quakers traditionally spurned sacraments "vain rituals," believing that true baptism was a visitation of the Holy Spirit and that true communion was unity of worship among believers. See James H. Moon, *Water Baptism: A Pagan and Jewish Ritual But Not Christian* (Fallsington: James H. Moon, PA. 1902).

36. AC to *FR* 38, no. 1 (9 August 1884): 13. An excellent discussion of the Ordinance Crisis is Hamm, *Transformation,* 130–37. Also see Moon, *Water Baptism.*

37. Minutes, SMM, 18 July 1885, printed insert, 206–7; AC to *FR* 39, no. 3 (22 August 1885): 47

38. AC to *FR* 30, no. 47 (7 July 1878): 746–47; ibid. 30, no. 5 (18 September 1876): 75. On 4 July 1876 several members of a black militia in Hamburg, South Carolina, were killed in cold blood by local whites, all of whom were acquitted in subsequent trials. See Foner, *Reconstruction,* 570–71.

39. Pearce, "AMA and the Freedmen Bureau in Arkansas," 260; MIYM, 1876, 39; ibid., 1877, 37.

40. *FR* 30, no. 5 (18 September 1876): 75; Amasa and Lydia Chace to *CW* 6, no. 22 (15 November 1876): 367–68.

41. MIYM, 1877, 35–36; "History of Southland College," 29; Stanley Pumphrey to *CW* 8, no. 19 (8 May 1878): 218.

42. AC to *CW* 7, no. 9 (18 February 1878): 99; Calvin Clark to Joseph Dickinson, 19 September 1877, inserted into Minutes, MB, 19 September 1877, 138–39.

43. AC to *FR* 30, no. 47 (7 July 1877): 747; MIYM, 1877, 36; Minutes, MB, 3 September 1877, 121; ibid., "Financial Statement, Southland College," 1 August 1876–31 July 1877, insert, 139; Calvin Clark to Joseph Dickinson, 19 September 1877, insert, 138–39, box 11, SP; Stanley Pumphrey to *CW* 8, no. 19 (8 May 1878): 218–19. See also advertisement for "Southland College and Normal Institute," *FR* 29, no. 15 (27 November 1875): 235.

44. CW 8, no. 15 (10 April 1878): 169; MIYM, 1878, 36–37; Minutes, SMM, 21 August 1878, 88–89.

45. MIYM, 1878, 33–35; Calvin Clark to James Dickinson, 16 September 1878, insert, Minutes, MB, 151, box 11, SP. See also AC to Rebecca Collins, 7 September 1878, quoted in *FR* 27, no. 6 (21 September 1878): 92.

46. AC to *FR* 30, no. 47 (7 July 1877): 746–47; ibid. 31, no. 24 (26 January 1878): 379–80.

47. AC to *FR* XXXI, no. 24 (26 January 1878): 380; AC to *CW* IX, no. 16 (17 April 1879): 185. Phillips County was one of the centers for the Liberian Exodus Arkansas Colony whose first convention was held in Helena in November 1877. Some local black ministers joined Alida Clark in denouncing this movement, but a group of families from Phillips County joined the ill-fated Arkansas West African colonizing expedition. See Adell Patton, "The 'Back-to-Africa' Movement in Arkansas," *AHQ* 51, no. 2 (Summer 1992): 164–77 and especially Kenneth Barnes, *A Journey of Hope: Arkansans and the Back-to-Africa Movement in the Late 1800s* (Chapel Hill: University of North Carolina Press, 2004).

48. AC to *FR* 31, no. 24 (26 January 1878): 379.

49. Minutes, MB, 25 September 1877, 130, Box 11, SP and MIYM, 1877, 38. For unknown reasons, Southland was shut out from a ten-thousand-dollar bequest of a

wealthy New Jersey friend "for the education of the colored people of the South." Minutes, MB, 10 October 1876, 118.

50. "Southland History," 35; Kirkman, "Southland College," 31.

51. Levi Coffin and Elisha Hathaway to Mission Board, n.d., in Minutes, MB, 31 January 1876, 88–90; MIYM, 1876, 39; ibid., 1877, 38. Hathaway's bequest was for the support of the Quaker mission at Maryville, Tennessee, as well as Southland.

52. Minutes, MB, 27 September 1878, 149; ibid., 16 December1878. Also see "History of Southland College," 31.

53. Minutes, MB, document signed by Joseph Dickinson, 26 April 1879, 155–56; MIYM, 1879, 49. Indiana Yearly Meeting settled with Hathaway's heirs for $250. See MIYM, 1880, 48.

54. MIYM, 1879, 49–50; "History of Southland College," 31–32; Minutes, MB, 156, including Mrs. Clark's detailed report of 23 April 1879, including a seven page list of contributors.

55. Stanley Pumphrey's description of the Southland campus in 1878, in a letter to *CW* 8, no. 19 (8 May 1878): 217–18 may be compared to the late-nineteenth-century idealized drawing of Southland.

56. AC to Joseph Dickinson, 21 January 1880, reprinted in *CW* 10, no. 7 (12 February 1880): 76–77.

57. Ibid.; *FR* 33, no. 27 (14 February 1880): 422–23.

58. *CW* 10, no. 7 (12 February 1880): 76–77; Note by Joseph Dickinson, *FR* 33, no. 27 (14 February 1880): 423.

59. *CW* 33, no. 32 (20 March 1880) 509–10.

60. Minutes, SMM, 18 February 1880, 107; ibid. (17 March 1880): 109–10; ibid. (19 May 1880) 113; MIYM, 1880, 52; AC to *FR* 33, no. 32 (20 March 1880): 509; ibid. 33, no. 40 (15 May 1880): 637; *CW* 10, no. 7 (12 February 1880): 76; ibid. 10, no. 27 (1 July 1880): 316.

61. Minutes, MB, 26 January 1880, 163; ibid., 20 April 1880, 164–65; "Southland College, Arkansas," *FR* 33, no. 40 (15 May 1880): 636–38; Minute 65, MIYM, 1880, 48. Beard may or may not have known that the University of Arkansas had been established at Fayetteville in 1876.

62. MIYM, 1880, 50; AC to *Friends' Review,* 31 May 1880, quoted in *FR* 33, no. 48 (10 July 1880): 764–65; ibid., 19 November 1880, quoted in *FR* 34, no. 22 (8 January 1881): 349.

63. Minutes, SMM, 16 June 1880, 115–16; ibid., 15 December 1880, 122–23; AC to *FR* 33, no. 48 (10 July 1880): 765.

64. *The Friend,* 1 September 1880, 246

65. MIYM, 1880, 49.

66. MIYM, 1880, 50; "History of Southland College," 35.

67. Letter from George Sturge, 2 September 1881, Minutes, MB, 31 October 1881, 179–80; *The Friend,* 1 November 1881, 301. See also Kirkman, "Southland College," 31–32.

68. More than half a century after Southland was closed, the Sturge Bequest still formed the largest portion ($28,500) of Indiana Yearly Meeting's Black Scholarship Fund of $43,645 from which aid was dispensed to deserving black college students. Letter from Charles E. McCracken (treasurer, Indiana Yearly Meeting) to the author, 27 November 1982.

69. Calvin Clark to Joseph Dickinson, 23 September 1881, Minutes, MB.

70. AC to Daniel Hill in *CW* 11, no. 27 (7 July 1881): 319; MIYM, 1881, 27; AC to *FR* 35, no. 20 (24 December 1881): 317.

71. AC to *FR* 34, no. 22 (8 January 1881): 348–49; Graves, *Town and Country,* 59–60.

72. MIYM, 1881, 22–26; A. Clark to Daniel Hill in *CW* 11, no. 27 (7 July 1881): 319.

73. *The Friend,* 1 February 1882, 36.

6.

1. *CW* 12, no. 13 (30 March 1882): 132; A. and C. Clark to Benjamin Webb, 21 March 1882, Minute Book, MB, insert, box 11, SP; Sarah Gooddard to *FR* 35, no. 36 (15 April 1882): 573; *The Friend,* 1 July 1882, 183–84.

2. Matron's Report, MIYM, 1882, 7–8.

3. Records of Southland Meeting indicate that George W. Bell became a member of the Society of Friends while he was a student in 1874. According to the records of the St. Louis Society for Medical and Scientific Education, Bell was born in 1864, but the Lincoln University *Biographical Catalogue* (Oxford: Lincoln University, 1918), 23, gives his birth year as 1857; the latter date seems more plausible although the assertion that he had been born in Abyssinia does not. There are a number of discrepancies in various sources regarding Bell's life and career. I am grateful to Dr. Walter L. Brown, professor emeritus at the University of Arkansas, for providing much of the information I was able to gather on G. W. Bell. These sources include James Leslie to Walter Brown, 6 May 1977; Audrey L. Berkley (librarian, St. Louis Society for Medical and Scientific Education) to Brown, 20 February 1978; Sophy H. Cornwell (special collections librarian, Lincoln University) to Brown, 19 April 1978.

4. *FR* 33, no. 48 (10 July 1880): 765; ibid. 35, no. 37 (22 April 1882): 586.

5. Mary Elizabeth Beck (1823–1903) was a teacher and recorded minister who traveled widely on religious missions in the Middle East, Scandinavia, and America. She reported on her visit to Southland in *TF* 1 February 1882, 36. I am grateful to Josef Keith at the Library of the Society of Friends in London was providing me with information about Mary Beck.

6. Extracts of letters from AC to Mary Beck, 1 November 1882, 6 November 1882, *TF,* 1 January 1883, 14.

7. AC to Mary Beck, 8 January 1884, *TF,* 1 March 1884, 72. Southland's curriculum, if always flexible, seems, at times, to have been quite exalted. In December 1882 Mrs. Clark emphasized a strong science component with "classes in Physiology, Zoology, Philosophy, Astronomy, Botany, Chemistry, etc." AC to *FR* 36, no. 20 (23 December 1882): 316. For Bell's subsequent impact on Southland, see below.

8. Extracts of letters, AC to Mary Beck, 1 November 1882, 6 November 1882, *TF,* 1 August 1883, 14; AC to *CW* 13, no. 13 (29 March 1883): 149.

9. AC to *FR* 36, no. 35 (7 April 1883): 556–57; AC to English Friends, *TF,* 1 August 1883, 209–10; *FR* 38, no. 28 (14 February 1885): 444.

10. AC to English Friends, *TF,* 1 August 1883, 209; Minutes, SMM, 18 July 1883, 171; MIYM, 1883, 10, 14.

11. MIYM, 1883, 9, 11, 14.

12. Lydia Chace to Calvin W. Pritchard, 4 January 1884, quoted in *CW* 14, no. 3 (17 January 1884): 39; AC to *CW* 14, no. 13 (27 March 1884): 196.

13. M. A. Marriage Allen, "The Coloured People of the Southern States," *Friends Quarterly Examiner* 18 (1884): 296–301, 390–99. Mrs. Allen's essay included an account of the Peabody Hotel in Memphis where "picturesque" black waiters carried trays of fruit through the dinning room. One of these waiters had been a student at Southland, and his fourteen dollar a month salary seemed to her an impressive fulfillment of the school's educational mission (299). See also Minutes, SMM, 17 October 1883, 176–77.

14. AC to *CW* 16, no. 13 (27 March 1884): 196–97. Mrs. Clark noted that 110 students were studying Julia Coleman's temperance lesson books and that the entire school was resolved into a Band of Hope every two weeks.

15. Minutes, SMM, 24 May 1884, 182–85; "Great Revival at Southland, Arkansas," *CW* 14, no. 22 (29 May 1884, 5 June 1884): 342, 355; *FR* 38, no. 1 (9 August 1884): 13; MIYM, 1884, 10. The traveling Quaker revivalists were Elwood Scott and William Penn Henley of Carthage, Indiana.

16. "Great Revival at Southland, Arkansas," *CW* 14, no. 22–23 (29 May 1884, 5 June 1884): 342, 355. See also AC to Mary Beck, *TF,* 1 July 1884, 187.

17. George Bell to *FR* 37, no. 32 (15 March 1884): 509, 519–20.

18. "Great Revival at Southland," *CW* 14, no. 22 (29 May 1884): 342.

19. AC to *FR* 37, no. 35 (4 April 1884): 556; "Great Revival at Southland, Arkansas," *CW* 14, no. 22 (29 May 1884): 342; AC to James Clark, quoted in *TF,* 1 July 1884, 186; AC to M. F. Beck, 28 July 1884, quoted in ibid. (28 July 1884): 241.

20. AC to *CW* 14, no. 35 (28 July 1884): 553.

21. Minutes, MB, 28 July 1884, 198; MIYM, 1884, 9.

22. While Bell was no longer on the school's faculty, in November 1884 he married Mattie Beesley, another Southland teacher and graduate. (See *TF,* 2 February 1885, 40). There was an outside possibility that complaints to the board may have concerned the visit of Joel Bean to Southland early in 1884 as he was considered unsound by many evangelical Friends (see chapter 5 above). This is unlikely, however, as Bean's ministry was openly acknowledged and highly praised in Mrs. Clark's report to Indiana Yearly Meeting. See MIYM, 1884, 10.

23. Minutes, SMM, 23 August 1884, 194; MIYM, 1884, 10.

24. Minutes, SMM, 23 August 1884, 194–95; AC to *FR* 38, no. 5–6 (6 September 1884, 13 September 1884): 76, 94; *TF,* 1 December 1884, 311; *FR* 38, no. 23 (10 January 1885): 364.

25. AC to *FR* 28, no. 28 (14 February 1885): 444; *CW* 15, no. 29 (16 July 1885): 365; "Temperance Report," Minutes, MB, 19 September 1885, insert, 151.

26. Alida Clark often spoke of Heneritta Kitterall as "our daughter" but there is no evidence of an official adoption.

27. *FR* 38, no. 23 (10 January 1885): 364; AC to ibid. 38, no. 42 (23 May 1885): 203–4.

28. AC to *FR,* XXXVIX, no. 3, 22 August 1885, 45–7.

29. Minutes, MB, 31 July 1885, 205–06, Box 11, SP

30. Minutes, MB, 30 September 1885, 206; ibid.

31. Bell's subsequent career is of considerable interest. After leaving Southland he graduated from the National Medical University in St. Louis and subsequently established a medical practice in Pine Bluff. From 1890 to 1894 he served in the Arkansas state senate. He married three times and his first two wives, Mattie Beasley, married in 1884, and Cattie Miles, married in 1889, died within year after marriage; very bad luck,

one must suppose. Eventually, Bell became one of the wealthiest black men in Arkansas. He also maintained the habit of making accusations again prominent individuals in positions of authority. See Gordon, *Caste and Class,* 103, 166–67, 167n73, for Bell's questionable attack on a Pine Bluff Catholic priest for an allegedly improper relationship with a female parishioner who had rejected Bell's own advances. Also see *Biographical Catalogue,* 23.

32. "Matron's Report," MIYM, 1885, 76–79.

33. One illustration of the Clarks' withdrawal from of even routine duties and activities was a two-year hiatus (23 May 1885–20 April 1887) in recording new members in Southland Monthly Meeting, a task heretofore meticulously performed under Mrs. Clark's supervision. From December 1873 to April 1885, 377 new members, including over 100 in 1884–85, were recorded. See "Record of Southland Monthly Meeting," box 12, SP, 15–35.

34. AC to M. W. Haines, 21 January 1886, HCQC.

35. AC to *FR* 39, no. 37 (15 April 1886), 589.

36. Calvin and Alida Clark to Joseph Dickinson, 20 April 1886, in Minutes, MB, insert.

37. Minutes, MB, 17 July 1886, 209.

38. MIYM, 1886, 54–58. See also Minutes, SMM, 18 September 1886, 216–18.

39. See chapter 7 below.

40. MIYM, 1885, 81; ibid., 1886, 58–59.

41. See chapter 8 below.

42. *FR* 40, no. 4 (26 August 1886): 56

43. Ibid. 40, no. 8 (23 September 1886): 127; ibid. 40, no. 50 (14 July 1887): 799.

44. Minutes, SMM, 20 October 1886, 219; ibid., 19 January 1887, 221; ibid., 21 September 1887, 227–28; Lydia Chace to C. W. Pritchard, quoted in *CW* 17, no. 4 (3 February 1887): 53. Apparently, while Lydia traveled about fulfilling her temperance duties, Amasa Chace stayed at the Clarks' new home.

45. Minutes, MB, 2 January 1887, 211; John Clark to Joseph Dickinson, quoted in *FR* 40, no. 27 (3 February 1887): 430; *CW* 17, no. 4 (3 February 1887): 56; Allen L. Herron to *CW* 17, no. 10 (10 March 1887): 111.

46. Minutes, MB, 1 February 1887, 212; ibid., 26 April 1887, 213.

47. A. L. Herron to *CW* 17, no. 21 (26 May 1887): 249; ibid. 17, no. 26 (30 June 1887): 311.

48. Sturge Fund Ledger, Box 17, SP, 11–13.

49. MIYM, 1887, 59–60; MB to Yearly Meeting, ibid., 59.

50. MIYM, 1887, 61–62; Minutes, MB, 15 October 217, 9 December 1887.

51. Minutes, MB, 30 August 1887, 216; FR 41, no. 12 (20 October 1887): 183; *CW* 17, no. 42 (20 October 1887): 497; MIYM, 1887, 63.

52. *FR* 41, no. 12 (20 October 1887): 183.

53. *FR* 41, no. 16 (17 November 1887), 254; Joseph Dickinson, "The Work of I.Y.M. in the South," *CW* 17, no. 51 (22 December 1887): 609. (This article had originally appeared in the *Richmond Palladium).*

54. Minutes, MB, 9 December 1887, 219–20; *FR* 41, no. 20 (15 December 1887): 317–18.

55. The yearly meeting held $4,000 in fire insurance, but the Freeport Insurance Company paid $520 rather than $1,000 on account of "an oversight by Calvin Clark"

of obtaining concurrent fire insurance without the knowledge or permission of the Freeport Company. These circumstances may have added to the lingering tensions between the Clarks and the mission board. See Minutes, MB, 3 January 1888, 221–22; "History of Southland College," 37–39, ECQC.

56. Lydia Chace, "The Fire At Southland," *CW* 17, no. 52 (29 December 1887), 615; *FR* 41, no. 21 (22 December 1887): 332–33.

7.

1. Letter Book (LB), Missionary Board (MB), 8 May 1888, 9, box 11, SP; *CW* 18, no. 6 (9 February 1888): 72; *FR* 41, no. 29 (16 February 1888): 461.

2. *FR* 41, no. 31 (1 March 1888): 492. The Clarks also indicated their eagerness to accept the Richmond Declaration of Faith, a Biblically-based creedal statement approved by Indiana Yearly Meeting in 1888 as an Orthodox response to the "Ordinance Crisis" initiated by the extreme holiness faction among Friends. See chapter 6 above.

3. LB, MB, 8 May 1888, 10–12, box 11, SP; *CW* 18, no. 20 (17 May 1888): 239; FR 41, no. 43 (24 May 1888): 685.

4. Minutes, MB, 30 April 1888, 224–25; LB, MB, 8 May 1888, 9–10; ibid., 15 June 1888, 35, Box 11, SP. Charles W. Osborne was the grandson of prominent Quaker abolitionist Charles Osborn.

5. LB, MB, Joseph Dickinson (JD) to C. W. Osborne (CWO), 29 May 1888, 23–24; JD to Elkanah Beard (EB), 11 June 1888, 32.

6. Minutes, SMM, 20 June 1888, 233–34.

7. LB, MB, JD to EB, 14 May 1888, 13; ibid., 15 May 1888, 15; ibid., 21 May 1888, 20–21; JD to EB and CWO, 30 May 1888, 26–27; JD to CWO, 8 June 1888, 31a.

8. Ibid., JD to EB, 14 May 1888, 13; ibid., 11 June 1888, 32.

9. Ibid., Certificate [of Indiana Yearly Meeting], 12 June 1888, 33.

10. LB, MB, JD to Cordelia Hadley, 11 July 1888, 42.

11. Ibid., JD to EB, 14 May 1888, 13; JD to CWO, 25 June 1888, 38; ibid., 16 July 1888, 44.

12. Ibid., JD to CWO, 11 September 1888, 49.

13. Minutes, MB, 30 July 1888, 226; LB, MB, JD to CWO, 21 September 1888, 53; ibid., 18 October 1888, 56; ibid., 30 October1888, 57; ibid., 28 November 1888, 57–58. There is no indication of any donations from local white people, but, in fact, a $500 subscription from Helena merchants would have allowed the missionary board to more than balance the budget for their building fund which ended with a deficit of $323.23. See Minutes, MB, 2 November 1888, 230.

14. CWO to *FR* 42, no. 1 (2 August 1888): 13; Minutes, SMM, 21 November 1888, 240.

15. Minutes, SMM, 15 August 1888, 236; ibid., 17 October 1888, 240; ibid., 21 November 1888, 240–41; *CW* 18, no. 43 (25 October 1888): 508; ibid. 18, no. 44 (5 November 1888): 552; *FR* 42, no. 13 (25 October 1888): 196.

16. Minutes, SMM, "Report of the Education Committee," 15 August 1888, 236.

17. C. W. Osborn [*sic*], "Southland," *CW* 16, no. 27 (5 July 1888): 317; Letter to *FR* 42, no. 8 (20 September 1888): 126

18. See below.

19. LB, MB., JD to CWO, 11 July 1888, 40–41; ibid., 30 July 1888, 45–47; ibid., 21 August 1888, 48; Minutes, MB, 30 July 1888, 228; CWO to *FR* 42, no. 8 (20 September 1888): 126.

20. Minutes, MB, EB to Missionary Board, 27 January 1889, 231. A hand drawn map of Slade land sales is inserted into ibid., 231. See also ibid., 30 April 1889, 325; LB, MB, "Description of land sold off the Slade land," 20 February 1889, 75; Minutes, MB, 11 March 1889, 233. In 1891 Emma France Lancaster, sometime clerk of Southland Monthly Meeting, purchased 45 acres of Slade land for $645. Minutes, MB, 20 April 1891, 250–51.

21. LB, MB, 28 January 1889, 68–69; Minutes, MB, 30 April 1889, 235.

22. LB, MB, JD to EB, 19 December 1888, 62; JD to CWO, 26 December 1888, 63; Minutes, MB, EB to Board, 27 January 1889, 231.

23. LB, MB, JD to CWO, 10 December 1888, 60, box 11, SP; CWO, "Southland College," *CW* 19, no. 4 (24 January 1889): 59; ibid. 19, no. 8 (21 February 1889): 123–24; Minutes, MB, 28 January 1889, 229–30.

24. Minutes, MB, EB to Board, 27 January 1889, 231; CWO to *CW* 19, no. 18 (2 May 1889): 278.

25. LB, MB, JD to CWO, 20 February 1889, 72; ibid., 13 March 1889, 80–81, box 11, SP.

26. Minutes, MB, 30 April 1889, 235–37.

27. LB, MB, JD to CWO, 21 May 1889, 88.

28. See L. M. Chase, "The Fire At Southland," *CW* 17, no. 52 (24 December 1887): 615, in which she called Principal R. E. Pretlow "an inspiration and strength" who had adopted himself admirably to the changed surroundings. There was no mention his dental practice.

29. LB, MB, JD to Irena Beard, 28 June 1889, 92–3, box 11, SP. See also ibid., JD to EB, 11 July 1889, 94–95, wherein Dickinson expressed the hope that Charles Osborne could "get over it without much damage to himself." Osborne apparently managed to do this and later served as a member of the missionary board.

30. LB, MB, JD to EB, 11 July 1889, 95, box 11, SP; E. Beard, "Southland," *CW* 19, no. 27 (4 July 1889): 426.

31. LB, MB, JD to EB, 12 August 1889, 98; ibid., 27 August 1889, 99, box 11, SP. Dickinson said that Charles Coffin's "nervous system is so broken down he will never again recover fully."

32. See Hamm, *Transformation,* 220n4. Among Coffin's questionable practices were granting of large unsecured loans to members of his family for speculative investments, watering the bank's stock, misrepresenting its assets and embezzling funds from trusts for which he was trustee. Because of these revelations and Coffin's subsequent bankruptcy, he was disowned by his own monthly meeting although never convicted of criminal wrongdoing.

33. LB, MB, JD to EB, 2 October 1889, 104, box 11, SP; *CW* 19, no. 42 (5 October 1889): 667–68; EB to *FR* 43, no. 5 (29 August 1889): 79.

34. Total enrollment increased from 189 to 224 and boarders from 62 to 102; it is, however, difficult to know whether this might be attributed to Charles Osborne's removal or to a relatively more prosperous year (that is, higher cotton prices) for black farmers and sharecroppers.

35. LB, MB, JB to EB, 3 June 1889, 10 June 1889, 11 June 1889, 89–91; ibid., 11 July 1889, 94; JB to Lucinda Hunt, 11 June 1889, 91, box 11, SP; MIYM, 1889, Report of Missionary Board, 73–74.

36. See Minutes, SMM, 19 June 1889, 244–45. Duncan Freeland joined Friends 19 June 1889. Record of Southland Meeting, 36.

37. Minutes, MB, 27 January 1890, 242–43.

38. Henry Stanley Newman (1837–1912), a minister and missionary from a weighty Quaker family, was editor of *The Friend* (London), from 1897 to 1912.

39. *The Friend* (London), 1 March 1890, 67.

40. Minutes, SMM, 17 April 1890, 250–51.

41. Minutes, MB, Report of John Henley on visit to Southland, 27 January 1890, 241–42; LB, MB, JD to EB, 27 January 1890, 116, box 11, SP.

42. LB, , MB, JD to EB, 11 January 1890, 113; JD to W. E. Henshaw, 29 January 1890, 117, box 11, SP. Henshaw's candidacy was further handicapped by the fact that he and his wife had only been Quakers "for two or three years." Minutes, MB, 4 March 1890, 244–45; ibid., 8 April 1890, 246. Thomas Hamm notes that the board's reservations were probably justified; in 1895 a W. E. Henshaw was convicted in Indiana of murdering his wife.

43. Letter from Elkanah Beard, *CW* 20, no. 15 (10 April 1890): 231; ibid. 20, no. 33 (14 August 1890): 519.

44. MIYM, 1890, 91–92.

45. LB, MB, JD to EB, 27 September 1890, 130.

46. *CW* 20, no. 42 (16 October 1890): 662–63; ibid. 20, no. 43 (23 October 1890): 683.

47. *CW* 20, no. 52 (25 December 1890): 828; LB, MB, JD to Wm. and "Bina" Russell, 9 March 1891, 141; JD to William J. Russell (WJR), 19 March 1891, 143.

48. See John William Graves, "Negro Disenfranchisement in Arkansas," *AHQ* 26 (Autumn 1967), 199–225. See also Fon Louise Gordon, "From Slavery to Uncertain Freedom: Blacks in the Delta," in *The Arkansas Delta: Land of Paradox,* Jeannie Whayne and Willard B. Gatewood, eds. (Fayetteville: University of Arkansas Press, 1993), 105–12.

49. See Graves, "Negro Disenfranchisement," 209–20; Gordon, "From Slavery," 107–11; Tom Dillard, "Madness With a Past: An Overview of Race Violence in Arkansas History," *Arkansas Review: A Journal of Delta Studies,* 32, no. 1 (August 2001): 97–98.

50. See John William Graves, "The Arkansas Separate Coach Law of 1891," *AHQ* 32, no. 2 (Summer 1973): 148–65. For Bell's picture and extracts for his ringing denunciation of the proposed segregation statute, see 159–161. Donahoo's remarks are quoted in J. Morgan Kousser, "A Black Protest in the 'Era of Accommodation': Documents," *AHQ* 34, no. 2 (Summer 1975): 169.

51. Roberts, "Desolation Itself," 93.

52. L. M. Chase [Chace] to *CW* 21, no. 41 (8 October 1891): 650.

53. Ibid.; *CW* 22, no. 13 (31 March 1892): 203.

54. LB, MB, JD to the editor of *FR* 45, no. 38 (14 April 1892): 605; JD to WJR, 30 May 1892, 177–78; Minutes, MB, 25 April 1892, 258–59; *FR* 45, no. 42 (5 May 1892): 642. Unfortunately, no copies of the Alida Clark memorial pamphlet seem to have survived.

55. *FR* 45, no. 6 (6 September 1891): 92; LB, MB, JD to Christopher May [Wray], 21 October 1891, 155–56, 158, box 11, SP; Minutes, MB, 21 October 1891, 256.

56. MIYM, 1891, "Report of the Missionary Board," 76–79; *CW* 21, no. 41 (19 November 1891): 739.

57. LB, MB, JD to Herbert Charles, 8 December 1891, 162; JD to WJR, 12 February 1892, 169.

58. WJR to *CW* 22, no. 13 (31 March 1892): 200–201; ibid. 22, no. 27 (7 July 1892): 425; MIYM, 1892, "Report of the Missionary Board," 80–83. See also *FR* 45, no. 51 (14 July 1892): 814.

59. LB, MB, Emma H. Thompson to JD, 18 July 1892, with a copy of Sarah Henley's Will and Minutes, MB, 28 September 1892, 260–61, box 11, SP. Sarah Henley also made provision for a Little Rock Orphans' Home and for the local branch of the Women's Christian Temperance Union with the remainder of the estate to be use to purchase a library for the use of Little Rock citizens, "regardless of sex or color," with books that were "soundly moral and . . . orthodox," including "the works of George Fox and other writings of the Society of Friends." To date, little information is extant regarding Sarah H. Henley or the final disposition of her will. Apparently, the righteous library was never built, either because the city of Little Rock did not provide a suitable building as specified in the will or because Henley's estate was not sufficiently large to complete all the tasks she assigned to it. There is some hint of the latter in LB, MB, JD to Emma H. Thompson, 14 October 1892, 187.

60. Minutes, MB, 28 September 1892, 260; *CW* 22, no. 42 (20 October 1892): 665; *FR* 46, no. 15 (3 November 1892): 234. The surplus for 1892 was $331.57.

61. LB, MB, JD to WJR, 4 October 1892, 186; *FR* 46, no. 13 (20 October 1892): 202; ibid. 46, no. 15 (3 November 1892): 234.

62. R. S. Russell to *CW* 22, no. 49 (8 December 1892): 773; LB, MB, JD to WJR, 13 March 1893, 200.

63. Minutes, MB, 7 February 1893, 263; Missionary Board, Correspondence, 1893, box 11-5, SP (hereafter as MB, Correspondence, 1893); WJR to JD, 15 February 1893; ibid., 22 February 1893.

64. MB, Correspondence, 1893, Herbert and Alice Charles to JD, 4 March 1893; ibid., EB to JD, 9 March 1893. For a report on Herbert Charles's controversial address, see William Russell, "Southland College," *CW* 22, no. 27 (7 July 1892): 425.

65. MB, Correspondence, 1893, WJR to JD, 13 March 1893.

66. Ibid.; WJR to JD, 3 April 1893; ibid., EB to JD, 11 April 1893. (Emphasis in original.) Total enrollment of 143 identified by department but without distinguishing between boarders and day students, see Minutes, MB, 10 March 1893, 264.

67. MB, Correspondence, 1893, Charles Hubbard to JD, 22 April 1893; ibid., WJR to JD, 15 February 1893; ibid., EB to JD, 2 March 1893; ibid., WJR to JD, 14 March 1893; Minutes, MB, 10 March 1893, 264.

68. MB, Correspondence, 1893, C. Hubbard to JD, 22 April 1893; MIYM, 1893, "Statistical and Financial Reports,"80. The statistical report did note, however, that the members were mostly young people and there were only eight families among them. See also Charles Hubbard to *FR* 46, no. 42 (11 May 1893): 668.

69. Minutes, SMM, 18 January1893, 272–73; ibid., 15 February1893, 273; MB, Correspondence 1893, WJR to JD, 15 February 1893; ibid., C. Hubbard to JD, 22 April 1893.

8.

1. MB, Correspondence, 1893, H. Charles to JD, 24 April 1893.

2. MB, Correspondence, 1893, WJR to JD, 3 May 1893, 12 May 1893; H. Charles to JD, 20 May 1893; WJR to JD, 3 June 1893.

3. MB, Correspondence, 1893, H. Charles to JD, 14 June 1893; MIYM, 1893, 77–79.

4. Minutes, MB, 16 June 1893, 266; *CW* 23, no. 43 (26 October 1893): 683–84. For Jacob N. Donahoo, see Tom Dillard, "Three Important Black Leaders in Phillips County History," *PCHQ* 19, no. 1 (December 1980): 10–23.

5. Continuing land purchases in the face of lingering fiscal problems seem oddly contradictory given the board's Quakerly concern about accumulating debt, but, as noted above, members of the board were perhaps inclined to believe in the enduring value of landed property.

6. "Friends Work at Southland, Ark.," *CW* 23, no. 42 (19 October 1893): 661; LB, MB, JD to WJR, 1 November 1893, 207.

7. LB, MB, EB to JD, 14 December 1893, 26 December 1893, 209; JD to EB, 19 December 1893, 209; JD to WJR, 29 May 1893, 221.

8. Minutes, SMM, 20 September 1893, 276; ibid., 20 December 1893, 21 December 1893, 278–79; ibid., 15 May 1894, 282–83; ibid., 15 August 1894, 285.

9. William Russell, "Southland College," *CW* 22, no. 27 (7 July 1892): 814; LB, MB, JD to WJR, 7 December1892, 189; MB, Correspondence, 1893, EB to JD, 14 December 1893.

10. William Russell, "Southland College," *CW* 24, no. 4 (25 January 1894): 59. J. N. Donahoo, editor of the *Helena Progress,* made a repeat appearance; the other speaker was George Chatters, "a staunch colored man" who was clerk of courts in Coahoma County, Mississippi.

11. William Russell, "Southland College," *CW* 24, no. 4 (25 January 1894): 59.

12. LB, MB, JD to WJR, 20 January 1894, 27 January 1894, 212–31; JD to EB, 27 January 1894, 214; William Russell, "Southland College," *CW* 24, no. 4 (25 January 1894): 59. See also R. S. Russell, "Friends Work at Southland," *CW* 24, no. 3 (18 January 1894): 34; William Russell to *FR* 48, no. 6 (8 February 1894) 131–32.

13. MB, Correspondence, 1894–95, EB to JD, 17 April 1894; Minutes, MB, 31 May 1894, 267–68.

14. LB, MB, JD to WJR, 2 June 1894, 223; MIYM, 1894, "President's Report," 83–87.

15. Minutes, MB, 22 October 1894, 271; ibid., 28 January 1895, 274; *American Friend,* 7 February 1895, 133. (In 1894 the *Friends' Review* and *Christian Worker* merged as the single national voice of Gurneyite Quakers in the United States.)

16. Minutes, SMM, 15 May 1894, 282–83; ibid., 15 January 1896, 299; MB, Correspondence, 1894–94, Elizabeth Bailey to JD, 28 November 1894; Minutes, MB, 28 January 1895, 272; *AF* (25 October 1894): 349.

17. Minutes, MB, 28 January 1895, 272–73; MB, Correspondence, 1894–95, WJR to JD, 24 February 1895.

18. MB, Correspondence, 1894–95, WJR to JD, 6 March 1895.

19. MB, Correspondence, 1894–95, WJR to JD, 7 February 1895, 11 March 1895; Minutes, SMM, 20 March 1895, 289; *AF* (28 March 1895): 303.

20. MB, Correspondence, 1894–95, WJR to JD, 7 February 1895. The story of this unfortunate young man is reminiscent of a similar childhood incident recounted in the "Reflections" of Laura Jane Moore (1870–1955), an English Quaker girl terrified by visions of hell-fire instilled by evangelical Quaker relatives. See Kennedy, *British Quakerism*, 99–100.

21. *AF* (28 March 1895): 303–4.

22. Minutes, MB, 28 January 1895, 274.

23. An idealized illustration of the five buildings on Southland campus was imprinted on the college's stationary, circa 1893–95 See illustration.

24. MB, Correspondence, 1894–95, Charles A. Francisco to JD, 16 April 1895; "Report of Edward Bellis and Charles A. Francisco," in *Southland College, 1864–1895: A Brief Sketch of Thirty Years of Missionary Labor,* Richmond, IN, 1895, 11–15, F PG II, ECQC; Minutes, SMM, 17 April 1895, 290; MIYM, 1895, 89–90.

25. "Report of the President," MIYM, 1895, 89; MB, Correspondence, 1894–95, Charles Francisco to JD, 16 April 1895.

26. "Report of Edward Bellis and Charles Francisco," in *Southland College* (1895), 9, 17–19; MB, Correspondence, 1894–95, Charles Francisco to JD, 16 April 1895.

27. MB, Correspondence, 1894–95, Charles Francisco to JD, 16 April 1895; ibid., WJR to JD, 8 May 1895.

28. Minutes, MB, 14 May 1895, 275–77; MB, Correspondence, 1894–95, WJR to JD, 15 May 1895; ibid., 21 May 1895; ibid., 5 July 1895.

29. MIYM, 1895, 86, 90–91.

30. Ibid., 86–88.

31. Ibid., 88–90.

32. See John William Buys, "Quakers in Indiana in the Nineteenth Century," dissertation, University of Florida, 1973, 180.

33. MIYM, 1895, 91. Even before Charles Osborne recommended more industrial-type training, Alida Clark, in her Report for 1885, noted that "the propriety and need . . . [for] more manual labor among our inmates" had led to their building a tool shop for training young men in manual arts as making provision for girls to be more systematically educated in laundry, "that very useful art." Ibid., 1885, 78–79.

34. James D. Anderson, *The Education of Blacks in the South, 1860–1935* (Chapel Hill: University of North Carolina Press, 1988), 103; "The Hampton Model of Normal School Industrial Education, 1868–1900," in *New Perspectives on Black Educational History,* Vincent P. Franklin and James D. Anderson, eds. (Boston: G. K. Hall, 1978), 61–85. Washington's famous speech was delivered on 18 September 1895. When Indiana Yearly Meeting met on 29–30 September, industrial education advocate Charles Osborne, apparently revitalized from his humbling personal experience at Southland, was appointed to the missionary board, MIYM, 1895, 79.

35. Anderson, "Hampton Model," 68. See also Butchart, *Northern Schools, Southern Blacks,* 102–3.

36. Anderson, "Hampton Model," 61–68, 84–85; *Education of Blacks,* 92–93; William A. Link, "Jackson Davis and the Lost World of Jim Crow Education," Special Collections Department, University of Virginia Library, May 2000.

37. Anderson notes that whereas Hampton and Tuskegee had received only 13 percent of Slater Fund grants in 1883, by 1902 their share was 50 percent of the total. "Hampton Model," 90.

38. Anderson, *Education of Blacks,* 85–86, 91; Link, "Lost World of Jim Crow Education." The Slater Fund later was a relatively minor source of funding for Southland while the General Education Board became seriously involved with Southland during its last years. For the Slater Fund, see Roy E. Finkenbine, "'Our Little Circle': Benevolent Reformers, the Slater Fund, and the Argument for Black Industrial Education, 1882–1908," in *African American Life in the Post-Emancipation South, 1861–1900,* Donald G. Nieman, ed. (New York: Garland, 1994), 70–86. Also see chapters 7 and 8 below.

39. A recent study of the early emphasis on literacy as the means to further professional training and economic advancement for freedmen is Heather Williams, *self-taught.*

40. Anderson, "Hampton Model," 82–86; *Education of Blacks,* 33.

41. MIYM, 1895, 88; *AF* (17 October 1895): 1010.

42. Minutes, MB, 4 October 1895, 281, ibid., 27 January 1896, 282; *AF* (19 December 1895): 1221.

43. Minutes, MB, 27 January 1896, 283; ibid., 27 April 1896, 285.

44. Minutes, MB, "Report of E. Bellis and Wm. J. Hiatt," 27 April 1896, 287–89.

45. Deed records of Phillips County indicate that William Russell was involved in numerous land transactions during and after his tenure at Southland.

46. Minutes, MB, "Report of E. Bellis and Wm. J. Hiatt," 27 April 1896, 288–89.

47. See especially W. E. B. Du Bois and Augustus Granville Dill, eds., *The Common School and the Negro American* (Atlanta: Atlanta University Press, 1911).

48. In 1890 Albert Smiley, a weighty eastern Quaker philanthropist, organized a conference at Lake Mohonk on the "Negro Question" to which no black person was invited. The all-white attendees, including S. C. Armstrong and former president Rutherford B. Hayes, chair of the Slater Fund, strongly supported the Hampton-Tuskegee Model as the future standard for black education. See Anderson, "Hampton Model," 88.

49. Minutes, SMM, 19 April 1896, 301.

50. MIYM, 1896, 81.

51. Minutes, MB, 27 April 1896, 289; ibid., 27 July 1896, 290–91.

52. Edgar Ballard to Eli and Mahalah Jay, 1 November 1896, 18 November 1896, ECQC. It is of interest to compare Edgar Ballard's remarks with the assessment, a few years earlier, of John Henley, another Indiana Friend, who commented that the conduct of Southland students in the class room as well as in meetings was "equal . . . to what is to be found in any Institution of white children in the Northern States." See Minutes, MB, 27 January 1890, 241–42.

53. Edgar Ballard to Eli and Mahalah Jay, 18 November 1896, ECQC.

54. Minutes, MB, Report of Edward Bellis (for the business committee), 2 March 1897, 295–96; MIYM, 1897, President's Report, 100.

55. Southland's total debt had grown to nearly $1,300. Minutes, MB, 2 March 1897, 296.

56. Minutes, MB, 2 March 1897, 296–97; ibid., 26 April 1897, 301.

57. Ibid., 26 April 1897, 299–301; MIYM, 1897, President's Report, 100, 102. The Russells remained in the Southland area for two decades, but eventually became alienated from Southland Monthly Meeting. See below.

58. "Report from Stanley A. Pearson," MIYM, 1897, 102.

59. See Anderson, "Hampton Model," 60–62, 73, 76. Shortly after Southland's experiment with industrial training, Isaac Fisher, a protégé of Booker T. Washington, became principal of the Arkansas state-supported Branch Normal School at Pine Bluff. With strong support from local white leaders, especially trustee William H. Langford, Fisher instituted a curriculum emphasizing industrial rather than academic education with a view to making the school an "Arkansas Tuskegee." This approach, however, aroused bitter hostility among black Arkansans which Fisher attributed to their jealousy at seeing a Tuskegee man make good. W. E. B. Du Bois later called Fisher a "white folks nigger." See Elizabeth L. Wheeler, "Isaac Fisher: The Frustrations of a Negro Educator at the Branch Normal College, 1902–1911," *AHQ* 41 (Spring 1982): 3–50; Thomas Rothrock, "Joseph Cater Corbin and Negro Education in the University of Arkansas," *AHQ* 30, no. 4 (Winter 1971): 310–11; Anderson, *Education of Blacks,* 108–9.

60. MIYM, 1898, "Report of the President," 96–97.

61. Minutes, MB, E. Bellis to the Board, 26 April 1898, 307; ibid., 308. The minutes (307) also note that Southland had received a $1,000 bequest, to be known as the "James P. and Julia Ann Boyce Fund," which was added to the school's endowment.

62. Minutes, MB, 10 February 1897, 304–5;ibid., 11 January 1898, 312. The visit of another minister, Ira Johnson, early in 1897 had resulted in requests from thirty-eight persons "to be joined in membership with Friends." Minutes, SMM, 17 February 1897, 314.

63. Minutes, SMM, 16 June 1897, 318; ibid., 17 November 1897, 323; ibid., 16 March 1898, 326; ibid., 24 September 1898, 330–31; Minutes, MB, 29 September 1898, 309. As previously noted, the inflated membership list of the Southland Meeting was unrealistic. Still, in 1898 (Minutes, SMM, 16 November 1898, 333) nearly forty members, all but a few black, were listed on active committees of the meeting.

64. Jeannie M. Whayne, "Laboring in the 'American Congo,'" 47–85 in *A New Plantation South* (Charlottesville: University of Virginia Press, 1996), 47–48. See also *Helena World,* 23 February 1898. Only the benches could be retrieved from the abandoned Beaver Bayou Meeting House. Minutes, SMM, 20 August 1898, 329.

65. Minutes, MB, 1 November 1898, 312–13; ibid., 31 January 1899, 314–15; ibid., 30 May 1899, 316–20; MIYM, 1899, 77–78.

66. Minutes, MB, 30 May 1899, 317–18; MIYM, 1899, 76.

67. Minutes, MB, "Thirty-Sixth Annual Report," n.d., insert, 324; MIYM, 1899, 73–74, 76. Caroline Cowgill was the sister of Martha Ann Macy who had accompanied Alida and Calvin Clark to Helena in 1864.

68. Minutes, MB, 26 September 1899, 321–23; ibid., 28 September 1899, 324–25; ibid., 1 May 1900, 324–25, 327; "Report of the Executive Committee," 30 April 1901, 336–37, box 11, SP; MIYM, 1900, 129–30, 132–33; MIYM, 1901, 47–48, 51.

69. Minutes, MB, 1 May 1900, 326; Eli Jay, "History of Southland College," handwritten, 1905, 41–42, ECQC. .

70. Minutes, MB, 5 July 1900, 328; ibid., 26 September 1900, 329–30; ibid., 2 October 1900, 332–33; MIYM, 1900, "Report of the Missionary Board," 130, 134; Jay, "Southland History," 41–42.

71. Minutes, MB, 1 May 1900, 326–27; ibid., 30 April 1901, 334–35; ibid., 28 July 1901, 338–39; MIYM, 1900, "Report of the Missionary Board,"130–31; MIYM, 1901, 47–50.

72. Minutes, MB, 29 April 1902, 345. See also Jay, "History of Southland," 42–43 who described the new structure as "handsome and commodious . . . up-to-date in all its apartments."

73. (Richmond 1906). Minutes, MB, 25 September 1901, 341–42; MIYM, 1901, 47; "Report of the Missionary Board," 53; MIYM, 1905, "Report of the Missionary Board," 57. As noted above, Eli Jay's handwritten manuscript "History of Southland College, Near Helena, Arkansas," is also preserved in the Earlham College Quaker Collection.

74. Phillips County Deed Records indicate that the Russells owned considerable land in the vicinity of Southland and that they were involved in numerous landed transactions between 1896 and 1908. An anonymous article in the *PCHQ* 9, no. 1 (December 1970) on "Postal Service in Phillips County," lists Ruth S. Russell as postmistress for Southland from 1897 to 1915 and William Russell from 1915 to 1917. The *Catalogue of Southland, 1911–1912* contains a half-page advertisement for "Wm. and R.S. Russell" as "Dealers in General Merchandise" at Southland, Arkansas.

75. *AF* (30 January 1902): 109, emphasis added.

76. Minutes, SMM, 15 August 1900, 343; ibid., 19 December 1900, 346. In August 1901, Drew's son William and his family followed Daniel and his wife Laura to Oregon(348). Daniel Drew addressed Oregon Yearly Meeting in 1901 and was listed as a minister by that meeting from 1901 to 1907 when he transferred his membership to the AME Church. Another prominent Southland Quaker family, Emma and Anderson Lancaster and their daughter Ruby, also migrated to Oregon. Emma Lancaster was a Southland graduate, teacher, and former clerk of the monthly meeting, but Anderson Lancaster was disowned for adultery by Southland Meeting in 1896 (*Record of Southland Monthly Meeting,* 20), an incident that may have influenced the Lancasters' decision to leave Arkansas. See Henry J. Cadbury, "Negro Membership in Society of Friends," *Journal of Negro History* 21 (1936), 206.

77. See above.

78. *AF* (6 March 1902): 227.

79. Minutes, SMM, 17 September 354; ibid., 15 October 1902, 354–55.

80. MIYM, 1903, "Report of the Missionary Board," 40.

81. Ibid.

9.

1. Buys, "Quakers in Indiana,"182.

2. *The Record of Southland Monthly Meeting,* 43, box 12, SP, indicates that Harry Wolford was the son of Charles T. and Malinda Hill Wolford and Anna's parents were James M. and Mary Elizabeth Kelley Barrnet, members of Whitewater Monthly Meeting. Harry and Anna Wolford had been received into membership of New Westville, Ohio, Meeting in 1898. The 1900 census indicates that Harry Wolford was a schoolteacher in Jackson Township, Preble County, Ohio.

3. Minutes, MB, 30 September 1903, 345–46. Westville Friends attended New Paris Meeting under the auspices of Whitewater (Indiana) Monthly Meeting

4. Minutes, SMM, 16 September 1903, 361; Minutes, MB, 30 September 1903, 345–46; ibid., 26 January 1904, 350. The furnace had to be moved soon after its installation to avoid its being flooded by spring rains. Ibid., 26 January 1904, 349.

5. MIYM, 1904, 46–47, 50

6. See Minutes, MB, 1 October 1905, 357; ibid., 30 April 1906, 358; MIYM, 1905, 57. Money from the sale of the land at Marvel was used to purchase a steam heating plant for the girls' dormitory.

7. MIYM, 1904, 48. See also Minutes, SMM, 18 March 1903, 355–57, wherein individuals from each of the above-noted families sought membership in the Southland Meeting. Record of Membership, Southland Monthly Meeting, 42–43, box 12, SP.

8. Minutes, SMM, 21 January 1903, 355.

9. Minutes, SMM, 20 July 1904, 365.

10. Ibid., 365–66. No minutes were recorded in the Southland Meeting Book between 17 August 1904 and 20 June 1906 or again between 18 July 1906 and 1 May 1907.

11. Minutes, SMM, 20 June 1906, 367.

12. MIYM, 1905, 57; Minutes, MB, "Report of Superintendent Harry Wolford, June 19, 1905," 355.

13. Minutes, MB, "Southland Commencement," May 1906, 359; ibid., 25 September 1906, 359–60; MIYM, 1906, 15–17.

14. MIYM, 1907, 16–20; Minutes, MB, 9 June 1907, 360, 362.

15. Minutes, MB, 27 September 1907, 362; ibid., 15 March 1908, 363–65; Edward Bellis to Mary A. J. Ballard and Edwin S. Jay, 2 May 1908, 365; ibid., 15 May 1908, 365; ibid., 24 May 1908, 365. MIYM, 1908, 16.

16. Minutes, MB, 24 May 1908, 365; MIYM, 1908, 16. For the list of needed improvements, see Charles O. Whitely, "Southland College," *AF* (17 September 1908): 608.

17. MIYM, 1907, 16–18, 21.

18. Minutes, MB, 15 March 1908, 363; Todd Everett Lewis, "Race Relations in Arkansas, 1910–1929," dissertation, University of Arkansas, 1995, 86.

19. The Orthodox Yearly Meetings attached to the Five Years Meeting were Baltimore, California, Canada, Indiana, Iowa, Kansas, New England, New York, Oregon, Western, and Wilmington, with headquarters in Richmond. The newly-formed Nebraska Yearly Meeting was added in 1909. In 1963 the Five Years Meeting became Friends Central Meeting. See Punshon, *Portrait in Grey,* 204–5.

20. Minutes, MB, 10 October 1909, 371; ibid., 30 May 1912, 380.

21. *AF* (17 June 1909): 380; ibid. (7 October 1909): 637–38; Minutes, MB, 23 May 1909, 368–66.

22. Minutes, MB, 21 September 1909, 369–70, box 11, SP. Available evidence seems to indicate that Davis left Southland abruptly after a dispute with one or both of the Wolfords. See Herschel Folger to Lydia E. Folger, 11 October 1909, Folger Letters (hereafter FL), Alumni Biographical Files (ABF), ECQC. Folger commented that while Davis "made a hit with the pupils," he was "not quite so pleasing to the powers that be."

23. Three weeks after arriving at Southland, Folger comforted a male relative, apparently over financial difficulties, noting that while "things may seem blue but you must remember the way this $40 [a month] job dropped down out of the skies." Herschel Folger to Wm. O. Folger, 1 November 1909, FL. I am grateful to Thomas Hamm for providing additional material about Herschel Folger and his family. For

information about the African American community in Carthage, see Stephen A. Vincent, *Southern Seed, Northern Soil* (Bloomington: Indiana University Press, 1999), 126–27.

24. H. F. Folger to Lydia E. Folger, Sat. Eve, October 1910, FL.

25. Herschel Folger to Wm. O. Folger, 8 October 1909, FL.

26. Herschel Folger to Lydia E. Folger, 11 October 1909, FL.

27. Ibid.

28. Herschel Folger to Miss Mary Folger, 15 October 1909, to Lydia Folger 18 October 1909, to Wm. O. Folger, 1 November 1909, FL.

29. Herschel Folger to Miss Mary Folger, 15 October 1909, to Lydia Folger, 3 November 1909, to Wm. O. Folger, 14 November 1909, to Folger, 17 December 1909, FL.

30. Herschel Folger to Wm. O. Folger, 22 November 1909, FL.

31. Herschel Folger to Mrs. Lydia E. Folger, 6 December 1909, to Wm. O. Folger 9 January 1910, to Mary Folger, 6 February 1910, FL. Folger was also impressed with the mail service at Southland, which had its own post office. Several times he remarked how letters from Indiana reached his remote location in one or two days. See Herschel Folger to Miss Mary Folger, 15 October 1909, to Mrs. Lydia Folger, 5 December 1909, FL.

32. Herschel Folger to Lydia Folger, 3 November 1909, to Mary Folger, 6 February 1910 (emphasis added), FL; "Southland College, Arkansas, Under Care of a Board of the Five Years Meeting," *AF* (10 April 1910): 155–56.

33. Minutes, MB, 1 May 1910, 371; MIYM, 1910, 19–21.

34. Minutes, MB, 1 May 1910, 371; MIYM, 1910, 20–21.

35. Minutes, MB, 1 May 1910, 371; ibid., 21 September 1910, 372; ibid., 11 October 1910, 372–73; ibid., 16 October 1910, 373; MIYM, 1910, 19–23.

36. *Catalogue of Southland College and Normal Institute,* 1911–1912, (Helena, 1911), following page 41.

37. Phillips County deed records indicate that in the period between 1909 and 1925, Harry and Anna Wolford were among the most active buyers and sellers of landed property in the county.

38. Members of the Roden family began to appear in Southland Monthly Meeting records in the spring of 1907. In the early 1980s Emma Roden Young was still living in the house built by her father. Interview with Emma Roden Young and Willa Burchett Graves, Southland, AR, 18 February 1982. Also see *AF* (16 October 1924): 800, for a note about Frank Roden.

39. Interview with Alfred L. Billingsley Sr., Southland, Arkansas, 19 February 1982. Also see Deed Records, 1909–1928, Phillips County Courthouse, Helena.

40. F. Raymond Jenkins, Wolford's successor as Southland's director, believed that Wolford charged high rates of interest. Interview with F. Raymond Jenkins, Richmond, IN, 9 June 1981. See also see below, chapters 10, 11.

41. See Voucher No. 19, "Probate Court of Phillips County, in the Matter of the Estate of H.C. Wolford, deceased. . . .," 18 December 1939, Phillips County Courthouse, Helena.

42. Interview with F. Raymond Jenkins, 9 June 1981, Richmond, IN.

43. Interview with Alfred L. Billingsley Sr., 19 February 1982, Southland, AR.

44. Interview with F. Raymond Jenkins, 9 June 1981, Richmond, IN. See also chapter 11 below.

45. Minutes, MB, 4 February 1911, 374–75; MIYM, *1911*, 20.

46. Minutes, MB, 4 February 1911, 374–75; *AF* (2 March 1911): 141; MIYM, 1911, 19–21, 23, 28–29. At the conclusion of the 1911 school year, the Wolfords announced they intention to bequeath their worldly possessions to Southland when they left its service. Minutes, MB, 9 June 1911, 376. However, the circumstances of their eventual departure negated this possibility. See chapter 11 below.

47. Minutes, MB, 23 July 1911, 377; ibid., 25 July 1911, 378. The missionary board had thought that the yearly meeting would permit them to borrow from the Metford Fund, which was overseen by the yearly meeting treasurer, but the trustees apparently decided enough was enough. See MIYM, 1911, 21.

48. Minutes, MB, 8 January 1912, 379; MIYM, 1912, 21–22.

49. Minutes, MB, 30 May 1912, 380; MIYM, 1912, 380.

50. Minutes, MB, 30 May 1912, 380; 16 August 1912, 382–83; ibid., 18 September 1912, 383; MIYM, 1912, 21–23.

51. MIYM, 1912, 23.

52. Edward Bellis, "Southland College," *AF* (17 April 1913): 247–48.

53. Minutes, MB, 30 May 1913, 385; ibid., 1 August 1913, 38; ibid., 2 September 1913, 24 September 1913, 388; MIYM, 1913, 43, 45.

54. MIYM, 1913, 43; Minutes, MB, 1 August 1913, 387.

55. Leo Mortimer Favrot (1874–1949) had been a teacher and school administrator in his native Louisiana before he joined the Arkansas Department of Education.

56. Leo Favrot to H. C. Wolford, 25 February 1914, SP; Favrot to Director, Jeanes Fund, 31 January 1914, quoted in *Educating the Masses: The Unfolding History of Black School Administrators in Arkansas, 1900–2000,* C. Calvin Smith and Linda Walls Joshua, eds. (Fayetteville: University of Arkansas Press, 2003), 43.

57. Noting the absence of any previous records for Southland in the Arkansas Department of Education files, Favrot asked Wolford to begin a file by completing a department questionnaire. Favrot to Wolford, 25 February 1914, SP.

58. Link, "Jackson Davis and the Lost World of Jim Crow Education," May 2002.

59. MIYM, 1914, 33. The board also noted the increase in faculty from six to ten as well as a rise of teacher-student ratio from 26 to 40, which was apparently viewed as an achievement.

60. Ibid., 33–34.

61. The average price of cotton was about thirteen cents before 3 August 1914 when cotton exchanges shut down for three months. Farmers, especially black farmers, were left at the mercy of spot buyers who sometimes offered as little as four cents a pound. Some growers could not sell their cotton at any price. See George B. Tindall, *The Emergence of the New South, 1913–1945* (Baton Rogue: Louisiana State University Press, 1967), 30–31.

62. *AF,* 31 December 1914, 845; MIYM, 1915, 42–43, 51–54.

63. MIYM, 1915, 44 (emphasis in original).

64. James Larkin and James Daniels, both accepted into Southland Meeting during the war, did real estate business with Wolford. See Minutes, SMM, 25 February 1915, 404; ibid., 15 July 1916, 408.

65. Phillips County deed records indicate Wolford sold ten tracts of land in Sections 15 and 16 between 9 November and 22 December 1916.

66. Interview with Russell and Tressie Ratliff, 9 June 1981, Richmond, IN. Russell

Ratliff did not reveal the nature of his illness, but malaria was still a concern for northern Friends. At least one candidate for a position at Southland withdrew his application "on account of fear of malaria." E. Bellis to M. J. Ballard, 19 May 1916, F PG II 2, ECQC.

67. Interview with Russell and Tressie Ratliff, 9 June 1981, Richmond, IN. Also see *AF,* "Southland College, Arkansas" (24 June 1915): 399.

68. *AF,* "Southland College ," 415.

69. MIYM, 1916, 39–49. The deficit for the year was $573.58.

70. "Southland Day," Third Sabbath in May, 1916, F PG II 2, ECQC . This four page notice included a letter about Southland by Anna Wolford that was to be read before the collection was taken; it was published in *AF* (24 February 1916): 132.

71. "Receipts From Bible Schools Observing Southland Day," Report of the Missionary Board on Southland College to Indiana Yearly Meeting of Friends, Richmond, Indiana, 1916, 8–11; MIYM, 1916, 39–49. Overall, cash donations were down by $200 from the previous year.

72. Harlow Lindley (1875–1959) was a much respected professor of history at Earlham College. In the 1860s his mother Martha Newlin Lindley had worked among freed blacks under the Western Yearly Meeting.

73. MIYM, 1916, 38–40, 49. Also see *AF* (5 October 1916): 774, for reference to the report by an unnamed government expert, possibly Leo Favrot, on expensive but necessary changes to bring Southland up to required standards.

74. See Tindall, *Emergence of the New South,* 56. Tindall notes that King Cotton had been restored to his throne by 1916 and that prices continued to rise until 1919 (60).

75. MIYM, 1920, 20; "A Salutation," *Catalogue of Southland Institute, 1917–1918,* 9–10; *Helena World,* quoted in *AF* (16 November 1916): 903.

76. See, for example, the list of 63 recorded members around 1910. Besides the Wolfords and other white faculty, the Southland congregation was largely composed of members of about a dozen families. The missionary board believed that for "the large majority of those who have spent any length of time in the institution, both Christian and moral character have been built into their lives." MIYM, 1914, 33–34.

77. Charles E. Tebbetts, "A Trip Through the South–Note by the Way," *AF* (5 April 1917): 272.

78. Interview with Russell and Tressie Ratliff, 9 June 1981, Richmond, IN. Local Friends attended Sunday morning worship services with Southland students, but also attempted with varying success, to keep alive the tradition of separate mid-week meetings for worship and business.

79. Interview with Russell and Tressie Ratliff, 9 June 1981, Richmond, IN. In this regard, it is of interest to note that over 20 percent of male Quakers in Wayne County joined the Ku Klux Klan in the early 1920s, although Prohibition rather than racism was probably the chief appeal. See Thomas D. Hamm, *Earlham College: A History, 1847–1997* (Bloomington: Indiana University Press,1997), 151–52; Leonard J. Moore, *Citizen Klansmen: The Ku Klux Klan in Indiana, 1921–1928* (Chapel Hill: University of North Carolina Press, 1991), 72–74.

80. MIYM, 1917, 20–22.

81. Ibid., 19–20, 32; Minutes, Five Years Meeting, 76, ECQC; *AF* (11 October 1917): 809.

82. Minutes, Five Years Meeting, 75, ECQC; MIYM, 1917, 21, 24–25.

83. "A Salutation," *Catalogue of Southland Institute, 1917–1918,* 9–10.

84. Minutes, Five Years Meeting, 16–22 October 1917, 76, ECQC.

10.

1. *Catalogue of Southland Institute, 1917–1918,* 12; E. Bellis to M. J. Ballard, 9 May 1916, F PG II 2, ECQC.

2. *Catalogue of Southland Institute, 1917–1918,* 11–12; Minutes, MB, Executive Committee, 18 October 1917, 3–4, Box 11–3, SP.

3. Minutes, Five Years Meeting, 16–22 October 1917, 76, 78, ECQC.

4. Minutes, MB, Executive Committee, 18 Oct 1917, 3 November 1917, 7 November 1917, 6–7.

5. Minutes, MB, Executive Committee, 3 December 1917, 8 December 1917, 10 December 1917, 9–10; MIYM, 1918, 24–25.

6. Minutes, MB, Executive Committee, 17 December 1917, 11–12; ibid., 32 December 1917, 13; ibid., 17 February 1918, 15–17; ibid., 4 March 1918, 18–20. See also *AF* (25 April 1918): 399.

7. Minutes, Permanent Missionary Board, 4 March 1918, 19–20 and 13 March 1918, 22–25, box 11–3, SP. Also see *AF* (25 April 1918): 339. Southland principal Russell Ratliff had suggested a mid-March closing without graduation, but Director Baldwin, citing the symbolic importance of commencement ceremonies for students and their families, insisted on the need for the usual graduation festivities.

8. Minutes, Permanent Missionary Board, 7 April 1918, 25 and 29 May 1918, 27.

9. Minutes, Permanent Missionary Board, 4 March 1918, 20 and 13 March 1918, 23.

10. Minutes, MB Executive Committee, 1 July 1918, 29–30 and 13 July 1918, 31.

11. For London Yearly Meeting's support of conscientious objectors and refusal to comply with government censorship regulations, see Kennedy, *British Quakerism,* ch. 9–11.

12. MIYM, 1918, 26. Mildred Baldwin's illness was mentioned in the missionary board minutes of 1 July 1918, but three weeks later John Baldwin seemed to be energetically carrying on his duties. See Minutes, MB Executive Committee, 25 July 1918, 31–32.

13. Mildred E. White, "My Year at Southland Institute, 1918–1919," 1, ECQC.

14. Minutes, MB, Executive Committee, 1 August 1918, 33–34; ibid., 13 August 1918, 35.

15. White, "My Year at Southland," 1.

16. MIYM, 1918, 92–93.

17. White, "My Year at Southland," 1.

18. Ibid. Mildred White's comments on the high standard of discipline at Southland were supported by Tressie and Russell Ratliff who also served under Wolford and remembered few disciplinary problems. Interview with Russell and Tressie Ratliff, 9 June 1981, Richmond, IN.

19. White, "My Year at Southland," 2. See also interview with Russell and Tressie Ratliff, 9 June 1981, Richmond, IN.

20. Interview with Willa Burchett Graves, 18 February 1982, Southland, AR.

21. White, "My Year at Southland," 1–2.

22. Ibid., 2–3.

23. Ibid., 3. Avery, from Greentown, IN, remained Southland's music teacher for several years and remained a firm Wolford loyalist.

24. White, "My Year at Southland," 3.

25. MIYM, 1918, 25, 27–28.

26. After Edward Bellis's recommendation, the Indiana Missionary Board asked the Southland board to approach the Home Missions Board (HMB) of the Five Years Meeting (FYM) to ask if this approach met the approval of the permanent board of Indiana Yearly Meeting. Subsequent to this approval, a plan for the transfer of responsibility was presented to the HMB of the FYM. This body, in turn, appointed a special committee to consider the proposal. After some deliberation, the special committee gave its approval and the Five Years Meeting and authorized the Home Missions Board to take charge of Southland with the proviso that it become an incorporated body before assuming this responsibility. See MIYM, 1919, 24–26.

27. MIYM, 1919, 26, 38.

28. Members coopted from the former Southland board of Indiana Yearly Meeting were Dr. N. S. Cox, chair of the new committee; Harlow Lindley; and Charles M. Jenkins. Three nationally weighty Friends, John Cary of Baltimore, Lewis McFarland of North Carolina, and Earle Harold of Wilmington, Ohio, made up the rest of the board. The longtime secretary of the old board, Edward Bellis, was an honorary and advisory member. MIYM, 1920, 33.

29. MIYM, 1920, 29

30. An informative discussion of the background to and effects of the Elaine tragedy is Kieran Taylor, "'We have Just Begun': Black Organizing and White Response in the Arkansas Delta, 1919," *AHQ* 58, no. 3 (Autumn 1999): 265–84.

31. The historical literature on events at Elaine is voluminous but entirely lacking in consensus as to the underlying cause of the violence, who was responsible for starting it, or how many individuals died in the fighting. While most sources agree that four white civilians and one soldier were killed, estimates of black deaths range from 25 to 856. In a deeply researched recent study, *Blood In Their Eyes: The Elaine Race Massacres of 1919,* (Fayetteville: University of Arkansas Press, 2001), 80, Grif Stockley asserts that the death toll among blacks was probably "in the hundreds" and that most of these were killed in cold blood by federal troops (34–60). Stockley's view on the complicity of the military in a massacre has been contested by other scholars, especially Jeannie Whayne ("Low Villains and Wickedness in High Places: Race and Class in the Elaine Riots," in *AHQ* 58, no. 3 (Autumn 1999): 285–313). An excellent summary of recent scholarly work on the Elaine race riots can be found in *Arkansas Review: A Journal of Delta Studies* 32, no. 2 (August 2001).

32. See Grif J. Stockley, "The Legal Proceedings of the Arkansas Race Massacres of 1919 and the Evidence of the Plot to Kill Planters," *Arkansas Review: A Journal of Delta Studies,* 32, no. 2 (August 2001): 141–48. For a detailed narrative of the legal proceedings arising from the Elaine riots, see Stockley, *Blood in Their Eyes,* 107–233. The murder convictions of all twelve men were eventually reversed by the either the Arkansas Supreme Court or the U.S. Supreme Court.

33. "Slavery in Arkansas," *AF* (11 December 1919): 1089; Whayne, "Elaine Riots," 305–6.

34. MIYM, 1920, 27–28, 35–37. See also Gloria J. Gentry, "The History of Lexa," *PCHQ* 17, no. 3 (June 1979): 19, who notes the "inaccessibility . . . of the dirt roads" around Southland that were often nearly impassable for several months of the year.

35. The Five Years Meeting's Forward Movement operated in conjunction with a general fundraising project of the Federal Council of Churches.

36. MIYM, 1920, 31–32; "Board of Home Missions Outlines Work," *AF* (3 June 1920): 529–30; *Friends Missionary Advocate,* November 1920, 351.

37. See chapter 8 above.

38. *Friends Missionary Advocate,* November 1920, 351, 366.

39. "Indiana Yearly Meeting," *AF* (2 September 1920): 788.

40. MIYM, 1920, 33, 36–37; RMS, "Four Days at Southland," *AF* (3 March 1921): 165. For Penn's future activities, see chapter 11 below.

41. MIYM, 1920, 24–28; "Report of Treasurer," Indian Yearly Meeting, August 1920, 110–11, 119, showing overdrawn accounts of over $6,000.

42. RM, "How Much for Home Missions?," *AF* (27 January 1921): 64.

43. "Betty of Southland," *AF* (27 January 1921): 65–66; R. M. Simms, "Home Missions," *AF* (27 January 1921): 64.

44. Anderson, *Education of Blacks,* 144.

45. "Southland Institute Survey," *AF* (17 February 1921): 135.

46. First Annual Report of Board of Home Missions, 1921, 20, SP.

47. Ibid., 21–22; Simms, "Four Days at Southland," 165.

48. First Annual Report of Board of Home Missions, 1921, 21; Simms, "Four Days at Southland," 165.

49. First Annual Report of Board of Home Missions, 1921, 22.

50. Simms, "Four Days at Southland," 165.

51. White, "My Year at Southland," 3; Simms, "Four Days at Southland," 165.

52. See First Annual Report of Board of Home Missions, 1921, 22, which notes payment of tuition in chickens, sweet potatoes, and other items.

53. "Meeting of the Home Mission Board," *AF* (26 May 1921): 410.

54. "Southland Institute, Announcements for 1921–22," F PG II 2, ECQC; "New Teachers for Southland Institute," *AF* (4 August1921): 625. For stories on and pictures of John W. Moses, see *AF* (4 August 1921): 625; "Away Down South in Arkansas," *AF* (3 November 1921): 882–83. See also Charles Wadelington and Richard F. Knapp, *Charlotte Hawkins Brown and Palmer Memorial Institute* (Chapel Hill: University of North Carolina Press, 1999), 120.

55. "Away Down South in Arkansas," 3 November 1921, 882. For a further discussion of Moses's credentials and career, see chapter 11 below.

56. "Away Down South in Arkansas," *AF* (3 November 1921): 882; John W. Moses, "Christian Work at Southland Institute," *AF* (3 November 1921): 883; "Thanksgiving at Southland," ibid., 8 December 1921, 999.

57. Anna Wolford's account of this incident "A Story of Southland," appeared in *AF* (9 March 1922) in tandem with John W. Moses's essay on "Our Southland," 187–88, 198–99. Her article was reprinted by the Home Mission Board as "Neighbors Unto Southland," copy in ECQC. Will Turner, killed on 18 November 1921, is identified in Todd E. Lewis, "Mob Justice in the 'American Congo': 'Judge Lynch' in Arkansas During the Decade After the World War I," *AHQ* 52, no. 2 (Summer 1993): 164. Also see *Arkansas Gazette,* 19 November 1921.

58. Ellison R. Purdy (chair of the Home Missions Board's executive committee) "A Statement and a Query," *AF* (10 November 1921): 905; Wilbur W. and Lois P. Kamp, "First Glimpses of Southland Institute," *AF* (24 November 1921): 950.

59. Undoubtedly, one important reason for the dearth of contributions was the serious theological disputes facing the American Quakerism at this time. Division between fundamentalist and modernist Friends reached a peak in the interwar years. Some evangelicals Friends wanted the Richmond Declaration of Faith to be adopted as a creedal statement for all Orthodox Quakers, and there was also strong movement to remove Walter Woodward as executive secretary of the Five Years Meeting and editor of the *American Friend* on account of his liberal views. See Elbert Russell, *The History of Quakerism* (New York: Macmillan, 1942), 537–41. See also Thomas Hamm *History of Earlham College* (Bloomington: Indiana University Press, 1997), 117–39, for a discussion of the attack in 1920–21 by holiness and other evangelical Friends on "unsound" teaching by Earlham faculty that brought on a special investigation of one Earlham teacher, which Hamm describes as a sort of heresy trial. These divisions would eventually reach Southland when some fundamentalist faculty accused the school's principal, Raymond Jenkins, of being theologically unsound. See chapter 12 below.

60. *AF* (2 February 1922): 95; "John W. Moses, "Our Southland," *AF* (9 March 1922): 198–99.

61. Second Annual Report of Board of Home Missions, *1922,* 16–20.

62. Ibid., 20.

63. *AF* (2 February 1922): 95; "Are Other Pastures Greener?" *AF* (20 July 1922): 578. The latter article was unsigned but internal evidence indicates that it was written by Atwood L. Jenkins, Richmond insurance man, former member of the Indiana Missionary Board, and the father of F. Raymond Jenkins, who was about to be appointed as Southland's new, reform-minded principal.

64. *AF* (1 June 1922): 439; Second Annual Report of Board of Home Missions, 1922, 20.

11.

1. Elizabeth H. Emerson, *Walter C. Woodward: Friend on the Frontier, A Biography* (Richmond: Privately printed, 1952), 155; Second Annual Report of Board of Home Missions, 1922, 18.

2. Minutes, Five Years Meeting (MFYM), 1922, 5–11, September 1922, 200, ECQC.

3. Second Annual Report of Board of Home Missions, 1922, "Southland, 1921–22," 18–19, 21.

4. Interview with F. Raymond Jenkins, 9 June 1981, Richmond, IN; Jenkins (FRJ) to Warren K. Blodgett (Hampton Institute), 27 October 1922, box 1, SP.

5. Second Annual Report of Board of Home Missions, 1922, 18–19; Third Annual Report of Board of Home Missions, 1923, 24–25; Emerson, *Walter C. Woodward,* 155–56. Other members of the delegation were Harlow Lindley, Earlham professor and head of the HMB's Southland committee; Charles A. Reeve, an Indianapolis ice cream manufacturer; and B. Willis Beede, an official of the Five Years Meeting's foreign missions board. Of these, only Lindley had previously visited Southland.

6. Emerson, *Walter C. Woodward,* 156. Elizabeth Emerson obviously had access to the full report, "What the Deputation Found at Southland, September 1922" by B. Willis Beede. This document was supposedly deposited with Walter Woodward's papers in the Earlham College Library. However, it is not presently in the Woodward collection nor is it included in a list of microfilmed official reports sent to the Home Missions Board.

7. Available evidence strongly suggests that John W. Moses was a very persuasive conman. See below, chapter 12.

8. FJR to Warren K Blodgett, 27 October 1922; Emerson, *Walter C. Woodward,* 156.

9. The Southland Committee of the Board of Home Missions, "An Important Crisis Passed at Southland," *AF* 2 November 1922): 879, 891.

10. *AF* (2 November 1922): 876–79.

11. Woodward's article was made part of a "Suggested Program for the Lesson on Friends and the Negro," see an undated mimeographed sheet, in file labeled "Negroes," F PG IV 2, ECQC. In fairness, it should be noted that Walter Woodward had been and would remain an outspoken advocate for racial justice. See, for example, his editorial "America the Beautiful," *AF* (6 April 1922), for a stinging denunciation of American race prejudice.

12. Woodward, "Down Among the Cotton" 876–79; Third Annual Report of Board of Home Missions, 1923, 24–25.

13. "An Important Crisis Passed," *AF* (2 November 1922): 891; Woodward, "Down Among the Cotton," 879. See below, regarding attempts to revive Southland Monthly Meeting.

14. See E. D. Proudfoot, Assistant to the Treasurer, Hampton Institute, to FRJ, 7 November 1922, Box 1, SP, who refers to their discussions, even before he visited the campus, of Jenkins's plans and ideas for putting things right at Southland.

15. Discouraged and upset by the protests against him, Walter Webb actually left the school briefly until Jenkins persuaded him to return. See Helen Hilts to Friend [Walter Webb], 23 October 1922; FRJ to W. K. Blodgett, 27 October 1922, box 1, SP.

16. Interview with F. Raymond Jenkins, 9 June 1981, Richmond, IN; Warren K. Blodgett (Hampton Institute) to FRJ, 23 October 1922; FRJ to Blodgett, 27 October 1922; Helen Hilts to [Webb], 23 October 1922, box 1, SP.

17. Helen Hilts, Negro Record Department, Hampton Institute, to FRJ, 9 November 1922, box 1, SP.

18. Minutes of Teachers' Meetings, 16 October; 23 October; 30 Oct; and 6 November 1922, box 10, SP.

19. Minutes of Teachers' Meetings, 23 October and 6 November 1922, box 10, SP; FRJ to Ruthana M. Simms (RMS), 18 October 1922, and to Harlow Lindley, 27 October 1922, box 1, SP.

20. Minutes of Teachers' Meetings, 30 October and 13 November 1922, box 10, SP; Mrs. Fannie Buford to FRJ, 29 October 1922 and FRJ to Mrs. Buford, 1 November 1922, box 1, SP.

21. The Home Missions Board hired a Kansas City Quaker accountant, F. A. Wright, to audit the books left by Harry Wolford. Wright personally visited Southland to check all past accounts. There were, for a time, some questions about the Wolford's ledgers, but eventually Wright's examination "showed that all financial transactions for

the past four years had been regularly and systematically handled" with careful records made of all receipts and expenditures. See F. A. Wright, C.P.A., to C.C. Brewer (Helena banker), 26 December 1922, to FRJ, 27 December 1922, and to Ellison R. Purdy (Minneapolis), 5 January 1923, box 1, SP.

22. Jenkins could not have been pleased when Wolford requested that he collect an account of $22 from an infirm elderly man who lived "away back in the hills" so as to save the old fellow a difficult trip into Helena. HCW to FRJ, 27 December 1922, box 1, SP.

23. FRJ to Harlow Lindley, 12 December 1922, box 1, SP. See below, chapter 12.

24. Minutes, Teachers' Meeting, 23 October 1922, box 10, SP; FRJ to Harlow Lindley, 4 December 1922, box 1, SP. See also FRJ to Mrs. S. H Bennet, Mr. Robert Darwin, Mrs. Mary Willis, and Jerry Tharp, 5 December boxes 1 and 2, SP, informing these parents that while "Southland cannot have boys and girls . . . who commit such actions," the guilty parties would be given another chance because "we had not done our part in warning the students." Curiously, the matter of student immorality was not discussed at a teachers' meeting on 4 December, Minutes, Southland Staff Meeting, 4 December 1922, box 10, SP.

25. FRJ to Harlow Lindley, 4 December 1922, box 1, SP; Third Annual Report of the Board of Home Missions, 1923, 28.

26. The Southland board informed Jenkins that they lacked the means to hire a special matron for the girls' dormitory. See Minutes, Southland Staff Meeting, 8 January 1923, box 10, SP; Atwood and Mary Jenkins, "Christmas at Southland–What Shall the Future Be?," *AF* (18 January 1923): 48.

27. For example, see Mrs. Lena Adams to FRJ, 15 November 1922; Almitta Anderson to FRJ, 16 November 1922; J. C. Bobo to President, 23 November 1922; Mrs. Estelle Flowers to FRJ, 20 and 23 November 1922, box 1, SP.

28. See Minutes, Southland Staff Meeting, 20 November 1922 and 29 January 1923, box 10, SP.

29. FRJ to RMS, 18 October, 21 November, and 11 December 1922 and to Harlow Lindley, 6 December 1922, box 1, SP.

30. See, for example, "Are There Thirty?" *AF* (7 December 1922): 987;Home Missions pamphlet, "Friends and the Negro Problem," in file labeled "Negroes," F PG IV 2, ECQC. See also FRJ to Mary Crossand, 8 December 1922; FRJ to RMS, 21 November 1922; and FRJ to Harlow Lindley, 20 December 1922, box 1, SP.

31. See Jesse Overman to FRJ, 9 December 1922, box 1, SP; Atwood and Mary Jenkins, "Christmas at Southland–What Shall the Future Be?" *AF*, (18 January 1923): 48; "Practical Help for Southland," *AF* (18 January 1923): 49, 59.

32. FRJ to RMS, 8 January 1923, box 1, SP.

33. FRJ to RMS, 25 January and 3 February 1923; RMS to FRJ, 29 January 1923, box 1, SP.

34. Wellford White to FRJ, 25 January and 3 February 1923, box 2, SP; RMS to FRJ, 29 January 1923, box 1, SP.

35. See FRJ to Mary M. Crossand, 8 December 1922, box 1, SP; Mildred White, "My Year at Southland Institute," ECQC. See also chapter 10 above.

36. FRJ to RMS, 8 February1923, box 1, SP. The first bell at Southland sounded at 6 a.m. See Etta Mae Robinson to Union Missionary Society of Short Creek, Cadiz, OH, 21 January 1923, ibid.

37. FRJ to RMS, 8 January, 25 January, and 3 February1923; RMS to FRJ, 29 January 1923; FRJ to RMS, 21 February 1923; FRJ to Harlow Lindley, 23 February (telegram) and 24 February 1923, box 1, SP; *AF* (15 February 1923): 129.

38. Ruthanna Simms complained that while student tuition rates had been left entirely in Wolford hands, he provided no clear information as to real costs. RMS to FRJ, 22 January 1923, box 1, SP. See also FRJ to RMS, 25 January 1923, ibid., in which Jenkins noted that he had accepted Wolford's accounts of charges, some of which were irregular because he "made group rates for families" and in a few cases allowed students to pay their way entirely with work.

39. Caroline Cooper to FRJ, 20 February 1923; Will Edwards to Mr. Gankis [*sic*], 31 March 1923, box 1, SP. See also Samuel Boldin to FRJ, 4 June 1923, ibid.

40. FRJ to C. C. Burchett, 23 February 1923, box 1, SP. Burchett later became a leader in a second community petition to remove Jenkins and restore Harry Wolford as Director, see below.

41. See Irene Utter, "Touching the Race Problem at Southland," *AF* (15 March 1923): 212; "The Sun Still Shines at Southland," ibid., 212–13.

42. Minutes, SMM, Statistical Report (inserted), July 1919, 24 September 1918, 425, 2, 9; ibid., 22 August 1922, 425–26.

43. Ibid., 27 October 1922, 428. See also Woodward, "Down Among the Cotton," 879, who noted the need for "deepening the spiritual life of the school."

44. FRJ to RMS, 25 January 1923, box 1, SP.

45. In the fall of 1923 the Social Service Committee of Indiana Yearly Meeting recommended the "elimination of present Quarterly Meeting correspondents for Southland Institute," an indirect admission that the Southland Meeting was no longer functioning as a viable congregation. See MIYM, 1923, 8.

46. FRJ to Charles H. Young, *Helena World,* 20 March 1923, box 2, SP; FRJ to Ann E. Colby, 29 March 1923, box 1, ibid.

47. *AF* (1 March 1923): 171; Minutes, Southland Staff Meeting, 5 March 1923, box 10, SP; Third Annual Report of Board of Home Missions, 28.

48. "Charles O. Whitely's reflections on his visit", 1923, box 2, SP; Third Annual Report of Board of Home Missions, 1923, 28; *AF* (5 April 1923): 268–69; ibid. (12 April 1923): 290; Etta Mae Robinson to Union Missionary Society, 27 March 1923, box 2, SP; MIYM, 1923, 31–32.

49. FRJ to Ann E. Colby, 29 March 1923, box 1, SP and to Nell Vore, 9 April 1923, box 2, ibid. See also see FRJ to RMS, n.d. [March 1923], ibid.

50. "Glory of Humdrum," *AF* (29 March 1923): 252; Minutes, Southland Staff Meeting, 23 April 1923, box 10, SP; J.W. Ramsey, Superintendent, Helena Public Schools, to FRJ, 27 April 1923, box 2, ibid.

51. See Wellford White to Southland, 10 May 1923, box 2, SP, asking for payment of wholesale grocery bill for March and April. Minutes, Southland Staff Meeting, 7 May 1923, box 10, ibid. See also Third Annual Report of Board of Home Missions, 1923, 25–26.

52. Petition to Home Mission Board of Five-Years Maturing of Funds [Meeting of Friends], 15 May 1923, box 1, SP.

53. See RMS to L. Hollingsworth Wood (LHW), 20 July 1923, L. Hollingsworth Wood Papers (hereafter as LHWP), Haverford College Quaker Collection (HCQC), for a detailed account of the Catherine Penney–Joseph Penn affair.

54. FRJ to Florence Jamison, 23 May 1923, box 1, SP; Ruthanna M. Simms, "Four Days at Southland," *AF* (3 March 1921): 165–66.

55. RMS to LHW, 20 July 1923, LHWP; FRJ to Florence Jamison, 23 May 1923, box 1, SP.

56. FRJ to Jamison, 23 May 1923, box 1, SP. See also Jesse Overman to Leigh Barrett, 16 July 1923, box 1, SP, in which Overman told of hearing that Penn and Walter Webb "had a scrap." Since Webb had also been accused of malfeasance by some members of the community, one may speculate that his dispute with Penn had something to do with the Catherine Penney affair. Webb apparently was somewhat more combative than the average teacher in a Quaker school. When he saw John Newsome, the man Raymond Jenkins called his "arch-enemy" in the local community, on-campus Webb threatened to beat Newsome up if he spread any more false rumors. RMS to LHW, 20 July 1923, LHWP.

57. Leigh Barrett to Mrs. Minnie D. Wells, 26 and 27 July 1923, box 2, SP; Florence Jamison to FRJ, 20 July 1923 and FRJ to Florence Jamison, 28 July 1923, box 1, ibid. Also see the poignant reply of Sam Judah's mother concerning her daughter's alleged misdeeds, Minnie Wells to Leigh Barrett, 28 July 1923, box 2, ibid.

58. On 24 June 1923, Jenkins received the following telegram from Joseph C. Penn: "Am Wiring Resignation. Better Offer. Send Check.," box 2, SP. There were also embarrassing repercussions during the next school year. Jenkins related to Ruthanna Simms the story of a male student who when confronted with the fact that he had impregnated a classmate told the director "that if Penn . . . could get by with it that he guesses he could." FRJ to RMS, 9 February 1924, box 5, ibid. Also see correspondence between FRJ and Clara B. Johnson of the Messenger Society of Friends Church in Lynn, IN, which had earlier taken an interest in Catherine Penney and wondered why she was not still in school. Johnson to FRJ, 28 September 1922 and 6 September 1923, ibid.

59. Interview with F. Raymond Jenkins, 19 June 1981, Richmond, IN. See also the case of Mary Lee Moore, below.

60. See Third Annual Report of Board of Home Missions, 1923, 28; *Friends Missionary Advocate,* [1923], 281.

61. Third Annual Report of Board of Home Missions, 34–35.

62. White's Institute, now White's Residential and Family Services, was founded in 1852 from a bequest of Quaker entrepreneur and philanthropist Josiah White (1780–1851) as a manual labor school for poor children under the care of Indiana Yearly Meeting. After a period as an Indian boarding school, since 1897 it has focused on orphans and wards of courts.

63. Third Annual Report of Board of Home Missions, 34–5; MIYM, 1923, 32–33; FRJ to LB, 28 July 1923, box 1, SP.

64. "Report on Meeting of Executive Committee of Board of Home Missions," *AF* (31 May 1923): 422–23; B[oard] H[ome] M[issions], "A Proposal From Southland College," ibid., 19 July 1923, 568.

65. RMS to LHW, 20 July 1923, LHWP.

66. LB to RMS, 25 May and 11 June 1923; RMS to LB, 29 May and 21 June 1923, box 1, SP; Welford White to Southland Principal, 7 June 1923, box 2, ibid.

67. LB to RMS, 8 July 1923; RMS to LB, 11 and 14 July 1923, box 1, SP.

68. See FRJ to Mrs. Malone, Poro College, St. Louis, 17 June 1923, box 3, SP; FRJ

to Mary D. Cox, High Point, NC, 22 June 1923; FRJ to Anna B. Griscom (American Friends Service Committee), 13 July 1923; FRJ to Dillard, 28 July 1923, box 1, ibid.

69. Surprisingly, there is no biography of Wood, but see the effusive appreciation of his work for racial justice by the National Urban League's longtime Executive Secretary, Eugene Kinckle Jones, who called Wood "a character patterned after no man, like unto whom there will be few to follow." Jones, "Phylon Profiles III: L. Hollingsworth Wood," *Phylon* 61, no. 1 (Winter 1945), 17–21.

70. See Minutes of the Southland Committee, 10 July 1923, LHWP; RMS to LHW, 13 July 1923 and to Carolena Wood, 13 July 1923; Walter C. Woodward to LHW, 16 July 1923, ibid.

71. See Jenkins-Moore correspondence, 21 May, 20 June, 29 June, 28 July, August 1923, and 14 September 1923, box 2, SP. See also RMS to LHW, 20 July 1923, LHWP; RMS to FRJ, 9 August 1923, 21 August 1923, 18 October 1923; FRJ to RMS, 13 August 1923, 25 August 1923, and 29 September 1923, boxes 1 and 5, SP.

72. The somewhat frantic last-minute efforts to hire needed faculty are reflected in FRJ-RMS correspondence: RMS to FRJ, 3 August, 7 August, 21 August (telegram), 21 August, 22 August, 5 September, and 11 September 1923; FRJ to RMS, 21 August, 25 August, and 8 September 1923, boxes 1 and 5, SP. See also see *AF* (22 August 1923): 661.

73. See FRJ-Webb correspondence, 28 July, 10 August, 20 August, 1 October, and 10 October 1923, boxes 1 and 3, SP; For Jenkins's esteem for Webb, see FRJ to Charles A. Reeve, 8 December1922, box 1, ibid.

74. FRJ to Florence Jamison, 11 July 1923; Jamison to FRJ, 20 July 1923, box 1, SP.

75. It was perhaps telling that, in contrast to the Wolford era, the new catalog contained no sponsoring advertisements by Helena merchants. Jenkins told an Indiana Friend that Southland's distance from the town and the fact it was a school for black children "makes it a little difficult in securing their co-operation and interest." FRJ to C. O. Snyder, 14 November 1923, box 5, SP.

76. Henry Patten and Wilhelmina Gronewald were volunteers teachers, and Eva Tharp was secretary and bookkeeper, while Peter and Rosa Fowler were superintendent of buildings and grounds and matron respectively. The Fowlers were accepted despite Charles O. Whitely's warning that Peter was a difficult man who might "add to your troubles." Whitely to FRJ, 6 September 1923, box 5, SP. See also Lester Perisho to FRJ, 30 August 1923, ibid.

77. "Southland Institute Catalog Out Today," SP; *Catalog of Southland Institute, 1923–1924,* F PG II 2, ECQC.

12.

1. FRJ to J. H. Dillard, 8 August 1923, box 1, SP. See also see Gertrude C. Mann to FRJ, 11 August 1923, ibid., with reference to the Slater grant.

2. See "Inventory," 31 August 1923, box 20, estimating the total worth of Southland's land, buildings, and equipment at $60,689.97. Enclosed in FRJ to RMS, 22 September 1923, box 5, SP.

3. FRJ to RMS, 21 and 25 August 1923, box 5, SP.

4. See Home Missions Board to C. C. Burchett (the first name on the petition) et al, 3 August 1923, and amended version, 28 August 1923, box 1, SP.

5. For Atwood Jenkins's authorship of the revised text of the letter, see RMS to FRJ, 3, 7, and 9 August 1923, box 1, SP.

6. It was perhaps indicative of northern Friends' tendency to generalize about the nature of black people and black culture that Ruthanna Simms, in recommending a Quaker minister who had worked in Jamaica for an evangelical mission to Southland, seemed to presume that experience with black Jamaicans somehow uniquely qualified this man to deal with black people in the Arkansas Delta who, culturally, might have lived on a different planet. See RMS to FRJ, 7 August 1923, box 1, SP.

7. FRJ to RMS, 13 August box 1, SP; 8 September and 18 September1923, box 5, ibid.

8. FRJ to RMS, 8 September 1923, box 5, SP. See also RMS, "Beginning Most Things New At Southland," *AF* (11 October 1923): 802–3. One of the new regulations was a requirement that all student tuition and board be paid in advance; this was obviously observed only in the breech.

9. FRJ to RMS, 29 September, 10 October, 12 October, and 3 November 1923, box 5, SP; FRJ to Jesse Overman, 10 October 1923, box 3, ibid. In one instance, at least, the higher level of morality was called into question when medical examination revealed one student had contracted gonorrhea and had to be send home as "dangerous to society." See FRJ to Will Davis, 2 October 1923, box 4, ibid.

10. RMS to FRJ, 11 September 1923; FRJ to RMS, 15 September 1923, box 5, SP.

11. See especially RMS to FRJ, 18 October 1923, box 5, SP.

12. FRJ to RMS, 12 October 1923, box 5, SP.

13. Minutes of Staff Meetings, 19 September and 1 October 1923, box 10, SP. For evidence of the Martin's support for Wolford, see M. E. and L. Martin to H. C. Wolford, 2 September 1923, box 10, ibid. It is not clear how this letter came into Jenkins's possession.

14. FRJ to Walter Webb, 10 October 1923 box 3, SP; FRJ to RMS, 12 October 1923, box 5, ibid.

15. Charles Carpenter, Treasurer, IYM to FRJ, 24 September 1923 box 5, SP; FRJ to IYM, 17 April 1924, ibid.

16. Dillard to LHW, 1 October 1923, LHWP.

17. Alden Knight to *AF* (25 October 1923): 845. Knight was obviously among those Midwestern evangelical Friends who believed that the Five Years Meeting and Home Missions Board were giving too great attention to "service" and too little to evangelicalism.

18. RMS to FRJ, 2 and 25 October 1923; FRJ to RMS, 2 November 1923, box 5, SP.

19. RMS to FRJ, 29 October 1923, box 5, SP; L. Hollingsworth Wood's "Account of Visit to Southland," November 1923, LHWP.

20. D. Elton Trueblood to LHW, 14 November 1923, LHWP.

21. For example, see RMS to LHW, 1 November 1923, LHWP, in which she noted that the board would need to borrow $1,500 from White's Institute just to cover Southland's immediate operating expenses.

22. Jackson Davis to LHW, 8 September 1923, LHWP.

23. FRJ to J. A. Presson, 19 October 1923, box 8, SP; Anderson, *Education of Blacks,* 141.

24. Presson to FRJ, 22 October and 20 November 1923, box 8, SP; RMS to LHW, 28 November 1923, LHWP; FRJ to LHW, 30 November 1923, SP.

25. Favrot to FRJ, 1 and 17 December 1923, box 4, SP; RMS to LHW, 28 November 1923, LHWP. See also Favrot's "A Study of County Training Schools For Negroes in the South," *Occasional Papers,* no. 22, 1923, Charlottesville, VA.

26. Leo M. Favrot, "Report on Southland Institute," typescript, 1–2, box 4, SP.

27. With regard to the possibility of a Rosenwald school in the vicinity of Southland, see Frances Shepardson, [Rosenwald Fund] to LHW, 21 November 1923, LHWP. For background on the Rosenwald Fund, see William A. Link, "Jackson Davis and the Lost World of Jim Crow Education," May 2000.

28. Favrot, "Report on Southland Institute," 2–3; Favrot to FRJ, 28 December 1923, box 4, SP.

29. FRJ to RMS, 30 November 1923 and 5 December 1923, box 5, SP. See also Minutes of the Staff Meeting, 5 November 1923, ibid., where a dozen possible night classes are listed.

30. Treadway to Phillips County Attorney, 29 December 1923, box 4, SP.

31. WCW, "In the Shadow of a Great Tragedy," *AF* (10 January 1924): 24–26.

32. Ibid., 25–26. The quotation is from Helen E. Hawkins to LHW, 11 January 1924, LHWP.

33. "Quotations from letters from Young Friends concerning Southland": Ethel H. Wall, Wilmington, OH; Mary A. J. Ballard, Colorado Springs, CO; Mark Macmillan, Piketon, OH, SP; Walter H. Wilson, West Branch, IA, to *AF* (7 February 1924): 116. With reference to Hicksites and Southland, see RMS to LHW, 31 January 1924, LHWP.

34. FRJ to RMS, 14 January 1924, box 5, SP.

35. RMS to FRJ, 17 January 1924, box 5, SP. See "If Winter Comes at Southland," *AF* (24 January 1924): 72.

36. FRJ to RMS, 23 January 1924, box 5, SP; FRJ to LHW, 31 January 1931, LHWP.

37. FRJ to RMS, 30 January, 5, 6, and 7 February 1924, box 5, SP. On 7 February 1924 the Helena Wholesale Grocery Company submitted an unpaid bill of $372.80, Wellford White to Southland College, box 4, ibid.

38. "Budget Report for Southland Institute, February 1st. 1924," 10 pp. (copy), LHWP.

39. Thorkelson's figures were, in fact, incorrect or incomplete, although the comparison is still revealing. According to the Minutes of Indiana Yearly Meeting, 1913, 43, 45, Southland's income for 1913 was $10,314.81, total enrollment was "nearly four hundred," and there was no budget deficit.

40. "Southland Emergency Campaign," 28 January 1924, LHWP and box 5, SP; RMS to FRJ, 9 February 1924, ibid.; RMS to LHW, 7 February 1924, LHWP; "*AF* (14 February 1924): 156.

41. RMS to Southland Multipliers, 13 February 1924, box 5, SP.

42. For Anna P. Strong see Tom Dillard's column Remembering Arkansas in *Arkansas Democrat-Gazette,* 15 July 2007. She was the daughter of Chandler Paschal one of Southland's first college graduates and a recorded minister of Southland Monthly Meeting; in 1924 Chandler Paschal was acting as pastor for the meeting. Anna Strong graduated from Southland in 1903. She subsequently continued her education at Tuskegee Institute and Columbia University, becoming one of Arkansas's most celebrated black educators for whom a new Marianna high school was named.

43. FRJ to Anna P. Strong, 20 January 1924, box 3, SP. Jenkins letter included a list of suggested "Points for Southland Alumni." Ruthanna Simms separately solicited help from Maggie Busby Jordan of Chicago, a daughter of one of Southland's staunchest black Quaker families. RMS to Maggie Busby Jordan, 21 January 1924, box 5, ibid.

44. For example, see Maceo V. Littlejohn to RMS, n.d. [February 1924], LHWP. See also "What Southland Means to Me," *AF* (7 February 1924): 108.

45. *AF* (15 February 1924): 156. Detroit alumni were organized by Grant Thomas, a former Southland teacher, who apparently withdrew his support after corresponding with Harry Wolford, see RMS to FRJ, 1 March 1924, box 5, SP; RMS to LHW, 3 April 1924, LHWP.

46. See RMS to FRJ, 26 January and 12 February 1924 and "Southland Alumni Exchange," n.d.; Tressie Ratliff and RMS to Southland Alumni, 24 April 1924, box 5, SP; RMS to LHW, 3 April 1924, LHWP; *AF* (1 May 1924): 349.

47. LHW to Harold Taylor, 23 February 1924; RMS to LHW, 25 February 1924, LHWP; RMS to FRJ, 27 February 1924, box 5, SP.

48. Favrot to FRJ, 8 February 1924, box 4, SP; FRJ to RMS, 12 and 19 February 1924, box 5, ibid.; RMS to LHW, 21 February 1924, LHWP.

49. FRJ to RMS, 9 February 1924, box 5, SP. See also FRJ's correspondence with Mr. and Mrs. Causell, 21–30, January 1924; FRJ to Lucien Darwin, 22 January 1924, box 4, ibid.

50. FRJ to RMS, 26 February1924, box 5, SP.

51. LHW to RMS, 27 February 1924, LHWP. There is a typed extract of this letter in box 5, SP. See also RMS to LHW, 29 February 1924, LHWP; RMS to FRJ, 1 March 1924, box 5, SP.

52. RMS to LHW, 29 February 1924, box 5, SP.

53. RMS to FRJ, 1 March 1924, box 5, SP; Minutes of Staff Meeting, 3 March 1924; Southland staff to RMS, telegram, 3 March 1924, box 10, ibid. SP.

54. RMS to FRJ, 4 March 1924, box 5, SP.

55. Agenda, Southland Committee, 5 March 1924; RMS to FRJ and Southland Multipliers, 6 March 1924, box 5, SP; "Young Friends Rise to Emergency," *AF* (6 March 1924).

56. RMS to FRJ, 8 and 18 March 1924, box 5, SP; RMS to LHW, 3 April 1924, LHWP. See also RMS, "Southland Shall Live and Grow Strong," *AF* (13 March 1924): 206.

57. FRJ to RMS, 11, 13, and 14 March 1924, box 5, SP.

58. Program, Booster-Anniversary Banquet, Saturday, 15 March 1924, box 10, SP; FRJ to RMS, 18 March 1924, box 5, ibid. Also see FRJ's invitation to Rev. Abernathy, New Light Baptist Church, and other Helena clergymen to the banquet, 12 March 1924, box 3, ibid.; "March and April at Southland," *AF* (1 May 1924): 349.

59. FRJ to RMS, 13 March 1924, box 5, SP.

60. FRJ to RMS, 18 March 1924, box 5, SP; FRJ to Charles Sylva, 18 March 1924, box 14, ibid. See also FRJ to RMS, 14 August 1923, box 1, ibid. Jenkins pointed out that poor lighting from the run-down plant added to the problem of supervising students after dark.

61. Montclair E. Hoffman to FRJ, 19 March 1924, box 3, SP. See also B. Willis

Beede to FRJ, 2 January 1924, box 5, ibid. The Southland Papers contain a considerable volume of correspondence between Jenkins and Derric's father Rev. Charles Sylva regarding his son's escapades.

62. FRJ to RMS, 18 March 1924, box 5, SP (emphasis in original).

63. RMS to FRJ, 20 March 1924, box 5, SP; RMS to LHW, 3 April 1924; LHW to RMS, 7 April 1924, LHWP. As regards incidents of immorality, Wood, a thoroughgoing man of the world, noted that while unfortunate they were not unusual.

64. LHW to RMS, 7 April 1924, LHWP. Ruthanna Simms added Wood's remarks in a letter to Jenkins, 8 April 1924, box 5, SP.

65. FRJ to RMS, 22 March 1924, box 5, SP and to Dr. James H. Dillard and J. A. Presson, 24 March 1924, box 9, ibid.

66. RMS to FRJ, 26 March, 7 and 8 April 1924, box 5, SP.

67. FRJ to RMS, 10 and 11 April 1924, box 5, SP. See also *AF* (1 May 1924): 344.

68. RMS to FRJ, 12, 14, 22 April and 7, 8 May 1924, box 5, SP; Special Meeting, Southland Committee, 18 April 1924, box 5, SP; LHW to RMS, 16 April 1924, LHWP. See also *AF* (1 May 1924): 349.

69. FRJ to RMS, 19 April and 12 May 1924, box 5, SP; Wellford White to Southland Institute, 9 April 1924, box 4, ibid.

70. Clarence Pickett to FRJ, 16 April 1924; FRJ to Pickett, 21 April 1924. box 5, SP.

71. See Staff Meetings for 7 April and 5 May 1924, box 10, SP, during which Jenkins reminded faculty of their responsibility to attend chapel.

72. RMS to FRJ, 19 April 1924, box 5, SP; RMS to LHW, 5 May 1924 and LHW to RMS, 7 April 1924, LHWP. Jenkins's letter on theological matters is not included in the Southland Collection.

73. RMS to LHW, 8 May 1924 and LHW to RMS, 12 May 1924, LHWP. In a letter of 7 May to Wood, Jackson Davis noted, "I have great admiration for Mr. Jenkins."

74. Leo Favrot to RMS, 13 May 1924, LHWP. It is likely that Hollingsworth Wood pressed Favrot to write with such unstinting praise. After the end of the school year, one of the teaching staff, Lester Perisho, wrote a long letter to Ruthanna Simms expressing the view that criticisms of Jenkins had been overblown and that, despite difficulties and dissent during the past year, any change of leadership would be a dangerous leap in the dark. Perisho to RMS, 26 June 1924, (copy), ibid.

75. RMS to LHW, 17 May 1924, LHWP.

76. W. W. Brierley to LHW, 2 May 1924 and LHW to RMS, 28 May 1924, LWHP. See also RMS, "Southland Progress Encouraging," *AF* (5 June 1924): 453.

13.

1. RMS and Helen E. Hawkins to Friends of Southland, 28 April 1924, box 5, SP; Fourth Annual Report of Board of Home Missions, 1924, 23; F. Raymond Jenkins, "A Message of Thanks From Southland," *AF* (1 May 1924): 350; LHW to Alice G. Gifford, 19 May 1924, LHWP.

2. FRJ to RMS, 20 and 22 May 1924, box 5, SP; RMS, "Southland Progress Encouraging," *AF* (5 June 1924): 453.

3. FRJ to S. L. Smith, Director, Rosenwald Fund and A. B. Hill, State Superintendent of Schools, 19 May 1924 and Mr. Childress, Negro Rosenwald

Building Agent, 27 May 1924; N. M. Whaley, Assistant State Superintendent, to FRJ, 20 May 1924; FRJ to Mrs. Saunders, Superintendent of Schools, box 4, SP. See also Favrot to FRJ, 22 May 1924, ibid.

4. Rosa M. Keplinger to B. Francis Wright (copy), 17 July 1924, box 5, SP. In fact, as noted above, the Wolfords had been members of New Westville meeting under the auspices of the Whitewater Monthly Meeting until their membership was transferred to Southland in 1903. When New Westville later became a separate monthly meeting, the Wolfords' names would not have been kept on is records. My thanks to Thomas Hamm for clarifying this matter.

5. C. Hawkins Brown to Principal, Southland, 25 July 1924; FRJ to C. H. Brown, 5 August 1924; C. H. Brown to W. C. Woodward, 15 August and 6 September 1924, box 5, SP. The nature of Anna Wolford's "criminal" relationship with Moses was not specified.

6. H. C. Wolford to Mr. Moses (copy), 26 March 1924, box 5, SP (emphasis in original).

7. William C. Woodward to C. H. Brown (copy), 8 September 1924, box 5, SP.

8. Charles Wadelington and Richard F. Knapp, *Charlotte Hawkins Brown and Palmer Memorial Institute* (Chapel Hill: University of North Carolina Press, 1999), 120–21. See also FRJ to B. Willis Beede, 6 December 1922, box 1, SP. New York City was John Moses's last known address.

9. H. J. Thorkelson to LHW, 27 May 1924, LHWP; RMS to FRJ, 29 May 1924, box 5, SP; RMS, "Southland Progress Encouraging," *AF* (5 June 1924): 453.

10. RMS to FRJ, 3 June 1924, box 5, SP; RMS to LHW, 22 April and 11 June 1924, LHWP. See also *AF* (29 May 1924): 427, for a report on the HMB executive board meeting and FRJ to Howard Gluys (Earlham College engineer), 12 June 1924, box 5, SP.

11. Davis to FRJ, 9 June 1924, box 3, SP. See also LHW to FRJ, 9 June [1924], box 5, ibid.

12. FRJ to RMS and Howard Gluys, 14 June 1924; FRJ to RMS, 18 June 1924; FRJ to LHW, 18 June 1924; FRJ to RMS, 26 and 30 June 1924, box 5, SP. See also FRJ to Howard Gluys, 12 June 1924, ibid., outlining Jenkins's innovative plan for a new campus sewer system.

13. LHW to FRJ, 20 June 1924 and Clarence Pickett (for the Southland Committee) to GEB, 26 June 1924, LHWP. See also RMS to Atwood L. Jenkins, 23 June 1923, box 5, SP.

14. RMS to Jackson Davis, 30 June 1924; RMS to LHW, 30 June and 8 July 1924; and RMS to W. W. Brierley (copy), 8 July 1924, LHWP; Favrot to FRJ, 8 July 1924, box 3, SP. See also RMS, "The Present Situation of Southland," *AF* (11 September 1924).

15. RMS to FRJ, 30 June 1924; FRJ to RMS, 5 July 1924; Atwood L. Jenkins to RMS, 5 July 1924 (copy in LHWP); "*AN OPTION*" to purchase land from T. H. Welsh, 8 July 1924, box 5, SP.

16. RMS to FRJ, 7 July 1924, quoting LHW; Atwood L. Jenkins to RMS, 10 July 1924 box 5, SP; FRJ to Favrot and Davis, 10 July 1924; Favrot to FRJ, 10 July 1924, box 3, ibid.

17. Favrot to FRJ, 14 July 1924 and Davis to FRJ, 19 July 1924, box 3, SP.

18. Southland Committee Meeting, 21 July 1924, LHWP.

19. FRJ to Favrot, 22 July 1924, box 3, SP. Jenkins was no doubt buoyed up by a

$500 appropriation from the Slater Fund, which had just arrived. See Gertrude C. Mann, Secretary, John F. Slater Fund to FRJ, 17 July 1924, box 9, ibid.

20. W. C. Woodward to LHW, 24 July and 4 August 1924, LHWP.

21. AMP Strong to FRJ, 19 July 1924, box 6, SP. In her letter Strong mentioned that she had talked to Jackson Davis at Hampton, and he had noted that the GEB were "going to get right behind you in your problems."

22. FRJ to Dr. George Phenix, Hampton Institute, 23 August 1924 and A. M. P. Strong to FRJ, 2 September 1924, box 6, SP. Anna Strong went on to obtain degrees at both Tuskegee Institute and Columbia University as well as well as honorary degrees from Arkansas AM&N College and Bishop College in Texas. See Dillard. "Anna Strong," *Arkansas Democrat-Gazette*, 15 July 2007.

23. FRJ to Dr. George Phenix and to Anna P. Strong, 8 September 1924, box 6, SP.

24. RMS to L. W. Reynolds (LWR), n.d., box 5, SP.

25. FRJ to Jackson Davis, 25 July 1924, box 3, SP.

26. FRJ to Eva Tharp, 4 and 7 August 1924, and Tharp to FRJ, 4 August 1924, box 3, SP; FRJ to Francis Wright, 22 August 1924, and FRJ to Woodward, 23 August 1924, box 5, ibid.

27. FRJ to RMS, 30 August 2 and 4 September 1924, box 6, SP.

28. For White's Institute, see above, chapter 11.

29. RMS to FRJ, 3 and 6 September, box 6, SP; RMS to LHW, 3 September 1924, LHWP.

30. Calhoun Institute was founded as a center for black industrial education in rural, poverty-stricken Lowndes County, Alabama, in 1892 by Charlotte R. Thorn (1857–1932), a wealthy Eastern socialite, under the direction of Hampton founder Samuel C. Armstrong and with assistance from Booker T. Washington. Sponsored by many of the same eastern chiefly Hicksite, philanthropists, who supported Tuskegee and Hampton, Calhoun survived until 1943. See R. H. Ellis, "The Calhoun School, Miss Charlotte Thorn's 'Lighthouse on the Hill' in Lowndes County, Alabama, *The Alabama Review* 37, no. 3 (1984): 183–201; Robert G. Sherer, *Subordination or Liberation? The Development of Conflicting Theories of Black Education in Nineteenth Century Alabama* (Tuscaloosa: University of Alabama Press, 1977), 68–69, 171n12, 171n14.

31. RMS to LHW, 3 September 1924, LHWP.

32. Gregg to LHW, 8 September 1924 and LHW to Gregg, 9 September 1924, LHWP.

33. See Davis to FRJ, 10 September 1924, box 4, SP; RMS to FRJ, 12 September 1924, box 6, ibid.

34. Staff Meeting, 10 September 1924 , box 10, SP; FRJ to RMS, 8 September 1924, box 6, ibid., which includes the list of faculty and staff for the 1924–25 school year. See also Ruthanna M. Simms, "Southland Opens," *AF* (2 October 1924): 797.

35. FRJ to RMS, 22 September 1924, box 6, SP; Jackson Davis to LHW, 17 and 24 September 1924, LHWP.

36. Ruthanna Simms, "Present Situation at Southland," *AF* (11 September 1924): 733; RMS to FRJ, 15 September 1924, box 6, SP; RMS to LHW, 27 September and 10 October 1924, LHWP. See also *News of Southland*, "September her Golden Month," mimeograph sheet, box 6, SP. Simms sent separate pleas for immediate help to wealthy Baltimore and Midwestern Friends. See RMS to Francis A. White et al,

15 September 1924, box 6, ibid.; RMS to Bertha Stubbs Sumpter, 27 September 1924, LHWP.

37. LHW to RMS, 30 September 1924, LHWP.

38. RMS to LHW, 10 October 1924, LHWP. See also FRJ to LHW, 14 October 1924, ibid.

39. LHW, "Southland Institute," n.d. [October 1924], LHWP

40. See FRJ to LHW, 22 October 1924, LHWP, for a list of contributions ranging from $5 to $500, totaling $1,100, that had been received by the Home Missions Board.

41. LHW to GEB, Attn. Mr. Thorkelson, 6 November 1924, LHWP. See also LHW to FRJ, 6 November 1924, ibid.

42. RMS to LHW, 14 November 1914, LHWP.

43. See Emerson, *Walter C. Woodward*, 157–58, for Woodward's account of how and others were "all but sweating blood to bring Southland out of severe crisis" so that it might "become a Quaker Hampton or Tuskegee."

44. The highest enrollment figure for the 1924–25 school year was 130 (only 87 had registered on 10 October 1924), an increase of over 25 percent from the previous year but much diminished from the 300–400 enrolled during the latter years of Harry Wolford's administration.

45. FRJ to Southland Staff, 9 October 1924 and L. Willard Reynolds (LWR) to Mr. and Mrs. Jenkins, 10 October 1924, box 6, SP. Alfred Barnes had already been sent home the previous August for challenging the authority of staff members. See B[lanche] O. H[udson] to Mary Mayer, 12 August 1924, ibid.

46. LWR to FRJ, 25 October 1924 and FRJ to LWR, 3 November 1924, box 6, SP. Jenkins wrote to Alfred admonishing him to submit to the staff's authority or be expelled. See FRJ to Alfred Barnes, 13 October 1924, ibid. See also LWR to FRJ, 19 November 1924, ibid.

47. FRJ to LWR, 24 October, 3 November and 8 November 1924, box 6, SP. Among Jenkins's ideas for the fundraising campaign was "to write a full and accurate account" of Southland's history. To this end he instructed Reynolds to sent him old letters and record books stored in Central Hall. This material and the copious correspondence from Jenkins's tenure at Southland were eventually stored in the attic at the offices of Friends Central Meeting in Richmond until the late 1980s when they were uncovered and subsequently returned to Arkansas and deposited in the Special Collections Department of Mullins Library, University of Arkansas. See FRJ to LWR, 14 October and 5 November 1924, ibid.

48. FRJ, "Southland is Surely Climbing," *AF* (16 October 1924): 823; "Kept Enough for a Pair of Pants," ibid. (23 October 1924): 856–57; "Do Friends Realize the Truth?," ibid. (30 October 1924): 877; "How Southland Helps to Pay Its Way," ibid. (13 November 1924): 913. See FRJ to LHW, 22 November 1924, LHWP, reporting a not-very-successful fundraising tour among Friends in eastern Illinois and western Indiana.

49. FRJ to LWR, 11 November 1924, box 6, SP; FRJ to LHW, 12 and 22 November 1924, LHWP; LWR to RMS, 24 November 1924, box 6, SP.

50. FRJ to Eva Tharp, 1 December 1924; "List of Accounts Payable," 1 December 1924, box 6, SP.

51. C. W. Garrison, M.D., to LWR, 6 December 1924; LWR to Arkansas State Board of Health, 22 December 1924, box 6, SP.

52. LHW to FRJ, 6 December 1924; FRJ to Favrot, 11 December 1924; Favrot to FRJ, 15 December 1924; and FRJ to LHW, 18 December 1924, LHWP.

53. FRJ to LWR, 15 and 20 December 1924 box 6, SP; FRJ to LHW, 18 December 1924, LHWP.

54. L. Willard Reynolds, "Christian Education At Southland," *AF* (18 December 1908–09); "Extend Sympathy," ibid.: 1009.

55. LWR to FRJ, 31 December 1924, box 6, SP.

56. Ibid. Southland was eventually billed $52 for repair to the car with which Moses collided. See J. D. Mays, Phillips County Sheriff and Collector, to LWR, 19 March 1925, ibid.

57. See FRJ to LWR, 13 January 1925, box 6, SP, in which Jenkins admonished Reynolds to ease up in his work after having had his tonsils removed.

58. Margaret Jones, "A Meeting of the Executive Committee and Several Friends from Richmond who are interested in Southland Institute," 6 January 1925, LHWP. Jenkins claimed that $63,000 was already available for this project, but this was misleading because he included the GEB's projected $20,000 as well $40,000 from Southland's largely restricted endowment fund.

59. Ibid.

60. FRJ to LWR, 13 January, 1925 and LWR to RMS, 15 January 1925, box 6, SP.

61. FRJ to LWR, 13 January 1925, box 6, SP; LHW to RMS, 19 January 1925, LHWP.

62. RMS to LHW, 21 and 23 January 1925, LHWP.

63. LHW to RMS, 27 January 1925, LHWP.

64. Fifth Annual Report of Board of Home Missions, 1925, 30–31.

65. RJ to LWR, 2 February 1925 and RMS to LWR, 22 January 1925, box 6, SP. See also "Southland Institute Again Reports," *AF* (5 February 1925): 112.

66. LWR to FRJ or Eva Tharp, 9 February 1925, box 6, SP.

67. LHW to FRJ, telegram and letter, 7 February 1925 and LHW to Wilbur K. Thomas, 7 February 1925, LHWP.

68. Minutes, Southland Committee Meeting, 9 February 1925, LHWP.

69. Ibid.; FRJ to LHW, 14 February 1925, box 6, SP; Wilbur K. Thomas to FRJ, 16 February 1925; Southland Committee Meeting, 17 February, 1925, LHWP.

70. LWR to FRJ, 30 January 1925 and FRJ to LWR, 7 February 1925, box 6, SP.

71. FRJ to LWR, 11 March 1925; FRJ to Southland Institute Staff and to Southland Students and Southland Friends, n.d.; LWR to FRJ, 18 March 1925, box 6, SP.

72. Board of Home Missions [Walter C. Woodward], "A Statement Concerning Southland Institute." See also Emerson, *Walter C. Woodward*, 157–58.

73. "Statement Concerning Southland Institute."

74. Mrs. Rosie Knox to Miss Tharp, 10 March 1925, box 6, SP.

75.B. W. Knox to President, 2 April 1925, box 6, SP. Knox, a resident of Excelsior Springs, Missouri, in 1925, was the husband of Henrietta Kitterall, one of the original orphans adopted by Alida and Calvin Clark, a member of Southland's first graduating class in 1876 and a longtime teacher at the school.

76. FRJ, "Telling the Students," *AF* (9 April 1925) 277–78. See also Clarence Pickett, "Southland Never So Needed As Now," ibid.: 277.

77. See FRJ to LWR, 18 April 1925, box 6, SP, with instructions on how to handle these new pupils during the final six weeks of classes.

78. See Southland Staff Meeting, 24 April 1925, box 10, SP; LWR to *Helena World*, 27 April 1925, SP.

79. FRJ to LWR, 25 April and 1 May 1925, box 6, SP.

80. B. Frances Wright to LHW, 13 August 1925 and LHW to B. Frances Wright, 17 August 1925, LHWP; "Minutes of Conference in the Interest of Southland," 18 September 1925 and LHW to RMS, 2 October 1925, LHWP.

81. Report on Board of Home Missions Meeting," *AF* (28 May 1925): 391, 395. See also Gilbert Bowles, "Some Thoughts on Closing Southland Institute," ibid. (30 July 1925): 544, 547; Bowles to LHW, 15 June 1925, LHWP.

82. RMS, "Lest We Forget Southland," *AF* (5 November 1925), 765. She noted in this article that the Southland account was, as usual, overdrawn.

83. Attached to a letter of RMS to the Southland Circle, 12 December 1925, LHWP.

84. Lester Perisho to RMS, reprinted in *AF* (26 November 1925): 816.

Epilogue

1. RMS to Southland Circle, 29 December 1925, LHWP.

2. Interview with F. Raymond Jenkins, 19 June 1981, Richmond, IN.

3. See Eugene Kinckle Jones, "Phylon Profile III: L. Hollingsworth Wood," *Phylon* 6, no. 1 (1st Quarter, 1945): 17–21.

4. Telegram (copy), Frank to Clarence Pickett, n.d. [1925]; Sixth Annual Report of Board of Home Missions, 1926, 3–4; Kirkman, "Southland College," 33; and Gentry, "History of Lexa," 19. The AME Zion Church paid $7,000 for the property.

5. Carolyn Cunningham of Helena, former editor of the *Phillips County Historical Quarterly*, kindly provided information about Southland's successor institution, including the *Bulletin, Walters-Southland Normal and Industrial Institute, 1937–38* and "A Brief History of Walters-Southland Institute" by Bishop W. W. Matthews who was chief administration officer at the school. See also Gentry, "History of Lexa," 19–20.

6. Gentry, "History of Lexa," 19–20.

7. Interview with Alvin "Buddy" Bird, 19 February 1982, Southland, Arkansas. In the early 1980s Mr. Bird owned most of the land that formerly comprised the Southland campus and farm.

8. Fifth Annual Report of Board of Home Missions, 1925, 39.

9. Circulars for Annual Reunion Picnic of the Southland College Club of Chicago, 1964 and 1966, gift to the author from Willa Burchett Graves. A fascinating aspect of the 1964 picnic was the appearance of Joseph Charles Penn, retired assistant superintendent of public instruction for the State of Illinois, as featured speaker. One may suppose that Catherine Penney did not attend this gathering.

10. Alfred L. Billingsley Sr. was honored by Pres. Lyndon Johnson by being appointed as the first black Farm Home Administration committeeman. See his obituary, *Arkansas Democrat-Gazette,* 27 May 2000.

11. Samuel Kountz, the son Jerry S. Kountz who graduated from Southland in 1913, became a pioneer organ-transplant surgeon who developed a widely adopted technique for controlling heart and kidney rejection. See David Taylor, "A Garden in

the Wilderness: The Role of Southland College in Early Negro Education," *PCHQ* 26, no. 1: 10.

12. Interviews with Willa Burchett Graves and Ernestine Pruitt Billingsley, Southland, AR, 19 February 1982.

13. Interview with Emma Roden Young (recorded as a member of Southland Monthly Meeting, 19 April 1908), Southland, AR, 18 February 1982.

14. Elbert Russell, *Friends at Mid-Century* (Richmond, IN: The Isaac T. and Lida K. Johnson Lecture, 1950), 15n.

15. Fifth Annual Report of Board of Home Missions, 1925, 30–31; Minutes, Five Years Meeting, 1927, 63–64; Interview with F. Raymond Jenkins, 19 June 1981, Richmond, IN.

16. Lydia M. Chace to Friends, 12 March 1878, *CW* 8 (3 April 1878): 158.

Bibliography

I. Manuscripts

A. M. Taylor Papers. Haverford College Quaker Collection, Haverford, PA.

American Missionary Association Archives. Arkansas History Commission, Little Rock.

Controversial Issues Involving Earlham, Race Relations and Policy. Friends Collection. Lilly Library. Earlham College Archives, Richmond, IN.

Deed Records, 1865–1928. Phillips County Courthouse, Helena, AR.

Dictionary of Quaker Biography. Haverford College Quaker Collection, Haverford, PA.

Edgar Ballard Letters. Eli and Mahalah Jay Collection. Friends Collection. Lilly Library. Earlham College Archives, Richmond, IN.

Elizabeth Edwards [now identified as Ruth Emily Edwards] "Diaries." Friends Collection. Lilly Library. Earlham College Archives, Richmond, IN.

Elkanah Beard Diaries. Friends Collection. Lilly Library. Earlham College Archives, Richmond, IN.

Enoch K. Miller Papers. Small Manuscript Collection. Arkansas History Commission, Little Rock.

Hadley, Job. "Reminiscences, 1883." Friends Collection. Lilly Library. Earlham College Archives, Richmond, IN.

Herschel Folger Letters. Alumni Files. Friends Collection. Lilly Library. Earlham College Archives, Richmond, IN.

"History of Southland College, Near Helena, Arkansas." 1905. Friends Collection. Lilly Library. Earlham College Archives, Richmond, IN.

Jay, Eli. "History (Southland Institute)." 1896. Friends Collection. Lilly Library. Earlham College Archives, Richmond, IN.

Judge James Millinder Hanks Diaries, 1865–1869. MC 1335. Special Collections. Mullins Library. University of Arkansas.

L. Hollingsworth Wood Papers, Ms. Col. 1175, Box 73. Haverford College Quaker Collection, Haverford, PA.

Mary Sale Edmonson Diary. Arkansas History Commission, Little Rock.

Minute Book of Board of Control for Freedmen's Relief Committee of the Ohio, Indiana, and Western Yearly Meetings of Orthodox Friends. Friends Collection. Lilly Library. Earlham College Archives, Richmond, IN.

Minutes of the Committee of the Indiana Yearly Meeting of [Orthodox] Friends on the Concerns of the People of Color [1851–1863]. Friends Collection. Lilly Library. Earlham College Archives, Richmond, IN.

Minutes, Indiana Yearly Meeting Committee for Freedmen. Friends Pamphlet Group I. Friends Collection. Lilly Library. Earlham College Archives, Richmond, IN.

Probate Records, 1939. Phillips County Courthouse, Helena, AR.

"Southland College" Friends Pamphlet Groups (F PG) II, III, IV. Friends Collection. Lilly Library. Earlham College Archives, Richmond, IN.

Southland College Papers. MC 577. Special Collections. Mullins Library. University of Arkansas.

White, Mildred E. "My Year at Southland, 1918-1919." Friends Collection. Lilly Library. Earlham College Archives, Richmond, IN.

II. Printed Sources

Abstracts of the Records of the Society of Friends in Indiana. Vol. 1, *Whitewater and Springfield Monthly Meetings.* Ruth Dorell and Thomas D. Hamm, eds. Indianapolis: Indiana Historical Society, 1996.

Annual Reports of the Board of Home Missions, 1921–1928. Five Years Meeting, Richmond, IN.

Arkansas Commissioner of State Lands. *The 1868 Report: A Collection of Historical Documents From Arkansas's First Land Commissioner.* Little Rock: Arkansas Commission of State Lands, 2002.

Arkansas Freedmen's Bureau. Records of the Bureau of Refugees, Freedmen, and Abandoned Lands. Record Group 105. National Archives, Washington DC.

Assistant Commission for the State of Arkansas. Bureau of Refugees, Freedmen, and Abandoned Lands, Misc. Records. Microfilm roll 52. National Archives, Washington DC.

Beard, Elkanah. *Journals, 1862–1864.* MS 484. Friends Historical Collection. Guilford College. Quoted in Daniel J. Salemson, "'to spend some time as a missionary among colored people': The Civil War Writings of an Indiana Quaker." *The Southern Friend* 20, no. 1 (Spring 1998): 3–75.

Biographical and Historical Memoirs of Eastern Arkansas. Chicago: Goodspeed, 1886.

Biographical Catalogue. Oxford: Lincoln University, 1918.

Catalogue of Southland College and Normal Institute, near Helena, Arkansas. (Helena, 1898–1899, 1911–1912, 1915–16, 1923–24).

Chace, Lydia. *The Autobiography of Lydia Meader Chace.* Quaker Heritage Press. www.qhpress.org/quakerpages/qwhp/lydiachace.htm (accessed 14 February 2003).

Coffin, Levi. *The Reminiscences of Levi Coffin.* Richmond, IN: Friends United Press, 1991.

Eaton, John. *Report of the General Superintendent of Freedmen, Department of the Tennessee and the State of Arkansas for 1864.* (Memphis, 1865).

Edgerton, Walter. *A History of the Separation in Indiana Y[early] M[eeting] in the Winter of 1842 and 1843 on the Anti-Slavery Question.* Cincinnati: Achilles Pugh, 1856.

"Final Report of the contraband Relief Commission of Cincinnati, 6 December 1864." Quoted in *Friends' Review* 18, no. 19 (7 January 1865): 294–95.

Freedmen's Bureau Record, Arkansas. *Records of U.S. Bureau of Refugees, Freedmen and Abandoned Lands.* Microfilm, 28 reels. National Archives, Washington DC.

Friends Association of Philadelphia. *Statistics of the . . . Friends Association of Philadelphia and Its Vicinity for the Relief of Colored People.* Philadelphia: Inquirer Printing Office, 1864.

John F. Slater Fund. *Reference List of Southern Colored Schools.* Lynchburg, VA: J. P. Bell, 1918.

Indiana Yearly Meeting Committee for the Relief of the Freedmen. *Annual Reports, 1862–1870.* Richmond, IN: Indiana Yearly Meeting.

Indiana Yearly Meeting. *The Discipline of the Society of Friends of Indiana Yearly Meeting.* Richmond, IN: E. Morgan and Sons, 1864.

"Memorial on Behalf of the Freedmen by Representatives of the Society of Friends, 14 December 1865, LR, commissioner, Bureau of Refugees, Freedmen and Abandoned Lands. National Archives, Washington DC.

Minutes of the Executive Committee on Education for all schools within the limits of Indiana Yearly Meeting, and under their control, 1869–1871. Richmond, IN: Indiana Yearly Meeting.

Minutes, Five Years Meeting, 1917–1928. Richmond, IN: Indiana Yearly Meeting.

Minutes of Indiana Yearly Meeting, 1862–1930. Richmond, IN: Indiana Yearly Meeting.

Pumphrey, Stanley. "Missionary Work in Connection with the Society of Friends." Philadelphia: 1880.

"Receipts From Bible Schools Observing Southland Day," Report of the Missionary Board on Southland College to Indiana Yearly Meeting of Friends. Richmond, IN, 8–11.

"Report of Indiana Yearly Meeting's Executive Committee on Freedmen." 30 September 1864. Quoted in *Friends' Review* 18, no. 13 (26 November 1864): 20–24.

Southland College, 1864–1895: A Brief Sketch of Thirty Years of Missionary Labor. Richmond, IN: Nicholson Printing, 1895.

U.S. Bureau of the Census. *Fourth Census of the United States, 1820.* Washington DC, 1822.

———. *Seventh Census of the United States, 1850.* Washington DC, 1853.

———. *Eighth Census of the United States, 1860.* Washington DC, 1864.

III. Quaker Newspapers and Periodicals

The American Friend (Philadelphia). 1894–1930.

The American Friend and Freedman's Record (Richmond, IN). 1864–1868.

The British Friend. 1864–1913.

Christian Worker. 1871–1894.

Friends Intelligencer. 1864.

Friends Missionary Advocate. 1885–1930.

The Friend (London). 1864–1925.

Friend's Review. 1864–1894.

IV. Secondary Sources: Books

Abbot, Margaret Post. *Historical Dictionary of Friends (Quakers).* Lanham, MD: Scarecrow Press, 2003.

Anderson, James D. *The Education of Blacks in the South, 1860–1935.* Chapel Hill: University of North Carolina Press, 1988.

Barnes, Kenneth. *A Journey of Hope: Arkansans and the Back-to-Africa Movement in the Late 1800s.* Chapel Hill: University of North Carolina Press, 2004.

Berry, Fred, and John Novak. *The History of Arkansas.* Little Rock: Rose, 1997.

Bolton, Charles. *Territorial Ambition.* Fayetteville: University of Arkansas Press, 1993.

Braithwaite, William C. *The Beginnings of Quakerism.* 2nd. ed. Cambridge: Cambridge University Press, 1955.

Budge, Frances Anne. *Isaac Sharp: An Apostle of the Nineteenth Century.* London: Headley Brothers, 1898.

Butchart, Ronald. *Northern Schools, Southern Blacks, and Reconstruction: Freedmen's Education, 1862–1875.* Westport, CT: Greenwood Press, 1980.

Chambers, Fred. *History of Black Higher Education.* Westport, CT: Greenwood Press, 1978.

Cimbala, Paul and Randall M. Miller, eds. *The Freedman's Bureau and Reconstruction.* New York: Fordham University Press, 1999.

Daniel, Pete. *The Shadow of Slavery: Peonage in the South, 1901–69.* Champaign-Urbana: University of Illinois Press, 1992.

Davis, David Brion. *The Problem of Slavery in Western Culture.* Ithaca, NY: Cornell University Press, 1966.

DeBlack, Thomas. *With Fire and Sword: Arkansas, 1861–1874.* Fayetteville: University of Arkansas Press, 2003.

Drake, Thomas. *Quakers and Slavery in America.* Gloucester, MA: Peter Smith, 1965.

Du Bois, W.E.B. and Augustus Granville Dill, eds. *The Common School and the Negro American.* Atlanta: Atlanta University Press, 1911.

Eaton, John. *Grant, Lincoln, and the Freedmen.* New York: Longmans, Green & Co., 1907.

Emerson, Elizabeth. *Walter C. Woodward: Friend on the Frontier, A Biography.* Privately printed, 1952.

Engs, Robert Francis. *Educating the Disfranchised and Disinherited: Samuel Chapman Armstrong and Hampton Institute, 1839–1893.* Knoxville: University of Tennessee Press, 1999.

———. *Freedom's First Generation: Black Hampton, Virginia, 1861–1890.* Philadelphia: University of Pennsylvania Press, 1979.

Fairclough, Adam. *Teaching Equality: Black Schools in the Age of Jim Crow.* Athens: University of Georgia Press, 2001.

Foner, Eric. *Reconstruction: America's Unfinished Revolution, 1863–1877.* New York: Harper Collins, 1988.

Fox, Henry Clay, ed. *Memoirs of Wayne County.* 2 vols. Madison, IN: Western Historical Association, 1912.

Favrot, Leo and Jackson Davis. *A Suggested Course of Study for County Training Schools for Negroes in the South.* Lynchburg, VA: J. P. Bell, 1917.

Fulop, Timothy E. and Albert J. Raboteau, eds. *African-American Religion: Interpretive Essays in History and Culture.* New York: Routledge, 1997.

Gertis, Louis S. *From Contraband to Freedman: Federal Policy Toward Southern Blacks, 1861–1865.* Westport, CT: Greenwood Press, 1973.

Gordon, Fon Louise. *Caste and Caste, the Black Experience in Arkansas, 1880–1920.* Athens: University of Georgia Press, 1995.

Graves, John William. *Town and Country: Race Relations in an Urban-Rural Context, Arkansas, 1895–1905.* Fayetteville: University of Arkansas Press, 1990.

Haiters, Erik F., James Mak, and Gary M. Walton. *Western River Transportation: The Era of Early International Development, 1810–1860.* Baltimore: John Hopkins University Press, 1975.

Hamm, Thomas D. *Earlham College: A History, 1847–1997.* Bloomington: Indiana University Press, 1997.

———. *The Quakers in America* New York: Columbia University Press, 2003.

———. *The Transformation of American Quakerism.* Bloomington: Indiana University Press, 1988.

Ingle, H. Larry. *Quakers in Conflict: the Hicksite Reformation.* Knoxville: University of Tennessee Press, 1986.

Jones, Rufus. *The Latter Periods of Quakerism.* Vol. 2. London: Macmillan, 1921.

Kennedy, Thomas C. *British Quakerism, 1860–1920: The Transformation of a Religious Community.* Oxford: Oxford University Press, 2001.

Knollenberg, Bernhard. *Pioneers Sketches of the Upper Whitewater Valley: Quaker Stronghold of the West.* Indianapolis: Indiana Historical Society, 1945.

Lemann, Nicholas. *The Promised Land: The Great Black Migration and How it Changed America.* New York: Vintage Books, 1992.

Lytle, William M. comp. *Merchant Steam Vessels of the United States, 1807–1868* ("The Lytle List"). Mystic, CT: The Steamship Historical Society of America, 1932.

Matthews, Donald G. *Religion in the Old South.* Chicago: University of Chicago Press, 1977.

McNeilly, Donald. *The Old South Frontier: Cotton Plantation and the Formation of Arkansas Society, 1819–1861.* Fayetteville: University of Arkansas Press, 2000.

Moneyhon, Carl H. *Arkansas and the New South, 1874–1929.* Fayetteville: University of Arkansas Press, 1997.

———. *The Impact of the Civil War and Reconstruction on Arkansas.* Baton Rouge: Louisiana State University Press, 1994.

Moon, James H. *Water Baptism: A Pagan and Jewish Ritual But Not Christian.* Fallsington, PA: James Moon, 1902.

Moore, Leonard J. *Citizen Klansmen: The Ku Klux Klan in Indiana, 1921–1928.* Chapel Hill: University of North Carolina Press, 1991.

Morris, Robert. *Reading, 'Riting, and Reconstruction: The Education of Freedmen in the South, 1861–1870.* Chicago: University of Chicago Press, 1976.

Nelson, Jacquelyn. *Indiana Quakers Confront the Civil War.* Indianapolis: Indiana Historical Society, 1991.

Newman, Henry Stanley. *The Young Man of God: Memoirs of Stanley Pumphrey.* New York: Friends Book and Tract Committee, 1883.

Nieman, Donald. *African Americans and Education in the South, 1865–1900.* New York: Garland, 1994.

Nickalls, John L., ed. *Journal of George Fox.* London: Religious Society of Friends, 1986.

Ownby, Ted. *Subduing Satan: Religion, Recreation and Manhood in the Rural South, 1865–1920.* Chapel Hill: University of North Carolina Press, 1990.

Punshon, John. *Portrait in Grey: A Short History of the Quakers.* London: Quaker Home Service, 1984.

Ratcliff, Richard. *Our Special Heritage: Sesquicentennial History of Indiana Yearly Meeting of Friends, 1821–1971.* New Castle, IN: Community Printing Co., 1970.

Richardson, Joe Martin. *Christian Reconstruction: the American Missionary Association and Southern Blacks, 1861–1890.* Athens: University of Georgia Press, 1986.

Roberts, Arthur. *The Association of Evangelical Friends.* Newberg, OR: Barclay Press, 1975.

Russell, Elbert. *Friends at Mid-Century.* Reprint of the Isaac T. and Lida K. Johnson Lecture, 22 October 1950. Richmond: Earlham College, 1950.

———. *The History of Quakerism.* New York: Macmillan, 1942.

Seabury, Paul. *The Waning of Southern "Internationalism."* Princeton, NJ: Princeton University Press, 1957.

Selleck, Linda B. *Gentle Invaders: Quaker Women Educators and Racial Issues During the Civil War and Reconstruction.* Richmond, IN: Friends United Press, 1995.

Sernett, Milton C. *Black Religion and American Evangelicalism: White Protestants, Plantation Missions, and the Flowering of Negro Christianity, 1787–1865.* Metuchen, NJ: Scarecrow Press, 1975.

Sherer, Robert G. *Subordination or Liberation? The Development of Conflicting Theories of Black Education in Nineteenth Century Alabama.* Tuscaloosa: University of Alabama Press, 1977.

Smith, C. Calvin and Linda Walls Joshua, eds. *Educating the Masses: The Unfolding History of Black School Administrators in Arkansas, 1900–2000.* Fayetteville: University of Arkansas Press, 2003.

Soderlund, Jean. *Quakers and Slavery: A Divided Spirit.* Princeton, NJ: Princeton University Press, 1985.

Spivey, Donald. *Schooling for the New Slavery: Black Industrial Education, 1868–1915.* Westport, CT: Greenwood Press, 1978.

Stockley, Grif. *Blood in Their Eyes: The Elaine Race Massacre of 1919.* Fayetteville: University of Arkansas Press, 2001.

Tallack, William. *Friendly Sketches in America.* London: A. W. Bennett, 1861.

Taylor, Orville. *Negro Slavery in Arkansas.* Durham, NC: Duke University Press, 1958.

Thornburg, Opal. *Whitewater: Indiana's First Monthly Meeting of Friends, 1809–1959.* Richmond, IN: privately printed, n.d.

Tindall, George B. *The Emergence of the New South, 1913–1945.* Baton Rogue: Louisiana State University Press, 1967.

Vincent, Stephen A. *Southern Seed, Northern Soil: African-American Farm Communities in the Midwest, 1765–1900.* Bloomington: Indiana University Press, 1999.

Wadelington, Charles and Richard F. Knapp. *Charlotte Hawkins Brown and Palmer Memorial Institute.* Chapel Hill: University of North Carolina Press, 1999.

Warner, Stafford Allen. *Yardley Warner: The Freedman's Friend, His Life and Times.* Didcot: The Wessex Press, 1956.

Weeks, Stephen. *Southern Quakers and Slavery: A Study in Institutional History.* Baltimore: Johns Hopkins University Press, 1896.

Whayne, Jeannie. *A New Plantation South: Land, Labor, and Federal Favor in Twentieth-Century Arkansas.* Fayetteville: University of Arkansas Press, 1996.

Whayne, Jeannie, Thomas A. DeBlack, George Sabo III, and Morris S. Arnold. *Arkansas: A Narrative History.* Fayetteville: University of Arkansas Press, 2002.

Whayne, Jeannie and Willard B. Gatewood. *The Arkansas Delta: Land of Paradox.* Fayetteville: University of Arkansas Press, 1993.

Williams, Heather Andrea. *self-taught: African American Education in Slavery and Freedom.* Chapel Hill: University of North Carolina Press, 2005.

Williams, Nancy A., ed. *Arkansas Biography: A Collection of Notable Lives.* Fayetteville: University of Arkansas Press, 2000.

Young, Andrew. *History of Wayne County, Indiana.* Cincinnati, 1872.

V. Secondary Sources: Articles

Allen, M. A. Marriage. "The Colored People of the Southern States." *Friends Quarterly Examine,* 18 (1884): 296–301, 390–99.

Anderson, James D. "Education as a Vehicle for the Manipulation of Black Workers." In *Technology and Education: Dissenting Essays in the Intellectual Foundations of*

American Education, edited by Walter Feinberg and Henry Rosemont. Urbana: University of Illinois Press, 1975.

———. "The Hampton Model of Normal School Industrial Education, 1868–1900." In *New Perspectives on Black Educational History,* edited by Vincent P. Franklin and James D. Anderson. Boston: G. K. Hall, 1978.

Aptheker, Herbert. "The Quakers and Negro Slavery." *Journal of Negro History* 25 (1940): 331–62.

Bean, Joel. "The Issue." *The British Friend* (March 1881): 49–51.

Bigelow, Martha Mitchell. "Freedmen of the Mississippi Valley, 1862–1865." *Civil War History* 8, no. 1 (March 1962): 38–44.

Bolton, S. Charles. "Slavery and the Defining of Arkansas." *AHQ* 58, no. 1 (Spring 1999): 1–23.

Brawley, Benjamin. "Early Effort for Industrial Education." *Occasional Papers,* no. 22, (1923).

Breckinridge, Margaret E. "Adventures on a Hospital Boat in the Mississippi." *PCHQ* (December 1962): 31–42. Reprinted from *Memorial of Margaret E. Breckinridge.* Philadelphia: J. Lipincott, 1865.

Cadbury, Henry J. "Negro Membership in the Society of Friends." *Journal of Negro History* 21 (1936): 151–213.

———. "Quaker Bibliographical Notes II. Anti-Slavery Writing." *Bulletin of Friends Historical Association* 26 (1937): 39–53.

Calvert, Pamela. "'How Blessed It is for the Sisters to Meet': Historical Roots of the Pacific Northwest Women's Theology Conference." *Quaker History* 92, no. 2 (Fall 2003): 19–51.

Coleman, Christopher. "A Contraband Camp." *Indiana History Bulletin* 1, nos. 11–12 (September 1924): 130–143.

Day, Deborah K. "'The Magic Awakening Touch': The interplay Between Spirituality and Public Activism: Quaker Women and Education in the South, 1865–1900." *Southern Friend* 18 (Fall 1996): 7–26.

Dillard, Tom W. "Remembering Arkansas: Anna Strong deserves more credit in black education." *Arkansas Democrat-Gazette.* 15 July 2007.

———. "Madness With a Past: An Overview of Race Violence in Arkansas History." *Arkansas Review: A Journal of Delta Studies* 32, no. 1 (August 2001): 97–98.

———. "Three Important Black Leaders in Phillips County History." *PCHQ* 9, no. 1 (December 1980): 10–23.

Du Bois, W. E. B. "How Negroes Have Taken Advantage of Educational Opportunities Offered by Friends." *Journal of Negro History* 7, no. 2 (April 1938): 124–131.

Ellis, R. H. "The Calhoun School, Miss Charlotte Thorn's 'Lighthouse on the Hill' in Lowndes County, Alabama." *The Alabama Review* 37, no. 3 (1984): 183–201.

Favrot, Leo M. "A Study of County Training Schools for Negroes in the South." *Occasional Papers.* No. 22. Charlottesville, VA, 1923.

———. "How the Small Rural School Can More Adequately Serve its Community." *The Journal of Negro Education* 5, no. 3 (July 1936): 430–38.

Finkenbine, Roy E. "'Our Little Circle': Benevolent Reformers, the Slater Fund, and the Argument for Black Industrial Education, 1882–1908." In *African-American Life in the Post-Emancipation South, 1861–1900,* edited by Donald G. Nieman. New York: Garland, 1994.

Finley, Randy. "In War's Wake: Health Care and the Arkansas Freedmen, 1863–1868." *AHQ* 51, no. 2 (Summer 1992): 135–62.

Foti, Thomas. "The River's Gifts and Curses." In Whayne and Gatewood, *Arkansas Delta,* 30–57.

Gatewood, Willard. "Arkansas Negroes in the 1890s: Documents." *AHQ* 33, no. 4 (Winter 1974): 293–323.

———. "Negro Legislators in Arkansas, 1891: A Document." *AHQ* 31, no. 3 (Autumn 1972): 220–33.

Gentry, Gloria J. Sands. "The History of Lexa." *PCHQ* 17, no. 3 (June 1979): 13–22.

Gordon, Fon Louise. "From Slavery to Uncertain Freedom: Blacks in the Delta." In Whayne and Gatewood, *Arkansas Delta,* 98–127.

Graves, John William. "The Arkansas Separate Coach Law of 1891." *AHQ* 32, no. 2 (Summer 1973): 148–65.

———. "Negro Disfranchisement in Arkansas." *AHQ* 26, no. 3 (Autumn 1967): 199–225.

Hackett, G. H., ed. "Diaries and Letters of Rev. Otis Hackett." *PCHQ* 1, no. 1 (Summer 1962) 23–46.

Hamm, Thomas D. "Hicksite Quakers and the Antebellum Nonresistance Movement." *Church History* 63, no. 4 (December 1994): 557–69.

———. "Joel Bean and the Revival in Iowa." *Quaker History* 76, no. 1 (Spring 1987): 33–49.

———."'New Light on the Old Ways': Gurneyites, Wilburites, and Early Friends." *Quaker History* 93, no. 1 (Spring 2004): 53–67.

Hamm, Thomas D., April Beckman, Marissa Florio, Kristi Giles, and Marie Hopper. "'A Great and Good People': Midwestern Quakers and the Struggle Against Slavery." *Indiana History Magazine* 100, no. 1 (March 2004): 3–25.

Hamm, Thomas D., Margaret Marconi, and Benjamin Whitman. "The Decline of Quaker Pacifism in the Twentieth Century: Indiana Yearly Meeting of Friends as a Case Study." *Indiana Magazine of History* 96, no. 1 (March 2000): 1–45.

Harvey, Hank. "A Beacon for the Needy." *The Blade* (Toledo, OH) (14 February 1999).

Holley, Donald. "The Plantation Heritage: Agriculture in the Arkansas Delta." In Whayne and Gatewood, *Arkansas Delta,* 238–77.

Hume, Richard. "The Arkansas Constitution Convention of 1868: A Case Study of the Politics of Reconstruction." *Journal of Southern History* 39 (May 1973): 183–206.

Johnson, Charles. "Minnesota Troops at Helena: Narrative of the Sixth Regiment." *PCHQ* 24, no. 3–4 (June-September 1986): 1–16.

Johnson, William. "Prelude to the Missouri Compromise." *AHQ* 24, no. 1 (Spring 1964): 47–66.

Jones, Eugene Kinckle. "*Phylon* Profile III: L. Hollingsworth Wood." *Phylon* 6, no. 1 (1st Quarter, 1945): 17–21.

Jordan, Ryan. "The Indiana Separation of 1842 and the Limits of Quaker Anti-Slavery." *Quaker History* 89, no. 1 (Spring 2000): 1–27.

Kennedy, Thomas C. "Another Kind of Emigrant: Quakers in the Arkansas Delta, 1864–1825." *AHQ* 55, no. 2 (Summer 1996): 199–220.

———. "The Rise and Decline of a Black Monthly Meeting, Southland, Arkansas." *AHQ* 50, no. 2 (Summer 1991): 115–139. Reprinted in *The Southern Friend* 19, no. 2 (Autumn 1997): 5–29.

———. "To Raise This People Up: The Early Years at Southland College." *Reflections* 12, no. 2 (Spring 1987): 1, 7–9.

———. "The Last Days at Southland." *The Southern Friend* 7, no. 2 (Spring 1986): 3–19.

———. "Southland College: The Society of Friends and Black Education in Arkansas." *AHQ* 42, no. 3 (Autumn 1983): 207–38. Reprinted in *The Southern Friend* and *The Phillips County Historical Quarterly*.

Kettler, Rose. "Schools of Phillips County." *PCHQ* 25, nos. 1–2 (December 1987, March 1988), 30–45.

Kirkman, Dale P. "Southland College," *PCHQ* 3, no. 1 (September 1964): 30–33.

Kousser, J. Morgan. "A Black Protest in the 'Era of Accommodation': Documents." *AHQ* 34, no. 2 (Summer 1975): 149–78.

Lemon, Lester C. "Black Public Education in the South, 1861–1920: By Whom, For Whom and Under Whose Control?" *Journal of Thought* 18, no. 3 (Fall 1983): 76–89.

Legan, Marshall Scott. "Disease and the Freedmen in Mississippi During Reconstruction." *Journal of the History of Medicine and Allied Sciences* 28 (1973): 257–67.

Lewis, Todd E. "Mob Justice in the 'American Congo': 'Judge Lynch' in Arkansas During the Decade After the World War I." *AHQ* 52, no. 2 (Summer 1993): 156–184.

Lindley, Harlow. "A Century Of Indiana Yearly Meeting." *Bulletin of Friends Historical Association* 12, no. 1 (1923): 3–21.

Lindley, Martha N. "Work Among the Contrabands." *Indiana Historical Bulletin* 1, no. 11–12 (1924).

Link, William A. "Jackson Davis and the Lost World of Jim Crow Education." Special Collections Department. University of Virginia Library, May 2000.

Lovett, Bobby. "African Americans, Civil War, and Aftermath in Arkansas." *AHQ* 54, no. 3 (Autumn 1995): 304–58.

Moneyhon, Carl H. "The Civil War in Phillips County." *PCHQ* 19, no. 3–4 (June-September 1984): 18–36.

———. "Economic Democracy in Antebellum Arkansas, 1850–1860." *AHQ* 40, no. 2 (Summer 1981): 154–72.

———. "The Impact of the Civil War in Arkansas: The Mississippi River Plantation Counties." *AHQ* 51, no. 2 (Summer 1992): 105–18.

Nicholson, N. "Work Among the Contrabands." *Indiana History Bulletin* 1, no. 9.

Patton, Adell. "The 'Back-to-Africa' Movement in Arkansas." *AHQ* 51, no. 2 (Summer 1992): 164–177.

Pearce, Larry Wesley. "The American Missionary Association and the Freedmen in Arkansas, 1863–1878." *AHQ* 30, no. 2 (Summer 1971): 123–44.

———. "The American Missionary Association and the Freedmen's Bureau in Arkansas, 1866–1868." *AHQ* 30, no. 3 (Autumn 1971): 242–59.

———. "The American Missionary Association and the Freedmen's Bureau in Arkansas, 1868–1878." *AHQ* (Autumn 1972): 246–61.

———. "Enoch K. Miller and the Freedmen's Schools." *AHQ* 31, no. 4 (Winter 1972): 305–27.

Porter, Rusty. "Railroads in Phillips County." *PCHQ* 26, no. 3–4 (June–September 1988): 1–26.

"Postal Service in Phillips County." *PCHQ* 9, no. 1 (December 1970): 1–10.

Redington, Capt. Edward S. "The 28th Wisconsin Infantry Regiment at Helena." Pts. 4–7. *PCHQ* 13, no. 2 (March 1973): 23–33; 13, no. 4 (September 1973): 7–17; 14, no. 1 (December 1975): 7–17; 14, no. 2 (March 1976): 30–40.

Roberts, Bobby. "'Desolation Itself': The Impact of the Civil War." In Whayne and Gatewood. *Arkansas Delta.* 70–97.

Robertson, Brian K. "'Will They Fight? Ask the Enemy.' United States Colored Troops at Big Creek, Arkansas, July 26, 1864." *AHQ* 66, no. 3 (Autumn 2007): 320–32.

Rothrock, Thomas. "Joseph Carter Corbin and Negro Education in the University of Arkansas." *AHQ* 30, no. 4 (Winter 1971): 277–314.

St. Hilarie, Joseph M. "Negro Delegates in the Constitutional Convention of 1868: A Group Profile." *AHQ* 32, no. 1 (Spring 1974): 38–69.

Salemson, Daniel J., ed. "'to spend some time as a missionary among colored people': The Civil War Writings of an Indiana Quaker." *The Southern Friend* 20, no. 1 (Spring 1998): 3–75.

Sarma, Jan, ed. "Civil War and Reconstruction." *PCHQ* 16, no. 3 (June 1978): 1–23.

Shirey, Mary Willis. "Young Stanley: Arkansas Episode." *AHQ* 3, no. 4 (1944): 356–72.

Spencer, Carole. "The American Holiness Movement: Why Did It Captivate Nineteenth Century Quakers?" *Quaker Religious Thought* 28, no. 90 (January 1998): 19–30.

Spencer, Carole. "Evangelism, Feminism, and Social Reform: the Quaker Woman Minister and the Holiness Revival," *Quaker History,* 80, no. 1 (1991), 24–48.

Stockley, Grif J. "The Legal Proceedings of the Arkansas Race Massacres of 1919 and the Evidence of the Plot to Kill Planters," *Arkansas Review: A Journal of Delta Studies,* 32, no. 2 (August 2001): 141–48.

Taylor, David. "A Garden in the Wilderness: The Role of Southland College in Early Negro Education." *PCHQ* 26, no. 1 (December 1987): 1–27.

Taylor, Kieran. "'We Have Just Begun': Black Organizing and White Response in the Arkansas Delta, 1919." *AHQ* 58, no. 3 (Autumn 1999): 265–84.

Walz, Robert B. "Arkansas Slaveholdings and Slaveholders in 1850." *AHQ* 12, no. 1 (Spring 1953): 38–74.

Washington, Booker T. "Industrial Education for the Negro." In *The Negro Problem,* edited by W. E. B. Du Bois. New York: James Pott, 1903.

Waterman, Robert E. and Thomas Rothrock, eds. "The Earle-Buchanan Letters of 1861–1876." *AHQ* 33, no. 2 (Summer 1974): 99–174.

Watson, Charles Robert. "Minnesota Troops at Helena." Pt. 2. *PCHQ* 25, nos. 1–2 (December 1986–March 1987): 1–29.

Whayne, Jeannie. "Low Villains and Wickedness is High Places: Race and Class in the Elaine Riots." *AHQ* 58, no. 3 (Autumn 1999): 285–313.

Wheeler, Elizabeth L. "Isaac Fisher: The Frustration of a Negro Educator at Branch Normal College, 1902–1911." *AHQ* 41, no. 1 (Spring 1982): 3–50.

"Wisconsin Troops a Helena" Pt. 11. *PCHQ* 15, no. 3 (June 1977): 5–19.

Wood, Richard. "Evangelical Quaker Acculturation in the Upper Mississippi Valley." *Quaker History* 76, no. 2 (Fall 1987): 128–34.

Worley, Ted. "Helena on the Mississippi." *AHQ* 13, no. 1 (Spring 1954): 1–15.

VI. Dissertations and Theses

Anscombe, Francis Charles. "The Contribution of the Quakers to Reconstruction of the Southern States." PhD diss., University of North Carolina, 1926.

Buys, John William. "Quakers in Indiana in the Nineteenth Century." PhD diss., University of Florida, 1973.

Drake, Richard B. "The American Missionary Association and the Southern Negro, 1861–1888." PhD diss., Emory University, 1957.

Fain, James Harris. "Political Disfranchisement of the Negro in Arkansas." Master's thesis, University of Arkansas, 1961.

Lewis, Todd Everett. "Race Relations in Arkansas, 1910–1929." PhD diss., University of Arkansas, 1995.

Nelson, Jacquelyn S. "The Society of Friends During the Civil War." PhD diss., Ball State University, 1984.

Walz, Robert. "Migration into Arkansas, 1834–1880." PhD diss., University of Texas, 1958.

VII. Interviews

Billingsley, Alfred L., Sr. Southland, AR. 19 February 1982.

Billingsley, Ernestine Pruitt. Southland, AR. 19 February 1982.

Bird, Alvin "Buddy." Southland, AR. 18 February 1982.

Graves, Willa Burchett. Helena and Southland, AR. 18 February 1982.

Jenkins, F. Raymond. Richmond, IN. 19 June 1981.

Ratliff, Russell and Tressie. Richmond, IN. 19 June 1981.

Young, Emma Roden. Southland, AR. 18 February 1982.

Index

THOMAS C. KENNEDY is professor emeritus of history at the University of Arkansas. *He is the author of The Hound of Conscience: A History of the No-Conscription Fellowship, 1914–1919* and *British Quakerism, 1860–1920: The Transformation of a Religious Community.* He has also written numerous articles on Southland College and Quakers in Arkansas.